THOSE DAYS

By the same author

VILLAGES
SHAHHAT, AN EGYPTIAN
THE GOLDEN BOWL BE BROKEN
THE LONG CHARADE
THE INDIAN REPORTER'S GUIDE

THOSE
DAYS

AN AMERICAN ALBUM

Richard Critchfield

ANCHOR PRESS/DOUBLEDAY
GARDEN CITY, NEW YORK
1986

Acknowledgments

The author wishes to thank the following individuals, publishers, companies and historical societies for the use of material in this book.

Photographs: For cover colored photograph, Bruce Wendt, Judson, North Dakota. Black and white: The Fred Hultstrand "History in Pictures" Collection, North Dakota Institute for Regional Studies, North Dakota State University, Fargo; Archives, North Dakota State University; State Historical Society of North Dakota, Bismarck; Dalene Battagler, Hunter, North Dakota; Wells County Historical Society, Fessenden, North Dakota; State Historical Society of Wisconsin, Madison; Buffalo Bill Museum, Le Claire, Iowa; Clay County Historical Society, Moorhead, Minnesota.

Songs: From *The Methodist Hymnal*, 1884 and 1905 editions:

"What a Friend We Have in Jesus," music by Joseph Scriven (1820–86), words by Charles C. Converse (1832–1918).

"Shall We Gather at the River?" words and music by Robert Lowry, published 1865.

"All Hail the Power," words by Edward Perronet (1726–92), alt. by John Rippon (1751–1836), music by Oliver Holden (1761–1844).

"Blessed Assurance," words by Fanny J. Crosby (1820–1915), music by Mrs. Joseph F. Knapp (1839–1908).

"Onward, Christian Soldiers," words by Sabine Baring-Gold (1854–1924), music by Arthur S. Sullivan (1842–1900).

"Lead, Kindly Light," words by John Henry Newman (1801–90), music by John B. Dykes (1823–76).

"Amazing Grace," words by John Newton (1725–1807), published 1779, early American melody with many arrangements.

"Blest Be the Tie That Binds," words by John Fawcett (1740–1817), music by Hans G. Nageli (1773–1836), arrangement by Lowell Mason (1792–1872).

"God Be with You till We Meet Again," words by Jeremiah E. Rankin (1828–1904).

Libretto of *Tristan and Isolde*, by Richard Wagner, quoted from *Stories of the Great Metropolitan Operas*, by Helen Dike, illustrated by Gustaf Tenggren, copyright 1942, Artists and Writers Guild, officially sponsored by the Metropolitan Opera Guild, Inc., used by permission of Random House, Inc.

Lyrics and dialogue for Mississippi medicine show adapted from material as appearing on Rounder Record 1023, "Gid Tanner and His Skillet Lickers—The Kickapoo Medicine Show," by permission of Rounder Records, Cambridge, Massachusetts.

"Saint Louis Blues," by W. C. Handy, permission by Handy Brothers Music Co., Inc. © 1914. Copyright renewed MCMXLI. With special thanks to Wyer Owens Handy.

"Come Home, Father," third stanza, by Henry C. Work © 1892 by Henry C. Work, quoted from performance of *Ten Nights in a Bar Room*, drama by William W. Pratt adapted from the novel by T. S. Arthur, first performed in New York in 1858.

"Oh, Promise Me," lyrics from second stanza, taken from original 1889 version by Clement Scott, music by R. DeKovan.

"The Letter Edged in Black," words and music by Hattie Nevada © 1897, quoted from original text. Song revised with a new arrangement in 1925.

Riverman's song quoted at end of Mississippi rafting chapter by Robert Rexdale as quoted in Walter H. Blair's *A Raft Pilot's Log*, published 1929.

"My Blue Heaven," words by George Whiting, music by Walter Donaldson © 1925, 1927, renewed Leo Feist Inc., 1953, 1955, renewed Donaldson Publishing Co. All rights reserved. Used by permission of Donaldson Publishing Co.

"How Ya Gonna Keep 'Em Down on the Farm," words by Sam M. Lewis and Joe Young, music by Walter Donaldson © 1919 by Mills Music, Inc. Copyright renewed 1947. Used by permission. All rights reserved.

"Lilac Days," words and music by James G. Golseth © 1932. Used by permission of the composer.

"Who Wouldn't?" words by Gus Kahn, music by Walter Donaldson © 1926 (renewed). Used by permission of Gilbert Keyes Music Co. and Donaldson Music Co. pursuant to sections 304 (c) and 401 (b) of the U.S. Copyright Law.

"As You Desire Me," words and music by Allie Wrubel © 1932 and renewed 1960 Words & Music, Inc., and Essex Music, Inc., New York, N.Y. Used by permission.

"Strike Up the Band!" words by Ira Gershwin, music by George Gershwin © 1927 (renewed) Warner Bros. Inc. All rights reserved. Used by permission together with following seven songs from Warner Bros. Music.

"Bye Bye Blackbird," words by Mort Dixon, music by Ray Henderson © 1926 (renewed) Warner Bros. Inc. All rights reserved. Used by permission.

"Hallelujah!" words by Leo Rubin and Clifford Frey, music by Vincent Youmans © 1927 (renewed) Warner Bros. Inc. All rights reserved. Used by permission.

"I Found a Million Dollar Baby (in a Five and Ten Cent Store)" words by Billy Rose and

"The Hanging of the Crane," by Henry Wadsworth Longfellow, published in 1874.

"Crossing the Bar," quoted from the *Works* of Alfred, Lord Tennyson, Vol. 8, p. 294, published in 1896.

Excerpts from marriage and burial rites are quoted from *Liturgy and Rituals,* the Methodist Episcopal Church, 1905 edition and *The Book of Common Prayer.*

The Lucky Strike radio commercial reproduced by permission, American Brands, Inc.

Pepsi Cola Radio Jingle, written and arranged by Austen Groom-Johnson and Alan Kent © Pepsico, Inc., 1940. Reproduced with permission.

Library of Congress Cataloging in Publication Data
Critchfield, Richard.
    Those days.
    1. Critchfield family. I. Title.
CT274.C74C74 1986   929'.2'0973   85-6021
ISBN 0-385-19969-4

Author's Note

As everybody who tackles biography must discover, the distinction between fiction and nonfiction doesn't always work well. Interviews and documents take you only so far. What follows is the story of an actual American family. I've drawn upon the lives of my grandparents, my parents and their children, friends and neighbors, but it could be any of tens of thousands of families in this country. All the characters were, or are, living people, just as Le Claire, Hunter, Maddock and Fessenden, like the Mississippi River and the North Dakota prairie, can be found on a map. No attempt has been made to preserve anonymity, with the exceptions of Norma Thorson, the Bauer family, David W., Sven Gustafson, Heinrich Krause, Gertrude Engelhart—not their real names—and a few minor characters. Otherwise, real names have been used. I have stuck to the facts as long as I could learn them. Yet, as the reader will see, there is much I was unable to know—not being born yet for a good part of the story—and I had to do a certain amount of imagining to put together what seems most likely to have happened. In most cases, enough was known that it did not take much imagination; it was like coloring in the spaces between the lines. There is some exploration of human feelings, even if what are presented as interior thoughts tend to be drawn from letters and interviews. Everything is true, if we can characterize as truth any account of very ordinary life so long ago and when so many of the participants are dead. However a mixture of truth and fiction, the purpose of this work is to portray the full life and character of these people, but as persons whose individuality and destiny is seen within the setting of the changing technology and culture about them. As the saying goes, it's a wise child that knows his own father.

RC

Contents

III AN OPEN PLACE

"Well, good people, let us go, it's
getting dark . . ."

Chekhov

Prologue

Memories of her wedding day, when they came back to Anna Louise many years later, somehow took on the character of old photographs; in her mind's eye she seemed to see it all in brownish-yellowish tints and white oval frames. She even imagined a faint musty smell of lavender and camphor, as if everything that happened that day had been carefully laid up, like old lace, in some inner place of her mind. She remembered herself, wearing a long white dress, in the parsonage garden, which was fragrant with newly cut grass, lilac bushes in full bloom and the pink and white blossoms of pear, plum and apple trees. She was cutting off lilac branches and putting them in a large wicker basket which she cradled in her arm. She had a slim waist and ample bust, as they used to call it in those days, and her brown hair was piled on top of her head. Her features were finely cut, her lips thin, her face broad and serious, her eyes a warm brown. Her expression was melancholy; so was the romantic poetry fashionable early in the century.

Let us imagine, too, that it was still the early hours of the morning so that drops of dew glittered on every leaf and petal. From a neighbor's yard a rooster crowed. Anna Louise, her figure erect and slight, had tucked her dress up out of the grass. The branches, snapping in her fingers, were wet. Her wedding day had arrived, and a clear, cool April day it promised to be. Pigeons were cooing on the church roof, disturbed by all the stir and bustle, and sparrows in the flowering trees chirruped without stopping, as if they, too, were caught up in the excitement.

From early morning, neighbors had come with daffodils and tulips, violets, ferns and lilies of the valley. Women were decorating the parlor bay window with a floral arch. A display of wedding presents, some of them practical, were laid out on white linen in the dining room. These consisted of towels, napkins and bed sheets, embroidered pillow covers, cups and saucers with a rose design, a bread plate and a set of napkin rings. There were a few ornaments for the parlor: a plain hooked rug from the Quaker cousins in Whittier, a settee of oak made by Anna Louise's father, a pair of brass candlesticks, a brass-bottomed lamp with a purple ground-glass chimney decorated with roses from Aunt Allie, and a precious family heirloom—a pewter platter handed down from her New England ancestors—from Anna Louise's parents. Her former beau at college, Forrest, had sent violets; he was not invited. In the kitchen, a repast was being prepared of hams, stuffed chickens, a variety of fancy cakes, and candied nuts and fruits. The wedding cake had been delivered by the baker and stood safely in the pantry, with its tiny bride and groom under a bell of pink and white icing.

From the cellar came the creak and groan of grinding ice and salt muffled by a wet gunnysack; Anna Louise's brother, Hadwen, down from his teaching job in Minnesota, was cranking out some tutti-frutti ice cream in the freezer. Jessie, their mother, was in constant demand. With a harassed expression, and breathless, she tasted the fruit punch in the pantry, glanced at the floral decorations, and hurried to the kitchen, where members of the Aid Society had been at work since dawn. Mary, the bride's pretty, sixteen-year-old sister, in her stays and petticoat covered by a loose wrapper, and her hair in paper curlers, flew out to the clothesline in the backyard, shrieking happily to Anna Louise. It was all very noisy; throughout the downstairs, there were cries and giggles. From time to time there was a chorus of exclamations; passersby paused by the wide-open gate; something unusual was astir at the Methodist parsonage.

Rev. Hadwen Williams, who had fled to the quiet of his study ostensibly to work on his next Sunday's sermon, was troubled. He gazed into space. He had given his sermon the title "Difficulties Ahead" and begun his outline, "There are always difficulties for God's people . . ." He got no farther. He tried to think of the journey of the children of Israel, of the conquest of Canaan, the expulsion of idolatry, but his own difficulties banished all others from his mind. In the bustle over Louie's trousseau, to which Jessie and the young women attached so much significance, he had scarcely been able to catch his eldest daughter alone since her return from Dakota just days before. The snipping of scissors, the rattle of the sewing machine, the smell of the flatiron, the fittings, pinnings and measurings, seemed to leave them all nervous and touchy. On top of that, visitors kept arriving—young women who had taught or gone to school with Anna Louise and several Quaker cousins—and these had to be amused, fed and lodged for several nights.

Lifting his eyes from his sermon outline, and turning to look out the study window, he saw Anna Louise out in the garden picking lilacs. She was alone. At once he got up and hurried outside to join her. His kind, troubled face grew tense. There was a time to keep silence and a time to speak. Thoughts rushed about in his head. He thought: "She's a right good girl, but I can't believe she understands what she is taking on in this young man she wants for a husband."

The reverend was very domestic and loved his family more than anything in the world. It wasn't easy for him to have the first permanent break in the family come with Anna Louise's marriage to someone he had met only the evening before.

He joined her and began breaking off lilac branches, unable to conceal his agitation. He said nothing, but met her eyes. And from the expression of her eyes he concluded that she understood his feelings.

He was mistaken. Anna Louise was paying hardly any attention to what was going on around her, so powerful was the feeling that had filled her being since the day when, as they rode in a buggy across that bleak northern plain, Jim had poured out his heart to her and she had agreed to marry him. In her emotions that day, her roots in Iowa had been torn loose and she'd begun to search for new ones up there on the prairie with him. Since she'd returned home, she'd felt dismayed at herself and at the new sense of indifference she felt to everything and everybody in her past. This estrangement wounded her mother, and now Anna Louise saw how much it hurt her dearly loved father, too. It was as if, by not marrying someone from the world they knew, she was somehow turning them down as well.

Sensing none of this, words kept coming into the reverend's head: " 'Whom God has joined together . . .' " "Lord," he asked silently, "are you joining them together, or is this just my daughter's plain old contrariness? Oh, I know she's always been the apple of *my* eye, and I kinda suspect she could have had her pick of the young men at Upper Iowa University, too. But who should she take up with but this North Dakota boy? He's got no prospects. Had to drop out of medical school a couple of years ago and took up farming. Now, we hear, he can barely make a go of that. He's sure no natural-born farmer, you can see that right off. From what Jessie and I could learn from folks who have been up there and have talked with those acquainted with the family, he's a reckless, harum-scarum sort of fellow— beer-drinking, cigar-smoking, poker-playing—oh, a good enough ballplayer when it comes to that, but, as the good Lord knows, how wild! Drunk, we've heard tell, when he was only fourteen years old. And always running around with older fellows. They say their people back in Ohio even raised racehorses. Gambled on them too.

"Why, Louise could have had Forrest Claxton just as well as not, and he has a good job in the Fayette bank and his father is the bank president and a trustee in the Methodist church. Forrest would have been well set up to provide for her. And Beecher Beal, before him, was another fine young fellow. Why she upped and ran off to North Dakota, breaking off her engagement to marry Beecher, is something I'll never understand.

"But no, she's just plumb lost her head over this Jim fellow. Why, he didn't get here until late last night on account of he was taking part in a bowling tournament! That's what he told Jessie. And him about to get married? What manner of man is that? Nobody else in his family came down from Dakota for the wedding. Just him . . . Well, have him she will, and have him it looks like she's going to . . ."

Unable, at last, to keep his silence any longer, Reverend Williams took Anna Louise by the shoulders and looked her right in the eyes. He saw a strange look of worry and radiance in them he had not seen before. Perplexed, he searched her face imploringly and said, keeping his voice down though Jim was still upstairs sleeping after his long train journey, "Louise, can you be yoked for life to somebody with such different ways, somebody who may not even believe in God?"

"Oh, Papa, why, of course he does!" she cried, flushing with vexation. "His family are all Presbyterians." In truth, it distressed her that Jim didn't seem to care about church. Once, after he'd missed several Sundays, he had told her, "I don't seem to get much out of it anymore." But she was confident he would attend every week with her when they were married, just like other couples.

"He'll go," she said. She wanted to say more, but, seeing her father looking so wretched, she held her tongue. Her face felt hot. To conceal her anguish, she bent low over a lilac bush just as if she were nearsighted, and made a show of examining the blossoms.

The reverend reminded himself that he was not a prophet. It was just that when he looked ahead he found it hard not to imagine trouble and heartbreak for his daughter, and for the young man, too. Their backgrounds were too far apart.

Anna Louise straightened up. She was very flushed, and breathed heavily with emotion, looking frightened. "He drinks a little," she confessed. It was her one doubt.

"A little! From what we've heard, he's cut up scandalous a few times already. Oh, Louie, I worry about things to come. That's what I worry about."

She stared at her father's loving, imploring face, heard the despair in his voice, and she was seized with panic, as if all her new life could still be snatched away. This life might be troubled or happy, but she did not know what it would be like and she could not think of anything, or want anything, that was not part of Jim. She was torn with remorse, feeling she was somehow being compelled to renounce her old life, and with it her family and her father.

"Well, Papa, I'm going to marry him—if he'll have me. Now I better go get dressed."

He blurted out the words without thinking. "I wish you were marrying Forrest instead."

She looked at him without understanding what he meant, then understood and turned to stone. He saw by her face that he should not have uttered those words, but still he went on. "I'm responsible, under God, for you both, because I'm marrying you." She turned away from him, heedlessly scattering some of the lilacs on the grass. As she went toward the house, Anna Louise was deeply hurt, with such wounded feelings as she had never known. Time would pass, and Reverend Williams would resign himself to the marriage, but her hurt feelings would not pass, but remain in her heart all her life long.

Jim came downstairs shortly before the late-morning ceremony in a new black worsted suit. Mary had pressed out the creases left from packing. He also wore a new black bow tie. He was almost two years younger than Anna Louise, and that day looked it. Flaxen-haired, clean-shaven and with pale blue eyes, he was short, muscular-looking and handsome. He greeted the Williamses respectfully, smelled of bay rum and, attempting to be staid and serious, stood about stiffly with his arms at his sides, like a soldier at attention. As soon as he relaxed, one saw from the swing of his shoulders and in all his movements, as in the sound of his laughter and his easy smile, the guileless, athletic and open character of a healthy young man pleased with life and used to being liked by everyone. He seemed unaware of any tension within the family. Indeed, Jim saw very little; he looked at Anna Louise without taking his eyes off her.

His gift to the bride was a pearl necklace. Just before the ceremony began, he slipped it over her head with trembling hands. Anna Louise—Jim called her simply Anne—gave him a tremulous smile, her face lighting up, and lifted her short veil of cotton while he fastened the clasp of the string of pearls. Her hair was dressed high under the veil, parted in the center and swept into a soft and wide pompadour. Her wedding dress was white voile, high-necked, trimmed with lace, half-sleeved and very simple; the rather severe-looking skirt reached nearly to the floor, where new high-button shoes could be seen. She clung tightly to her modest bouquet of trailing lilies of the valley with baby's breath and tiny ferns. She looked serene. The faint frown and set lips could possibly be blamed on tight stays or stiff new shoes that pinched, and they soon gave way to an expression of radiance that grew more and more pronounced as the ceremony went on.

The Williams family were all in their best. Hadwen wore his Prince Albert coat, now so worn it looked sadly ministerial. Jessie, with her pure white hair and erect posture, was quite regal in a dress that had taken sixteen yards of gray silk. Her youngest daughter, Helen, was beside her. Hadwen, Jr., the only son, was to give the bride away. Three former fellow teachers from the nearby town of Elma, all smiles, whispers and confusion, were the bridesmaids. Young Mary, in pink lace, after pulling out some stops, played soft music, pumping away on the wheezing old parsonage organ.

> "Oh, promise me that you will take my hand,
> The most unworthy in this lonely land . . ."

Jessie, deeply moved, chose this moment to burst into tears, and Mary had to stop playing the organ, for her eyes were filled with tears too, and she could no longer see the keys. Breathless excitement stirred the wedding guests in the parlor, who didn't want to miss anything.

"Dearly beloved, we are gathered here in the sight of God, and in the presence of this congregation to join this man and woman in holy matrimony." Reverend Williams spoke the accustomed words, though he seemed to breathe a little heavily and once or twice his lips trembled. ". . . And therefore is not to be entered into by any inadvisedly, but reverently, discreetly, and in fear of God . . . James, wilt thou have this woman to be thy wedded wife, to live together after God's ordinance in the holy estate of matrimony? Wilt thou love her, comfort her, honor and keep her, in sickness and in health, forsaking all others, keep thee only unto her, so long as ye both shall live?"

"I will."

"Anna Louise . . ." Softly she repeated the vows after her father, and then Reverend Williams had Jim take her right hand in his right hand and say after him, "I, James, take thee, Anna Louise, to be my wedded wife, to have and to hold, from this day forward, for better, for worse, for richer, for poorer, in sickness and in health, to love and to cherish, till death us do part . . ."

Anna Louise and Jim, feeling very close, kept holding hands through their barely audible responses, not letting go until time for the ring—he gave her a simple gold band. Then Reverend Williams said, "With this ring I thee wed, with my body I thee worship, and with all my worldly goods I thee endow," and at that moment they both stopped smiling and turned a little pale. Jim pulled himself together first, repeating the words in a firmer voice than before. He gave a small, reassuring smile to Anna Louise, who now wore a touchingly solemn expression, a feeling that spread to his face too. They bowed their heads and clasped their hands for the final prayer, which Reverend Williams delivered in the most gentle voice. "Those whom God hath joined together, let no man put asunder . . ." After a soft whisper from him, they stood together and carefully exchanged the bridal kiss, a very modest, reserved kiss, and Jim gave her his arm. Mary, who had stopped crying, began to play the organ again, and in a much louder, livelier fashion than before.

"No love less perfect than a life with thee;
Oh, promise me, oh, promise me . . ."

The bridal couple kneeled to say The Lord's Prayer, and after Mendelssohn's rousing recessional, everybody rushed up to shake hands. The women embraced, and some of the men kissed the bride. Anna Louise took off her little veil but clung to her bouquet. She seemed dazzled by it all, with a happy glow lighting up her face, and when some of the young women whispered in her ear and burst out giggling, she said something to Jim and he nodded in agreement. Soon she was hurrying up the front staircase, a graceful figure holding up her long white skirt and clutching the bouquet of flowers. At the top she turned, hesitated, leaned over the banister, and threw it down to the shrieking girls, who crowded at the foot of the stairs, all jumping and jostling and squealing with their arms outstretched, vying to become the next bride.

A big dinner was soon set out in the dining room, and besides four courses and all kinds of side dishes, there was wedding cake, and Jessie had also decorated the ice cream with scalloped grapefruit and real yellow flower petals. The guests ate, chatted and creaked their chairs. Someone played the organ from time to time. The neighbor women extolled the married couple. Members of his congregation gathered around the reverend. There was loud talk and periodic outbursts of laughter, and a good deal of noisy confusion. Soon a photographer set up his tripod and camera to take the wedding pictures before the whole crowd went down to the railroad station to see the newlyweds off. There was to be no honeymoon. As everyone had read in the local paper, the groom had to go straight home to look after his stock, as he was "a well-to-do farmer, who owns and works a large grain farm near Hunter, North Dakota." It was a place no one but Anna Louise had seen. But they all felt they knew quite enough about it, especially since there were rumors that the groom was not well-to-do at all and that his farm was on a treeless plain, horribly flat, and in winter nothing but miles and miles of howling winds and unbroken reaches of snow. Who would dream of going to live there?

The wedding pictures today are faded sepia images on discolored, yellowish paper, still fixed in place by black mounting corners, but creased and covered with fine cracks after so many years. The red satin cover is foxed with brownish spots of mildew and the silk cord which, laced through round metal eyelets, holds the album together, is frayed and knotted. A smell of must and something bitter and aromatic, which might indeed be lavender and camphor, wafts off the heavy black pages. Dried flowers and stalks, perhaps, were once laid among them. So many pages have torn loose, one must turn them very gingerly. Beneath a picture of Anna Louise and Jim, shown in a dark and gloomy-looking Edwardian interior, someone has written in stiff, careful letters, "Mom & Dad, their wedding, inside the Methodist parsonage, Sumner, Iowa, April 19, 1913." Other photographs were taken outdoors in bright sunlight. A number were posed on the wide steps of the parsonage front porch, where the wedding party, all of them women except for the groom and the bride's father and brother, are seated in rows, squinting into the sun.

No one is smiling. Reverend Williams is actually frowning at the camera, his forehead sharply wrinkled in the harsh light and the corners of his set mouth turned down. Jessie Williams looks grim too. Indeed, there is a certain cast of pride, piousness, self-righteousness perhaps, about all these stern Iowa faces. Jim alone, in the pictures he is in, stands out as somebody different, as somehow not belonging to the rest. He stares right at the camera, intently, his brown hair, bleached by the sun during fieldwork, looking blond in the bright light. He is clean-shaven—he has yet to grow the mustache he will have the rest of his life—and his slightly cleft chin is tilted confidently upward—or is his stiff collar too tight? He has never looked so handsome in photographs; he never will again. He seems too boyish to be twenty-three. Already his hair is ruffled, cowlicks have sprung up, his bow tie is askew.

Looking at these pictures is to sense, once again, how much we are bound to our pasts, captives of those habits we call culture. Jim, half-Irish with a mother of Celtic peasant descent, inherits traits on his father's side handed down from English convict to Virginian foot soldier to Ohio frontiersman, transplanted after a few more generations to the raw, wind-chilled North Dakota prairie, there to take root among Scandinavians and German-Russians with Old World customs of their own. Except to be educated in Minneapolis, Jim never left the prairie; there is nothing to suggest he ever wanted to. This journey away from North Dakota for his wedding was a rare one. He must have found it strange among these judgmental and self-righteous, if kindly and gentle, Iowa Methodists of New England Quaker stock. Two highly divergent American cultural strains met, clashed and—in Anna Louise and Jim—united in marriage.

She, familiar with both worlds, was making the clearest choice. Yet, how much freedom to choose do we have? How much of what we do is decided by our culture and time? And how much by the essence of our own nature unaffected by culture and time? The answers, if answers are to be found, must lie in the years that went before, and would come after, this, the happy couple's wedding day. Was Reverend Williams right?

The youngest member of the wedding—nine-year-old Helen—in the framed photographs a frowning little pixie face framed in braids—was to recall the day most vividly some seventy years later. It was the only time her mother ever slapped her, for one thing. Jessie's nerves snapped coming home from saying good-bye at the railroad station. Stunned and hurt, since she'd hardly been naughty, Helen burst into tears. She sobbed to her mother, "Jim never paid any attention to me. He didn't care anything at all about being friends . . ." Remorseful, Jessie packed the child off to the hitherto-unknown pleasures of the town's newly opened nickelodeon. And so the wedding day for the little girl ended in the thrilling animated projection of horses galloping and men running about just as if it were happening in real life. Long afterward, when she thought of Louie setting out on her life with Jim, Helen could almost hear the frantic plinkety-plink of the pianist trying to keep up with the action and see the silently pounding hooves in the dust as Broncho Billy Anderson rode across the screen, guns blazing.

I

PREACHER'S
DAUGHTER

Saints . . .

If man is a mystery to be solved, clues lie with earlier generations. Who were those strangers who helped to make us what we are? Where to begin?

The story of Anna Louise goes back to her family's New England Quaker origins. The earliest family records to escape mildew, vermin and time are a few yellowing receipts dated 1765. They say that a Dr. John Hadwen, a Quaker who practiced medicine in Newport, Rhode Island, gave so many shillings for cheese, cloth and candles. More revealing is a letter from a group of London Friends, dated November 1774, urging the doctor and his relations to stay out of the Revolutionary War:

"If ever there was a season that called for a deep and humbling sense of the need we have for divine support, the present seems, indeed weightily, to call for such a disposition to be served . . . When men give themselves up to the guidance of their fears, their fashions and interests, observe the injunction of our Lord, 'When ye hear of wars or rumours of wars, see that ye not be troubled.' . . . Tenderly we advise you . . . Mix not in the various consultations . . ."

Rhode Island was a religious sanctuary after it was founded by Roger Williams when he was banished from the Massachusetts Bay Colony. He took into Rhode Island Jews and Quakers, who were being persecuted by the Puritans. Elsewhere in the colonies, outside of Pennsylvania and Quaker William Penn's City of Brotherly Love, Quakers were hounded, jailed, hanged, pilloried, flogged and accused of witchcraft, lucky just to get their ears cropped or their tongues bored with a hot iron. Massachusetts fined a hundred pounds anybody caught bringing a Quaker into the colony. On Boston's State House grounds today you can see the statue of Mary Dyer, a Quaker, with the inscription: "Witness for Religious Freedom. Hanged on

Boston Common, 1660." Her crime: teaching that "There is that of God in every man." Virginia passed its Act for Suppressing Quakers the same year. Just eight years had passed since the day a barely literate cobbler and sheepherder, George Fox, had gathered a few hundred of his fellow peasants together at a place called Pendle Hill in northern England and declared them to be "Children of Light." Promptly jailed in Derby, Fox told the judge he ought to "tremble before the word of God."

"Ha!" the judge sneered at him. "You are the quaker, not I." It stuck.

In no time at all, these zealots, calling themselves Friends, were threatening the established order. They invaded churches and demanded that congregations forsake the "steeple-house." They refused to pay tithes to worldly Oxford- and Cambridge-educated vicars, like those in Trollope's Barsetshire novels, or even let them perform marriage ceremonies. They declined to swear oaths or remove their hats to officials. They scorned the newly fashionable plural "you," used since the royalist cavaliers to show respect to single persons of rank; instead they clung to the old-time singular "thee" and "thou" of their peasant villages, where an older English was used in ordinary rustic speech.

Fox had left work and home when just nineteen to ask himself about the meaning of existence. As he wrote about it in 1647, after wandering about for several years, ". . . when all my hopes were gone, so that I had nothing outwardly to help me, nor could tell what to do, then, O then, I heard a voice which said, 'There is one, even Christ Jesus, that can speak to thy condition,' and when I heard it my heart did leap for joy."

None of this went down well in England or its American colonies. Only in tolerant Rhode Island and Pennsylvania did Friends flourish, run in elections, win them. By the Revolutionary period their numbers had grown to about fifty thousand in a total American population just over 2.5 million.

The Quakers were torn by the war. Most of them sympathized with the colonial cause; they were colonists themselves. Over five hundred were expelled from their meeting houses for enlisting on the American side (just six were expelled for joining the British). George Fox had opposed all war and revolution, preaching, "Whatever bustlings or trouble or tumult or outrages should rise in the world, keep out of them . . ." Most Quakers stayed pacifist, refused to be conscripted or pay war taxes; many were wrongly attacked as British sympathizers, a few were victims of mob brutality.

Like Fox, they had a remarkably simple, serene, unwavering faith. All that mattered was an individual's own direct experience with God. Christianity was not an outward profession, but an Inner Light by which God directly illumined the human soul. This Inner Light could come to anyone prepared to sit quietly, with an open heart. Nothing else was needed—no churches, no sacraments, no preachers, not even the Bible. At first, the early Quakers, most of them peasants, met in fields and huts. Later they built plain white frame meeting houses. There a group of them sat in silence. Sometimes two or three might speak out, sometimes not. A farmer might talk of a moral decision, another quote from the Bible, a woman pray for peace. They might say nothing.

It was a religion formed in the mind of an unlettered but serious and contemplative villager, apprenticed as a boy to a cobbler, who went off on a quest for spiritual enlightenment when he was still only nineteen. It grew up among a peasant people with rural tasks and values, who lived in villages and cultivated land. It is not surprising that, within a Christianity that had already firmly become a religion of the urban, educated middle class, Quaker fundamentalists kept arising from time to time to demand a return to the original faith of George Fox. One of these, Francis Williams, was the son of Dr. Hadwen's daughter Ruth. He was to become the grandfather of Anna Louise. The influence of his beliefs, though not he himself, runs like a thread throughout our story.

After the Revolution, the Hadwen family prospered. A native of Lancashire, England, where his family traced its ancestors in the county back to the fifteenth century, Dr. Hadwen had come to America as a young man in 1743. He died of "an apoplectic fit," reported the Newport *Mercury,* September 15, 1804, "his soul unsullied by a single vice." One of the doctor's sons, Benjamin, became a sea captain. A daughter, Dorcas, married Obadiah Brown, the son of the legendary Quaker merchant and philanthropist Moses Brown. Together with Samuel Slater, Moses Brown introduced the Arkwright waterwheel to New England, giving birth to its cotton industry. He also experimented in education and astronomy and dabbled in medicine, promoting inoculation for smallpox. Largely through his influence, Rhode Island College—later named Brown University in honor of his brother Nicholas—was moved to Providence in 1770. He contributed generously to the college and donated the land for the Moses Brown School in Providence, a preparatory institution for boys established by the Quakers in 1819. Obadiah Brown continued this philanthropy, endowing the Friends Boarding School on Nantucket Island with a hundred thousand dollars in his will, a huge sum at the time. Hannah, a sister of Francis Williams and Obadiah's niece, was educated there.

In spite of the illustrious Brown and Hadwen connections, the Williamses, like nine out of ten American families as the nineteenth century began, were rural people. Their ways and views, like those of the early

Quakers, were shaped by village life and cultivation of the land. It is not surprising that farming skill and practical trades, together with religious orthodoxy, were what counted. Though their letters make them seem amazingly literate by today's standards, they saw little need for higher education.

Francis, born in Newport, Rhode Island, in 1811, must have been a typical product of his culture and time. He went West as a boy with his family, driving a team of horses in a caravan of covered wagons. The family cleared land and settled in Bridgewater, in western New York State, which still survives today as a village of about fifteen hundred, fourteen miles south of Utica. Francis worked first at farming, also making harness, and gloves, mittens and mocassins from deerskin. When deer grew too scarce on the settling frontier, he turned to farming full-time and married. His bride, Mary Owen, was of Welsh ancestry and, like him, had a Rhode Island Quaker background. Her grandfather had pulled up stakes and headed West after being expelled from his meeting house for enlisting as a militia lieutenant in the Revolution.

A packet of letters from members of his family, evidently saved by Francis Williams, was handed down several generations. The author, as a boy of twelve, rescued the letters from extinction one summer day when his mother was about to throw them away along with some other old, mildewed letters, himself putting them away in an attic and forgetting about them. An aunt fortunately found them and preserved the lot. The first, dated March 1836, is from Francis' father-in-law, Aaron Owen, who, as was common along the steadily expanding frontier, had moved farther west to Jacksonville (now Ithaca), New York. He urges Francis to join him and buy land, saying, "Joseph Tripp's farm should be considered. His price is 50 Dollars an acre, but he is not disposed to sell except to a Friend . . . It is our united opinion and that of your friends that you had better come out here this spring. I could employ thee, Francis, at good wages."

Francis evidently jumped at the offer, as he and Mary went West at once. His mother, Ruth, writes to congratulate him: ". . . We think thou has made rather a bold shake at last." She appears to keep close ties with the Rhode Island branch of the family and has just been to Providence to visit relatives and get "Dorcas's things to rights as her health is delicate yet." At home the wheat crop has been "much damaged" by lack of rain. "Ours is green through the middle, but appears to be dead on the sides," she tells Francis. "Thy father said when he gets done with the spring ploughing, if it did not come right, he should plough it up . . ."

A gossipy correspondent is Francis's sister Catherine, who writes about who has come and gone "in the stage" and says the tavern in the Hollow is being repaired. "Elder Eaton," she reports, "has hired a gentleman from Hamilton to teach school in the basement story of the Meeting House so this summer there will be six schools in the Hollow, quite a seat of literature, we think." She, too, writes much about farming: "Father thinks we shall not have green corn for two weeks. He says the wheat is pretty good, but it is rather thin now the heads are long. Barley is good, oats also, and the grass abundant, 2½ tons per acre in the lower meadow and the rest will average 2 tons."

Although Cyrus McCormick's reaper has just been invented (he built his first one in 1831), the Quakers, like most farmers of the times, still harvest by hand with a sickle or scythe. Catherine writes that "a hired man from Oswego" has been taken on to cut grain with a cradle scythe for twenty dollars a month, a bargain wage. "R. Sweet gives H. Judson 26 Dollars a month & in Winfield I hear several have given 28 Dollars. Father thinks he is very fortunate in his man. Says he is the handsomest mower of barley he ever saw." Threshing is still done by beating the sheaves with flails or by horses or oxen that trod out the grain. A ring of threshers thumping flails on the straw-littered wooden threshing floor inside a barn with the doors open is a common rural sight. To winnow, it is tossed in the air so that the chaff is blown away from the grain. Catherine says the wheat and barley yield is fifty bushels an acre.

This early-American rural life is not crime-free. Another sister, Margaret, writes Francis that a store in the Hollow has been broken into and robbed of four hundred dollars. The money, soon found, has half of it been buried in a box in a farmyard and the rest in one of the culprit's "innocent father's house between the ceiling and chamber floor." A whole gang of young Quaker men is involved, and "more names are coming out daily."

"Catherine says she never saw so many teams as yesterday with all the sheriffs and guards. They have got some in irons and are obliged to keep guards for there is such a company of swindlers, or blacklegs as they call them, that they are afraid others will try to rescue them. Only think, such a class of respectable and wealthy parents! They must have really been possessed of the Evil One . . ." Margaret also writes about the family's high-spirited horses, "so full of capers that Father can hardly manage them." She gossips: "I believe I wrote last winter about Charlotte Monroe's losing her reason, did I not? Well, a week ago they missed her, sent round the neighborhood, looked up in the orchard, and at last into the well where they saw her. A man went down immediately & she was drawn up, but life had fled. Poor little thing, she shortened an unhappy life . . . Edwin Palmer was married a month or two ago to David Randall's daughter. She was a tailoress. Fisk's wife says she is 42 years old, but others say 33. At any rate she is quite too old for him . . ."

An amusingly eccentric correspondent is an older brother, James, who has borrowed thirty dollars from Francis and finds it "very pleasant to find my application for relief so cheerfully & promptly acceded to." He demands more letters, saying, "Well, Francis, do write & induce Catherine. She wields a good pen. Drum her up, instill a little energy into her system. Nothing else is wanted to make her a very eligible correspondent & now postage being a mere nothing, let me know how you are & often. All those little particulars are so interesting. Does Mother get out often to Meeting? & Father, too? Anything pertaining to either, I am pleased to learn & we shall not have them with us long to write about."

James has sent his son Henry, seventeen, off on a four-day journey by foot to stay with some cousins who have a tutor. "I treat it as a very good place for him to improve . . . He will never shine, but may perhaps pass; he will never be splendid in anything, but will rather be noted for application . . ." He is just as cheerily pessimistic about other offspring: "Our Maria has 14 pupils, gets 5/- a week to teach small ideas how to sprout. Our Susan, her husband & daughter, 5 years, are now at our gate, going to Meeting with Maria. They live on Shore place, have 350 sheep and are farming it on the driving credit system & I confidentially believe will make a deep slump of it shortly. However, I hope I am mistaken . . ."

All their letters dwell on farming, still the livelihood of over eight out of ten Americans. James himself has rented his land and stock to a tenant, Frederick, for a hundred dollars a year. He finds crop prospects "rather encouraging, except grass, which is short. Apples, not one. Frederick this day mows some yellow daisies & June grass. It has rained some 4 days in succession and is now clear & hot. As this is not worth an answer, send an old newspaper in acknowledgement. I greet you & fare you well."

In another letter, this time in winter ("No snow, good walking, hard frozen ground"), James says he has taken up chemistry, astronomy and magnetism, the last "a new and governing science for shortly most others will be indebted to it & controlled by its multifarious and powerful inventions." With characteristic élan, he declares that every child, "by hook or by crook," should study it and "adults like myself who have seen near 60 winters may find much that is interesting . . ." He goes on to say, "You may judge us by the papers we take," naming New York's "Evepress, Independent, Tribune & Evening Post," which he trades with a cousin for the "Phia Saturday eve post & American Union & Harpers magazine." He sees progress all about. "Our city 2 miles off is getting to be an important place,

3 or 400 inhabitants & there are 8 meeting houses within 6 miles of us. Six miles to a plank road & on that 8 or 9 miles to a railroad. Stage twice a day & has been for 2 or 3 years. We are approximating the center of civilization & who can say we are not in the focus . . ."

The last of these surviving letters to Francis is quite different. It is from another older brother, Henry, and dated October 3, 1848:

"Thou alluded to your Meeting-house troubles. I am so little of a Society man and . . . I am miserably qualified to give any advice. But when we reflect upon the nature of divine worship and the impossibility of approaching the Almighty unless every worldly thought and idea be prostrated before Him, might it not be safest at times to yield more than we think is right for the sake of peace?

"Now, my Dear Brother, is it not time for us to come to a pause, a solemn pause?"

In this remarkable letter, Henry Williams is trying to avoid a breach in the family, divided by what is known in Quaker history as the Wilburite-Gurneyite separation of 1845. This religious crisis had its roots in the evangelical revivals and tent meetings that were sweeping the frontier. Some members of the Society of Friends were turning to preachers and hymn singing, scripture reading and sermons. In Providence and Newport, where the Quakers were more urbane, widely traveled and better-read, the lack of a definite creed and regular ministry was not felt. But in small, isolated backwoods meetings, like those in Bridgewater or Jacksonville, where farmers arrived tired from clearing and working the land, the Quakers' silent meeting for worship sometimes became an empty form. In one of her letters, Catherine Williams mentions members falling asleep.

The quarrel was touched off by the tour of American Quaker communities by Joseph Gurney, a rich, aristocratic Englishman who urged more interest in education and the Bible. His presence stirred an evangelical revival among Quakers in frontier areas, who tended to discard many of the old forms and distinctions. Gurney's liberal interpretation of Quaker doctrine and practice was soon challenged in New England by a young Rhode Island schoolteacher, John Wilbur. Finding Wilbur an embarrassment, urbanized New England and New York Quakers tried to disown him, while Wilbur's adherents, many of them country people, set up a new yearly meeting in protest against what they considered dangerous departures from the teachings and ways of George Fox and the early Friends. Soon families were split, lawsuits contested community property, cousins avoided each other, and men and women averted their faces while driving their buggies past rival meeting houses.

Francis Williams joined the Wilburites. He was now thirty-four and had farmed in Jacksonville nine years and was making payment on his land. Like other local adherents of John Wilbur, Francis began to talk of going West to help found a colony of conservative Friends. His brother Henry tried to dissuade him:

"There is no doubt that the operation of Divine Light is much clearer on some minds than upon others . . . Deference, respect and esteem is due any conscientious man. If Joseph Gurney suggests that it might be profitable for some to pray every day, or three times a day, does it become me to say I cannot fellowship with those who advocate such sentiments? Would it not rather cause me to ask why I am not more often in a condition to pray?"

We do not know how Francis responded to this gentle plea for tolerance. He remained a Wilburite but stayed on in Jacksonville. It was not until 1859, fourteen years later, that he sold his farm and took his wife, Mary, and their ten children to the newly settled Wilburite village of Whittier in Iowa. It was named, like the one in California, after the Quaker poet John Greenleaf Whittier, who was then just reaching the height of his fame as the voice of the preindustrial New England villager and farmer. As so often with Americans, the vision of a purer, simpler society took Francis and his family West. Earlier, the Yankees from New England and New York had come by way of the Erie Canal into northern Ohio, but now they could make the trip by rail, traveling from Chicago on the first passenger train to go as far as Mount Vernon, Iowa. There they got off to make the last few miles of the trip to Whittier by oxcart, oxen then generally being used to draw the plows used to break the virgin prairie sod. Among the Williamses bouncing along over the rutted mud track was little Hadwen, aged four. We can only imagine how he felt sitting there, bone weary and wide-eyed, hearing the cart's wooden flanks groaning and creaking. Perhaps they rode through newly cleared forest. Did he think about Indians, blizzards, rattlesnakes and all the wonders and horrors that awaited those who "went West"?

From a few cabins huddled together in woods and cleared patches of land, Whittier had already grown into a village, with its own mill and store, a blacksmith and tanner, a cooper, wheelwright, cabinetmaker and cobbler. The plain language—everyone saying "thee"—and the plain gray, black or brown dress, the men's broad-brimmed hats and the women's bonnets, showed at once it was no ordinary little farming community. Hadwen attended its school of about thirty pupils. It had its own strict rules about what to wear. Silk, ruffles, ribbons, hats, rings, pins or any jewelry were forbidden. So was "all unnecessary noise, such as whistling, singing, or loud, boisterous laughing, or hallooing." Rather, pupils were "tenderly advised to check the arisings of pride in their hearts, and cherish instead a true regard for truth, that no desire may be fostered to imitate the ever-changing fashions of the world inconsistent with that simplicity heretofore rejoined . . ." All the pupils were required to go to Meeting House.

At first, the Williams family lived in a carriage house. The sale of the farm he'd built up in New York enabled Francis to buy forty acres of still-virgin land in advance of his arrival, and now he purchased four horses, three milk cows and some pigs and chickens. A thrifty soul, he kept all his savings in gold, hidden at home. He and his two oldest sons, Aaron and George, cleared the land and built a spacious white frame house with seven bedrooms (which, over a century later, is still standing, lived-in and looking as sturdy as ever). As a home it must have been austere. There were few books—George Fox's *Journal,* Robert Barclay's *Apology,* the works of William Penn, Isaac Pennington and other early Friends, the family Bible, and Whittier's *Legends of New England, Snow-bound* and *Maud Muller,* all with faded black and brown bindings. The Quaker wall calendar substituted numbers for the pagan names of months and the days of the week, so that February became the Second Month, Monday the Second Day and so on. Hadwen came to use the conventional names away from home, but in letters to his mother he kept to Quaker custom as long as she lived.

In 1864, Francis Williams crushed his right knee while felling a tree on a woodlot. Amputation, though so common among soldiers in the Civil War, was not attempted. The wound never fully healed, and Francis spent the last seven years of his life crippled and in pain. As his granddaughter Helen recalled, "Father had no memory of anything but a cross, grumpy invalid."

Whittier—they'd settled a mile north of the Meeting House—remained a world apart, over the years its people gaining a reputation as the ultraconservative Wilbur Friends. As late as 1914, a Quaker historian was to observe that Whittier's people had "succeeded in preserving the peculiarities, not to say the eccentricities, of Quakerism as it appeared three-quarters of a century ago."

Soon after his father's death in 1871, Hadwen, seventeen, talked his mother into letting him go to college. For Mary Williams it was a daring break with tradition. Nobody in Whittier had gone before. His two older brothers—Aaron and George—were unlettered farmers, though some of his sisters had gone to boarding school in New England so they could teach. Mary herself had encouraged Hadwen's scholarly bent.

Inscription by Mary Williams in notebook filled with 150 Quaker poems she had copied in longhand, presented to Hadwen June 11, 1872:

". . . Please accept this small token of affection from one who cradled thy infancy, watched over thy youth, and now in maturer years would crave that the protecting care of the unslumbering shepherd may be as a hedge about thy pathway, and the reward of a well spent life may be thy happy portion. Mother."

The poems, some by Whittier, have titles like "Thoughts in a Religious Meeting of Friends," "The Quaker of Olden Time," and "Thoughts in Silent Meetings."

A sample:

> "While others labor in thy cause
> With words of power and skill,
> Be it but mine to know thy laws,
> To love thee and be still . . ."

Despite its austerity, farm life in Whittier was evidently pleasant. At least George, who went off to California as a young man, remembered it with nostalgia in a letter home fifty years later:

". . . The dear old garrett, the old wooden clock . . . my mind often wanders back to the blackberry patch, the pasture by the creek and the cornfields. After the house was built and sand from the cellar was piled outside, Hadwen and I dug trenches in it and threw up breastworks and built forts. We all wanted to be soldiers in the Civil War . . . And I haven't forgotten plowing corn when I'd drive the oxen and Hadwen would tend the plow . . ."

At last she agreed to let him go, on condition that Hadwen pay his own way and, until he was twenty-one, the wages of a hired man to take his place on the farm. The United Brethren had started a school, Western College, near Cedar Rapids. Hadwen worked and worked, sometimes dropping out to "hire out" on a farm for some months or to teach school until he had enough to study again, but he couldn't always find the money.

From a letter by Hadwen Williams to his family, November 1874:

"Dear ones all at home—I had a fine time eating the things you brought, especially the peaches. I do not know that I said hardly enough about my going to school next term. If you can spare me, anyway, I want to go. It seems as if I only got started. I could finish Grammar, take Algebra and some other new study."

He offers to sell his horse, Dolly, and promises that he can teach school again

*in the winter and "the first dollars that I earn shall pay the one who sends me
to school."*

"So in view of all these facts, I ask, beg, plead, beseech, implore, entreat,
petition, and urge that you decide to let me go next term . . ."

*They did. A physician's certificate dated January 1887, and presented to Dr.
Hadwen Williams, thirty-two, of Martelle, Iowa, reads:*

"The holder, a native of New York state, having given satisfactory evidence that he has been engaged in the practice of medicine and surgery for
five years and that he received a diploma from the Medical Department,
State University, at Iowa City, the first day of March, 1882, is legally autho-
rized to practice Medicine and Surgery in the State of Iowa under the laws
of 1886."

*The menu of the Medical Department's Twelfth Commencement Banquet,
1882, shows that raw, fried or scalloped oysters were served, along with beef
tongue, sugar-cured ham, pressed corn beef, lobster and boned turkey with
apple jelly. President Pickard spoke on "The Physician as a Citizen," and the
barbershop quartet sang, "What Beams So Bright?" "Come, Jolly Comrade"
and "Crabbed Youth and Age." One H. Williams is shown as the president of
the graduating class.*

Hadwen and Jessie

From the Hawkeye-Record, *Mount Vernon, Iowa, October 3, 1884:*

"Last Thursday evening about 30 guests assembled at the Warren Richardson home in Linn Grove to attend the solemnization of the wedding rites of Dr. Hadwen Williams, who practices medicine in Martelle, and Miss Jessie Johnston, sister of Mrs. Richardson. At 8:30 P.M., while Miss French played Wagner's Wedding March . . ."

Same newspaper, "Local Items" column:

". . . Evolution has done wonders for him. Haddie was so bashful at one time that the sight of a piece of calico made the blushes come and go and his face to resemble a fiery furnace. Bon voyage, Haddie."

Same paper:

"Eli Johnston is among us for a few days. He came up, not from Egypt, but from Kansas, to be present at the marriage of his daughter, Jessie . . ."

Letter to Hadwen, Martelle, Iowa, from Eli Johnston, Emporia, Kansas, July 30, 1884:

". . . My daughter Jessie is to me a *precious treasure* and I hope you both have fully weighed the responsibilities resting upon you in celebration of the nuptial rites . . . May the God of peace and mercy direct you both to remain true to your vows and to do your duty in this life and prepare you for that life beyond the grave . . ."

From Eli Johnston's journal; in its pages was a yellowed "certificate of exemption" from military service in the Civil War "on account of having furnished a substitute":

". . . When I was a boy I went to the school of 'Lickin and Larnin'. Our teacher would wield a birch in the air and cut it to make a figure 8, but he couldn't tell the difference between Simon Barjona and Simon Jobarny. My seat was a slab off a sawed log . . . This school was a loud school. When it came to the spelling lesson the pupils used their muscle. One would be spelling 'baker,' another 'cessation,' another 'liability,' and another 'incomprehensibility' and all hollering at the top of their voices . . .

"My occupation has been varied. Since 1847 I've spent my winters trying to 'Keep school' and my summers farming. I moved to Iowa in 1858 and in 1861 bought a home in Linn Grove across from the churchyard which had 40 acres of prairie and 10 acres of timber. I have that land yet and have added to it 80 acres more of good valuable prairie . . . My parents were pious people and raised me up in the nurture and admonition of the land: 'Fear God and keep his commandments' . . . In the winter of 1850–51, while living in Indiana, I accepted the truth of divine revelation, 'Except ye repent ye shall all likewise perish.' While shouting was common during that protracted service and it is a practice I would not condemn, the 'still small voice' impressed me more . . . May God help me at all times to do my duty."

Jessie's mother, Margaret, died of consumption in 1867, leaving Eli, who soon remarried, with three small children. In her last letter, sent from her parents' home in Ohio, the dying Margaret wrote:

". . . I think my health is improving some . . . I can hardly stand it these hot days with my flannel jacket on. Mother is very careful of me, will not even let me wash the dishes . . . I wish it were so that I could be at home with you. I want you to keep in good heart . . . trust in the Lord and all will be well. Write me twice a week if you can. Goodbye, Mag. P.S. Did you set out any hedge?"

Family tradition held that Margaret was the great-granddaughter of a celebrated Colonel Joseph Reed, an Anglophile who was George Washington's private secretary in 1775 and later accused of treason by Alexander Hamilton, Dr. Benjamin Rush, General John Cadwalader and others. Washington defended his adjutant and promoted him to general in 1777, though it took over a century before Reed, who died in 1785, a mere forty-four, was absolved by historians. Astonishingly, alas, it turned out that there were two Colonel Joseph Reeds in the Revolutionary War, both of them Ulster Scots. The family connection seems more likely to have been a much less dashing figure of unsullied patriotism whom the 1783 tax rolls show at age fifty having fathered nine children and possessing a mill, a hundred-and-sixty-acre farm in York

County, Pennsylvania, three horses and a bank account of over two hundred pounds. But to return to the wedding. What follows are extracts from a journal kept by Hadwen and Jessie from their wedding day, September 25, 1884, and kept up with less and less frequency for forty-two years. Only the occasional entry is reproduced here. The initial ones are all by Hadwen:

"The early part of the week was almost continual rain, but today was very pleasant and fair. Desire Kyle, Amy French and Jennie Carpenter prepared the floral decorations in the parlor during the afternoon. A fine arch spanned the bay window supporting a large wedding bell. The guests arrived promptly and were seated in the parlor at the appointed hour. Jessie's Pa has been in Kansas but came home yesterday. The guests were as follows: Pa, Warren & Allie, Aaron & Libbie, George & Ola . . . The groom wore a suit of Prince Albert cut . . .

". . . The wedding party entered the parlor and took their places under the bell where Rev. Porter pronounced them man and wife. After congratulations we enjoyed a bountiful repast prepared by Allie and the bride. Pa brought peaches and apples from Kansas for the occasion. The evening passed pleasantly with music. The guests departed about midnight. We sat up for some time longer and waited for a chivari which had been promised, but were disappointed. After Jessie had retired, the Dr. removed a splinter 5/8th inches in length from beneath her finger nail which she accidentally thrust in her finger about noon today. We will not mention the list of presents . . ."

From the Hawkeye-Record:

". . . The presents were numerous, beautiful and useful: a bracket, silver cake basket, silver pickle castor, cup and saucer, butter knife, napkin rings, butter dish, fruit knives, paper holder, bedspread, half dozen napkins, bread plate, rocking chair, Nathaniel Hawthorne's *The Scarlet Letter* and the collected poems of Elizabeth Barrett Browning . . ."

Hadwen continues the journal:

"Sept. 26—Jessie kicked me out of bed because I slept on the rail. She could not resist the temptation . . ."

"Sept. 27—This evening we came home to Martelle. We shall keep house where I am now, living over the Post Office. We have 3 rooms, besides a woodshed . . ."

"Oct. 6—Have been away on calls all night. A house fire. This is the first time Jessie was left alone . . ."

"Nov. 27, Thanksgiving—Had Warren & Allie here for dinner. An A No. 1 Turkey. It cost six cents per pound live."

"Dec. 23—Went to Anamosa today. Jessie went along. Very cold and snowing. Wore my buffalo coat for the first time."

"Dec. 24—Helped make a Christmas Cross at the church today. About eighteen degrees below all day. House nearly filled at evening entertainment. The cross well filled with presents. Your humble servant officiated as Santa Claus. Wore buffalo coat, comic cap and fur-trimmed boots."

"Jan. 1, 1885—Although the mercury was 20 degrees below this morning, we went up to Mother's in Whittier today. A long, cold ride we had, too, but we enjoyed ourselves when we got there. Went in the buggy as there is not enough snow for sledding. Roads very rough."

The first entries from Jessie:

"Mar. 25—Sent off the first carpet of my own manufacture to the weavers today.

"Apr. 1—I gave Hadwen buckwheat cakes for breakfast today. Extra fine. Used a cloth."

From Hadwen:

"Apr. 9—I was called to see J. C. Peet last night between eleven and midnight. He was suffering from a severe hemorrhage of the lungs. Had another at 8 A.M. this morning & 2 P.M. this afternoon. Had Dr. Blakeslee of Anamosa in for consultation. Am staying with Mr. Peet all the time."

"Apr. 10—Am still staying with Mr. Peet at his farm. He had one hemorrhage at 4 P.M. and one at 7 P.M. He is very much alarmed & has given up all hope . . ."

"Apr. 11—Am still here & no prospect of getting away. He does not want me to leave. Jessie drove home alone today." *Jessie adds:* "I'm so lonesome and tired of living alone I can hardly stand it."

Hadwen goes on:

"Apr. 13—Am still holding the fort but hope I can get away soon. Jessie complains bitterly of being alone. Came home this evening at 11 P.M. & promised to return at an early hour." *Again Jessie adds:* "I don't think I complain more than the occasion warrants."

This episode of Mr. Peet—Hadwen continues to visit him on his farm almost every day through April—is typical of Hadwen's entries about his patients. Happily, Mr. Peet made a surprise recovery and his story ends: "J. C. Peet paid his bill today. $78.75. This is the largest bill I ever received at once." *There is a lot of sickness and death among children. Hadwen examines Jessie's fifteen-year-old half brother, Frank:* ". . . Very feeble. A temperature of about 102. Pulse 120. Probably has a tubercular deposit in lungs—*

prognosis unfavorable." *Young Frank soon dies, as does the infant daughter of Hadwen's brother, Aaron, in Whittier:* "Little Mary died today. She was about 16 months old. Very sweet & pretty babe. Fair as a lily. She will be buried at the Friends Meeting House . . . ."

Hadwen goes on:

"May 5—Since last entry cleaned house. We papered the walls & put down new carpet in the sitting room—a great improvement . . . Heard bobolinks yesterday. Had a very hard rain last night with much lightning. Oats are not all sown . . . Yesterday heard of suicide of Joel Beaver of Viola. On Saturday he took strychnine. Cause supposed to be disappointed love."

"May 7—Froze last night hard enough to bear up a man on soft mud. Ice in a bucket ¾ths of an inch thick. Oats are not all sown yet . . ."

"May 12—Went to Whittier to Mother's today . . . Had a very pleasant time. Got garden seeds & got home about 10 P.M.

"May 13—Made garden today. Planted corn, peas, beans, potatoes, lettuce, radishes . . ."

From Jessie, May 20:

"We went to Cedar Rapids today. Hadwen had to attend the State Medical Society Convention and I just went along for fun. We had a very nice time. Among other extravagances we sat for some cabinet photos. And had some ice cream, strawberries and new onions. We also did some of our spring trading. I went to the afternoon session of the convention but decided doctors do not make first-class orators. They mumble so . . ."

Hadwen:

"July 4—Did not celebrate today except to fire 13 rounds at sunrise . . ."

"July 30—Hottest day of the season so far, 104 degrees in the shade . . ."

"Aug. 26—Went to Lisbon to a Camp Meeting in the evening. Saw W. J. Beatty & wife. Did not get any supper before sermon. Got a lunch of Bologna, cookies, cheese, pears & peaches—cost 45 cents . . ."

"Nov. 3—ELECTION DAY."

Jessie:

"Nov. 19—Hadwen bought me a new sewing machine today. Very good one, I think. Price $85."

"Nov. 22—John and Lizzie Boxwell have had their breach of promise trial. John was fined $300.

"Dec. 8—This has been a busy day for Hadwen. He was at Gus McCall's from midnight until morning. They have a new baby boy. He went on the 7:20 train to the Rapids to attend Medical Society, where he read an essay, also bought himself some new clothes: coat, overcoat, vest & underwear. He came home on the 10 P.M. train and immediately went to Ed Lathwell's to deliver another baby. They also have a little son. He stayed until morning. It snowed enough last night & today to make sleighing."

Hadwen:

"Jan. 10—Very cold weather for three days. Sunday Mrs. Fred Leaper died 12:30 A.M. Went to Leapers on horseback. Cut about a dozen fences to get through the snow. Mercury fell to 18, 24 and 30 below zero on the 8th, 9th and 10th respectively. Very blizzardy."

"Jan. 31—A somewhat unusual occurrence took place this A.M. with the arrival of an 8^{14}/$_{16}$ths lb. boy. He has dark brown hair and blue eyes. Is strong & hearty. Mrs. Dell Armstrong & Dr. H. Williams officiating . . .

"Feb. 1—Pa and Ma came today from Linn Grove. They were somewhat surprised at the size of our family."

From Jessie, Apr. 4:

"Little Had is nine weeks old today. Weighed him yesterday. He weighs 14½ pounds. Hadwen very busy now, is gone a good deal. I would be very lonesome if it wasn't for my boy. The roads are very bad and have been indoors for some time."

Hadwen:

"May 16—Mrs. C. E. Brady died today. A good woman is gone."

"Aug. 20—Went to Camp Meeting last evening and this evening . . ."

"Aug. 22—Today we went up to Des Moines to attend Methodist Quarterly Meeting. A nice cool day. Drove two horses with our new harness. Had our buggy painted last week." *Since their marriage, Hadwen, who still sometimes goes to the Quaker Meeting House in Whittier, and Jessie, raised a Presbyterian in Linn Grove, have joined the Methodist church in Martelle and steadily become more active in it.*

From Jessie:

"Sept. 25—We have been married two years tonight. Our boy commenced to stand on his feet yesterday by holding on to a chair. Today he has cried a good deal more than common & we think his teeth are hurting him. He has none through yet . . .

"Jan. 31—This is little Hadwen's first anniversary. Our baby is a big boy 'one going on two' now. He walks more than he creeps now. Can talk but very little. Just 'Mamma,' etc. and can patacake . . ."

The entries become less frequent now. Here Jessie writes on Sept. 23, 1888, after four years of marriage:

"It has been a long time since there has been anything written in this journal . . . The second day of December, little Anna Louise was born. She is now nine months old and a round fat little dumpling she is. She has two teeth, stands up to chairs but does not walk yet. She is quite small for her age, brown-eyed and petite. Haddie has grown quite fast, and thinks sister Anna very nice indeed. Yesterday he was naughty and I told him he was a bad boy. Whereupon he remarked that he was 'Cain.' I must have told him Cain was a bad boy . . ."

"Dec. 25—Well, Christmas has come round again, and a grand time the babies have had of it. There was a Christmas tree at the church last night—at which Haddie gazed in silent ecstasy, and old Santa Claus brought him just what he wanted, a watch and a little wagon full of blocks, also quite a number of other small things—a book, bank, dishes, cup, etc. And Anna received a doll, which she clasped lovingly to her bosom upon receiving it and which has been christened Orpha. They have had a merry time of it today. They found some things in their shoes this morning—candy, little dolls and handkerchiefs. They think Santa Claus a lovely old Saint . . ."

"Jan. 1, 1889—Another year has come. The time rolls round very rapidly indeed . . . Anna is already beginning to display her feminine vanity. I made her a new pink calico dress and tried it on her today. When I took it off, she wept energetically, went and got it, and tried to put it on again."

There is no further entry in 1889. The next is Jan. 2, 1890, from Jessie:

"It has been a year since there has been anything written in this journal. Hadwen went to Chicago in April and was gone nearly six weeks at Dwight Moody's school . . ."

Life for Jessie has taken an unexpected turn. Some months earlier, Hadwen surprised her by announcing he felt called to become a medical missionary to China. To gain support from the Methodists' Foreign Missionary Board, he first had to enter the ministry. As it so happened, just at this time, in early 1889, Dwight L. Moody, the famous evangelist who was then at the peak of his popularity, called for a gathering in Chicago to "train young men and women in Christian work and to teach the Gospel." Hadwen went, and though the meeting led to the founding three years later of Moody's Institute, Moody's immediate purpose was quite different. Chicago's new industrialists, led by Cyrus McCormick, whose McCormick Harvesting Machine Company in Chicago was now producing over a thousand of his horse-drawn reapers a year, feared worker unrest. It was just three years since the city's Haymarket

Square riot of 1886, when seven policemen and four workers were killed in
violence and a bomb explosion after anarchists gathered to protest an earlier
fray between police and strikers outside the McCormick plant. They also
demanded an eight-hour day. The Communist Manifesto *had been published*
in 1848, and as the reputation of Karl Marx spread with Das Kapital—*the*
first volume came out in 1867—so did public fear of his ideas and the cry
"Workers of the world, unite! You have nothing to lose but your chains!" Now
McCormick, who gave $100,000, and other Chicago industrialists who helped
finance it, backed a new effort of evangelism by Moody among the city's
slum-dwelling workers. Nearly five hundred idealistic young men and women
responded to Moody's appeal to attend the Chicago convention from April 4 to
May 10, 1889, and be trained as "Christian workers," especially to save the
heathen "masses" of the cities. The thirty-five-year-old Dr. Williams was
among them. The emphasis in every session was on, in Moody's words, "the
surrender of the will" and to "sacrifice all for the Master."

Excerpt from Dwight Moody's opening address at the Chicago Avenue
Church, April 4, 1889:

". . . Work and work is the keynote of this convention. God sent you
here . . . The Haymarket Riot showed how urgent is the task. Either these
people are to be evangelized or the leaven of communism and infidelity will
assume such enormous proportions that it will break out in a reign of terror
such as this country has never known. It don't take a prophet or a son of a
prophet to see these things. You can hear the muttering of the coming
convulsion even now, if you open your ears and eyes . . . What is needed is
men who know the Word of God and who can go into the shops and meet
these bareheaded infidels and skeptics and appeal to them in the name of
Jesus Christ so that their hearts will soften under His precious Gospel . . .
Never mind the Greek and Hebrew. Give them plain English and good
Scripture. It is the sword of the Lord and cuts deep . . ."

Letter by Hadwen in Chicago to Jessie in Martelle, April 24, 1889:

"Dwight Moody came to our meeting tonight and at last I have had the
opportunity of seeing him in a revival myself. The key to his success, I
think, is to be in *deadly earnest* and to have a variety of *illustrations* by short
story narrative. The first of course can only come from a man who fully
believes that he has a divine message to a dying world, and who talks as if
this was his last opportunity. The second, I think, comes from the rare
faculty of being able to apply the right story or illustration to the right place
so as to make it of the most effect . . . Next week we are to have a man

who is to give us a few talks with special conference to dealing with those smart skeptics & atheists & Ingersolites. He comes from Oregon . . .

"I have found a number of little books here that will be of great help in Bible studies. It would be perfect to get three or four of them. One is a text book of references for use in preparing Bible readings, sermons, etc., another is *Bible Readings by Various Authors* . . .

Hadwen is sorry Jessie doesn't want to join him in Chicago. He wants to know how her expenses at home are running, as "it makes some difference with me in deciding how long to stay." The letter also includes some household instructions:

". . . You ought to drive a nail above the south window of the east bedroom. You remember I raised it with an axe & I never did anything about it afterward. Look after the coonskins & gloves now-days as this is the time for moth millers. If you have any doubts about their safety get some camphor & put some small pieces in with them. Look after the buffalo coat also . . ."

The rest of Jessie's Jan. 2, 1890, entry:

". . . Through the summer Hadwen preached a few times and October 7th he entered the ministry of the Methodist Episcopal church in Iowa City on trial by the Conference. He was given this place, New Hampton, to preach. So here we are."

Extract from interviews with Anna Louise, daughter of Jessie and Hadwen Williams, recorded seventy years after the events described:

"Poor Mother. Dad felt he must preach. Mother liked being a doctor's wife. Dad was just thirty-five and successful in his medical practice. But he wanted terribly to be a missionary. It was a great disappointment to her. He was never to have very big towns: Postville and Le Claire were about the biggest. And there was never going to be much money. We always had a cow. And we ate a lot of meal, cornmeal mush. How Mother hated cornmeal . . ."

From interviews with Helen Williams Collins, youngest of the four children of Hadwen and Jessie, ninety-four years later:

". . . To a good Quaker, becoming a Methodist preacher was abandoning your faith, it was apostasy. Father was pretty nearly in disgrace with his family in Whittier for going into the ministry. Mary Williams set the tone of that family and Father practically idolized her. I won't say he was exactly an outcaste, but Grandmother would have found it easier if he'd become a saloonkeeper . . ."

"Mother was high spirited. My goodness, she must have loved Father a lot. They about starved the first year or two. Father'd worked so hard for his education and in seven years as a doctor he'd built up a good practice and made plenty of money, only to realize he could no longer ignore the Call to preach. As I tell young people, if it's a *true* Call, you cannot run fast enough or far enough . . . Of course, when you got married that long ago, it was generally for keeps. Mother'd been brought up a Presbyterian. That was part of her life. She used to feel something was missing because she hadn't had that electrifying Call . . ."

Journal entry by Hadwen:

"Jan. 9, 1891, Volga City, Iowa—I went to Annual Conference in Decorah in October and was given this charge, Volga City. We stayed in New Hampton just one year. I built a parsonage 26 × 26. Raised $526 toward paying of same. Went into debt on it $550 . . ."

From now on, Hadwen's entries chiefly concern his new career of preaching and evangelism. This entry typically continues:

". . . Held revival at Williamstown for a week. Brother Orvello preached for me one night. Eight professed conversions but none could be induced to unite with the church. Held a revival the first three weeks in January in New Hampton, assisted by Rev. O. B. Waite. Seven professed conversions . . . December, 1890, commenced revival meetings assisted by Brother Perry of Elkader . . ."

Anne

From interviews with Anna Louise, 1959 and 1982; she describes her first memories:

There was a picket fence between two houses. One of the slats was loose. A little girl and I would slip through to see each other. One day there were tiny toads along the picket fence, on the crossbar. I never saw such tiny toads before or since. And there was a big fat man and he came up and said, 'Hello, little girl, I'm going to grease you all over and eat you up!' I was scared to death. I ran screaming into the house.

Our house was next to a church. There was a grave in our yard. A Catholic who'd married a Protestant. She couldn't be buried in the Catholic cemetery. Every time Haddie and I ran out of things to do, we'd have a funeral and sing over her grave. Right next to the church was a small-town hotel. It smelled strongly of old pipes and tobacco. They sold awfully good bubble gum. I took some money and bought some. Mother was upset. I wasn't supposed to go shopping on a Sunday . . ."

Entry in family journal by Jessie, 1891:

"Aug. 10—Yesterday was Sunday. Somebody gave Anna a penny in church and after the meeting was out, I was talking and didn't think much about her. She slipped out and across the street—to the hotel—and invested in three sticks of candy . . ."

Anna Louise, ninety years later:

It was chewing gum, not candy. That hotel had awful good chewing gum.

Jessie:

". . . and I didn't know she had gone until she got back and I enquired where her candy came from.

"This evening she sat upon the floor talking about Heaven. 'There won't be any naughty people up in Heaven, will there, Mama?' she asked. 'No,' I said. 'But I'll be there, won't I, Mama?' 'Yes, if you're a good girl.' 'Jesus will take his gun and shoot all the naughty people, won't he, Mama?' . . ."

Entry from Hadwen, March 1892:

"People from Elkader have been in the habit of coming to Volga City & selling liquor whenever any public dance was held. We grew tired of it & on the evening of St. Patrick's Day we seized their stock & afterward condemned it and poured it out. The constable, his deputies and myself did the work."

Jessie:

"Aug. 29, 1892—Our little boy started school this morning. I feel as though he were starting out alone in life now. The first time he has ever been from under our eye for even a few hours. May the Lord who loves him even better than I do, be with him and guide him through all the coming days, and years . . ."

Hadwen:

"Oct. 25, 1893—Jessie and I went to the World's Columbian Exposition in Chicago Oct. 10 to 19. Celebrating the discovery of America by Columbus 400 years ago. We left Anna at Aaron's in Whittier and Haddie & Allie came with us. Everybody's calling the fair "the White City" on account it's got hundreds of acres of white, classical buildings. It's all electrically lit up at night. We never saw anything to beat it. They show Westinghouse's new electric dynamo and alternating current generator. The whole White City is made of a kind of white plaster but inside, where they've got the exhibits all laid out, the steel girders are bare. Some compare it to the 'Heavenly City' toward which John Bunyan's Christian strove, or to a 'New Jerusalem.'

"Dwight Moody held tent meetings to vast crowds every night at the world's first Parliament of Religion. Some say he's drawn as many as two million people. I took Jessie to hear his famous talk about the Prophet Daniel. The big tent was packed with thousands of people and, speaking just like he was the King of Babylon, Moody leaned over the side of the pulpit and called, 'Oh, Dan'l, servant of the living God, is thy God able to deliver thee from the lions?' Then Moody spoke with a voice as if he were down in the pit, 'Oh, King, live forever. My God has sent his Angel and stopped the lions' mouths!' There was nothing theatrical, nothing irreverent about the way he did it. This was the word of God, but it was so vivid to Mr. Moody he made us feel we were right down there in the lions' den with him."

Jessie adds:

"I never saw such crowds. They say Hamlin Garland wrote his folks in North Dakota, 'Sell the cookstove if necessary and come!' I enjoyed the Midway, where Negro bands played some kind of wonderful new music with raggedy piano playing, and the view from the giant Ferris wheel. It was also my first experience with 'Black Tea,' and I dearly loved it; all we can get is green tea here at home. Hadwen took us to see Buffalo Bill's Wild West Show. I sure was tickled to see Annie Oakley, 'Little Sure Shot.' They had wonderful acts—the Pony Express, an attack on the Deadwood Stage, bucking broncos and a buffalo hunt. Sitting Bull was with the show one season before he got killed by the police in that Sioux uprising three years ago . . .

What Jessie heard at the Fair would soon be known as ragtime.

"Feb. 14, 1894—Anna had a fine time of it on the 14th. Old St. Valentine was very lavish with his love tokens. She received 12 altogether. She and Haddie have decorated the organ with them . . ."

Entry by Hadwen Williams, Jr., age eight:

"Feb. 25, 1894—We had an exhibition here last night. One of the things was Mother Goose. Nobody came as her. But we had Jack and Jill, Old King Cole, Beggars, When I Was a Boy I Lived by Myself, Little Miss Muffet, Polly Flinders, Simple Simon, Little Boy Blue, Tom the Piper's Son, Old Mother Hubbard, Little Bow Peep. I was Simple Simon. Anna was Jill. Lena Degro was blacked up to be a Negro. I said a piece about a Little Bird Tells Anna. We had food. That is all I can write tonight."

Postscript by Anna Louise:

"SIX YEAROLD ANNA

RIDGEWAY IOWA

WINN CO XXX"

Hadwen's increasingly rare journal entries now run entirely to dates of revival meetings and numbers converted, with the occasional comment like "a great outpouring of spirit." But in a letter to his mother, Mary Williams, in Whittier, in March 1895, he worries about Jessie's health:

". . . Jessie was taken sick Second Day night with Grippe. I was at Ashley canvassing for a new church and arrived home the same night I got the news . . . Today Lena is here and is baking, etc. . . . So things are all right again. Jessie is able to sit up a little today but is very weak. As usual with Grippe, she is much prostrated in the muscular system and gives out quickly if she tries to get about—even when she feels pretty strong lying down. For breakfast she ate a glass of milk and the white of an egg and a dish of canned peaches . . ."

A year later, Mary Williams herself died, aged seventy-eight. Hadwen's older brother, Aaron, wrote him on May 7, 1896, about their mother's estate:
"Dear Brother,

The estate figers as follows
Whole amt. $5301.90
Reserved   100.00
               $5201.90

Martha wrote me she would let thee have what thee wanted at 6 per cent so thee can send her a note for $349.77 dated March 1, 1896. The $100.00 I reserved to pay for perfecting the title and will divide what is left. I bought the grass seed and sowed on the two pieces of oats on thy place and it is up. Aint we having a lovely spring? Has rained some this A.M. Sheared my sheep myself. Dinner is nearly ready & we want to go to Springville this afternoon.—A.K.W."

Newspaper clipping found in journal:
"Last Saturday as Rev. Williams was studying his sermon, he suddenly stopped—not perplexed, but a good deal surprised—when the door opened and in walked about fifty of his friends. A little inquiry disclosed the fact that it was his fortieth birthday. Rev. Klemme, on behalf of those present, presented a nice rocking chair to him and a purse of money to Mrs. Williams. Those present with one accord all united in wishing Rev. Williams many happy returns of the day."

From Anna Louise:
After we left Martelle, we lived in New Hampton for a year, Volga City for two years, and Ridgeway for five years. They were all little towns in northern and eastern Iowa; there were to be fourteen in all. Life was quite placid and pleasant in those days. Our Quaker cousins in Whittier had a saying for it: "Leave the jostling to the masses. Take your time and shine your glasses." The most exciting things were presidential elections. When I was nine, William Jennings Bryan ran against McKinley . . .

From Bryan's "Cross of Gold" speech, Democratic Convention, 1896:
". . . Burn down your cities and leave your farms, and your cities will grow up again. But destroy your farms and the grass will grow in every city in the union . . .

"You shall not press down upon the brow of labor this crown of thorns. You shall not crucify mankind upon a cross of gold . . ."

Anna Louise:

. . . and there was a torchlight parade in Ridgeway and afterward a rally where Hadwen and a boy named John Baker were supposed to sing a duet. They were just ten years old. The song poked fun at Bryan. John sang first: "Oh, where have you been, Billy Boy, Billy Boy? Oh, where have you been, charming Billy?" And Haddie was supposed to answer. But he had fallen asleep. Which of course made it all the funnier. The crowd just roared. McKinley favored gold over silver and gold was supposed to be symbolic of big business and city interests. Dad was a staunch Republican and he painted a big bug gold. When McKinley won, everybody said it just went to show how many people had left farms for the city.

There was never much excitement, just ice-cream socials and sometimes visiting tent shows. Once, *Uncle Tom's Cabin* came to town. Posters were plastered all over Ridgeway promising "A High Tone of Morality Will Be Rigidly Maintained" and urging, "See ELIZA'S ESCAPE ON THE FLOATING ICE, followed at full speed by the Furious Pack of Panting Bloodhounds, goaded on to Madness by their Savage Masters. THE MOST THRILLING SCENE EVER DEPICTED!" The troupe staged a parade. Mama and I went to watch it and there was a big float pulled by two teams of horses with a little cabin on it. An old black Mammy was sitting in the cabin door, and when the float went by, she waved at us and cried, "Hello, Mama!" It was Haddie, working his way into the show.

I just loved it. Topsy saying, "Golly, I'se so wicked—I is. I's mighty wicked," and her "Never was born. I 'spect I just growed." It was horrible when Simon Legree flogged Uncle Tom, hitting him three times with a snake whip around the body and snarling with each stroke, "Take that! And that! And that! I'll take every drop of blood you have!" And Uncle Tom looking at him and saying, "You may kill my body, mas'r, but you can't kill my soul." And all the booing and cheering.

It seemed like once I started bawling, I never did stop. Little Eva on her deathbed, looking heavenward and St. Clair asking, "Oh, Eva, tell us what you see!" And Eva gasping, "Love, joy, peace!" and dying. Or George, holding Uncle Tom in his arms, and pleading, "Dear Uncle Tom, speak once more! Here is Mas'r George. Your own little Mas'r George. You mustn't die! I've come to buy you and take you home." But he's too late and Uncle Tom replies, "Oh, Mas'r George, the Lord has bought me and is going to take me home—and I long to go. Heaven is better than Kentuck." For days afterwards, Haddie and I would act out all the parts. I'd be Eliza, leaping with wild cries and desperate frenzy from one cake of ice to another —stumbling, leaping, slipping, and springing up again! Blood marked every step, I'd see nothing, until dimly, as in a dream, I was on the Ohio side and a man was helping me up the bank.

Mama did not share our enthusiasm about *Uncle Tom's Cabin.* She wanted us to develop a taste for good literature. When I was ten or eleven, she forbade reading the Elsie Dinsmore books, saying they were wishy-washy. Years and years later, when I was past seventy, I came across *Elsie Dinsmore* and took it home and read it. I got as far as the scene where Elsie is ordered by her father to sit down at the piano and play and sing; it is Sunday:

"She sat down, but raising her pleading eyes, brimful of tears, to his face, she repeated her refusal. 'Dear papa, I *cannot* sing it today. I *cannot* break the Sabbath.'

" 'Elsie, you *must* sing it,' said he, placing the music before her . . . Elsie sat with her little hands folded in her lap, the tears streaming from her downcast eyes over her pale cheeks . . ."

Mother herself was an avid reader. She was very fond of Dickens; her favorite was *Pickwick Papers.* When each of us was about ten, the day would come when Dad would put a book in our lap and say, "Now it's time for you to read *David Copperfield."* Mother also loved the historical novels of the time—Hall C. Cain's story of settling the West, *The Crossing;* an account of the plague in Philadelphia called *The Red City; Janice Meredith,* set in George Washington's time; and *Alice of old Vincennes,* about pioneers in Indiana. Like many ladies of her day, Mother also memorized long passages of poetry, mostly John Greenleaf Whittier and Longfellow. When Helen was born, she loved rhythm and Mother used to read her poetry instead of singing lullabies.

Mother sang beautifully, the stalwart of the choir. But Dad's singing was pitiful. He couldn't carry a tune. If he sang at all, he sang badly. He knew only two songs well and he used to sing us to sleep in thundering tones:

"Twenty-five blue bottles hanging on the wall . . ." Or: "John Brown's at your stable door. Where's your mule? I'll ride him till his back is sore and leave him at some stranger's door . . ." They went on and on. It was either these or nothing. He used to sing them when putting us to sleep. Those two songs were all he knew. Yet Dad was just starved for music. His idea of a perfect Sunday afternoon was to gather the family at the piano to sing so he could sit back and listen. "You're Not the Only Pebble on the Beach" was a popular tune.

Dad kept up with the newspapers. Besides subscribing to papers from Chicago, Des Moines, Springville and Mount Vernon, he got the New York *Advocate,* Epworth *Herald, Northwestern Christian Advocate,* the Presbyterian *Interior,* the anti-Catholic *Menace*—a priest lent him the Catholic paper—and Mother clandestinely bought copies of *The Saturday Evening Post,* which was considered too worldly and frivolous for a preacher's wife. Mother liked me to read authors like Louisa May Alcott and Nathaniel Hawthorne. My favorites over the years were Edward Lear's "The Owl and the Pussy Cat," "Froggie Went A 'Courtin Ride," *The Brownies Through the Union, Uncle Remus,* and later on *Little Women* and Horatio Alger's *Ragged Dick* novels. Best of all were Margaret Sidney's Pepper books—*The Five Little Peppers and How They Grew, The Five Little Peppers Midway* . . . all the Pepper books.

Excerpt, opening passage, Five Little Peppers; And How They Grew, *published 1880:*

"The little old kitchen had quieted down from the bustle and confusion of mid-day . . . The father died . . . Mrs. Pepper had had hard work to scrape together money enough to put bread into her children's mouths and pay the rent of the little brown house . . . 'Poor things!' she would say to herself . . . 'I must get learnin' for 'em someway, but I don't see *how!*' "

From Jessie, 1897:

"Feb. 7—Our little Mary is four and a half months old and we think she is a most wonderful baby. Especially Haddie and Anna admire her. Round and fat and we think very sweet but quite a sober baby. Does not laugh without she thinks she has a good reason . . . Hadwen has been holding a tent meeting . . ."

From Hadwen, 1898:

". . . Main Street is all aflap with American flags and the grocery ads in the paper say, 'REMEMBER THE MAINE.' On April 30th, Commodore Dewey's squadron steamed into Manila Bay. War bulletins seem to have become the town's meat and drink . . ."

In October 1898, Hadwen went to Waterloo, Iowa, to hear President William McKinley speak to a rally. The previous April, the Washington Post *had warned, "The taste of Empire is in the mouth of the people even as the taste of blood in the jungle." Hadwen quoted from McKinley's speech in the journal:*

". . . We mean to sustain our boys in blue that are carrying our flag, whether in the Philippines or here in Iowa . . . The question is: shall we stand together until the job is finished? . . . Our flag in the Philippines waves not as a banner of imperialism . . . It waves as it waves here and everywhere, the flag of freedom, of hope, of civilization . . ."

From a letter by Hadwen to Jessie from Elwood, Iowa, where he has just been assigned to preach. As usual, he has gone ahead to fix up the parsonage, and Elwood is hilly enough "to keep one going up and down all the time." More spectacularly, it has just been devastated by a cyclone. Dated Nov. 19, 1898:

". . . The track of the cyclone is only two miles south of town. The stories they tell are marvelous. Houses and barns were lifted into the air and ground to kindling. People at a distance say that buildings went into the air as if they had been tumbleweeds in a whirlwind. Pieces of a house as large as a whole side could be seen going around. Sometimes they would come to the outside of the whirl where they could be seen only to disappear again in an instant. Being drawn in again and again until all was ground to pieces. One man has a pair of shears with one handle broken off, a wire from a pail handle wrapped twice around it, then the wire is stuck through the ring of the remaining handle and wrapped round again. Buggy tires were found wrapped around trees. It would take volumes to tell of the marvelous things the people speak about . . ."

Entry by Jessie, 1899:

"Feb. 25—We moved here to Elwood after Conference. Like it pretty well . . . There is a great deal of sickness right now, mostly La Grippe . . . Father died December 7 in Linn Grove . . . One by one we are being taken away . . . The children are growing up so fast. We will soon have a young man & woman instead of a little boy & girl, and Baby is going on three years old and as full of cunning ways as she can be. Ma lives alone in Mount Vernon . . ."

Further comment from Helen Collins:

". . . After Grandpa Johnston died, Harriet Varner, his second wife, became almost a recluse. She liked to lie in a hammock in the summer and read and study. She had inherited plenty of money from her father, who'd owned a big farm, and she went to Louisiana every winter. She had a passion for jigsaw puzzles and all over the house were little cloth bags with puzzles . . . When she and Grandpa went down to teach in Cherokee Territory one time, Harriet used to pull all the blinds. She'd tell Grandpa, 'I don't want all those eyes peering in at us.' "

Jessie's February 1899 entry continued:

". . . Hadwen is going to Yosemite by train and taking his bicycle to ride about the park. He has worked so hard. I'll stay home and look after the children. Baby has a very peaceful disposition—tho just now she is having a tantrum. Haddie is 13 and Anna 11 . . ."

From a letter by Hadwen to Jessie, March 17, 1899, during his bicycle tour of Yosemite Valley. Naturalist John Muir's first book, The Mountains of California, *published five years earlier, has awakened Americans to the beauties of the Sierra. In his letter, Hadwen describes the valley's broad, parklike floor, its massive, rounded domes and granite cliffs, and the high, free-spilling waterfalls. Most awesome, he finds, are the Sequoias:*

". . . 'And there were giants in those days . . .' Just think of it, Jessie, the Sequoia tree was in its prime, swaying in these same winds, when Christ walked on earth. They are the oldest living things. Muir says he has counted more than four thousand annual rounds in one tree. Cycle through the woods here and God's work overwhelms you everywhere. As Muir wrote to Emerson, at Yosemite one is mostly in Eternity . . . There are trunks as tall and stately as granite pillars. With the humblest of violets growing around the feet of these giant redwoods. Their roots strike deep in the soil but they persist in soaring towards Heaven.

In 1955, the bristlecone pines of eastern California were proved to be older, up to 4,200 years.

From Anna Louise:

In Elwood there was only one other little girl my age, Edith Linbaugh, and we had to walk about half a mile to school and a mile to church. There was a Dr. McKenzie, with three sons: Albert, John and Charlie. They had three horses. Like Indian broncos. I rode with those boys all the time with my pigtails sticking straight out behind. Dr. McKenzie and his family were the elite of the town. In 1900 their oldest daughter returned from college and married a prominent lawyer. After the wedding everyone talked about the marvelous new dessert they'd served. It was called Plymouth Rock Gelatin and was made in pink and white. You had to put in your own fruit flavors. The groom later cheated an old lady and was disbarred. One of Dr. McKenzie's brothers came back from the Klondike and told marvelous tales of the gold rush. He showed us our first gold nugget.

Everybody walked to church. One day, a Mr. Potter, an elderly man, was walking and got caught on the railway bridge and was killed by a train. Mary was just four or five years old and was very perturbed about it. She asked where Mr. Potter had gone. Mama told her, "We assume Mr. Potter went to Heaven." Mary said, "Well, his legs didn't go. I saw them hanging out the back of a truck."

When I was thirteen I had quantities of hair. It used to get snarled on top. Once, while moving, Mother didn't comb it and I got terribly, terribly sick and almost died. It turned out that the hair was alive with lice. Mother had always heard that lice came from the body of a dead person and thought what a terrible thing it was. Father got some green soap but they thrived on it. So he made a solution of carbolic acid. It killed the lice but we still had to get the eggs out. We could have cut it, but nobody had short hair in those days. Aunt Allie and Aunt Margaret were coming and Mother thought it would be a horrible disgrace if I didn't have long hair.

Father was a very good man. And kind. He did much good in the community. And gave sympathetic, soothing funerals. He was a fundamentalist, preaching about the Bible, not about improving one's character or personality. He was strongly evangelistic and as a country preacher with a rural circuit in 1898 he made a huge tent out of duck canvas on Mother's sewing machine. He hired Haddie and me to sew around the holes for the tent pegs and Mother helped on her machine. The Methodist District owned one, but he wanted his own and he used it for summer revival meetings for over twenty years. On hot nights, they put up the sides to let the breeze through. He preached a lot out in the country, mostly in the evening after the farmers had finished their chores. He made notes but never wrote out a sermon. He held revival meetings every summer, with what they called "spiritual experiences." But Dad spoiled me for a lot of ministers. He gave you something you could use to live by through the week.

He'd wanted terribly to go to China. But when the time came, the Great Panic of 1893 was on. Armies of people marched on Washington for relief, Coxey's Army all the way from Ohio. There was no money in the country. Missionaries were being called home. Then, in 1900, the Boxer Rebellion broke out. There were reports, which proved false, of Americans and Europeans being massacred in Peking. Later, the children came and Mama wouldn't go to China with babies. The farthest Dad ever traveled was twice to California. For fifty years he also talked of going to Alaska as a medical missionary to work with the Indians. Instead, he spent his life preaching in one little Iowa town after another. Mama said she got so tired, every time we moved to a new town, of hearing the last congregation sing, "God Be with You till We Meet Again." Papa wasn't diplomatic enough to climb high in the ministerial profession, but he was well liked by his congregations.

Statement by H. W. Troy, Presiding Elder, Decorah District, 1899 Methodist Quarterly Conference:

"Let me say that if Methodism has a self-sacrificing, hard-working pastor, it is Hadwen Williams, and I doubt if the Home or Foreign field can produce a more conspicuous example of Christian heroism and devotion. At

Elwood, Rev. Bro. Williams, following the example of the Apostle Paul, constructed a tent with his own hands, in which he held revival meetings at Lost Nation and near the Godard church during the summer with good results, if no great religious awakening."

Sermon titles, listed under "Elwood Revival," found among Hadwen's papers:
". . . July 14, 'What Think Ye of Christ?;' July 15, 'He Leadeth Me,' Psalms 23 & 1; July 16, 'Wilt Thou Be Made Whole?' John 5:6; July 17, 'Accepting Christ,' Luke 15:18; July 18, 'Christian Soldiers,' Ephesians 6; July 21, 'Earnestness,' 2 Kings 9:20; July 22, 'What You Were Made For;' July 23, 'Secret Sins,' Psalms 19:12; July 24, 'Besetting Sins,' Hebrews 12:1; July 25, 'Love Your Enemies,' Matthew 5:44; July 28, 'Sermon to Young Men,' Genesis 3:19; July 29, 'Difficulties Ahead,' Hosea 7:9; July 30, Stormed, No Service . . ."

"Tent Dimensions," also found among his papers:
". . . Tent 40 × 60 ft. Wall pieces 6 ft. 9 in. Hem 1½ in. at each end making pieces 7 ft. when cut. 72 of these wall pieces with 4 extra for laps, 29 in. × 7 ft., 8 oz. Wall roped at top & bottom. Roof 24 ft. from eave to ring on gore pieces . . . Reinforced by piece of duck canvas 8 × 6 ft. at each pole and rafter . . ."

Journal entry from Hadwen, Dec. 31, 1900:
". . . Tonight I watched the sun set for the last time in the 19th century . . . It is a bright, moonlight night, dry and bracing. I am preparing my watchnight sermon to welcome the new century in . . ."

Hadwen

"What a Friend we have in Jesus,
  All our sins and griefs to bear!
What a privilege to carry
  Everything to God in prayer . . ."

Sometimes the singing was more like caterwauling and more than a little off-key. No matter, it was lusty and in earnest. I took pleasure in the sturdy old-time hymns with some "go" in them, those that came straight from the human heart, seeking after the Lord, if haply it might find Him.

This revival meeting opened the Week of Prayer. Not in the tent I'd made for summer camp meetings. Now the crops were in and the corn husked. Snow would soon be on the ground. All most folks had left to do was feed the stock and do the chores. It was a good time to hold prayer meetings. So this was in the church, with its cushioned pews, preacher's rostrum, the altar rail and memorial windows with red and purplish panes. Teams from the country were outside and blanketed. We'd have the meeting after chores five nights this week—Saturday I needed to work up my outline and scripture for Sunday morning. I'd use the same text when I walked out for services at Pleasant Grove and the Moody and Summit schoolhouses later in the day.

The first part of tonight's meeting was like any other, the prelude, the Call to Worship, singing and praying and reading out of the Bible. "The Lord is in his Holy Temple; let all the earth keep silence before Him." You could feel the anticipation for what was to come after. At a revival, my sermons followed the same pattern: fearful warnings to sinners; hopes of salvation to those as forsook their evil ways; mention of the Lord's forgiveness and mercy; appeals to come forward to the altar rail and repent before it was too late. Every sermon on secret sins hit its target. I'd first talk about sins in public life—vote buying in politics, secret rebates in railroad rates, adulteration of food in groceries and packinghouses, graft in officeholders. As soon as I got to little personal sins like harboring a grudge or gossiping uncharitably about a neighbor, I'd see a good many in the congregation squirming and looking around furtively, like they had a skeleton in the closet. "God finds us in our sin," I'd remind them, "no matter how secret it is in our thoughts. Won't you come that your heart may be at peace? Won't you come?"

The choir, always out in full force at revivals, filed into their loft behind the pulpit, and Sister Bessie Sykes took her seat at the pipe organ and started pulling out the stops and working the pedals, her head tilted back and arms outstretched; Bessie was getting awful nearsighted. The first hymn began with a loud peal, one of those hymns that always seemed to me instinct with the heart's devotion, a favorite of Dwight Moody's that Ira Sankey used to sing:

> "Shall we gather at the river
> Where bright angel feet have trod . . ."

In the Meeting House in Whittier, no opening hymns were sung. There was no organ, nor any pictures, lamps, no ornaments of any kind to attract the eye or disturb meditation. There were no announcements, no scripture reading, no morning offering. Silence prevailed, and in this silence each one present listened to the bidding of the Inner Light, unaided by any contrivances, just his own mind and heart. Many a time Aaron, George and I sat side by side the entire meeting without a word being spoken. If somebody, man or woman, felt moved by the Holy Spirit to speak, he or she got up, took off his hat or bonnet, and proceeded with an exhortation, usually unstudied but touched off with a spiritual freshness I have seldom, if ever, reached in my own sermons.

When the exhortation ended, it was again silent, unless another felt moved to speak. If somebody offered a prayer, everybody got up, the men on our side and the women on theirs, we took off our hats and turned our backs to each other until the petition ended, and all again were seated. So it went until he who sat at the "head of the Meeting," the one we called "the timer," felt that the hour had come for the Meeting to close. When he turned to his neighbor and shook hands, we knew the service had broke.

> "Yes, we'll gather at the river,
> The beautiful, beautiful river . . ."

Now, at a revival meeting, after the opening hymns were sung—old timers like "The Old Rugged Cross," "This Is My Story," "Work for the Night Is Coming"—some retired preacher who would help, like Brother Orvello here in town or Brother Perry from Elkader, would begin his testimony in the habitual way. It would be something like, "Fellow sinners and unredeemed friends. It's been forty years since the Lord, for Jesus's sake, spoke peace unto my soul." I'd only listen with half an ear, knowing they'd always end up with the same words: "Pray for me, brothers and sisters, that I may always serve God with rejoicing and meet you all in Heaven, our final lodging, where we shall strike glad hands, where parting is no more, where we shall be granted a holy rest and peace at last . . ." If it was Brother Perry, he might talk some about Charles Darwin and his daffy notion of men descended from monkeys, or the foolishness of another one of those Englishmen, John Tyndall, who proposed a "scientific" experiment be tried of all the world praying for patients in one ward of a hospital and not praying for patients in another ward, to prove the power of prayer. As Matthew tells us, if the blind lead the blind, both shall fall into the ditch.

For these were dirt-farming country people who felt very close to the Lord, almost like He was one of the neighbors. They were satisfied with His goodness in the natural order. God walked with men. He showed them mercy and comfort, though he could be wrathful, too. He treated all alike and loved his enemies—every one of them. And he loved the poor and humble—and they knew it. For them, the heavens bent down. They were the salt of the earth.

> "All hail the pow'r of Jesus' name!
>   Let angels prostrate fall;
>   Bring forth the royal diadem
>   To crown Him, crown Him, Lord of all . . ."

When the time came, I read the scripture about the Prodigal Son from St. Luke and how there is more joy in Heaven over one sinner that repenteth than over the ninety-and-nine that never go astray. I began my sermon: "Unconverted friends, you love sin. But you know from your own lives that a sinner *tires* of his sin, it becomes *hell* to him. Duty and indulgence don't make good companions. One cannot do one's duty and indulge in sin.

"Heed the advice of your mother, your Sunday School teacher, your Pastor. Accept Christ. You say people will laugh. They will criticize a convert. Your love of sin shows always. You will say, 'I will repent after a while but not just now.' Ask instead, 'How shall I accept Christ?' For Christ says,

'Without me, you can do nothing.' You must give your whole self. Don't keep back a part or you will have it all back.

"Repent." I gave them a good long pause here.

"Think of God.

"Think of Christ.

"Trust God for Salvation.

"Work for Salvation.

"Sinners do not want their consciences aroused. They do not want change. They love conditions of sin. They are languid, easy-go, bone-tired. They want to be left alone. They claim this is religious liberty. Sinners think they are too poor, too ignorant, too busy, too weak, too young, too old, too sinful to serve Christ. They think Jesus will torment them with extra work and they are so tired. They think He will bring them more care and they have too much care now. They think He will bring them responsibility and they want to be free. But *saved* men think the opposite of this. Which is the wisest course?"

Most of the congregation listened attentively. But way in the back of the church, where it was darker, away from the overhead gas lamps, I saw some wiggling and whispering going on in what we called "the seat of the scornful." Here sat the rawboned country boys who were just starting to grow whiskers and chew plug without turning green, the boys who found everything funny and could say, "By God!" and "Give him hell!" and who were trying out other profanity, not without a vague fear of getting struck by a thunderbolt. When they were together they were always up to some stunt, or looking for something to fight or something to laugh at. And just to show how much pluck they had, how much mischief Satan can find for idle hands to do, all the time I was talking about sin, they were scuffling with each other, and poking and tickling and snickering.

Sometimes during a revival, I'd get kinda provoked, and when the church stalwarts were giving their exhortations and I was free to sift through the congregation, I'd make a surprise stop by these boys. What a serious place now! God forbid anybody was going to sass the preacher now. I'd ask one of the boys, "Brother, have you accepted Christ?" And he'd hem and haw and turn red and his Adam's apple would bob up and down. "Well, no sir, I'm not ready yet," he'd stammer, knowing that if he could only hold out, he was sure of approval when I'd gone away. "Not ready? Why not ready?" I'd say in my sternest voice. "We never know when our turn will come. The Devil may be struggling for your soul this very night. How will it be if you don't come to Jesus?"

Now I spoke to this last pew directly. "Take heed of warnings. Your safety depends on it. For, as the Bible says, 'He that taketh warning shall deliver his soul.' There are many kinds of warnings: Railroad crossings. Road signs. Bells. Crossbars. Lighthouses. Buoys. Foghorns. Tide whistles. There can be wholly unexpected warnings: a sandbar looms up in the Mississippi. A man appears in the night with a lantern. Warnings are not always heard. We are too preoccupied with our own affairs. Or warnings are heard, but not believed, like the Johnstown flood. Or the warning may be neglected until it is too late. Obstacles loom up everywhere. Life is not a toboggan slide."

I'd caught the eye of that back row and saw a line of faces looking down sheepishly, each one stealing a glance at the others, ready to poke fun if they did. But they all stayed looking grave. It didn't do to cut up too much in church—the fly in the ointment of that was the threat of getting hauled out to the woodshed back home for a hiding from Pa's razor strop.

If I could, I liked to stress God's goodness and mercy, not retribution and Hell Fire. I talked some about how we overcame obstacles when we followed the Golden Rule and loved not only our neighbors but our enemies, too, and did good to them, and also cared for children and showed a regard for women.

I turned to those older folks who seemed to be listening so attentively. "Let us take the example of the Apostle Paul. Paul was the greatest gift to the infant church. He was a conscientious man, both as a Jew and as a Christian. He possessed a clear light, a comprehensive range, a broad knowledge, an intense soul and a mighty will.

"Now, what do we mean by these?" I warmed to a favorite subject. "First, his clear light: Paul never doubted for a moment his Call to serve Christ. All else bent to this one thing in his life, the Gospel of God. We know why he called himself the 'servant' of God. For a servant in those days meant a slave, a slave bought for a price. Slavery was a common condition. Paul meant he felt himself to be entirely given up to God's work.

"Second was his comprehensive range: Paul saw all that God had done for the world. He saw a great past history. He saw a mighty Gospel. He saw the future and the many lands and races won by Christ. Third, he had broad knowledge. His early schooling and learning fitted him for his work. He had known both Jew and Gentile, Greek as well as Roman. There is an inference for us in this. We, too, must know all sorts of people, from all walks of life, strangers as well as kinfolk and neighbors.

"Fourth, Paul possessed an intense soul. This means someone who has an intense interest in the work he has chosen to perform. Finally, Paul had a mighty will. As a Jew his will was governed by his conscience. As a Christian, he had the added light of the Holy Spirit. Christ's will was Paul's will. He knew no other Master.

"What conclusions can we draw from this? We can imitate Paul's submission, the variety of work he undertook and the variety of people he came to know and understand. We can imitate Paul's humility and his patience under trials. We must know that a spiritual life is possible and that God expects it. Christ says, 'Without me, you can do nothing.' Paul says, 'I can do all through Christ who strengthened me.' A man must see the guilt and shame of living in sin and falling from grace. Physically to remain a babe, as we see in the feebleminded, is sad. Spiritually to remain unconverted is sadder yet. It is one step between the lost and redeemed. The Holy Spirit leads. Let us take that step . . ."

Sister Sykes swung into another hymn as I sat down and, with their habitual coughing and throat-clearing and the scraping of chairs, the choir rose for a hymn.

> "Blessed assurance, Jesus is mine:
> O what a foretaste of Glory Divine!"

I asked Brother Perry to lead us in prayer. He was gifted as an evangelist of the old school. He began slowly. "Holy, everlasting, almighty God, unto whom all hearts are open, all desires known, cleanse the thoughts of our hearts with the inspiration of Thy Holy Name, through Jesus Christ Our Lord." The choir chanted an Amen. His formal prayer of confession over, Brother Perry became more impassioned. His voice fell into an old-time swing, almost a chant. "There's sinners here tonight that's halting between two opinions. There's sinners here tonight that are swinging to and fro, like a door on its hinges. Wake them up, O Lord!"

"Amen, a-a-a-men!" came voices from the congregation. "Praise the Lord!" "Hallelujah!"

"Let them feel, O Lord, the awful peril they are in, like Brother Williams says, like men walking in a fog on the brink of a terrible cliff who don't take heed of warnings, who don't see the road signs, hear the foghorns or the bells. Wake up these sinners in time, O Lord, and let them see where they are at! O Lord, hang them over Hell Fire for a spell, give 'em a good strong whiff of brimstone!" The organ swelled in the background, deepest bass to highest treble.

> "Onward! Christian soldiers, marching as to war,
> With the Cross of Jesus going on before . . ."

With Brother Perry's every petition, there arose a louder encouraging approbation. "Amen!" "Praise His Name!" The emotions, the sympathies of the congregation were all stirred up by his words and the militant, warlike beat of the hymn. Two older women, both of them church regulars, came forward to the altar rail and kneeled. I make haste to say these weren't new penitents; this was priming the pump. One of them prayed, "O Lord, be with our Loved Ones wherever they may be, even in Oregon and California." That tickled me, though I knew she had kinfolk out West. Very often the prayers of the old folks at one meeting were pret' near the same as the meeting before.

More prayers. More hymns. "Rock of Ages." "We have an Anchor that holds the Soul steadfast and firm while the billows roll . . . ," "Lead kindly Light . . . The night is dark and I am far from home . . ."

"Isn't there another?" I called from the pulpit. "Will you enlist? Shall God put your name on the book tonight? I ask all those who earnestly want to follow Christ to join me at the altar. Let God and your neighbors know you humbly repent your sins and earnestly want to come to Christ. Isn't there another?"

"Amazing grace! how sweet the sound
That saved a wretch like me . . ."

I've often felt when I heard that hymn that, then and there, the Holy Spirit was abroad, just like it moved a man back home at Meeting. It was an echo of the melody chanted by those white-robed multitudes which no man can number, strumming on their golden harps.

"I once was lost, but now am found,
Was blind, but now I see . . ."

One young man, coming hesitantly down the aisle, stopped, passed a hand over his face and, suddenly as if breaking away from past sin and shame, he almost ran to the altar rail. "God bless you, brother," I told him. Soon there was another. And another. Before long I counted eight kneeling, six of them new penitents. Brother Orvello stood by to get their names and addresses.

"That's it! That's it!" I cried. "Isn't there one more? We are going to pray soon for these penitent souls, that they may know their many sins are forgiven. Who else will come? Ah, here is one for whom many have been praying. Right here, brother, kneel right down here. God bless you." I kneeled beside him, feeling it was a good revival meeting, not like so many where the people were few and generally quite old. "Come unto me, all ye who are weary and heavy laden, and I will give you rest . . ."

"The Lord has promised good to me,
His word my hope secures;
He will my shield and portion be
As long as life endures."

It was under Dwight L. Moody's inspiration that I first made up my mind to give my heart to Christ and my service to the church, and his sermons have been a means of grace to me all these many years. We had a great outpouring of spirit at that 1889 meeting in Chicago, gathering in many anxious souls, and Moody founded his Bible Institute for Home and Foreign Missions. Moody's formal education was limited. Some said his father's death ended it at fifth grade. Moody possessed no special talent, natural or acquired. But he saw the Invisible God and became great. He said when he got the Call, "I want to see what a person who gives his entire life over to the Lord can accomplish." And he accomplished a great deal. I think your ideal Christian is somebody who has a clear idea of God. He can respect himself because he obeys the will of God. You take Peter. He was just a fisherman, unskilled, rash in judgment. But he saw the Invisible God and followed in His service. And God honored him. God rescues man from himself.

I can see Moody now, at the World's Fair in 1893, telling how his long-gone brother came home, at last, to their gray-haired mother in Massachusetts. Moody shouted to that vast crowd: "Sinner, do you believe she was ready to forgive him? But her joy was nothing compared to the joy in Heaven tonight if you come up to be saved. Your Father wants you. Come home this very night!" Moody showed how you need directness and speed to get your message across. Velocity counts. It is the swift express train we prize. We have shotguns for rabbits, but rifles for lions; a Krag-Jorgensen is awkward, but it is very sudden and will kill three men in a row. Moody preached his Old Fashioned Gospel. He stuck to the five points of the Niagara Conference: upholding the Bible's divine accuracy, the virgin birth, the deity and second coming of Christ, and that He died to lift our guilt of Sin. Shortly before he passed on in 1899, Moody said, "Human nature hasn't changed in the last nineteen hundred years. Preach a different Gospel from that successful in apostolic days? Oh bosh." Moody's gone to glory now these many months. I bet he's one of the brightest-looking angels there.

It was while hearing Moody I knew I could no longer ignore the Call to preach. I can tell you the exact minute and hour I first heard that Call. I was still in school and I'd gone out to our big old barn in Whittier so I could practice for the debating society, the acoustics were so good. I was loudly demanding of the pigeons and barn swallows and my imaginary audience in the haymow, "Can we resist the fascination and flattery of modern society? Can we withstand the temptations of money-getting in this nineteenth-century business age?" It was there the Lord placed His hand on my shoulder. It was just as plain as if I heard a voice speaking to me. How I was to do God's will wasn't yet clear to me, and as a student of medicine, I was unlearned in theology. But I knew all John Wesley asked was a "yes" to the question, "Do you love and serve God?" If doctrines meant less than spiritual life to Wesley and Francis Asbury, who brought Methodism to America, it's not surprising that Moody, in the way of the old circuit-riding preachers, cared little for theological abstractions. Peter Cartwright, the godfather of our Iowa Methodism, said that most country people just wanted "a preacher that could mount a stump, a block or a log, or stand in the bed of a wagon, and without note or manuscript, quote, expound and apply the word of God . . ." Of course nowadays a parson's all decked out in a Prince Albert coat, shapeless as it may be, and he's got sermons to write, babies to baptize, sickbeds to visit, revivals to lead, couples to marry, old folks to bury, a church in town and two or three country charges besides . . .

Oh, but they had good times in religion in those days. When men like Cartwright, steeled with conviction, rode out to solitary places, saving sinners, they say you could hear the redeemed for miles around, for those were the days of "shouting Methodists." The old men dreamed dreams, and the young men saw visions. Traveling the forest trails on horseback, preaching every day and twice on Sundays, those circuit riders converted many, exhorting until they dropped with weariness. They were in a hurry, as the end of the world was thought to be at hand. Nobody asked if the whale really swallowed Jonah or the Red Sea parted for Moses. You didn't have all this "higher" criticism of the Bible or the tomfoolery about evolution, as if Satan himself planted all these fossils to tempt man into disbelief.

You might say of those folks in the ever-advancing settlements, with their log huts and coonskin caps, that the end of the world they knew *was* at hand. In truth, those were the last days of their age. How I envy the young circuit riders, far-visioned and heroic, filled with a young man's fervency of spirit. Thousands of miles they rode each year, sleeping wherever night overtook them, sometimes out in the woods, sometimes in crowded cabins.

Jessie's Pa said their normal stipend over in Indiana when he was young wasn't more than fifty–sixty dollars a year, and that they had to find themselves. Conference sets my salary at eight hundred dollars, plus another hundred for rent, providing I can collect it all. According to the 1900 census, four hundred dollars is close to the average wage, so I can't complain none. A parson ought to get a decent salary. Nobody likes a sponge or a deadbeat. We respect the man who pays as he goes.

But it was for no earthly recompense that those circuit preachers served. What pay could tempt a fever-stricken man to lie for weeks in a frontier cabin, among fast guns and Indians on the warpath, among unbelievers, maybe being persecuted for his faith? Starved out sometimes, they located until they could get new garments and grub and a fresh horse and then— back to save souls! Many died young, but never were such words of comfort spoken, such miracles wrought and great truths promulgated, never was there such a spreading of the Gospel. They often builded better than they knew. Nowadays we're but frail and feeble folk beside them. Theatergoing, cardplaying, billiards, gambling, dancing and other debauchery of the baser sort are no longer sinful to some folks, even churchgoers, and the buying and selling of spirituous liquors is plentiful. Seems like every town has got to have its saloons, full of beery smells and intoxication, and with innocent children going in and out with their buckets and pitchers, working the growlers for their dads or some labor gang. The "Battle of Old Jim Crow" is far from won. Jessie tells me as how in some of the Mississippi River towns, she's never seen so many old men and so many saloons, both. She says, "Maybe they're all pickled in alcohol."

They were unlearned men, those circuit riders. Pa says they "murdered the king's English at every lick." It was a time of doubt and shifting. So is our age. So is every age. But they had power to move the hearts of men. Such power as we can only guess at when we hold our tent meetings, all too often poorly attended and mostly by old folks at that. And not all our praying and hymn-singing and exhortations can in the least degree bring about the Great Awakening we seek.

The tales you hear! How if the rowdies came out of their saloons and brought their bottles and drunkenness with them to the camp meeting, so much the better. A mighty power could smite them senseless to the ground, if not a preacher's fist, and only the Master Mechanic can mend broken bones. John Ruble, the first circuit-rider to marry, die and be buried in Iowa, when he passed on to glory in 1836 aged just twenty-six, died a real Christian soldier, crying out, "The will of God is done! Welcome, Death, I am prepared to go!" Mahlon Day Collins, a Quaker turned Methodist like myself, took his whole family on the circuit with him, in a surrey in summer and a bobsled in winter. They say that during blizzards, while his wife and children huddled under buffalo robes, Mahlon braved wind and snow, tramping ahead of the team to break a way through the drifts.

You'd think it needs must be that an age thus ushered in should be the grandest that the world has ever seen and not all this thunderation we've had since science got so big, with less and less talk about God, and more talk about men than is good for 'em. Why, glory be, some stargazers and prognosticators are starting to say that the teachings of Jesus and the Bible don't work in our new industrial society, and that the Book of Genesis is only some kind of metaphorical fairy tale, as if the King James Bible don't mean exactly what it says. Those old circuit preachers were the true voices in the wilderness, crying, "Repent ye, for the kingdom of Heaven is at hand!" And like the man of Nazareth, plain-spoken and humble as they, there came a time when they saw with sorrow that they must decrease, and what they had foretold must increase.

Jessie complains sometimes about moving from parish to parish with such regularity, and to parsonages with their damp fishy smells and drafts, and all too often leaky-roofed, sooty from smoke and shabby. We try to make each parsonage homelike with our solid old furniture and books, but it takes a lot of housecleaning. Jessie says, "If I ever go crazy, Papa, I'll just be sweeping and sweeping and never get the pile of dirt in one place." It surely is no picnic with small children, married to a country preacher with a rural circuit, after she started out as a doctor's wife and comfortably fixed. But how I longed to go out among the heathen of the East with my medical skills and the circuit-preacher's fervency and all the good, hard common sense and affection that was his.

Well, many are called, but few are chosen. Life is not a question of what we would like to do. It is a question of duty to be done. Not everybody can be a Moses, David or Paul. God has need of humble workers. Mankind has need of humble workers. We must gird our loins to go forward, holding fast to Wesley's motto as we labor in the Lord's vineyard: "The best of all is, God is with us." But what would those pioneer striplings make of the folks at Conference who shake their heads and deplore "the tendency of the age," as if God were an old man now, no longer knowing His business!

Anne

Elwood was a peaceful little burg. Where we moved now—Le Claire on the Mississippi River—would compare to Sodom and Gomorrah.

From the Le Claire news column of the weekly Globe, *published across the river in Port Byron, Illinois:*

"July 2—ESCAPED CONVICT CAPTURED ON LEVEE"

"July 16—SHOT A COON; Mate on Steamer Shoots Black Roustabout"

"Aug. 13—In a street fight Friday, Charlie Graham had his collarbone broken."

"Aug. 20—Three enterprising young men of Le Claire forced an entrance into the saloon at White Horse Crossing and appropriated four quarts of whiskey, one box of 10¢ cigars and $2.15 in money . . ."

"Nov. 19—FATHER, 70, SEVERELY BEATEN BY SON"

"Jan. 30—At Saturday Night's Masquerade Ball at the Auditorium the 150 costumes went from Uncle Sam and the Chinaman to a 'culled pussun.' "

"Mar. 7—DAN BREEN STABBED BY NEGRO ROUSTABOUT"

"Mar. 14—Rev. Williams began a series of revival meetings at the Methodist Church Sunday evening. All friends of religious work are invited. You don't have to put on your 'store clothes' to go to the tent meeting. Just come as you are . . ."

Father went ahead, taking the household goods in a boxcar. I drove the buggy, a surrey with a fringe on top. I was always the horseman. It was a fifty-mile trip and took about ten hours. We got there after dark. Facing the Mississippi was a tall, three-story brick house looking like an old store. Here the Clarks, a good Methodist family, were waiting for us; we stayed for supper at their house and all night. The next day, we moved into the parsonage. Just the view of the Mississippi from the front stoop of the church set Le Claire apart from anywhere I'd ever lived.

It was a river town with a roaring and bawdy past—there'd even been floating brothels—but it was starting to quiet down now that its logging and piloting role had just about run its course. The town was situated on a point; the Mississippi made a sharp turn there to run southwesterly about fifteen miles, a stretch known as the Rock Island Rapids in those days. Fast currents, high rocks and a narrow, twisting channel—what the local Indians called *pau-pesha-tuk*, "agitated waters"—made them dangerous to navigation. At low water, packets and floating rafts and stern-wheelers anchored overnight at Le Claire before tackling the rapids by day. Steamboats needed a special rapids pilot to run them. In 1901, the year we moved to Le Claire, there were still about forty captains, pilots, engineers and clerks in the river trade living in town, including Aaron Russell, whose piloting skill was used on the Nile when they tried to rescue General Gordon at Khartoum.

These rivermen mainly lived in big brick or frame Victorian houses, usually with scroll-sawed porches, lots of wooden gingerbread, hydrangea bushes and gardens with pink, red and white hollyhocks, sweet william, marigolds, lady's slippers and violets. These fancy houses rose on a steep hill above stone retainer walls the first block or two from the main street, a string of wooden shops known as Cody Road. This was because Buffalo Bill had been born in 1846 in a log cabin just west of town. He'd gone off at the age of eleven, though, to drive stock, join the Pony Express and kill thousands of buffaloes. Now he was in his fifties. The folks had seen his show at the World's Fair in Chicago eight years earlier. Lillian Russell was local too; she'd been born in Clinton, just twenty miles upriver.

Right from the first day, Haddie and I loved to go downtown. So much was going on. Smoke would be pouring from the Clarks' lime kiln, with men and wagons milling about the quarry. Near the water's edge on the levee was the biggest old rock elm tree you ever saw. Its trunk was thirteen feet around and it spread its branches out in such a huge, mushroomed-shaped canopy, stranded raftsmen often just slept under it. There was always some cook, fireman or deckhand sobering up there. It was known all along the upper Mississippi as the "Green Tree Hotel." In 1901 there were still over seventy stern-wheel rafters moving logs on the Upper River and also sixteen packet boats, thirty-five pleasure boats and all kinds of barges. Some steamboats were from the White Collar Line, like the *Jenny Lind, Sucker State, Canada, Greek Slave* and *Tishemengo*. Others, like the *Mary Morton, Dubuque, Sidney, Quincy* and *St. Paul*, were from the Diamond Jo Line, soon to be made famous when William Handy wrote "St. Louis Blues" in 1914:

"You ought to see dat stove pipe brown of mine
Lak he owns de Dimon' Joseph line . . ."

On the levee near the Green Tree there were always great heaps of sacks
—onions or potatoes or something else waiting for shipment. Over by the
coal yards, barges would load to go upriver. There was a packinghouse, a
boatyard with clanging mallets and caulking irons, two sawmills with buzzing saws, and the pounding of hammers on metal from a plow factory.
Down at the Kattenbracker Foundry, men built and repaired steamboat
machinery; farther down, men loaded wagons at the icehouse. Other men
worked at the limestone quarry, where Haddie was to get summer jobs.
With the ferry going back and forth to Port Byron, rafters calling in for
supplies and pilots, and the ringing of engine bells and the whistles of packets, there was always plenty of noise and excitement down by the Green
Tree. People still ran toward the levee if a whistle was heard and the drayman shouted, "Steamboat a'comin'!" The boat from St. Louis came around
the bend at four o'clock in the afternoon, just as the smoke of another from
St. Paul was usually in sight. Coming from school, we'd join the crowd
hurrying down to the riverbank to watch the boat hands bring the ship in, to
see who'd arrived, hear upriver and downriver news and gossip, and see
what cargo was dragged on and off by the roustabouts—we called them
"roosters." Out on the Mississippi, there were tugs and barges and men
poling small rafts down the river or fishing or gathering freshwater clams
and mussels to supply the button factories. Everybody was always looking
for pearls; some were worth as much as a thousand dollars.

Downtown, the sidewalks were of foot-square red tiles with patterns
pressed into them. All the stores advertised. Signs in the drugstore window
urged Hood's Sarsaparilla for heart trouble and Hale's Honey of Horehound
for consumption. At the bicycle shop, one said, "Don't hang up your wheel
this winter. Buy the ice attachment and ride your bicycle on the frozen
river." And at the livery stable, "Carriages for parties and funerals a specialty. Enjoy fine horses and a fine rig." The provision store had a smiling,
black-hatted Quaker Oats man in the window who Haddie claimed was
William Penn, and there were big glass jars of jelly beans, Tootsie Rolls,
licorice whips and other penny candy. Inside, there were mounds of cheese
and butter, bins of sugar and flour, nuts and raisins, barrels full of apples
and oatmeal, and the smells of dried codfish, pickles, smoked ham, kerosene, vinegar, sausage, onions and molasses. Lee's Lice Killer was sold by
the quart. Lump soft coal was twelve and a half cents a bushel. There was
"formaldehyde gas" to disinfect a house after diphtheria. In a shed outside,

they had new horse-powered threshers. So many changes were coming in farming now as self-binders were replacing reapers, steam threshers were taking over from treadmills, and bigger, heavier draft animals were being brought in for farm work.

Despite all its bustle and money, Le Claire was backward in some ways. The streets were poorly surfaced and often heavy with dust or deep in mud if it rained. There were livery-stable smells and swarms of flies, big Mississippi shad flies, which buzzed around the streetlamps after dark. Once I started getting invited inside the grand-looking houses, I found they were often cold and damp and drafty, with poor sanitation or, often as not, no plumbing at all. Le Claire was a terribly tough town, more like an Old World town. Every Thursday night, Papa preached up the river at a little place called Princeton; he took the team and buggy. The first time, Mother left me at home baby-sitting with Mary, who was four years old—I was now going on fourteen. Mother found out a few days later that the next-door neighbors had two sons, one in jail for rape and the other just freed on the same offense. I never baby-sat again.

In January there was a Masquerade Ball in the Auditorium, which backed up to our kitchen. Father would have died if I'd ever gone to a dance in Le Claire. They were just rotten. Some of the Methodist ladies complained about bawdy dances so close to the church; they called the fiddle "that instrument of the Devil." One man at all the dances, Tobias Carp, kept pulling the cloth off a table without spilling anything. His wife died and everybody said it must have been the happiest day of her life. Tobias was said to be as mean as dirt and as ornery as sin. In Le Claire, nice people were supposed just to attend to business, farming, housekeeping, or piloting rafts, or whatever, and try to be good. They went to lectures at the literary and temperance societies, weekly musicales, school exhibitions, church services and revival meetings; girls were expected to learn painting, music and embroidery. The rough element—what Mama called "the submerged tenth" —went in for dances, cards and dime novels; they went to horse races, gambled and got drunk in saloons, and their ladies wore a lot of artificial flowers, ruffles and beads and all such doodads.

Almost everybody in town worked on the Mississippi River boats. They'd go all spring and summer and come home in the fall with money. Families would eat steak then, but by spring, when the rafting season was about to begin again, just about the whole town ate liver, at ten cents a pound. It was even free. There were so many saloons in Le Claire that some raftsmen would end up dead broke after only a week's carousing. Dad said there was no tougher creature than a raftsman. His job was so harrowing and dangerous, it made for recklessness. On the raft, the roosters would drink whiskey, curse, work long hours, never shave and rarely bathe. When we'd walk home from school, they'd sometimes hoot and holler at us across the water. We paid them no attention.

I spent three years at Le Claire's Limestone Academy, where besides Latin and classical studies, we learned about art in Egypt, Greece and Rome, and great painters like Millet and Rembrandt, and we also studied operas like Wagner's *Tannhäuser* and *Lohengrin*. Haddie went to the Port Byron Academy, where they had lectures on the Roman Forum with stereopticon slides and readings from Homer, Goethe and Schiller. Haddie rowed a quarter of a mile across the Mississippi every morning, though once it got cold and froze, he just walked across. Port Byron was as dry as Le Claire was wet. It had no saloons at all, while we had the First Chance Saloon at the south end of town and the Last Chance Saloon at the north end and too many in between to count. One boy at school went downtown and had a beer every noon; he told me it was to last him until school was out. But there was very little cigarette smoking. We called them "coffin nails." One or two of the smokers we knew were tubercular and dying anyway.

Dad was what he liked to call "a flaming evangelist for temperance" in Le Claire. He'd say, "A teetotaler means T-totally or total with a capital T. Observe this: The Saloon Must Go! Our target is Total Temperance from whiskey and hard liquor, and also from beer, wine and hard cider . . ." Or he'd tell the men, "What is it to change from sin to righteousness? It is for the drunkard to abandon his liquor, the smoker his cigar, the chewer his plug, the blasphemer his profanity, the thief his robbery, the back-biter his scandal . . . To hear about a raffle or dance, saloon or gambling is no sin. To buy the lottery ticket, do the two-step, drink the peg of whiskey or sit down at the card table *is* a sin. We pay for it with a troubled conscience, a dwarfed character, a starved life and a lost soul . . ." Le Claire's W.C.T.U. ladies didn't invade the saloons and smash up their stock and fixtures with a hatchet, the way Carry Nation was doing down in Kansas, but they did stand outside and sing psalms and pray for Prohibition to become law. We all had to sign pledge cards saying, "I hereby solemnly promise, GOD HELPING ME, to abstain from all distilled, fermented and malt liquors, including wine, beer and cider; and to employ all proper means to discourage the use of, and traffic in, the same."

Dad said all those patent remedies that traveling tent shows sold down by the Green Tree had a strong dose of corn whiskey in them. Haddie and I would sneak down to watch the Kickapoo Indian Medicine Show, which had a fiddler and banjo and guitar players, and they'd sing and crack jokes and peddle bottles of wonderful medicine that would cure everything from ingrown toenails to baldness. Doc, who did most of the talking, said even Buffalo Bill endorsed his famous Kickapoo Tonic, "one of the greatest remedies ever to be placed before the American public." He highly recommended it for "sluggish liver, bilious blood, headache, bad breath, pain or burning in the stomach, dark around the eyes, pain around the heart or kidneys, constipation, loss of appetite, muscular lumbago and neuralgia, and a bad feeling on rising in the morning." They'd sing about how you could tell a Methodist preacher by the bottle hid in his pocket or how they'd named their cow Temperance because she was always dry. Once in a while, one of them would shout from the crowd, "Say, Doc!" And he'd say, "Yessir, what's a matter now?"

"That sure is good medicine what you got there. Yeah, it's good for horses, too. Yeah, I give my old horse a dose of it last week."

"Well, I'm sure it cured him, didn't it."

"I don't know. We ain't *caught* him yet!" And they'd all start fiddling and singing like crazy:

> "Beefsteak when I'm hungry
> Whiskey when I'm dry
> Water when I'm thirsty
> Heaven when I die."

There was a *real* crazy man in Le Claire, Snick Van Duzer. He wore three overcoats, usually the shortest one on top. Snick Van Duzer fancied himself a preacher and he'd go out and preach sermons in a ravine west of town. One Sunday, he went to church in Port Byron and when a visiting preacher didn't show up in time, Snick impersonated him and started to give the sermon. The janitor at school was named Scenthouse and the Presbyterian minister, Mr. Pugh. Father did the funerals for the old drunken reprobates. He was more popular with them than Reverend Pugh because he didn't lambast them so much.

Once when Reverend Pugh was preaching, there was an old lady in the congregation, Aunt Jenny Jack. She was deaf. When Reverend Pugh declared, "Everybody who wants to go to Heaven, stand up!" Aunt Jenny asked her niece, "What'd he say? What'd he say?" By the time the niece explained, Reverend Pugh was calling, "Everybody who wants to go to Hell, stand up!" Aunt Jenny popped up, the only one in the church. When she found out what had happened, she was terribly mortified.

There was an elegant lady who lived across the street. Mrs. Headley was her name. Sometimes when we'd be hanging out our clothes, we'd call back and forth, you know, things like, "Well, I see I got my washing out first today." One Sunday morning, Mr. Brown, the milkman, suddenly died. The next Sunday, Mrs. Headley suddenly died. At the Presbyterian service that night, Reverend Pugh took off his eyeglasses, waved them at the congregation and said, "Last Sunday when I came home, what do you think happened? They told me Mr. Brown was dead! Tonight when I came home, what do you think happened? They told me Mrs. Headley was dead!" It was very dramatic. Or would have been had he not flung his arm out so exuberantly his glasses went spinning off into the congregation. After a moment's shocked silence, everybody went into hysterical laughter. They couldn't stop. It only seemed funnier when Reverend Pugh tried to quiet them down. He finally had to pronounce the benediction and end the service. Churches were very friendly in those days. And Reverend Pugh was always so deadly earnest, no sense of humor at all. It was terribly funny.

When we got bored in Le Claire, Haddie and I would go down and see Ma and Pa Bowden, professional beggars from England. We'd tell Mother we wanted to take them food. Actually, we were filled with unholy glee because the Bowdens wore cast-off clothing and we'd try to guess whose it had been. "This union suit used to be Captain Tromley's, didn't it?" or "I know this petticoat was Mrs. Clark's." The Bowdens had a cat named after their dead son, Thomas. Mrs. Bowden made wonderful bread; she wrapped the dough in her petticoat at night and kept it in the warm bed to raise. Old Lady Bowden was against drinking. One time, she grabbed the arm of a young man just as he was about to go into a saloon. She dragged him over to the town pump and said, "Here, young man, drink this." But it was cold weather and the pump had frozen.

We rode horseback an awful lot in those days. My first date was with a boy who rowed over to school in Port Byron with Haddie every morning. Like everyone else in town, we owned our own rowboat, with two sets of oars. There was going to be a Halloween Party with a Ghost March, fortune-telling and a performance of the witch scene from *Macbeth* ("When shall we three meet again, in thunder, lightning, or in rain?") Hadwen was taking Alice Stoker, my best friend. He fixed me up with this boy, named Jimmy. Jimmy came and everybody was in the living room: Dad, Mother, the Methodist district superintendent, I don't know who all. Jimmy was equal to the occasion. He had four gold teeth in front. He looked horrible. But I wanted to go to that party.

Being a P.K.—preacher's kid—never cramped my style. Mother spanked me only once. When I was nine years old. I'd kept rattling the leaves of the hymnbook in church after she'd told me not to. It was harder for Haddie. At school he was always raising Cain. When he was sixteen, the folks sent him to the Methodist Academy at Cornell College in Mount Vernon, where they'd bought a house the year before with an inheritance from Mama's father. It was near campus, 525 West Sixth Street North. Mount Vernon was just a few streets of gracious old houses spread along a wooded ridge and, except for the chapel bell tower and some church steeples, almost hidden by trees. They rented it out over the years, though it never came to much.

Headline in the Cedar Rapids, Iowa, Republican, October 22, 1903:

"STUDENTS IN A RIOT: CORNELL MEN
IN INCIPIENT UPRISING LAST NIGHT"

From a letter by Hadwen, Jr., to Anna Louise:

" 'Stuff 'em! Stuff 'em! Stuff 'em!' We were all hollering and we chased this fellow to get up a little excitement and ran him down in front of Main Building. 'Stuff 'em!' everybody was shouting. It means catching a Senior alone, rolling him in the campus leaves and upholstering him by means of the aforesaid leaves stuffed down his shirt and into his clothes. It's a lot of fun.

"Then came Professor Freer. Could hardly keep his coat on. But he couldn't get close enough in the dark to see the fellows who encircled him. He went back inside and got a lantern. 'Ah,' says Freer, 'we can tell who you are now. Cowards, all of you! There's not a single one of you that dares to come up and identify yourself!'

"Some of the older boys are chanting, 'Riff, raff, ruff! Don't forget that we can stuff . . . the FACULTY!' Prof. Freer in a black Derby hat is holding his lantern and looking like Diogenes. The girls are out in full force and a certain group of ladies are exclaiming, 'Just hear—!' 'Just look!' 'I wonder what's doing?' Boys are running about, shouting, 'Stuff 'em!' 'Get FREER!' 'He'll get your name!' And all the while Professor Freer is shouting, 'COWARDS! COME, OH, COME. YOU ARE AFRAID TO STEP UP AND BE IDENTIFIED!' Then somebody threw a clod of dirt at his lantern and broke it and Freer got really mad and cried, 'YOU DARN DIRTY BLACK COWARDS!' It is reported that Prof. F. pinched his chin all night to make it well. Probably not."

Haddie goes on to describe a chemistry test, on the "Law of Definite Proportions," the "Law of Multiple Proportions," the "chemical and physical properties of Hydrogen" and "on and on." The letter ends:

". . . We made Chlorine in the Laboratory and I have not yet recovered. Cough! Cough! Cough! The Small Pox Boys in infirmary may have lots of company . . . Sunday we got a call up from the College Office. About a dozen of us. 'In Union there is Strength.' We are all offenders and law breakers. With so many of us we get off easy. This is the second call up of my 'career.' "

From letter by Jessie to Hadwen, Jr.:

". . . Glad you were vaccinated & hope it takes but am afraid it won't. As you & I never seem to have very good success in that line. But I have always heard that if the vaccination wouldn't take, smallpox wouldn't either. I hope it won't spread much either way. We have never been so much afraid since we had so many cases around us in Elwood. Still, be careful, if you can . . . I'm having as bad a toothache as never before in my upper jaw. Isn't that funny? Your Pa looks 'scandalous.' He has had another spell and shaved off his mustache . . ."

Further comment from sister Helen Collins, seventy-eight years later:

". . . Mother was a handsome woman. She had beautiful carriage. Her mother had died of consumption when she was just four, and that hung over her all her life. If she'd get the least little cough, it'd scare Father half to death. She had done deep breathing exercises from the time she was a girl. Father used to say he didn't have a girl near as good-looking as she was. He'd say, 'You know, times I'll be out making calls, and off a couple of blocks I see this lady walking along and I think, my, that's a handsome lady. And when she comes closer, well, I see it's Mama!' He always called her Mama. The only time he ever called her Jessie, it'd be when we had company. When he'd come home, he'd open the front door and call, 'Mama! I'm home!' "

Anne:

Our first year in Le Claire, Queen Victoria died. Two years later, in 1903, the Wright Brothers made their twelve-second flight at Kitty Hawk. The year after that, when I was sixteen, they announced they were going to show twenty-five automobiles at a bicycle picnic—Fords, Oldsmobiles, Packards, Buicks, Cadillacs and Studebakers. I got sick and couldn't go. I cried my eyes out, thinking I'd never get a chance to see so many cars again.

Chewing gum was newly popular. Dad hated it. He'd say, "The only thing that really unhinges me when I'm preaching is some woman sitting right down in front and chewing on that confounded gum." Mama said it couldn't be a lady down in front and that he must be thinking of the more doubtful folks who crowded into the back of the church. Dad always kept his study at home. If some woman came to pour out her troubles, he made sure Mama was in the house. The folks never made any effort to shield us. Dad was always trying to help some illegitimate child. One mother was practically an outcast when everybody knew it was the banker. There were drunkards in Le Claire who regularly beat their wives and children; they'd come to the house at all hours of the night. One time when Dad was out of town they came running for Mother to come and give some man last rites down at one of the sawmills. A buzz saw had cut him right in two and there wasn't a preacher or priest around—everybody had gone—and finally somebody said Mrs. Williams would be better than nothing.

It seemed like we always had company, mostly missionaries who went around trying to raise money. I never knew but one time that Mother turned anybody away. She was doing her spring cleaning. There was an old missionary who used to come and stay and stay. Finally Mama told Dad she'd had enough. "I'm not cooking dinner today," she said. Mother was more apt to fly off the handle. Dad became just perfectly furious at anybody abusing stock or children, and one time he chased a thief who took a chicken from our front porch way down the street, but otherwise he never got mad. He was very even-tempered.

A terrible thing happened the summer of 1903. One Sunday night, Mary, who was six, and I drove up with Dad in the buggy to Princeton. Haddie stayed home and went to the young people's meeting, the Epworth League. It was in the Methodist Church basement, which was lighted with a group of five kerosene lamps in a holder, suspended from the ceiling by a rope in the corner, held by a weight. You lowered it by rope to light it. Haddie and Mary and I practically always sat right underneath this lamp. That night, because we'd gone with Dad, Haddie sat with some friends in the back. Instead, a young girl, Nellie Knapp, who was attending Epworth League for the first time, was sitting there.

During the benediction, the rope broke and the lamp fell with a tremendous crash, drenching Nellie with burning kerosene. Her clothes ignited and in a moment she was a flaming torch. She rushed wildly into the open air. Mother was sitting a few yards away on the parsonage porch. She grabbed a rug and ran to Nellie, who was a mass of flames and screaming in agony. Some men, dashing from the church, threw the rug about her, brought her down and rolled her on the ground to put out the fire. They carried her into the Headley house and the doctor was summoned. She was horribly burned and suffered terribly. In the early morning, she mercifully lost consciousness and died. She was twenty-three.

After that, Mother, who was pregnant, was terrified of fire. Six weeks later, Helen, her last child, was born. When the baby was three days old, a Mrs. Criswell came over to do the washing. About midmorning, she went back to her own house on an errand. I went into the summer kitchen and found the clothes basket behind the woodstove was blazing. Some fiery coals had fallen in. All I could think about was how to get that flaming basket away. Mother had just seen a girl burn to death. If she'd known there was a fire, she'd have jumped out of bed. She was ill from the delivery and it could've been the death of her, too. So, not wanting to make any noise, I picked up the flaming basket and carried it out the back door. I set it down and came running back and picked up the washtub with four pails of water in it and emptied it on what fire was left. My hands and arms were throbbing and there were large red patches on them. When the fire was out, I went into the house and sat down and cried. I had to tell Mother.

I became violently ill. They thought I was going to die. The doctor said it was peritonitis, caused by the burns and the strain of lifting. I was out of school nine weeks. A boy I knew came to the house and saw Mother weeping and Dad looking so grim he concluded the worst. Soon word went around the Limestone Academy that Louise Williams had passed on. The girls sang, "We shall not meet, but we shall miss her . . ." It became my song for the rest of the year.

From letter by Hadwen, Jr., in Le Claire to Harriet Varner Johnston, Jessie's stepmother, in Mount Vernon. It is dated Christmas Day, 1903:

". . . Mama thanks you for the bedroom slippers and Louise is very much pleased with her shawl. Mama says, 'Tell Grandma that her present to me has filled a long felt want and now I'll be able to keep my pedal extremities warm enough.' Last night they had a Christmas entertainment at church. They had a red brick fireplace but no Santa Claus as some did not think it would be right. Bags of candy and peanuts. I got a match scratcher.

"Louise and her chums are going to have a party at our house tonight. They have got some mistletoe but I am inclined to believe that they will be afraid to hang it up and if they do they won't go anywhere near it. We're going to play finch, pit and other games. It is snowing this morning and is rather cold. After lunch we are going coasting . . ."

Anne

In 1904, the year I was sixteen, rafting was still going strong. Maybe the old "joyous and reckless crews of fiddling, sing-song, whiskey-drinking, break-down-dancing rapscallions" had been replaced by "quiet, orderly men," as Mark Twain lamented in *Life on the Mississippi,* published in 1883, one year before *Huckleberry Finn.* It was just as well for me. For the folks let me go that summer when Captain George Tromley, Jr., a Methodist and a friend of Papa, invited my friend, Bess Moore, and me to come along on a ten-day trip upriver to Lansing and back. Bess's brother, Rob, was his chief engineer. The captain's father had been a legendary French-Canadian raft pilot. Our steamer was to be the big *J. S. Van Sant II,* famous for towing the biggest lumber raft ever brought down the Mississippi, just two years before.

For three years I'd been watching lumber rafts float by: two or three acres of logs, or white, sweet-smelling boards in each raft, a crew of ten or twelve men, a stern-wheeler with its prow pushing from behind, and a second, smaller steamer going back and forth across the front of the raft, steering it. I never expected to go on one. We were first to make a one-day steamer trip upstream to Lansing, where we would pick up the raft and bow boat, the *Lydia Van Sant,* which had been built in Le Claire. Captain Tromley said the river was exceptionally low and steamers were forced to run slowly. There were many bars and snags and he planned to drag three lines. He warned us that with such low water the raft was likely to get grassy and be full of water snakes.

It was the first week of September. Rob Moore, who was twenty-six and a muscular fellow of six foot, showed us our stateroom. He had climbed Mount Rushmore, a feat pictured in the Photograph Gallery of Fred

Schworm's store downtown, where the river pilots whiled away their time in winter.

Fog stayed with us the whole trip to Lansing. Three bells sounded to signal our departure. Once out on the water, we lost sight of everything. I thought of Huck's words: ". . . I shot out into the solid white fog, and hadn't no more idea which way I was going than a dead man." For fleeting seconds, a dim, yellow sun came out, then gray mist blotted it out again. The hurricane deck was wet with fog. All we could see below the railing was muddy water as it gurgled and swirled, sliding us along. Captain Tromley stayed at the big wooden wheel in the pilothouse, which, on a clear day, would have offered a sweeping view in all directions.

Once, Rob guided us down several decks to see the engine room, with its big moving machinery, hissing steam and the red glare from furnace doors. We watched the sooty, sweating firemen as they stoked up the fires to keep the big paddle wheel moving. The boilers supplied high-pressure steam to the engines, and Rob had to be ready to respond to orders from the pilot-house.

The *J. S. Van Sant* had a sizable crew, but it was not at all like traveling on one of the big packets, all white-painted steamboat-Gothic gingerbread and carrying up to a thousand passengers. Mama and I had made day trips downriver to Davenport, and the big boats made frequent stops to take on wood to feed the boilers. Wooding up was always a good chance to stretch your legs if the bank wasn't too mosquito-infested. It was amusing to see the men and boys among the steerage passengers work—helping to carry wood aboard was part of their fare. Some worked like beavers; others just dragged along a stick or two until the mate hollered at them to scramble.

All the way to Lansing, we kept hearing the deep-clanging roof bell, a smaller bell from the pilothouse and shouts from the hurricane deck.

"Labboard lead, there! Stabboard lead!"

The cries of the leadsmen came out of the fog, hoarsely repeated in the shouts of the word-passers.

"M-a-r-k three! M-a-r-k three! Quarter-less-three! Half twain! Quarter twain! Mark twain!" Which of course meant two fathoms deep.

Pilots were said not to mind low water or any kind of darkness, but fog really stopped them. All steamboats were dangerous. Just that summer, more than a thousand died in the *General Slocum* steamboat disaster in New York State. We were forever hearing of boats that exploded, burned or collided, struck sand flats, or mud flats, or had their bottoms torn out by drowned trees or snags. The average life of a steamboat was said to be only four or five years.

It wasn't until we neared Lansing that evening that we first saw—above the roofs, treetops, steeples and cooking smoke of the town—the magnificent limestone bluffs that overlook the Iowa side on that stretch of the river. Behind them was Iowa's Allamakee County, a wild-looking backwoods of hill farms and dark, ragged timber. Across the river stretched the flat Wisconsin bottomlands.

That night, Bess and I stayed up to watch the roustabouts haul wood aboard. The "roosters" were the common laborers of a steamboat. They loaded and unloaded freight; every time the boat came in for a landing and the gangplank went down, they went into action. But their big job on the rafter was to keep all those logs floating along in an orderly way. Rob said it was a devil of a job, but these men would be doing strenuous work anyway; better to do it, they felt, on a steamboat than on shore. Wooding up in the dark was exciting, as it was done by the light of bonfires, torches and cressets—big iron fire baskets filled with burning oil-soaked wood. From the deck, we could eavesdrop on the profane and uproarious shouting of the roosters: "Fetch a torch or a chunk of fire here, boys!" "Lend a hand, you bloody son of a wildcat!" "Where the *hell* you going with that barrel, you *blankety-blankety-blank* coyote?"

Once enough cordwood was taken on, the *J. S. Van Sant* steamed off before dawn to a slough, the quiet-water side of an island where logs were made into rafts. As we left Lansing, the town still slept. When everything was ready at the slough, the steamer took its place behind the raft—river towboats always pushed their tow. The bow boat, steering, went crosswise way out in front across all the floating logs and lumber. Captain Tromley rang for power on the paddle wheel, the departure bells clanged and, blowing its hoarse whistle and puffing steam, the *J. S. Van Sant* began its downstream journey. As we headed for Prairie du Chien it started to drizzle; the air on the river was hot and muggy.

Ahead of us floated just about three acres of lumber—logs and boards both—moving at about two and a half miles an hour, carried by the slow current. The huge raft was steered around the bends by the bow boat and great sweep oars. These, some twenty to thirty feet long, were fastened to the front and rear of the raft. "Bucking the oar" was the raftsman's toughest job, and the ones doing it looked as though they could take a dozen men apart in a fight. The roosters wore spiked boots and walked out on the logs, which were chained together to make fifty-foot pens with loose logs and lumber floating inside. Most of them carried long pike poles or those heavy wooden staffs with hinged metal hooks rivermen used to handle the logs and called peavies. Up in the pilothouse, the captain kept an eye out for sand-bars and snags and studied the current and the wind.

Rob said Captain Tromley was celebrated for his knowledge of the river's bed, its bars and crosscurrents and how to manage both the raft and the roosters in dangerous situations. "He never has broke up," the young engineer told us. "He knows his channel and knows how to keep his boat and tow in deep water. The captain's father and uncles were all masters and pilots, and veterans of the old floating days when rafts were run without steamboats. Oh, he takes his chances and gets into tight places, but he always gets out right side up." The captain suggested that Bess and I sleep late in the mornings when it was cool. But bells were always ringing for changes in the watch or to summon "off-watch" men to meals and we hated to miss anything. The galley's cooking was so good I must have put on ten pounds. Rob said cooks sometimes got thrown overboard if it wasn't. Captain Tromley said, "I want to pay my men well, feed them well and work them like hell."

Through the Winneshiek Bottoms the current was fairly strong. Our course to Prairie du Chien was along a deeply worn channel which wound in and out of many islands. The Iowa bank was high and steep, with pale, greenish-white bluffs and overhanging trees, while Wisconsin was low and flat, with a thick cover of willows. French fur trappers named the landing "Prairie of the Dog," but it was not barking, but the shrill, fluty sound of a steam calliope that greeted us as we came in. Soon a big white steamboat came into sight at the levee and Bess shrieked, "It's the *New Sensation!*" We could see the ornately painted paddle boxes and double smokestacks and the ornamental steamboat cannon on the forward deck. It was one of the show-boats that came every year. Captain Tromley said the actual boats kept changing but some floating paddle-boat palace called the *New Sensation* had been steaming up and down the Mississippi for fifty years. Prairie du Chien itself looked sadly in decay; old yellow limestone buildings crumbling on a decrepit levee. I tried to imagine smoke rising from tepees, squaws with papooses, French traders haggling with Indians over rum and furs and French priests trying to save the red man's soul. It was so long ago.

Since we had time, the captain let Rob take Bess and me to that evening's performance on the *New Sensation*. Like the *Floating Palace*, which also came to Le Claire, it put on vaudevilles and melodramas like *East Lynn*, *Tempest and Sunshine* or *Parson's Bride*. That night there was to be a performance of *Ten Nights in a Bar-Room*. It was exciting, dressing up and going around the public rooms with their wood paneling, cut-glass chandeliers and ornate Victorian furniture—Turkish carpets, marble-topped tables,

gilded looking-glasses and velvet drapes—with "mosquito bars" over all the
windows. Once again we watched as poor Joe Morgan staggered into the
saloon to spend his last penny on whiskey, fallen as he was and powerless in
the clutches of demon rum. Remember elocution class? CUR-few shall-l-l-l
not Har-rrringngng toNIGHT! That's how the actors talked. Joe, the
drunkard, took a great gurgling swig out of the bottle he kept in his pocket.
Then in through the swinging doors came Little Mary to sing: "Father, dear
father, come home with me now." The fire was out, the house all dark, poor
Benny was so sick in Mother's arms. Of course Joe didn't go, just stayed
swilling down more liquor. At last Little Mary came back to sing the final
verse:

> "Father, dear father, come home with me now!
>   The clock in the steeple strikes three;
> The house is so lonely—the hours so long
>   For poor weeping mother and me.
> Yes, we are alone, poor Benny is dead,
>   And gone with the angels of light;
> And these were the very last words that he said,
>   'I want to kiss Papa goodnight.' "

The next day, at the spot where Marquette and Joliet first saw the Mississippi, we drifted lazily over whirlpools and eddies as the brown mud of the
Wisconsin River mingled with our olive green. All of a sudden everybody
started shouting—there was a railroad bridge dead ahead. The logs and
lumber had to be quickly arranged so that the raft could be split lengthwise;
each half had to go separately through the narrow passages between the
piers of the bridge. The roosters were furiously working with their peavies
and pike poles to shift about three acres of logs with stubborn ideas of where
they wanted to go. To guide the logs, the towboat was drawn with cables at
an angle to the raft, like a big rudder. As the steamboat strained and huffed
and churned, the raft slowly swung the right direction. At the same time, in
answer to Captain Tromley's whistle signals and shouts from one word-
passer to the next, the bow boat drove its paddle wheel forward and then in
reverse, pulling the head of the raft the right way too.

Captain Tromley said any big log raft was ornery. If you unexpectedly hit
an island or bar, the river might suddenly be full of stray logs and dunked
raftsmen. "To get through a railroad bridge without injury," he said, "you

must start right and stay right." He recalled that when the railway was first built, some pilots used to spit at it.

The next day, Rob took us in a skiff; two men came along to help row it and pull it ahead of the tow. The captain wanted Rob to post some mail and buy ice, meat and fresh vegetables. There were signs, "Boat Store," in all the little river towns, showing who catered to the river trade.

"There's always time to go ashore when we're going as slow as we are now, simply towing in a low river," Rob said. He laughed. "One time, two fine young ladies from Muscatine made a trip from Beef Slough to Lansing with Captain Tromley and they always wanted to come along when we took the skiff to shore. All of a sudden they quit coming. It turned out some of the roosters had told them I wasn't safe, that I'd been a real bad corpse-maker in Illinois with a criminal record that long . . ." Rob said he sometimes worked as an engineer as far as St. Louis, where he'd ship his kit home and take deck passage on a northbound steamer.

"You'll always find several raft crews on an upstream steamer," he said. "They'll all have money. Just been paid for the down trip. Every boat has a bar, and 'red liquor' is in hot demand. We used to have some high old times. Of course, most of the fighting is confined to the lower decks."

Guttenberg, where Rob bought the stores that day, was like a little German town: wide-eaved, steep-roofed houses, women wearing shawls, and red-cheeked, fat old men smoking long porcelain pipes and drinking beer from steins. Everybody complained in heavy German accents that they'd never seen the weather hotter, the river more dangerous, the fishing worse, or the mosquitoes more vicious.

After Guttenberg the current was stronger as the river flowed through a rock-walled, steep-sided valley for a stretch. One morning, a slightly built rooster offered to let me wear his spiked boots so I could go out on the logs in the raft. I did, carrying a pike pole for balance; it was thrilling. Once you were out on it, the raft was a bobbing mass of sweet-smelling logs, mostly pine. Scattered across the logs, here and there, were the surefooted roosters, poised and agile, leaning on their peavies. They'd cut their pants off just below the knee or wore them tightly stuffed inside their spiked boots. We were floating along so slowly it was only by looking at the bank that I could tell we were moving. The roosters were calling and cheering me on, but one slip and you were in the river, and I was teetering so precariously, I was just as glad to get back to the *J. S. Van Sant* without a dunking.

Dubuque, which we drifted past next, was blistering hot. "Wonderful corn weather," people kept saying. A little ways downstream, I went with Rob to fetch fish and ice at Sabula, which was swarming with mosquitoes;

great clouds of them buzzed around us and we saw all we wanted of the town at a glance. There were so many like it along the Mississippi, clusters of houses pinched under a limestone bluff, or straggling up a steep gully, with steamboat stores and warehouses down by the riverbank, and maybe shantyboat squatters' colonies, the kind of tough river world Huck and Jim kept floating into.

After Dubuque the river changed. On the Iowa side, rocky bluffs gave way to gently rolling hillsides dotted with small farms. The Illinois bank became woods and marshes. Evenings, the crew gathered on the forecastle to sing—roar, you might say, as few of the songs were meant for the parlor —"Buffalo Gals," "Raftsman Jim," "Big Maquoketa." One about the great Mike Fink, who could "outrun, outdrink and outfight any man on the river." And the *Prairie Belle*'s engineer, Jim Bludso, who, when it caught fire, kept the engines going while the passengers scrambled to safety, giving his life to make good the promise:

> "I'll hold her nose agin the bank
> Till the last galoot's ashore."

Some of the songs Bess and I pretended not to hear, being, as we were, proper Methodist young ladies who couldn't bear the least bit of obscenity and who thought anybody who took a drop of liquor was dissolute and bound straight for hell. I noticed that while at home Dad spoke of "wet," "dry," "a union of forces" and "local option," the roosters talked just as enthusiastically about "bootleggers" and "speakeasies" in places where they'd already "voted dry."

Soon Bess and I were humming all the tunes. ("He weren't no saint— them engineers is pretty much alike . . .") We spent hours and hours on deck in the shade of a tarpaulin, catching the breeze, watching the river, half in a dream. Sometimes a buoy would shoot by with a gurgle of water, or a small tug drift past pulling a string of barges. After steaming over enough muggy river miles, a kind of lassitude creeps over you. Mudbank follows mudbank, and trees and rubbish float by in the greenish-brownish water—so much water, always on the move. Clinton came and went, a glimpse of wharves and smoke. We took the skiff into Camanche one sundown and were greeted on the levee by some townspeople who couldn't see us plainly in the dark and were too busy slapping mosquitoes to care much about anything else anyway. That night, our last on board, we stayed up on deck late, listening to the roosters sing what had become my favorite of their songs:

"I was standing by my window yester morning
Without a thought of worry or of care
When I saw the postman coming down the pathway
With such a happy smile and jaunty air.
Oh he rang the bell and whistled while he waited,
And then he said Good morning to you, Jack;
But he little knew the sorrow that he brought me
When he handed me a letter edged in black . . ."

What a sad, sweet song, I thought. Rob Moore had a desperate case on me. He wrote and proposed regularly for the next few years.

That night, during the blackest hours, all thoughts of sleep were driven away by the noisiest storm we'd had all summer. The wind blew, hot and stifling, lightning flashed, thunder rolled, but not a drop of rain fell. I got up before daylight. Stars still shone. There was a sliver of moon in the sky, its silver light reflected in the muddy Mississippi. Cool breezes played over the water's surface. An air of expectancy hung over everything. Even the mosquitoes seemed to be waiting for something, probably new travelers with fresh blood in their veins, now that they'd drained ours. In the east, the sky grew light. A startled bird fled scolding into the air. An old man in a rowboat held up a string of catfish to show me his night's catch. We passed Princeton, where Dad preached and had held a tent revival that summer. We were almost home.

"I'll tell you the story as best I can,
For I'm only a weather-worn river man . . .
And I miss the crews that will sail no more,
As I miss the face of a girl on shore . . ."

Rob softly sang as he helped us carry our baggage down the gangplank to the levee. The *J. S. Van Sant* was going on to Muscatine and St. Louis with its raft of lumber. He looked around, taking in the levee, the Green Tree, the wooden store fronts on Cody Road, the big houses of the pilots up in the hills. Rob sighed.

"You know, bit by bit the old place seems to be sinking back into the rocks from which it came. Well, good-bye, Louise. I'll miss you."

A month later, Father was reassigned to a new church in another peaceful little inland farming town, this time named Monona.

Anne

Entry by Jessie, 1905:

"Oct. 31—It has been a long time since we have written in this journal . . . Little Helen is just as full of mischief as Haddie ever was. But cries more. Has been a great bunch of nerves. But is such a cute little thing, rosy-cheeked and dark-haired. She talks a good deal now quite plainly. Gets lots of bumps . . . Mary gets along nicely in school . . . Haddie is principal of the school in Ridgeway where he started as a First Grader 13 years ago . . . Papa has just come in from milking . . . Anna Louise teaches at Hardin, a one-room schoolhouse way out in the country. She has only 47 pupils so far, with more to follow in winter . . ."

Anna Louise:

Just after Christmas the year we moved from Le Claire, I enrolled in the Upper Iowa University Academy in Fayette, a Methodist school not far from Monona. The next summer, I went to the Teachers' Institute and took the examination. I was now seventeen.

Extracts from Report of the Superintendent of Public Instruction, State of Iowa, Section B1:

". . . Neither certificate nor diploma shall be granted when the candidate falls below 75 percent in any of the following branches: Arithmetic, English Grammar, History of the United States, Orthography and Geography; or below 65 percent in any of the following: Reading, Writing, Bookkeeping, Physiology, Algebra, Botany, Natural Philosophy, Drawing, Civil Government, Constitution and Laws of Iowa, and Didactics; or below 60 percent on any of the following: Geometry, Trigonometry, Chemistry, Zoology, Geology, Astronomy, Political Economy, Rhetoric, English Literature and General History . . . Applicants must in all cases present a certificate of good moral character . . .

"The following lists of questions are to be used at examinations for certificates:

ORTHOGRAPHY
TIME, FORTY MINUTES

"1. Put into proper shape as to punctuation, capitals and versification the following:

to be or not to be that is the question whether tis nobler in the mind . . .

PENMANSHIP
TIME, ONE HALF HOUR

. . . 5. Illustrate *slant* and form all the capitals which require the *capital* stem, the *direct* oval, the *reversed* oval . . .

ARITHMETIC
TIME, TWO HOURS

. . . 6. Of two pieces of land, the one a circle of 17 rods in diameter, the other a triangle whose hypotenuse is 30 rods and whose base is 24 rods, which is the larger, and by how much? . . ."

Anna Louise:

And so it went. My head was soon swimming. Physiology ("State what fluids or juices are secreted by the system for the digestion of food and give the particular use of each"), History ("Name five important events in Andrew Jackson's administration"), Algebra ("Find G.C.D. of $x^3 + 5x^2 + 10x + 8$ and $x^5 + 2x^4 - x - 2$"), Natural Philosophy ("What is a molecular force?"), Drawing ("Draw a figure and locate horizon line, vanishing point, point of sight, line of view, point of view, point of distance, and base line"), Psychology ("What is the arrangement of the white and gray matter in the brain? In the spinal cord?"), Civil Government ("Give the duties of the President"), and Geography ("Locate Savannah, Glasgow, Tokio, Timbuctoo, Madras, Sitka, Santiago, Vera Cruz") . . .

I was dead sure I'd failed when notification came four weeks later that I'd passed. There was a shortage of teachers at the time. So I got the post at Hardin, just a few miles from Monona, where Papa arranged for me to stay at the home of the Vic Pierson family. Mrs. Pierson was an enormous woman, so fat she'd once been offered a job with a circus. She was warmhearted and told me, "You got my sympathies, Miss Williams."

Hardin was very primitive, mainly poor backwoods farming families. I was paid fifteen dollars a month and gave the Piersons five of it for board. They couldn't get anybody for less. Even so, a good many of the men in Hardin seemed to feel women weren't supposed to have money to fling right

and left in the foolish way women will when they're not looked after—
which to them meant new shoes for the baby and a new calico dress every
two or three years. Many farmers did have to struggle, with wheat not yet a
dollar a bushel, eggs only six for a quarter and taxes of four or five dollars to
pay on an eighty-acre farm every year. Land, for the few who could afford
it, was going for fifty, sixty, up to two hundred dollars an acre. Most of it
around Hardin went for less, for it was hilly and stony or, if flat, poorly
drained. The poorest farmers were mainly tenants and their landlords didn't
want to spend money to tile the land. The local people worked terribly hard
for little return, and about all a person could rightly expect in these rural
districts was a simple one-room school, with desks, benches and a stove in
it.

On the fateful morning, I was up at the crack of dawn, washing and
putting on new bloomers and a camisole. I held the bedpost as Mrs. Pierson
laced up my corset from the back, pulling it from top and bottom to middle,
then hooking in her fingers to twist it real tight. On went a second starched
petticoat, my black skirt that skimmed the floor and crackled a little, and a
new white shirtwaist with leg-o'-mutton sleeves and a high collar with an
ascot tie at the neck. I'd swept up my long hair into a "Gibson Girl"
pompadour, too, but when I went out and stood in front of the Piersons'
parlor mirror, I still saw a scared seventeen-year-old girl not long out of
pigtails.

Later on I got a horse, but that day I walked to the schoolhouse, about a
mile over a dirt track. It was set out in the middle of nowhere, surrounded
by a pasture and woods in an acre of open ground. There was a big play-
ground, two privies smelling of lime with the usual spiderwebs and a big
daddy longlegs, a coal shed and just outside the schoolhouse door a water
pump and wooden platform, with a bucket and long-handled tin dipper so
the children could drink.

The schoolhouse itself was airy and light, with three big paned windows
across the back wall. There were four rows of wooden benches and desks,
whittled and carved with rude initials; two pupils shared each desk. The
blackboard wasn't slate like we had at the Limestone Academy, but just
wood painted black, which was cheaper. On it, written in chalk in Spence-
rian teacher's script, was, "I pledge allegiance to my flag and to the Repub-
lic for which it stands; one nation, indivisible, with liberty and justice for
all." Below this, the previous teacher had also written out the first stanza of
"My Country, 'Tis of Thee," which the children sang every morning, just
after the pledge to the flag. The song was my cue to give the signal that the

lesson was about to start by clearing my throat and saying, "Class, may I have your attention, please."

Over the teacher's desk was the familiar framed print of Gilbert Stuart's unfinished portrait of George Washington. Hanging over it was the flag, with a star for each of the forty-five states. There were also chalk, a floor that needed a broom, a recitation bell, a shelf full of books, a pot-bellied stove, maps, a dustpan, a bench with a washbasin and a cake of homemade lye soap, and hooks along the southern wall for coats and caps, with room to set overshoes underneath. A member of the school board had brought me over and given me the keys a couple of days before; I'd seen there was no wall clock and brought a wind-up alarm Mama had given me.

I was terribly excited. I hung up my new wool cape, lined with plaid flannel, along with my shawl, and looked for the coal shuttle, poker and broom. School began at nine, so I had just an hour to get the fire going to take the chill off and set the place to rights. I opened the flue on the chimney pot, put in some dried leaves and straw and a little kindling on top of that, and some smaller pieces of dried wood somebody had left in the woodbox. Then I struck a match and, thank the Lord, it went right up. When the fire got really roaring, I closed the damper at half mast. I soon learned to close it entirely about an hour before school ended each day so the fire would die. If I forgot, it meant staying on long after school until the fire was out or very low. In Hardin it seemed like I always smelled of smoke.

As nine approached, I watched children heading my way, little figures picking their way along the rutted road or cutting across fields. The first to arrive was a small boy in cowhide boots, his head amost hidden in a gritty old cap with earlaps, and his little sister, bundled up in a shawl, trudging right behind him. As they came in, they chirruped, "Good morning, ma'm!" in heavy accents. I soon discovered that many of the children spoke German or Czech, Norwegian or Swedish at home. Most had been up for hours, helping with chores.

From Norman Borlaug, who grew up on a small farm about forty miles from Hardin and went on to receive the Nobel Peace Prize; a 1985 interview:

". . . The little one-room country schoolhouse I went to up there—of course that was fifteen years later—it was still half-Norwegian, half-Bohemian (they didn't like to be called Czechs). Just to the north, the second little town over was Spillville. That was pure Bohemian. Antonin Dvořák spent a summer there to capture the feeling for his *New World Symphony.* "Going Home," that's one of my favorites . . . Our farm, Dad owned just fifty-six acres and the rest was Granddad's that he rented, another forty-nine acres. We had chickens. Sold pigs and eggs for cash. There was a little crossroads, Saude, with a co-op creamery, general store, blacksmith and machine shop, feed mill for grinding your oats and corn, the Lutheran church and that was it. You'd take eggs and buy what you needed. If they were worth more than what you purchased, you got a due bill. It showed how much you got for the eggs, how much you bought and what you had 'due.' In the winter you'd go down to the river and haul back a sledload of ice. Each fall we'd sell six or seven head of beef, drive those cattle thirteen miles into Cresco. Generally you and the neighbors at the same time . . . All Norwegians. With the Bohemians on one side and the Irish on the other . . ."

That first day, the children came in quietly, about the only time they ever did. There were forty-seven of them, from mere babes to lanky boys as tall as I was. They carried their lunches in tin buckets: potato cake, baked johnnycake and bread, maybe a vegetable and a little lard. Sometimes apple butter or honey for the bread or a bit of cold fried ham. There were also apples that fall, winesaps and Grimes Goldens and Whitney Crabs you'd wait to eat until they were ripe and mushy. Mrs. Pierson pickled them whole and left the stems so you'd have something to hold onto. For a treat, she might make apple fritters, frying some in a small cake of batter in deep fat and sprinkling them with sugar. We all drank from the pump, using the bucket and dipper, which made the cool water taste of tin.

High up on one wall—I'd have had to stand on a chair to reach it— hanging across two nails was a hickory stick. We all knew what that was for, but I never used it. There was rarely any need for discipline with children of immigrant parents; they got so much of it at home. Oh, sometimes if some- body was a little naughty, I'd make him sit in the corner or maybe stay inside during recess. Most of the time, everybody behaved, except for a little whispering and squirming, and a stare usually stilled that. People driving past the schoolhouse usually just heard, aside from the creak of their buggy wheels, the hum of recitation.

What trouble there was came from the big fellows in the back seats, as did the apple cores and spitballs. They were with us just the three or four coldest months. Since the 1879 Bennett Law, every American child had to spend at least twelve weeks in school each year learning four subjects: read- ing, English, mathematics and American history. In Hardin, that was all the bigger boys got; as soon as they could, their fathers pulled them out to work on the farm. Sometimes I met them at parties, but I wouldn't date them. A teacher was talked about too much. Those parties were something; at one, a girl passed around a dishpan full of water instead of finger bowls.

Just once I was afraid. Clem, who stood nearly six foot and came from a poor sharecropper family, got out his jackknife one day and started carving up his desk. Clem had a bad reputation and he didn't know more than the law allowed. I went right back and held out my hand and said, "Clem, you give me that knife." He grinned but he didn't budge. Brute strength for brute strength, he was more than my match. But I knew I had to prove myself or slink off home and hide. In Le Claire, with all those tough rivermen, Dad had been forever preaching about the manliness of Jesus, how he displayed "a marvelous knowledge of men, was keen and sharp in debate, could face a mob calmly and speak to the point when rebuking sinners." Nothing intimidated *him* . . . The silence in that room was awful. *"Clem, you give me that knife,"* I repeated. He slowly closed it and gave it to me. After that I never had another bit of trouble with him.

To the school board, learning by memory was what mattered: history dates, multiplication tables, combinations of numbers, verses from the Bible in alphabetical order. So was penmanship. The children practiced ovals and more ovals and how to write with their feet flat on the floor and the paper at just the right angle. For geography, we had a wooden map case, with roll-down maps of all the continents—only, mice got in and chewed the Atlantic coastline off North America.

A teacher was judged most of all by how well she knew arithmetic. At school the children ciphered through their lessons and handed in their sums to me. I'd say I'd take them home and look them over when I had more time. As if that fooled anybody. I *had a key!* The answers were all there in the back of the teacher's book. Friday afternoons we ciphered. We'd also choose up sides and have spelldowns. We used *McGuffey's Speller,* beginning with *a-b ab, e-b eb,* and *i-b ib,* and building up by stages to such twisters as "gas-tro-no-mic," "su-per-flu-i-ties" and "ec-sta-sy." Our McGuffey Readers also had exercises in pronunciation, especially how *not* to pronounce words. I would read: "Do not say *ed-dy-cate* nor *ej-ju-cate* for ed-*u*-cate; *vic-ter-y* for vic-*to*-ry; *pop-py-la-tion* for pop-*u*-la-tion. . . ."

We memorized poetry, too. We got examples of good English from stories in our readers like Dickens' "Death of Little Nell": "She was dead. No sleep so beautiful and calm, so free from trace of pain, so fair to look upon . . ." But at the Limestone Academy, we'd had Latin and English literature, and at home we'd grown up with the King James Bible, not to speak of Shakespeare, Longfellow and the rest. I found few of the Hardin children opened a book at all outside school. What to do? I wrote Mama and she sent me a book titled *Graded Selections for Memorizing.* Mama wrote, "What they don't keep in their houses, they can keep in their heads." The author was

John D. Peaslee, A.M., Ph.D. In his Foreword, he wrote: "These memory gems may be guiding stars to our children for life, for what one learns as a child one never forgets . . ." Professor Peaslee rarely quoted a whole poem or speech from a play, just passages. Soon the schoolhouse rang with quotations: "This is the forest primeval. The murmuring pines and the hemlocks . . . ," "The quality of mercy is not strained . . . ," "Blessings on thee, little man, barefoot boy, with cheek of tan!" "By the shores of Gitchee Gumee . . . ," "This above all: to thine own self be true . . . ," "The curfew tolls the knell of parting day . . . ," "Of all sad words of tongue or pen . . . ," "Home is the sailor, home from the sea . . . ," "Listen, my children, and you shall hear . . ." Of the poetry we memorized, my favorites came to be Bryant's "Thanatopsis," Field's "Little Boy Blue," Tennyson's "Crossing the Bar," Leigh Hunt's "Abou Ben Adhem" and the Twenty-third Psalm.

Of course I also taught the children sayings from the Bible—"A prophet is not without honor, save in his own country . . . ," "The race is not to the swift. . . . ," "Go to the ant, thou sluggard . . . ," "They shall beat their swords into plowshares . . ." The children loved to hear the stories of David and Goliath, Samson and Delilah, Moses in the bulrushes, Hagar in the wilderness, and Joseph's coat of many colors. And with the six-year-olds it was mainly trying to get them to sing, "Jesus Loves Me," and to sit still and not suck their thumbs or swallow the chalk.

Unless it rained or sleeted, I'd send the children outdoors for recess every day. The girls would play shinney or blackman or, for the little ones, drop the handkerchief, or they'd solemnly chant as they held hands and circled, "Here we go round the mulberry bush." The boys would be at baseball, marbles, pom-pom-pull-away, or "I'm the king of the castle and you're the dirty rascal."

They loved it when the snow came, holding out their mittens to catch the big wet flakes. Or they'd turn their faces to the sky, mouths open wide like the beaks of hungry baby birds, eyes squinty as the snow clung to their eyelashes, tongues stuck out to catch the flakes. Sometimes they'd lie down on their backs in the snow and move their arms up and down to make angel's wings. If there was enough unbroken snow, they'd make a big wheel, with spokes in it, by tramping around, to play what they called "Fox and Geese." Some would give chase, if they were the fox, trying to "kill" the geese by jumping over them, and get back to the top of the wheel. Some would run away, squealing and shrieking, if they were the geese, dodging about to try to trap the fox by surrounding it. If snow fell during the night, I'd find the schoolhouse surrounded by a pure white, crusty expanse when I arrived in the morning. After the hour-and-a-half noon recess, when I'd go to tap the window with my ruler, what had been a field of white was a crisscross of gray foot tracks, body impressions, beaten paths and potholes. If there was enough snow, the boys tried to wash the girls' faces in it. If I heard a lot of yelling, it meant they were having a snowball fight, which was great fun until somebody got hit in the ear. Then they'd come running in to me, sobbing.

I always gave them a good long recess, because outdoors the children could whoop and holler and carry on as much as they wanted to. Afterwards, all the boys and girls would come trooping in, breathless, and puffing from exertion. I'd hope they'd spent all their energy, but they always seemed to have plenty left, bumping through the aisles, knocking books and papers off desks with an "ex*cuse* me!" and falling into their seats and sniggering. "Boys! No roughhousing!" I'd have to call. "And girls, stop that giggling!"

The year passed quickly. Winter left us at last; one day, the snow had gone, except for dirty banks along the road, and slush and mud; it thawed in the afternoon and froze up at sunset. During recess, the girls started jumping rope and I could hear them chanting, "Pease porridge hot, pease porridge cold, pease porridge in the pot, nine days old . . . One potato, two potato, three potato, four . . ." Or the boys, playing marbles, arguing excitedly over a highly prized shooter: "Heck! He always wants to play for keeps!" Shrill cries of "You're it! You're it!" and "Tommy's it and had a fit and couldn't get over it!"

Rainy days now, they got restless. Oh, not the little ones. If there was thunder and lightning, I'd have to gather them all around the recitation bench and hold as many as I could get in my arms. How they crowded up! But an older boy, fearless in the peals of thunder, might be standing by the stove, grinning and not thinking of anything in particular and another boy would hit him a clout on his back and tell him to "pass it on." And he'd pass it on. Soon there got to be such a chasing over benches and maybe upsetting the water bucket, and tearing up generally, I'd have to shout, "Boys! Boys! If you can't play more quietly, I'm going to fetch down that switch." There may be a boy somewhere who always wipes his feet before he comes in and who never sasses his teacher; it's just that I've never found him among my pupils.

At first we used slates, but that meant enduring the squeaks of gritty pencils, and they just seemed to invite games of tick-tack-toe, three in a row. So I bought some paper and the children supplied their own lead pencils, pen holders and points. The school board bought certain supplies—ink, coal, chalk, erasers, a dictionary, recitation bell, spindle, flash cards for arithmetic, the water bucket, dipper, dustpan and broom, and now and then a book or two. But the children loved to draw. So I bought crayons and paper myself. I also asked Mama to send me a chart and taught them the scale: *do re mi fa sol la-a-a-a.* Just about the only songs they knew were hymns they'd learned as little tads in Sunday School: "Work, for the Night Is Coming," "Brighten the Corner Where You Are" or Martin Luther's battle cry, "Ein Feste Burg." Hardin taught me resolve. Some of these farmers brought up their children to know little but work. They used to come to the school, lean, unshaven work-worn men and hold up the poems or crayon drawings in their nail-blackened, hard-callused hands and grumble, "What's the use of this?" I'd stammer some foolish reply. But these children were up at five every morning to go way out into the pastures to fetch the cows, come back to carry water and firewood, slop the hogs, curry and harness horses, heaven knows what all. Home meant never-ending chores. It was up to school to show them there was something to life besides work.

In Le Claire, I'd always been busy. Now, waiting for the children to come in the morning or the fire to go out at night, I had more time to be conscious of things. That red flash was a friendly cardinal and I'd come to know a whole family of woodchucks. Nature was close in Hardin; it made you think.

The day came when the heat that yesterday felt so pleasant was now too hot for endurance. The younger ones came in from recess with flushed, red faces. One boy, bolder than the rest, was usually found to plead, "Miss Williams, m'am, cain't we have the windows open? It's awful hot!" With these drafts! But I'd open one and right away the outer world, kept out so long, came into the schoolroom: the crowing of roosters, the creak of the pump, the rumble of a passing wagon, the chirruping of birds, the whistle of the Milwaukee's No. 11 headed for Chicago, all blending together in the soft spring air. Spring deepened, and who cared for ciphers or spelldowns now? The girls, once so eager and alert, now sat staring with vacant, dreamy faces out the windows. I'd read: "A farmer sold sixteen bushels of wheat for sixty-six cents a bushel; how many . . ." but I could plainly see that the boys' minds were out in the woods, where they were going fishing when the chores were done. The teacher should have looked stern and rapped the ruler for attention, but she, too, I must confess, was thinking of a young man who was coming over to Pierson's after supper to take her to a basket social at the church. I wondered . . . I wondered . . . would the money I'd saved be enough to go to college and not have to teach again next year?

That summer, Mama had a worrisome cough and Dad proposed they take a railroad trip to California. They could go through the Canadian Rockies and Lake Louise and Banff. I said I'd look after Mary and Helen. I had decided to enroll as a freshman at Upper Iowa University in Fayette in the fall. It was seven years since Father's tour of Yosemite Valley on his bicycle. Mother's cough soon cleared up, but a visit to San Francisco, nearly destroyed by its great earthquake that April, left them both awed and shaken.

From a letter sent by Jessie from Oakland, the "City of Refuge," to her daughters in Iowa, August 1906:

". . . Papa and I went out to Cliff House yesterday. A damp, chill fog was rolling in from the Pacific. I've never been so cold in all my life as since we've been here. I just can't get warm. By sheer grit, laughing in the face of Fate, they're cheerfully and quickly rebuilding, but it still looks like a dead city, not a city recently dead, but one destroyed hundreds and hundreds of years ago. Like Pompei, dug out from its lava. Down on Market Street you can see fragments of wall, twisted columns, great broken chunks of stone, pipes, crazy walls, everything covered with a grayish, yellowish dust. The hills go up and down so steeply, and it's all so quiet. Just ruins and silence, that's about all . . .

"All Chinatown was burned. The site is in demand for business use and the Chinese may be forced to rebuild elsewhere. The St. Francis Hotel stood the earthquake shock, but fire consumed most of the surrounding district. We saw lots of small tents with imposing signs for businesses and hotels. And little booths for cooking. A monument in Union Square commemorating Admiral Dewey's victory at Manila Bay was shifted from its base and tilted at an angle of ten degrees . . .

"From the top of Nob Hill, almost everything you can see, except for the Ferry Building, was destroyed or badly damaged by fire. Way down across the Bay you can see Oakland, where Dad and I are staying . . . Everybody still talks about the violence of the earthquake. And the noise. The falling bricks and girders made a terrible sound, people say. One man who helped give chloroform told us how they were aroused at 5 A.M. by the violent shaking and how the buildings all made such a terrible roar as they came down and the screams and cries of those buried beneath them and how silent it was afterwards. All the normal sounds of the city died, you see. They say people came rushing out into the streets. The streets were full of people. But the odd thing was—and everybody says the same thing—that the people were silent, absolutely silent. I guess hardly any of them could speak in the first few minutes. And no wonder . . ."

Extract from a sermon delivered by Hadwen at the Methodist Church in Monona, Iowa, September 18, 1906:

". . . One day it was the most lighthearted city on the continent, the joyous city by the Golden Gate, the gateway to the Ocean of Adventure; the next day it was in ruins. Friends, in Christian literature, from Dante's Inferno to Bunyan's Vanity Fair, hell has been represented as a crowded city. And hell is what San Francisco became. The earthquake that killed hundreds and shook all the lowlands was followed by a fire, perhaps the greatest fire in history. There was no water to fight the fire and most of the city burned.

"Flames rolled down the city's streets, destroying everything in their wake. People told us how the great and honorable, the learned and the wise, fled before the fire with the beggar and the thief. All were alike. As the earth shook and flames swept through the city, it was like Judgment Day. Neither the mayor, nor the mighty men, nor the wise men, could stop its destruction. Many who were worth millions were left paupers. Friends, when the Day of Judgment comes, there will be no difference. And if it was a terrible thing in the days of earthquake and fire in San Francisco, it will be far more terrible for us to go down in our sins to a Godless grave . . ."

Hadwen

Jessie says, "Papa, I'm not going to ride in one of those contraptions any farther than I know I can walk back." I make haste to say she means one of those new Fords that accommodates two passengers at such an imposing height and has Prest-O-Lites for driving after dark. I saw a fellow start up one on Main Street just the other day. Some farmers who'd brought their teams and wagons to town all gathered around to watch this fellow nearly break his arm turning the crank. At last, when the engine shuddered just right, he raced around and hopped on the running board and leaned over to move the spark and throttle. We all leaned over too, trying to figure out what in tarnation he was doing. Once he was at the wheel with the engine roaring and all set to go, a lady climbed in and sat down beside him, looking so grand with a veil tied to her jaw. It was a pleasure seeing them drive off, both trying not to let on how they were tickled to death.

Seems like you don't hear folks shouting, "Get a horse!" like they used to. I recollect how Jessie and I and the children saw our first automobile at the County Fair when we were living in Ridgeway. They called them horseless carriages in those days. Most of them were steered by a lever and had one-cylinder engines, with a chain-and-sprocket drive on regular carriage wheels. They had a Stanley Steamer at the Fair they claimed had entered races against gasoline-powered cars and won every time. That day, it went halfway around the racetrack and got stuck. Everybody had a good laugh. They said we'd never get away from horses.

If a person could afford it, an automobile sure would come in handy, wouldn't it? Myself, I'd be glad to settle for a Red Ball Motorcycle. One of the Sunday School missionaries comes around riding one. It's been one of the few times since we've been married that Jessie absolutely won't go along with me. What would people say, she asks, about a preacher who came to tent meetings in a duster and goggles and cap, roaring down the country roads like a "pleasure driver" on Sundays and maybe causing runaways? I reckon an automobile would make more sense. But even if a person had the money to buy one, where would he keep it? It would be the dickens trying to find a place in winter or if a bad storm blew up.

"Give me a team of horses any day," you hear a lot of folks say. Yet there's plenty of botheration with horses, too. To be looked after properly, horses have got to be fed well, watered, curried, shod, harnessed, exercised and taken to the vet. There's nothing that puts my dander up quite so much as people who are abusive to their horses. Then of course you've got a feed bill for hay and oats, same as you'd have for gasoline. And when an automobile acts stubborn, a man can reckon why. If a horse gets skittish, sometimes it takes another horse to know the reason.

Trouble is that Iowa did away with its old law that every automobile driver had to phone ahead to the next town that he was coming, so if your team was apt to shy you got some warning. These days maybe you're out in the buggy and you and Jessie have on your Sunday best and are going at a pretty good clip, when a real "hellwagon" wheezes by, engine sputtering full blast and the driver squeezing one of those rubber-bulb honkers loud as he can—Poop-poop! Honk-honk! POOP-POOP! HONK-HONK! Blinding dust flies up in your faces. AAr-r-r-ggghhh! The team rears on their hind legs, whinnying, backing, ears flattened and teeth bared with fright. "Whoa, whoa there! Steady, steady!" you're shouting, hoping the buggy don't upset. After you get the horses calmed down in the next quarter mile or so, there is Jessie with that awful glint in her eye that spells deadly rivalry, saying, "Why, the idea! Hadwen, did you see who that was? They're *Presbyterians!*"

So, good land a mercy! The world can't wait one minute before it changes ten thousand ways. I'm handy enough with a dripping faucet and can tinker with a lawnmower and put the storm windows on. But how in the blazes would you fix an automobile? There's the carburetor, gears, axles, tires, controls, chassis and the seating arrangements, all getting fancier every year. And even if you do get glass screens, hoods and side curtains fitted to protect you from rain, wind and snow, what if your motorcar should break down far from home, among strangers, on a dark and stormy night? Me in the mud on the flat of my back, crawling under the machine with a monkey wrench, my glasses skewgeed, hands streaked black as tar and face not much better? It would surely be no picnic. Why would anybody want an automobile, with all the mental anguish it entails?

In 1910, Hadwen bought a secondhand 1904 Ford, replacing it in 1915 with a brand-new Model T. A letter from Hadwen to Jessie, September 1920:

". . . Mrs. Murdock's funeral went all right until it turned out the cemetery was about a mile out of town. Wouldn't you know they'd have an old-fashioned, horse-drawn hearse! What a time I had coming behind it in the Model T. I had to keep running in low and water got to boiling in the radiator. Those horses looked so jumpy I was scared they'd bolt . . .

"Put in most of today on the car. Fixing the brakes I disconnected. Doing without them nearly cost me harmful trouble. Had to take off both rear wheels. I got it fixed right, I guess, as it cranked smooth with good compression.

"Started home 2 P.M. Stopped awhile at Whittier. Got away 3:40 P.M. Dust ruts very bad. Prevented high speed. At South Point put on headlights. At Arlington, the dad-blamed emergency brakes jammed so the high-speed lever refused to work. As I had a good foot brake, I removed the loose fins from the brake rods & cut the brake out. Took 10 minutes in the dark, as I had no torch light or lantern. Drizzled several times. Muddy streak at Clermont but narrow. After two miles came to mud & new grade, which was awful. Got into hitch & skid in front of Hawkins. New grade & square bank with step & wheel guard solid against it. Hard pull to get out. Finally backed to the place I went in and the wheels held in the old tracks & got out. Dark as Egypt. Home 10:20 P.M. Car worked all right in the cylinders and lubrication. Hope you are fine. Papa"

Anne

The Upper Iowa University Collegian *of October 6, 1906, shows that Louise Williams—she has dropped the Anna now—was elected secretary of the freshman class. Like Cornell in Mount Vernon, U.I.U., as many called it, was a small Methodist college in the northeastern Iowa town of Fayette. Male students boarded with families; there was a girls' dormitory. Tuition was $23.75 per term, plus laboratory fees of $5, less for a preacher's daughter. Each student was assigned to a numbered seat at Chapel, where the day began with hymns, prayers and a sermon. A popular hymn was "When the Roll Is Called Up Yonder."*

Farmers sent their daughters to U.I.U. to become schoolteachers or find husbands, their sons when they could spare them from fieldwork. Enrollment, over three hundred in winter, fell under two hundred during fall harvesting and spring planting. Fayette was one of those gracious little Iowa college towns: quiet, leafy streets, gardens, big, well-tended lawns, white frame Victorian houses with bay windows and wide front porches. It was just a short train trip to Monona through wooded, rolling farm country, with Venetian red barns, windmills and houses half-hidden by clumps of oaks and cottonwoods.

Social life at U.I.U. revolved around sports, dances, the Methodist church, the Y.M.C.A. and Y.W.C.A. and two debating societies, each with male and female wings: the Philos and Aonias and their rivals, the Zeths and Zetas. A debate might be: "Resolved, That a college education unfits a girl to be a farmer's wife"; it would get pretty lively, each side cheering its debaters with "yells" and trying to drown out the opponents, and, after popcorn or watermelon, there was usually a skirmish over caps and umbrellas in the cloakroom. I stayed terribly busy. There was tennis, skating, chafing-dish parties. I acted in *She Stoops to Conquer,* joined the Glee Club, played girls basketball in heavy-ribbed woolen stockings beneath blue serge bloomers. In the Lyceum series, Ernest Thompson Seton came from Canada to talk about wild animals and Frank W. Gunsaulus of Chicago gave his famous lecture on "Savonarola." I went to my first dances. Two-steps and waltzes. "Baby Mine" was popular. It was joyous. I wrote Mama all about it, but said she'd better not tell Dad.

In January there was a week-long Methodist revival and the college authorities claimed more than a third of the student body had been newly "converted." Sometimes alumni who'd become missionaries came back to speak, trying to raise money. One, a girl named Mabel Lossing, Class of 1903, who was going to India, said, "I don't want any of you to feel sorry for me because I am going to do God's work." I did feel sorry for her, though, so pretty and rosy-cheeked and so likely to come back all worn and thin and yellowish, as so many of them did. Somebody was always up to mischief. After the Chapel steeple got draped with a freshman banner, Dr. Bassett, the college president, demanded it come down at once. Instead, the culprits dug a mock grave in front of Science Hall and put up a cardboard tombstone reading: "U.I.U. born Jan. 1st, 1857, died Oct. 12th, 1906, its Spirit gone to Rest."

It was during "class scrapping" that I met Beecher Beal. Every year, the freshmen tried to hold their annual banquet in secret; the sophomores tried to prevent them. Ours was to be at Jim's Hotel in the next town of West Union. It got rough. When some sophomores descended on one boy, Harry Griffith, in his room before breakfast, he pulled out a knife and slashed two of their overcoats. Another freshman was waylaid when he went to start a fire in the bookstore where he worked; he was taken by sleigh to a farmhouse three miles from town. Some freshman boys got wind of it and charged after them with a fast team and bobsled and set him free. As luck would have it, that afternoon I was going to class when Frances White and Carrie Comstock came by in a cutter and gave me a lift. Before I knew it, I was their prisoner. They tied my hands firmly and drove me out to Lillian Green's house on the edge of town and didn't let me go until seven o'clock that evening. My captors and I walked back to campus to find, just as they'd planned, that the freshmen had already left in four sleighs for West Union.

I was terribly let down until one of the seniors—Beecher Beal—offered to drive me over in his cutter. We set out at eight wrapped in warm buffalo robes, but it was Beecher's first trip to West Union, and in the dark he lost his way. It was one of those clear cold winter nights when the whole world seems lighted by stars. Beecher was a sturdy farmer's son, a young man of twenty-one, with a handsome, ruddy face and dark eyes. At school he dressed in a college blazer, but you could tell from his muscular physique that he was used to farmwork. That night as his horses sank deep into the snow and we lurched this way and that, I had to keep clutching his arm to avoid falling out. Beecher was embarrassed about being lost in open country. I didn't mind. We reached Jim's Hotel too late for dinner but in time for the toasts. Everybody cheered when we came in, red-faced from the cold and all bundled up.

After that, Beecher and I went to all the debates and hayrides, sleighing parties, basketball games, dances and oyster suppers together. Beecher had a habitual expression of dignity that seldom left his attractive face. He liked serious argument, such as the difference between moral law, as in "Thou shalt not kill," bad in itself, and sins made so by God, such as "Remember the Sabbath, and keep it holy."

One time he drew up a set of rules for taking meals in his boardinghouse: "Fines are to be imposed for making cutting remarks, using slang or incorrect grammar, disorderly conduct, laughing at one's own jokes, eating too many pieces of pie or cake, drinking more than two cups of tea or coffee, tipping things over, or leaving the table without being excused. Fines for one week will be limited to twenty-five cents. After that the culprit will be ostracized—no one is to speak to him for seven days." When a boy named Jack Kauffman was ostracized, Beecher amended the rules: "Nobody can take the pie or cake of an ostracized person."

He was always up to something. To advertise the Glee Club's spring concert, Beecher came into Chapel one morning blacked up as a Negro and handed a poster to Dr. Bassett. Beecher sang baritone and was fond of such songs as "Blow, Bugle, Blow" and "Home They Brought the Warrior Dead." In the spring Oratorical Contest, Beecher gave his oft-repeated talk on the Negro, "Emancipated—but Still in Chains." When everybody applauded, I noticed for the first time that a kind of self-satisfied, replete expression sometimes came over Beecher's face, just as if he had that minute finished dinner. He took part in track meets and baseball games, we went on picnics and bicycle rides. Then, one muggy June day, Beecher joined his fellow seniors to march two abreast in caps and gowns down from Old Main to bleachers set up in Elm Grove. Dr. Bassett called for No. 564 in the Methodist hymnal and we all sang, "God Be with You till We Meet Again."

Some of his classmates planned to spend the summer working at a lumber camp in Minnesota and they wanted Beecher to join them. He refused, telling me, "Those lumberjacks are good-hearted boys, Louie, but they know no end to profanity, card-playing and whiskey-drinking. I'd rather earn less helping Pa on his farm and work among gentler folks."

Comment by Beecher B. Beal, Class of 1907, under his picture in the Upper Iowa University college annual:

"My connection with the Y.M.C.A. has been a great inspiration to me through meeting the men in Christian fellowship, and not only the men of the college, but the very many other prominent association men it has been my privilege to meet and hear in the past four years. I also believe in a good healthy class scrap occasionally."

From a letter to Anna Louise by Beecher in Greene, Iowa, July 15, 1907:

". . . We have a load of hay to put up. The crops are all looking fine, the corn being too large to plow last week. A good oat crop. Dad has a hundred hogs to feed and sixteen cows to milk, also calves to be fed and milk to separate, so I have plenty of chores . . . I was given A+ in Botany, Zoology and History and an A in German, B+ in elocution and the same in church history . . . We spent 'a safe and sane' Fourth . . . Gosh, I go to church and to town once in a while and that's about all. I miss you . . ."

Anna Louise:

That summer I came down with diphtheria. A bad case, yet I recovered quickly. It was an epidemic and several young people and children in town died suddenly of that awful croup. For a time I only wanted to eat apricots and my voice was affected; never in my life could I really sing again.

In August, Beecher was offered a teaching job in the town of Elma, not too far from Fayette. He said there was an opening for me, too, if I wanted it. Haddie was talking about going back to finish college at Upper Iowa and I knew money would be short. I talked it over with Mama and Papa and applied and was accepted. I never thought too much about the future in those days. Like all my friends, I wanted to teach school and I wanted to marry and have four or five kids. It would be a town school, not like Hardin. And, of course, Beecher would be there.

Anne

Ta-rah, ta-rah, boom! The pupils from all four rooms, upstairs and down-stairs, marched out of the schoolhouse in single file, keeping step to the loud drum beat. This was something new for Elma, one of Beecher's innovations. Each day, at noon and four, a favored boy was chosen to beat the snare drum and we all paraded in soldierly fashion out to the wooden sidewalk that ran around the schoolyard. Beecher was no longer the carefree student, tearing around campus in his gray flannel blazer, rusty black bow tie and crimson-and-white Upper Iowa cap. In Elma he'd been principal and now he was Superintendent of Schools. This made his monthly salary a hundred dollars, more than Papa was getting. My own salary as Assistant Principal in the Elma High School, starting at twenty-seven-fifty a month in 1907, had risen to fifty-five dollars by the winter of 1909–10, enough so I was able to lend some to Haddie.

After his promotion, Beecher bought me a diamond ring. We were en-gaged to be married in another year or two, just as soon as we'd saved up enough to afford it. I was in no hurry. My work kept me busy. Now I examined seventh- and eighth-graders in algebra and geography, heard Latin recitations of Cicero, Caesar and Catullus *("Ave atque vale . . .")* and in civil government had made mock ballots for the 1908 elections (Taft 14, Bryan 6).

We went bicycling so much I paid twenty-five dollars for a new Crusader, which Beecher pronounced "a first-class wheel." When we visited Fayette or my folks, Beecher's sister, Bertha, came along to chaperone. From Monona, Dad had been given a parish at McGregor, back on the Mississippi. Then they'd been reassigned to Lime Springs, a small farming town just south of the Minnesota border. Mama wrote that the people were mainly Welsh in town, though they'd see plenty of Norwegian and Irish farmers if any of the drugstores got a permit to sell "medicinal" liquor.

Haddie had just finished at Upper Iowa. He'd always been up to something devilish there. Once, he put pajamas on a statue of Andrew Carnegie. Another time, he and his friends got into the tower of Old Main and rang the bell like mad. The payoff came at commencement time in June. The college had just installed plumbing in the girls' dormitory and they stored the chamber pots they'd taken out of the rooms in the attic. Hadwen's gang found them and one night they strung the pots up high on wires, right where the commencement procession was to take place the next day. The custodians had to break all the chamber pots by throwing rocks at them. But they left some of the handles still hanging. Years later—some thirty or forty years later—Hadwen found the remains of some of the pots hanging there.

Our life outside school was also placid. Beecher and I went dancing, but not on Sundays. He'd say, "I can't see any religion, Louie, for a person who goes to church in the morning to worship God and that night goes waltzing." We saw our first moving picture show, *The Passion Play*. Beecher bought a Victrola and we listened to "Red Wing," "Holy City," "Asleep in the Deep," "Old Kentucky Home" and "Merry Widow Waltz." William Jennings Bryan came to town and gave his famous chautauqua lecture "The Prince of Peace" (". . . If this invisible germ of life in the grain of wheat can thus pass unimpaired through three thousand resurrections, I shall not doubt that my soul has the power to clothe itself with a new body, suited to its new existence, when this earthly frame has crumbled to dust . . .") Beecher rode into Elma on the same train as Bryan by chance, and he was thrilled to see the great man sound asleep in his coach seat and loudly snoring just like an ordinary mortal.

Like every girl, I just expected to marry and raise a family. There were no wars, nobody went to foreign lands. We were entirely preoccupied with our own country and our own lives. Even at home there was still a wide gulf between town people and country people. Newspapers wrote about "The Country Life Problem." Beecher had our pupils debate: "Resolved, That life in town is preferable to life in the country." We were used to sidewalks, electric light, water from faucets, going to the library. Farmers had no mail delivery, no electricity, they only came to town on Saturdays to shop. Some people in towns called them "hicks" or "hayseeds." Rural schools just went up to eighth grade. If you went to high school, your folks had to pay your tuition and board in town. President Roosevelt appointed a Commission on Country Life, and in 1908 they sent every teacher a questionnaire. The commission's report, when it came out the next year, recommended better schools, better roads, parcel post, more credit, diversified farming, agricultural extension, rural cooperatives and government control of monopolies—things farmers had been wanting for years. The President warned Congress that progress in the cities wasn't enough and that our civilization rested on life in the country. He said, "The men and women on farms stand for what is fundamentally best and most needed in American society."

The report particularly blamed country schools and churches for "ineffective farming, lack of ideas and drift to towns." Dad was stung by this criticism, after fighting for better roads and schools for years. He roused himself to the country preacher's defense.

From a talk, "The Rural Pastor and his Church," given by Reverend Williams at the Country Life Conference, Ames, Iowa, June 24, 1910:

". . . For twenty years we've watched a steady exodus from the land. Country churches are the despair of many a pastor. How often have I walked seven or eight miles on a Sunday evening just to face a few elderly souls whose young folks have gone to the city? Some argue that we ought to consolidate the rural churches and schools, and cluster them, together with stores and the homes of farmers, at railroad stations, as I hear tell they do in Europe. Now, while I'm strongly in favor of school consolidation, I reject the rest. The course of American history suggests no such future peopling of the land. It falls to the church to serve the farmer where he lives, and that is going to continue to be in scattered homesteads . . . We all know the main reason young people move to town: money. In 1882, the average farmer's income was $252 a year, compared to the city worker's $572. By 1900, the city worker was making $622, but the farmer just $260 . . .

"I've been the son and brother of farmers, been their doctor, farmed myself, and now I've been a country preacher with a rural circuit for twenty years. And I tell you our country life is still much affected by the pioneer's individualism. But maybe what was a means of survival on the frontier has become, when working together works best in town, a cause of rural decay . . .

"It may sound like evangelism to some, but the American moral code grew out of our country life and reading the Bible. The New Testament, in the story of Jesus and the Gospels, the Apostles and early church, teaches a melting of the heart, the love of God and one's fellow men. Simple. That's all there is to it. If country people can be brought the story of the Master's life from birth on to his crucifixion and resurrection, with all His teaching, it will abide with them in all they do . . .

"The Old Testament, too, was written for a rural people. Its hymns, what we call psalms, are the songs of country men and women who love their plains and hills and mountains. Its doctrine of Divine Providence is best told in that simplest of psalms about the shepherd who leads his sheep onto green pastures and beside the still waters, watching over them even in the Valley of the Shadow. The Old Testament prophecies and sermons were preached by great souls made anxious by the exodus from the land into cities. Isaiah denounces practices common in Iowa today: the evils of absentee landlordism; the large numbers of tenants and sharecroppers; the idleness of the retired farmer; the pitiful condition of hired men who must work twelve hours a day and seek refuge in the intemperance of the saloon . . . Why, we've got landlords who won't tile poorly-drained land and blame poor crops on lazy tenants. I say to them, 'When you tile your land, you get your man. Not before.' "

He says country preachers ought to attend Farmers' Institutes to keep up with new farming practices:

"No rural pastor ought to be ashamed if he can help a young farmer's wife dispense with parasites among her poultry or help her husband cure abortion among his cows. To know about soil conservation, balanced rations and improved livestock ought not to impair any man's ability to present a strong Gospel . . ."

He advocates using "the road grader and King Drag" to improve roads and says, "many an obscure pastor has earned a good record in the Book of Life" by helping farm boys and girls get into high school and college. Hadwen warns that current emphasis in Methodism on "large endowments, commodious new churches and columns of converts" makes "the adding machine supreme."

". . . Our poorest country people are worthy soldiers of the cross, as faithful as any who adorn the Lord's vineyard. With them there is no doubt . . . I agree with the Commission on Country Life that scientific farming, good roads and good schools are the key to rural revival. But let it be a Gospel of both mind and soul . . ."

From a letter by Hadwen in Sumner, Iowa, September 1910, to a fellow Methodist minister in Lime Springs:

". . . In Lime Springs they just had dog and pony shows, little circuses and those traveling theatrical troupes. Remember the time they put on *Ben Hur* and they did the chariot race on the stage? And the Magic Lantern Show with stereopticon slides? How the crowd liked to sing, 'The Old Flag Never Touched the Ground, Boys!' Do they still sing it?

"Well, Sumner has a *picture show*. Every Friday and Saturday night, five cents admission. And I tell you, Brother Perry, I saw three evils right off. First, the nickelodeon is situated in an old storeroom right in the middle of Sumner's five saloons, which do their best to attract those coming and going from it. Second, the works of the Devil multiply under cover of darkness; the danger of dimly lit theaters to weak-willed young folk can hardly be exaggerated. Last, and the real trouble, is the films themselves.

"No sooner did I preach against having movies on Sunday, too, when the nickelodeon manager come over and offered to provide us with free films to raise money for some badly needed church repairs. With a leaky roof I didn't hardly feel I could turn his generous offer down. I selected a couple of films from the list he provided. One of them, "Our Country First," sounded all right. Well, good land a mercy! What do we get but white slave traffic, gin-crazed fiends and gambling hells. Some of the Aid Society ladies upped and stamped out halfway through it, demanding I call down fire and brimstone on the head of that theater owner. But the poor fellow didn't have any more idea of what we were going to see on that screen than I did.

"So the next time we had a fund-raiser for the church we ordered four one reelers, two cowboy and two comedy. Well, one cowboy reel packed more violence than any dime novel would dare to print. I've come around to thinking that those folks in New York who make the films must have one idea only: how to provide thrills. Hate thrills, love thrills, nothing but thrills. Intemperance, gambling, wild chases, firing guns right at the audience, they show just about every sin a person can think of. One film advertised outside the theater showed two speeding locomotives hurtling right at each other on the same track and about ten feet from a head-on collision. But right through that ten-foot gap is rushing a large automobile steered by a pretty girl. It says, 'The most Powerful, Most Exciting, Most Stupendous Chapter Play Ever Filmed, Full of Action, Punch and THRILLS, THRILLS, THRILLS!' When I complained about it to Jessie, it turned out she'd snuck in to see the blamed thing! I tell you, Brother Perry, it sometimes seems like a losing battle over these picture shows . . . We finally settled for *Her First Biscuits* and *The Violin Maker of Cremona*, with little Mary Pickford . . ."

From *Anna Louise:*

The summer of 1910, while Beecher farmed with his Dad, I helped the folks move down to Sumner, Dad's new parish. It was like any other summer; I helped Mama put up preserves, Dad held revival meetings in a tent by the tennis courts, Beecher came down several weekends and we swam and bicycled and played croquet or lawn tennis and sat out on the hammock. Beecher had purchased a new photographic apparatus, a Kodak, which he put on a tripod and, with a hood over his head to improve the visibility of the image, he'd say, "Please have the goodness to look fixedly at one object and call up a pleasant expression on your faces." We all had to stand perfectly still, holding our breaths, posing for him. Despite our engagement, I felt vaguely discontented and dissatisfied. Not with Beecher. It was just that life itself was passing so quickly and uninterestingly. I wondered if the whole world was like Iowa, and felt ashamed. I kept asking myself: Why have you grown so weary and bored? You've had a tranquil, untroubled life; so why does it seem all wrong?

On an impulse, without telling anybody, I wrote to the Andrew Love Agency in North Dakota. Andrew, an Upper Iowa graduate, had gone to Fargo, the largest town in that remote and empty state, to open a teachers' placement bureau. He soon replied. Yes, he wrote, there was a fall opening to teach seventh and eighth grades, but not in Fargo itself. It was in a rough little prairie town of about four hundred people forty-one miles to the north. It was called Hunter and hadn't been settled more than thirty years. He didn't think I'd like it.

Mother was dead set against it. All she could talk about was the Dakota Territory's terrible blizzard of 1888, when snow covered whole barns and over a hundred people died. "Oh, Louie, I've heard so many tales of those awful blizzards and how so many people are always freezing to death," she said. "There was a trainload of Texas long-horned steers. The train was wrecked and cattle got scattered all over the countryside. When they found them, most were frozen stiff. Don't go!"

Haddie was more adventurous. "Go ahead and apply anyway, Louie," he said. "It's seventy-five dollars a month. That's twenty more than you're getting now." He made a pun on a Methodist hymn. "Oh, do not fear to follow when Love leads the way."

Even Mama had to laugh. "Don't joke," she said. "Some of those hymns are real Sunday School ragtime. 'Leaning on the Everlasting Arms' makes an awful good two-step."

Beecher admitted we couldn't afford to get married just yet, but he wanted me to stay by his side in Elma as Assistant Principal. When I said, "I want a little adventure in my life, Beecher," he looked so anguished I almost relented. "What's better than making a home and bringing up your children and living a good Christian life like your folks and mine?" he asked. "All I want, Louie, is for you to have a little patience." I felt ashamed to make him so distressed. We talked and talked and took long walks and sat for hours swinging idly on the front-porch hammock. Before Beecher went home, we'd compromised. He'd agreed to let me take the job for a term or two, if I really had my heart set on it. But that was to be all. We were still engaged, the same as we ever were.

In his letter of recommendation, Beecher wrote that Miss Anna Louise Williams had given "excellent satisfaction" and was a "pleasant and effective" teacher:

". . . In discipline, I would place her upon a par with the best, having won the esteem and high regard of her students. She is cultured, discreet, of good poise, and a lady in every respect . . ."

Further comment from Helen Collins:

". . . I could never understand Louie going off like that. Beecher was so proper. And well thought of. I heard they named a school in Hibbing, Minnesota, after him. When they were in Elma, Beecher used to send me all the new sample readers he got at the school . . ."

From a letter by Jessie in Sumner to her sister, Allie, in Linn Grove:

". . . Beecher looked confident when he left, as if it'd all been settled to his satisfaction. I wonder. Louie had become such an unfailingly correct and gracious young woman over in Elma. We just assumed she and Beecher were happy together and wedding bells were a matter of time. Now she slouches around the house all day, fretting and looking pale and with her hair in disorder. It gives me the melancholy feeling, Allie, that everything in the world comes to an end, no matter how long it may last.

"Last night I got them all to go out for a walk—Haddie, Louie, Mary and little Helen. As soon as I was alone with Hadwen, I told him how concerned I was. He said Louie was a remarkable girl. 'Yes, she is remarkable,' I agreed, with a nervous glance out the window to make sure they didn't all come trooping back in. 'You'd have to look a long time for such a girl. Even so, Papa, I'm getting anxious. If you count Hardin, she's taught school four years already. That's long enough for anybody. She's twenty-two and it's time she was thinking seriously of herself. If a girl spends all her time with books and schoolchildren, she can find that life slips away without her being aware of it. What I'm saying, Papa, is this: she ought to get married.'

"Hadwen looked at me so kinda surprised. He said, 'But she *is* going to get married. She's engaged to marry Beecher. You couldn't find a more proper and upstanding young fellow. They'll make a fine couple. She can settle down and look forward to a quiet, peaceful life.'

"M-hm-m-m. Well, yes, I thought to myself, maybe that's just the trouble . . ."

Anne

Clickety-clack, clickety-clack, clickety-clack . . . The green rolling hills, with their woods and fields and farms, swept past to the rumble and lurch of the train and the clickety-clickety clatter of the wheels. My excitement made me aware of everything. There would be the roar of an approaching train, the deafening shriek when it passed, and the loud rumbling of wheels over bridges. Time flew by, imperceptibly, and it seemed that seldom more than a few minutes passed but the train seemed to stop at a station, and at each stop could be heard doors slamming and people shouting. The clanging of the bell, the conductor's whistle, the footsteps running up and down the brick platforms, the noise, the coal smoke, the smell of tobacco that drifted back from the smoking compartment—all these things seemed heightened by my anticipation.

Perhaps because the trees, telegraph poles, and farm after farm kept flitting past my eyes, all sorts of disconnected ideas came rushing into my mind. I worried about my trunk back in the baggage car. What was I to do with Papa's big buffalo coat? (They'd insisted I somehow needed it to keep from freezing to death.) Had I packed everything else in? Stockings, thread, gloves, hankies, the bunting and hatpins, the tailored white shirtwaists and dark skirts for everyday, the brown wool suit with the satin-lined jacket and gored skirt, the brown hat that went with it with real egret feathers, the white chiffon afternoon gown with blue flowers, the cream-colored gingham, the plaid blouse with the sailor collar, the lace cuffs and collars, the split skirt for riding, the fur muff for cold weather, the petticoats, camisoles and muslin drawers and underskirts, the extra silk chiffon veiling and the ribbon with the satin stripe, the parasol . . . In Minneapolis, when I changed trains, I followed the Negro redcap down the stuffy aisle of the Pullman sleeping car. The berths were nearly all made down and he set my hatbox and wicker suitcase below some dusty green curtains buttoned to a seat at the farther end.

"Now, yo' berth's ready any time, Miss," the porter said. When at last I climbed in, I found I had very little room to undress. Squirming and fussing, I unlaced my shoes and took them off, along with my stockings and some new elastic garters I suspected impeded circulation. Off came the long pleated skirt and starched shirtwaist to be hung up right away so they wouldn't look too wrinkled and rumpled in the morning. With relief I unhooked the front of my corset. Mama had helped me lace up the back as tight as I could stand it; the salesman claimed the stays were real whalebone, not reed or steel. I got out my dresser set, with hairbrush, mirror, comb, soap and toilet water for the morning, and a wrapper to wear over my nightgown in case I had to get up at night. At last, my hair brushed a hundred strokes, I was ready to lie back and sleep. I couldn't.

The faded green plush was permeated with coal dust; it tickled my nose. Even the starched white linen of the pillow felt gritty. I was thirsty. A draft from the window poured over my exposed shoulders. I pulled the scratchy Pullman wool blanket up. Little by little, in spite of these discomforts, I could feel a heavy lethargy take possession of me. I lost the desire to change my position. The rails roared in my ears. I thought guiltily of Beecher. I imagined getting into my warm, soft bed at home, and pulling the bedclothes over me. Suddenly I missed Mama and Papa and felt terribly homesick. *Clickety-clack, clickety-clack* . . . At last I fell asleep . . .

When at length I lifted up my head and blinked open my eyes, the sleeping car was flooded with bright daylight. The train wasn't moving. I'd slept very soundly. I peeked out the drawn green curtains. The train was standing in front of a red brick Great Northern station. To the right was a wide street with brick buildings and electric trolley lines. Though it was early, people were already going about their business, and buggies and spring wagons and Ford automobiles were going up and down or standing at the curb. Red, white and blue bunting was draped about the streetlights, and a big banner hung across the street, saying, "WE LIKE YOU, TEDDY." The conductor came along the corridor calling, "Fargo!" and sometimes stopping to punch the tickets of passengers getting off. The porter came to tell me we would be staying in the station for some time and that he would fetch water if I wanted to go to the washroom. I contrived to have a good wash, though the basin water quickly turned a milky gray from the soap and coal dust. But the smell of camphor, tar and pine needles from the greenish-white soap seemed clean and I rubbed my face and hands so vigorously they had a pink glow. I brushed my hair for some time before carefully pinning it back up in a pompadour; then I rehooked the corset over my camisole and got all dressed again, fastening the lace collar at my throat with a cameo pin. I also pinned my money inside, thinking of the saying that a woman put money in her sock, but a lady stuffed it down her bosom. For my arrival in Hunter, I'd bought a black cape trimmed with beaded ribbon, black gloves, and a black suit hat, trimmed with a taffeta bow and black silk pyroxilin braid.

All dolled up at last, I went back to my seat, which the porter had made up. A vendor came through selling copies of the local weekly, the Fargo *Forum*. I bought one and sat back to read it, stiffly erect, as if to show the world that a good Iowa upbringing, with sensible corsetry, could fortify a young lady against anything North Dakota could bring. The newspaper was dated September 9, 1910, and the front page carried a photograph of Theodore Roosevelt wearing a black silk top hat. He'd visited Fargo, given a Labor Day speech and laid the cornerstone for a new Andrew Carnegie library. A story told how Roosevelt recalled coming to the Badlands as a young man to hunt buffalo in 1883 and how he ended up staying and ranching until 1886. The *Forum* quoted him: "If it had not been for what I learned during the years I spent here in North Dakota, I never in the world would have been President of the United States . . . I feel that I'm at home again." The paper also carried a text of his speech, a now familiar appeal for the revival of country life.

I hastily glanced at the world news ("Society Girls Fly with Aviator," "Suffragettes Smash Windows") and turned to the local stories. What was life going to be like here? "Penniless and Half Starved," said a headline. "Worry Drove Him to Death," "Went Crazy and Tried Suicide," "Settler Dies Alone on Claim." Awful, if the *Forum* was to be believed. "Brutal Wife Beating," "Child Trampled by Horse," "Farmer Hangs Self." It went on and on. "DON'T TREAT THE DRUNKARD LIKE A CRIMINAL" commanded an ad for a "three-day cure." The advertisements for Moody's and deLendrecie's department stores told a different story: chandeliers, Haviland china, brass jardinieres, a complete set of the Elsie Dinsmore books. I saw Buffalo Bill was coming to town on his "Farewell Retirement Tour." With the conductor's call, "All aboard!" and a screech and a lurch, we were moving again. I put the paper aside. I'd have to see for myself.

As we left Fargo behind and entered the open countryside, gaining speed, I leaned forward, eagerly looking out. Once more the landscape flew by to the rhythm of the train wheels, with their clickety-clack, and screeching and pounding as the cars jumped along the steel tracks. This was my first good look at North Dakota. It was like nothing I had ever seen before. The sky was cloudless and a pale blue, almost grayish-white. An unusually fierce and glaring light; I had to squint. The rolling green hills were gone. Now instead, on all sides, left and right, wherever you looked, stretched a perfectly flat and empty plain. It beggared all description. No roads, no hills, no farms, no bluffs, no creeks, no rivers. Nothing at all.

God had leveled the whole country out with a rolling pin. It was so horribly flat. My spirits sank. It was too big and flat and brown and cheerless. The light was too harsh. There were no trees. It was like being on the edge of the world. I was struck with awe and anxiety.

Even the grass beside the railroad tracks looked dead. Here and there was a patch of plowed land and the blackest soil I'd ever seen. There was virgin prairie grass, too. And wheat. Some of it still standing, but much in shocks, yellow shocks of wheat marching across the perfectly flat fields in long rows, waiting for threshers. Once, the train mounted a wide curve and I could see ahead. Where the tracks straightened out again they just kept going in two straight lines until they disappeared on the horizon. Telegraph poles with two wires on them stretched along one side of the tracks to what seemed like infinity. The poles grew smaller and smaller until they were thin little sticks. Crows and blackbirds sat on the wires and looked indifferently at me and the train. You could go on and on in North Dakota and never see where the horizon began and where it ended.

We hadn't gone far before the train slackened speed, there was the noise of the bell and iron scraping iron as the brakes screeched, and the conductor called, "Casselton!" Here I was to change to a local train for the last twenty miles to Hunter. Casselton had a few brick buildings and some tall trees, but its mainly clapboard houses, painted white, looked badly weathered by the sun, wind and prairie dust. The Hunter train didn't leave for some time, and after I saw to my trunk I sat inside the small, boxlike depot. There were the usual farmers' grain elevators alongside and a stockyard, where huge fat pigs, pink and revolting, were wallowing in the mud.

The local, when it came, creaked and swayed on the track, but some of its windows were open, and the air, gritty as it was, seemed wonderfully fresh. In Iowa, even the smallest towns were now getting paved streets; people demanded better roads for their automobiles. In Casselton, there weren't even sidewalks—just wooden planks on the side of a rutted track. That was downtown; farther out, there was neither paving nor planks.

"Hunter!" The short journey took no time at all. As the conductor took my bags, I glanced in the mirror over my seat. The plumed hat was a mistake, too grand for the traveling salesmen with their derbies and battered sample cases, and the unshaven farmers in overalls and sheepskin jackets and their tired-looking wives and children. "Hunter!" All I could see was the same old plain. A copse of cottonwoods flitted by. A windmill. At last, looking ahead, I could see some steeples, three or four grain elevators and the tops of trees. Beyond them was the unending plain. The huddled mass of trees and buildings broke the prairie hardly more than the stand of cottonwoods.

We pulled into town. A few big handsome houses, white-painted Victorian mansions. The rest were bleak frame shelters. A road sign flashed by: "NO HEAVY TEAMING." To my relief I saw some box-elder trees, lilac bushes and gardens of zinnias and hollyhocks. The train drew into the station. After Casselton I was prepared. The center of Hunter took up one side of a wide dirt road; it was two blocks long, facing us, a single row of one-story wooden shanties with false, square fronts and dusty awnings over a wooden, partly covered, plank sidewalk. The depot was flanked by several big elevators, a potato warehouse and a well and horse tank. I saw the shops included a lumberyard, an implement dealer, a feed mill, a pool hall and bowling alley, a machine and blacksmith shop and a garage and livery stable. That was it.

The train jerked to a full stop right in front of the squat little red frame station. "Hunter! Hunter!" The conductor swung open the door of the coach to the platform. At once a cloud of dust and whirling flecks of straw blew in, forcing the passengers crowding in the aisle to squeeze their eyes shut and choke and cough.

We'd left cabs and redcaps far behind. After arranging for a drayman to bring my trunk, I set off on foot, bag and baggage, for the hotel. The depot agent pointed it out across the tracks and west of the coal chute and water tank. It was big and decrepit, a sprawling, two-story wooden building so unpainted and weathered the grain in the siding stood out in relief. Several men in overalls and boys in caps and knickers sat hunched up on the hitching rail, like so many black crows. They all gaped at me when I passed, and not one so much as tipped his hat. The screen door slammed behind me. I found myself in a big lounge. I quickly took in the flyspecked windows, caked with dust, the bare and unswept floor, the soiled leather chairs, the ink-stained writing desk with an advertisement for the Gale & Duffany Hardware & Lumber Company on its glass-covered back. A sign commanded, "USE THE SPITTOON," but the disgusting yellow tobacco stains on the rugs, floors, windows and shirt fronts and beards of the men I'd seen showed few of them did. A room beyond seemed to serve as both dining room and saloon; I saw a bar, dirty tablecloths, catsup bottles. Somewhere a dog barked, and an angry screech could be heard, such as cats give when their tails get stepped on.

The proprietor hastened to tell me that two other lady teachers would be staying at the hotel. With the land boom, he said, a person was lucky to find any accommodation. Every day, two or three carloads of men pulled into town. "Some," he said, "are just land-jumpers, fly-speculators, claim-soakers, men looking for a quick profit, ma'am, not a home. But there's also real settlers who plan to bring their wives and children." God help them, thought I.

We ascended a steep, narrow wooden staircase, and the room he showed me upstairs and in the back was small—and grim, too. I'll tell the world. It had discolored flowered wallpaper and cracked linoleum, a brass bed with a patchwork quilt, rag rugs, a wallboard with clothes hooks, a dresser with towel, pitcher, soap dish and basin, slop jar, and a gaslight. He said he'd take out a hideous velvet claw-foot settee to make room for my trunk. A small bathroom down the hall held a commode, or chamber pot mounted in a chair with a cover, in case you got sick or there was a storm and you couldn't make it out back to the privy. There was also an iron tub; with advance notice, hot water could be hauled up in pails. The privy for ladies was way out behind the hotel, reached across wooden planks. Be careful, the proprietor warned, not to step off the planks if it rained; the local black soil, called gumbo, stuck to your feet like glue. The room's small stove burned lignite coal; North Dakota had no wood to speak of, just a few trees on the tree claims or in towns. A thin, lumpy mattress lay on the bed; I was glad I'd brought Papa's buffalo coat after all.

I found a good many men crowded about at the hotel, since the proprietor ran a "blind pig" for illicit liquor sales on the side; the whole place reeked of whiskey, tobacco and sheepskin. A lot of young roughnecks hung around and voices kept shouting confusedly, "Did you see his poker hand, Jake?" "Look here, by God!" "Why, that son of a bitch!" "What's up?" "And I told that damn spike pitcher, 'I'll get you!' " The other teachers and I might be drinking tea while farmers at the next table were swilling down beer and perspiring freely from the suffocating heat of the hotel's kitchen range. The roar of conversation was steadily interrupted by the banging of a swinging door as Olga, the tough waitress, hurried in and out. The sound of an accordion came through a partition wall, an endless sound.

Sometimes I got a headache from all the noise and profanity. I also found that the change of climate from the gentler Iowa weather—I was to hate wind for the rest of my life—made me continually drowsy. This sleepiness, and homesickness for Beecher and my family, helped me to overlook the crudeness of the hotel. One Sunday afternoon, a land agent who stayed there, Carl Danskin, invited me to go for a joyride in his open roadster. Sixty miles an hour in an open automobile for a mile! It was thrilling. I badly missed Iowa, but it was older and more settled. As rough and raw as it was, there was something a little more free about life in North Dakota. Somehow it spoke of the future.

The hotel's frequenters, if they had too much to drink or were suddenly surprised, might explode into a torrent of foul language. If Danskin or any of the other young men I knew were present, they would shout angrily at the offender, "What do you mean by all that dirty language? Keep your tongue in your head. Can't you see there's a young lady present?" Often, the one who swore, noticing me for the first time, would dissolve into confused apologies: "Good afternoon, ma'am. Excuse me, I didn't take no notice of you sitting there. I didn't mean no harm." And I'd say, "Not at all. Thank you kindly." Many of the hotel's clientele were harmless. One very small man, who was pockmarked and blind and made a precarious living tuning pianos, had a habit of ordering raw eggs. Olga said he'd once had her break twenty-five eggs into a jar and he swallowed them in a single draught.

The swinging door kept continually banging, crowds kept coming in and going out, the accordion kept playing and one night there was a pounding on the door of my room. A drunken voice shouted, "Let me in, little teacher! Let me in!" After that, I decided it was a horrid place for a nice girl to stay.

Noon. A hot wind was blowing. I was coming back from school. Even the five-minute walk from the schoolhouse was oppressively hot. Dust rose in rolling clouds. Scraps of paper, bits of straw and tumbleweed whirled along. I crossed the tracks and started up the board sidewalk, which, with a wooden hitching rail, ran past the hotel. The whole town looked dead, as if it had gazed out on nothing for too long and had given up hope anything interesting would ever happen. I could scarcely see for blowing dust.

Ahead, just beyond the hotel door, two idlers were sitting on a wooden bench they'd tilted way forward, so their shoulders rested against the wall and their boots were up on the hitching rail. I was aware of the noonday hush. Usually Hunter had a variety of sounds: the murmur of human voices, the squeak of a gate, the stamping of a horse, dogs howling, carts rattling, hens clucking . . . Now there wasn't a thing to be heard but the sound of the wind and my own footsteps.

The young men, boys, really—they were two or three years younger than

I—had the wind-burnt faces and dust and chaff on their hair and shirts of threshers. Their faces and forearms were burned a dark reddish-brown color, and their white foreheads showed they were farmers. They were looking at me, but I ignored them and stepped briskly along the wooden planks. Just as I reached the hotel and went to open the door, what I'd dreaded happened: a sudden gust of wind sent my skirts flying, wrapping them and my billowing petticoats up around my ankles. I gave a little shriek and dashed inside the door.

"Now *she's* got damn good-looking legs," one of them said.

Horrid North Dakota boy, I thought, I won't notice him. I'd glimpsed the speaker: a dusty cap perched jauntily on the back of brown hair, which was wet in front and sticking every which way on his forehead. A faded shirt, streaked dark and light blue with perspiration, a muscular build. Blue eyes. He was chewing a blade of grass. Our eyes had met just for an instant and I'd seen something lively, boastful and challenging in his, as if he were about to say, "Just a minute there, ma'am, and I'll tell you something that will make you split your sides laughing." As the door banged shut, he *did* laugh. I heard him exclaim, loud enough so I would hear:

> "When the wind blows a girl's skirt high,
> Dirt gets in the bad man's eye . . ."

I forgot the incident by the time I reached my room. The smart rascal.

Anna Louise, sixteen years old.

Hadwen and Jessie Williams, 1885.

The Green Tree on the levee at Le Claire, 1901.

The steamer *J. W. Van Sant II* pushing a lumber raft down the Mississippi, 1904.

Roustabouts on the levee.

A one-room country schoolhouse. (Fred Hultstrand Collection)

Three teacher friends and Anna Louise.

Class of 1904, Limestone Academy, Le Claire.

Beecher Beal and Anna Louise swimming.

Beecher Beal and Anna Louise, summer of 1910.

Jim, sixteen years old.

Dr. Henry Critchfield, his father.

Lillie Critchfield, his mother.

The Critchfield family, Hunter, about 1900. Jim stands with his arms crossed between his mother (in black) and his father. Harry and McLain, the twins, are seated on each side of girl at left, Ray is shading his eyes and Burke is standing far right. His hand rests on shoulder of Judge Lyman Critchfield, Henry's brother from Ohio.

Jim, on his pony, Snowflake, with his father in front of their home in Hunter, 1902.

The old swimming hole. (Fred Hultstrand Collection)

Buggies going to church on Sunday. (Clay County Historical Society)

Skating on the Red River. (Clay County Historical Society)

II

THE NORTH
DAKOTA BOY

... and Sinners

They weren't all saints. Remember Samuel Johnson's low opinion of the early Americans? ". . . a race of convicts who ought to be thankful for anything we allow them short of hanging." It went with a claim that four of every ten Englishmen who came here between 1607 and 1776 were in trouble at home: convicts, debtors, drunks, runaways.

Having Quakers on one side, it seems fitting to have convicts on the other. Actually, family legend doesn't say what Amos Whitfield had done, whether he'd committed a crime or simply been shanghaied, just that he was an impressed seaman in the British Royal Navy, serving on a frigate. Thought to be a native of Wales, he jumped ship off the coast of New Jersey in 1746 and made his way to the backwoods frontier country of Virginia and Delaware, there to assume the alias Critchfield. It is conceivable that he made it up, but more likely he heard it and took it as his own name.

The history of the Critchfields in America, or at least that particular branch that began with Amos Whitfield, really begins with his offspring, including a son, Nathaniel. (Four other sons, Joseph, Samuel, John and William, have come to light; Amos had thirteen children in all.) As an old man in Ohio in 1832, Nathaniel applied for a veteran's pension. Barely literate and a casual speller—he sometimes dropped the "t" in Critchfield—he said he'd enlisted in the Continental Army three times, first in April 1778, when he was seventeen, in Colonel Evans's Virginia Regiment, and reenlisting for two more hitches in 1780, this time with Colonel Piper's Pennsylvania Regiment. He served a total of sixteen months and stayed a private the whole time.

Contemporary accounts show that the lot of the common soldier during the Revolution was not easy. They were often hungry, cold, sick or bored.

Pay was poor and usually in arrears. The officers may have been sympathetic, but detached; wrote one colonel: "Part of the troops are so ill furnished with shoes and stockings, blankets, etc., that they must inevitably perish in this wretched weather." While none of Nathaniel's letters and very few of any enlisted men's survive from the Revolutionary War, entries in the diary of another private, Zebulon Vaughan, give us a pretty good idea of conditions (particularly if a reader has ever been an enlisted man himself). The boredom, for example; look at this week in August 1777: "27 wensday we Ly in Camp; 28 thursday we Ly in Camp; 29 friday we Ly in Camp; 30 Sartaday we Ly in Camp; 31 Saborthday we Ly in Camp . . ." Two of Private Vaughan's favorite terms for daily army life: "Nothing Strang" and "Nothing Remarkebul."

His first battle: "We Cold See the dead men Lay plenty piles of them hove into a Swamp hole . . . it was an ofull Sight to see." He has no love of officers. When twenty men are killed and more wounded in an ambush, he rages it is "all for the Sake of Col. Thompson an old fool." When it comes to provisions, "the officers comley tak all and Solders Starve . . ." Once, to punish some soldiers who fire their guns to celebrate New Year's Day, 1779, his regimental commander has each of them flogged ten stripes on their naked backs. Zebulon Vaughan's fury is intense: "Cus all such men and Let the Cus foller them to thare grave and six feet under ground." As the war drags on, stealing and desertion "prevale gratley among us"; several men are hanged.

His company is inoculated against smallpox, causing the men to fall ill. Vaughan reports a week goes by before "the Simtoms Come on me Very hard with pain in my head and Boons." A few days later the pain has "gone off" and the "pox kome out." He says, "We Remane with very sore throts . . . we can Scars Eat or drink or tok or Swaller without groning."

Winter is the harshest time; food and clothing can be in short supply: "Snowey day and one half of the Rigment is Bar footed." Conditions worsen. "Remane bare footed and a grat many Bar ass and bare back the Like i Never See Bee fore in this worl for the want of Clothes and non to Bee had . . . Snow nee deep . . . Cold weather and no hous to Live in . . . we Sufer gratley . . . We go hungrey every day Lik dogs and Dum Beasts . . . hard times for Solders . . ." At last provisions come. Outfitted with new jacket, breeches, shoes and stockings, with a half pint of rum, "plenty of flour and midling good Beef," Private Vaughan's morale miraculously recovers. There is "no gromblem when provishon is plentey among Solders." He philosophizes, "All we want is for this troblasom war to end . . ."

When the "troblasom" war did at last end, young Nathaniel struck out at once for the western Pennsylvanian frontier. Not to settle for good, though. Like so many, he, too, would get "Ohio fever." Under the treaty that ended the Revolutionary War, the British gave up their lands northwest of the Ohio River and east of the Mississippi. The Continental Congress in 1785–87 legally opened up this land for settlement, and despite famine and Indians, the rush was on. By the first decade of the nineteenth century, whole towns in New England were pulling up stakes and heading for Ohio. Many were like Francis Williams and his Quaker neighbors in Whittier; they mixed a religious zeal to live without sin and do God's work with a shrewd appreciation of the prosperity to be gained by clearing and cultivating virgin land.

Migrants like Nathaniel, coming from the backwoods of Pennsylvania, Virginia and the southern coastal states, were of a different breed. Many, like him, were individualistic, barely literate veterans of the Continental Army, crack shots and hardy enough to survive on a frontier. In 1806, Nathaniel, now forty-five, headed West through the Cumberland Gap into Kentucky and down the Ohio River, finally setting out into the Ohio woods on foot with two of his grown sons, carrying guns, ammunition and tools for work. He was soon joined by his wife, Polly, and the rest of their large brood of children, and they cleared a tract of bottomland and sowed it with crops. At some point, at least two of Nathaniel's brothers, Joseph and William, who had both also been foot soldiers in the Revolution, migrated with their families to the same farming area in Ohio, what later became Knox County. Working small dirt farms in southern Ohio, they were perhaps typical of the many poor whites who settled there, having little and asking for little—just enough land to clear and till so they could feed their families and be let alone. As Private Vaughan's diary conveys, their experience in the Revolution would have left such former enlisted men more crustily independent than ever and more suspicious of the American officer class and its ethics and laws. These frontiersmen would pass such values down to their children; the war had taught them to shoot straight and to depend on themselves to survive.

As an old man, Nathaniel Critchfield got his pension, enjoyed it for only five years, and died in 1837. His tombstone, in Shrimplin Cemetery in the town of Howard, Knox County, reads: "With Washington at Valley Forge." The year Nathaniel died, one of his great-grandsons, Lyman, who was to become Ohio's attorney-general in 1861, when he was only thirty, had just turned six. Well over a century later, at this writing, one of Lyman's grandsons, who was twenty-two when Lyman died, is still alive, a vigorous ninety.

Thus one can quite easily span the entire two-century history of the United States in three lifetimes.

It took many more generations. One of Nathaniel's sons, William (1782–1867) married an Elizabeth Troutman, and *their* son, Reuben (1805–97), and a Nancy Hardesty, were Lyman's parents. Reuben himself stayed a poor farmer and sometime cabinetmaker and mechanic (though a brother served and died as a post surgeon in Tennessee during the Civil War). It was his wife, Nancy, a Quaker from Maryland, who felt she had come down in the world and fought to get her two sons educated. She did. Both became wealthy lawyers, and with them the Ohio Critchfields left farming and rural life for good. They prospered, shared an addiction to fast horses—handed down, according to family legend, from Nathaniel, the Virginian—and ran for public office.

Lyman himself lived on until 1917, dying at his desk right in the middle of writing a legal brief when he was eighty-six. A Populist and Democrat in a Republican state, he ran and lost races to Congress, argued cases before the Supreme Court in Washington and was an early champion of the eight-hour day. He was a lifelong admirer of William Jennings Bryan and, alas, Bryan's oratorical style. (A sample from an 1896 speech on Pioneer Day: "Before the gigantic savage Indian chief, painted hideously for war, and armed with gleaming instruments of revenge and death, the pioneer was the disarming angel of a new covenant of the family, religious faith and liberty . . .")

It was a strangely ill-fated family. Lyman's wife, Adelaide (". . . a queenly stateliness equaled by few," intoned the 1910 *Wayne County History),* died terribly, burned to death after her dress caught fire from a gasoline-stove explosion in 1895. (A younger brother of Adelaide's, Hartley Shaffer, the black sheep of the family, went West the same year—we will encounter him briefly.) One of her daughters, Addie, died young too, of meningitis at twenty-four. The old family mansion on North Bever Street in Wooster, Ohio, went up in flames in 1978; one of Lyman's great-grandsons died in the fire. Premature death seems to have cursed the family.

Lyman Critchfield had five daughters and two sons. The younger son, who appears but once in our story, fought in Cuba in 1898 and later became a Wooster judge. He is chiefly quoted in the family for a remark he made to the young Scandinavian bride of a honeymooning young nephew from North Dakota: "You are the first person of Swedish descent," said the judge, "that I have ever met who is not of the domestic class." Aunt Irene never forgot it. She was still talking about it when she was eighty years old. The other son, Henry, was the author's grandfather. Born in 1861, he went to

Ohio's Kenyon College and then, seeking to become a doctor, he became a medical apprentice to an established physician, in the custom of the times, first in Middleburg, Ohio, then in Minneapolis. He'd finished up at the University of Minnesota just as Hadwen Williams—seven years older, but he'd worked his way through—was getting his medical degree in Iowa. As a young doctor, Henry met and married a pretty Irish girl, Lillie Ray, who ran a sewing school in downtown Minneapolis. Her parents had come from Cork during the potato famine. Lillie's father knew Andrew Burke, another Irishman who'd gotten into banking in Dakota Territory and later was to become North Dakota's second governor. With Burke's help, in 1886 Henry was offered a section of land—six hundred and forty acres—in the Red River Valley just across the Minnesota state line, if he would set up a medical practice in a brand new town, Hunter. It had been created just six years earlier, in 1880, when the Great Northern Railroad extended a branch line that far. Hunter was on the edge of the extinct, prehistoric Lake Agassiz; its black soil, left by glaciers, was said to be wonderfully fertile.

In those days, with everybody talking about getting rich from wheat and land speculation, Dakota Territory was the place to go. In the Twin Cities it was talked about not as the big, empty and dry prairie that it was, but as the empire it could become in twenty or thirty years—the main passenger train to cross it was called the Empire Builder. The last of the buffalo herds were gone, but their bones were still scattered about. Wild elk were abundant, so was game. Ten years had passed since Little Bighorn. The Indians were vanquished at last. One could be in on something.

Extract from a compendium of current biography in North Dakota, 1900:

"Dr. Henry Critchfield, M.D., is one of the most widely known physicians and surgeons of Cass County, and has resided in Hunter and followed the practice of his profession there for fifteen years . . . The great-grandfather of our subject, Nathaniel Critchfield, was a native of Virginia and one of the first settlers of Ohio . . ."

No mention of poor Amos Whitfield. A granddaughter of Dr. Henry Critchfield from Minnesota gives us a last look at Nathaniel's descendants who stayed in Ohio:

"We visited them some years ago. We stayed in town at the Judge's big house on the hill. And they had a horse farm where they had dug their own lake and kept trotters in beautiful white barns, surrounded by green fields and white fences. Their horse, Demon Hanover, once won the Hambletonian. They were people who had a lot of money and who showed they had a lot of money and their conversations were about things that had to do with money and football and horses . . ."

Jim

There was the hiss and scrape of the runners on the frozen crust and it sounded like glass being crushed underneath until you hit the rumble of the railroad tracks or a stretch of deep and heavy snow. The bells on the shaft rang out sharply. *Jing-jing, jing-jing.* I squinted into the glare. The whole countryside was blinding white in the bright winter noontime. Not a cloud in the whole blue prairie sky. Fine snow sifted across the tracks ahead. It was so cold! I was all bundled up except my nose and warmed by the straw under the buffalo robes, snuggled against my father's knees in the sleigh.

The mud had hardened into icy ridges on the frozen ground. When we struck a rut, the sleigh would lurch and bump, grinding and creaking. Father steadied me and called, "Whoa, there!" Clouds of breath steamed from the nostrils of his favorite black span, and you could hear their hooves pounding on the hard-packed snow. "Breathe through your scarf, Jimmy," he said. "That way you won't burn your lungs with this icy air." I did, but felt it stinging anyway. There was also a steady drop of water turning to ice at the end of my nose. Father didn't seem to feel the cold. He was singing in his hearty baritone, breathing out the frosty air. His mustache was covered with icy rime, white against the ruddiness of his face.

> "In the sky the bright stars glittered,
> On the bank the pale moon shone . . ."

Father sang all the time. Mother would play and he'd sing. "I'll Be Seeing Nellie Home," "In the Gloaming," "I Love You Truly," all those old songs. He was a tall man, a six-footer, and he looked even taller in his plucked-otter coat and its big fur cap. Under it he wore, as he always did, a boiled shirt, wing collar, cravat and silver tiepin, just as his father and brother did back in Ohio. He was the only man I ever heard about who combed his hair before he went to bed at night. I was rigged for the weather too: flannel underwear, long woolen stockings and pants, a sheepskin reefer, scarf and knitted cap. Even so, I kept holding my mittens up to my ears and I'd slap myself to keep the blood going—that hard, crackling cold went clear to your bones. Father's specially built sleigh had two runners and a box on top, with sliding doors and a big, six-foot-wide glass windshield. It was packed with straw and old blankets and buffalo robes.

Claus said it must be thirty below. He was our hired man and always rode with Father if there was a call out in the country in winter. Enveloped in his ample sheepskin coat, Claus would stay out to walk the horses so they didn't get too cold and stiff. He was a big, sturdy man, maybe forty, with rough fair hair, and came from Norway. There wasn't much Claus didn't know. One time when it got real cold he told me not to touch metal with my tongue. Oh, boy, I couldn't wait until I tried it on the edge of the snow shovel. When it stuck I got scared and pulled it away and it took all the hide off and bled a little. Claus said if I was ever such a damn fool again to keep breathing on it until it thawed off so it would stop sticking and let go.

In the whole frozen prairie nobody else was in sight, there wasn't a sign of life, not even a dog running out to bark. They were all keeping warm by the kitchen stove. That snow reflected the sun like a mirror; so did the brass railings of the sleigh. When Father stopped singing, the only sound was the *jing-jing* of the bells and the scrape of the runners as we jolted along. Once, when we passed a homestead, a woman came out, waved, and looked at us as if to say, "Good Lord! I wonder who sent for the doctor," and hurried back inside her warm house with a bucket of coal, slamming the storm door.

I wondered where we were headed anyhow. It was the worst cold snap that winter. Before long, Father turned into a deeply drifted lane. Way back was a solitary house looking so bleak with its windbreak of thin, small trees. Icicles hung from the gutters of the roof, but thick smoke was coming from the chimney. Father set me out and I stamped my tingling feet to get the numbness out of the toes. The porch steps squeaked with frozen snow, and a cold entry was piled with overshoes. Once inside, I made a beeline for the stove, which was glowing with a crackling fire, while somebody cried, "My land, boy! Out with your Pa on a day like this?"

As soon as I was nine or ten, I used to go out to the barn and harness and hitch Father's team for him, standing on a box to reach over the horses' backs. Sometimes, one of my brothers would beat me to it. There were four of them, Burke and Ray, who were bigger, and the twins, Harry and Mc-Lain, one dark and one light, and six years younger than me. Ray, who was the oldest and three years ahead of me, could swear and chew tobacco and play hooky and everything. He knew plenty of bad words, too. Burke, he was bossy and might tattle on you. You couldn't beat Burke when it came to just plain being ornery. I had one sister, Kathryn, too, but she didn't come along until I was fourteen.

People in Hunter said Father had the fastest horses in the county. He kept about a dozen at a time out in the barn, mainly trotters, standardbred and blooded stock. When I was four, he took Mother to the 1893 World's Fair in Chicago and came back with a Hambletonian breed mare, Signa. Cost him eight hundred dollars. He brought back a Henry B. Miller upright black walnut piano for Mother, too. All she could talk about when she got home was how the White City looked all lit up at night and hawkers on the Midway who went around hollering, "White Cross Buns!"

Signa's daughters, Sunshade and Playmate, became our best trotting mares. You never had to worry about them straying off the road or anything. If you'd leave a barely tense line, Playmate would keep to the track and drive just as nice a trot as could be. The minute you pulled up on the lines, she'd go. She had spirit. Father got her down to where she could do three-fifteen on the racetrack outside Hunter, which is pretty fast. With Sunshade and Playmate, Father could make the twenty miles to Casselton in eighty minutes. People would say, "All you can see of Doc is a streak across the sky."

He'd come in on Main Street from a call out in the country and not even turn to go over to our house. Come in very fast, in a cloud of dust and pounding hoofbeats, the horses foaming. Claus would be standing there with a fresh team of trotters and another buggy. And Father would just leap out of one and into the other and shout, "Giddi-ap!" and that buggy would give a piercing scream and away he'd go, the horses wide-eyed, their manes flying. And everybody would say, "Boy, that's moving!" and, "What a beautiful team of bays!"

A speed of seven miles an hour was thought to be good time for a team in cool weather and good roads; Father generally did fourteen. Of course, if it was muddy he'd have to slow down to three or four, just like anybody else. Hunter only had single-lane dirt roads; if you passed another buggy or cart, one of you had to go out on the grass.

My own pony, Snowflake, was a medium-sized Indian spotted horse. Sometimes Father bought mustang broncos right off the range, mostly for work or driving; few ever made saddle horses. They were small, wild, or half-wild plains horses descended from Spanish stock and rounded up in western North Dakota; as soon as I was big enough, I joined Ray in breaking them in. Out in the barn behind the house in Hunter, which was about eighty feet across and had twelve stalls, Father kept his favorite stallion, Reddy. Reddy was in a paddy stall at the back; he was a real outlaw. A bay with white front feet, he'd defy any move you made to work with him. He'd bite, kick, strike his front feet, squeal, whinny. When I was first around him, Reddy would see me and snort, wheel, and with his ears flattened back and white teeth bared, he'd rush and lunge right at me. He was quick as lightning and looked like he'd as soon snap my arm off as look at me. I believe he would have, too. Everybody was ready to give up on him. But Father liked Reddy's disposition. He'd take him out to the racetrack and drive him hard. Father would come in feeling good, and Reddy all in a lather but well under control. He eventually mellowed into a reliable workhorse, but for a long time he wouldn't let anybody else touch him, harness him up or drive him— just Father.

Father wasn't one to spare his sons, either; we all had to work on the farm he rented—one hundred and sixty acres—to provide feed for his horses, though he hired men to do the plowing, planting and harvesting. Father did no physical labor himself; I never saw him do any kind of manual work. Never. I guess he didn't have that background back in Ohio. As a doctor, he was too busy. And all those drives we took with him as boys over winter roads, banked high with snow, the wind biting your face and steep, unexpected pitch holes looming up; when the runners dipped into one of them, it could snap your head off. All the farmers kept two or three dogs, and sometimes they got together and ran in a pack. Some men carried Colt six-shooters to scare them, but except for a sixteen-gauge shotgun he used for hunting, I never knew Father to carry a weapon. Why, he didn't know what fear was. One time, we were way out to hell and gone and about a dozen dogs came leaping out of the fields at us, as though from ambush, all howling and barking—*Rrrr-r-r-gh!* All of them ran right beside the buggy, with their shaggy muzzles and fiery red eyes, jostling each other, fierce as anything. It seemed like they were ready to tear us to pieces, the horse, the buggy, anything. Father seemed delighted, and with a satisfied expression he bent over and lashed at the dogs with his whip. The dogs barked more frenziedly than ever, the terrified horses fled on, and staring down at the dogs' eyes and teeth, I reckoned that if I fell off they'd instantly tear me to bits. But I tried to look at them the same way Father did, and I wished that I had a whip in my hand.

From a taped interview with Harry Critchfield, one of Jim's twin younger brothers, eighty years later:

". . . When Father got ready to go anywhere, they'd hitch the horses onto the buggy. The barn doors were always closed, because a lot of his horses were fiery. The minute those doors swung open, out they'd go, sometimes on their hind legs. And he liked that. He liked spirited horses. He wanted horses that would pull on the lines . . ."

The only time Father ever laid a hand on me was once when Burke hit me with a spitball and I chased him through the surgery just as Father was lancing an abscess on a patient's swollen, purple arm. Boy, did I get whipped! After a big fire destroyed most of Main Street when I was ten—Father discovered the fire at four o'clock in the morning when he was going out on a call—he built a surgery and consulting room north of the parlor and began to receive patients at home. Accident cases, sutures and all, came to the house.

I never saw him refuse a call, day or night, no matter what the weather. Many a time, he didn't get back for supper or we'd hear the rattle of buggy wheels late at night. Sometimes I'd see a German or Norwegian farmer sitting in his overalls by Father's desk, speaking with low tones and painful difficulty about his wife or child who'd gone sick again. When I was twelve, Father let me hold the smoky kerosene lamp while he washed and stitched. At first, the moans of the patient and the sight of blood made me sick to my stomach. Father taught me if you take a gulp of water you recover fast. Later, under his direction, I learned how to dress wounds and carry out minor procedures. I guess, after that, like Ray, I just never thought about becoming anything else.

The dead of winter. Late afternoon. A blizzard was blowing up. That morning, I'd watched it start. There'd been a strange, violet-blue sky. Moist air. The branches of trees looked wet. It got misty and very still. About noon, in a very short time, the mist turned to rain, the rain to snow. A wind came up and shifted direction. It started coming from the northwest, straight out of Canada, and the velocity increased, driving boiling gray clouds toward Hunter.

I stayed indoors. The windows were frosting up and great flakes of snow, flashing white, darted against the glass. You could hear the wind shake the storm doors and windows. It howled in the chimney and whistled through the furnace registers. The whole house creaked. Ray and Burke brought the cows back to the barn and said the snowflakes were shooting in level lines and it was getting hard to see. Mother was worried about Mrs. Muir, a neighbor who was alone that day, and sent Ray and Burke over to look in on her.

In our house it was safe and snug. Mother lit the lamps. Father was in his surgery. Claus brought in a scuttle of coal and poured it with a clatter into the top of the kitchen stove. He adjusted the damper and drafts and was about to go back for another scuttle when the telephone rang. Father took the call, a woman was bleeding after delivery. It was a farm fifteen miles north of town.

"I'll leave now," Father spoke into the phone. "I'll tell you what to do until I get there." He gave instructions. Claus bundled up, Father put on his fur coat and hat and told Mother he was going to stop off at the Larson farm five miles out; it was on the way and the father had flu. I went out to help Claus hitch the team. The minute you stepped outdoors, an icy wind got hold of you and snowflakes hit your face like hissing slivers of ice.

Father told me to tie a rope from the barn to the back porch in case it got much worse. "It looks like a real blizzard," he said, very solemn. When he and Claus were ready in the sleigh, I opened the barn doors; the timbers creaked with cold, like river ice. The sleigh headed out, circling around a big snowdrift. I watched it through eyelashes to which snowflakes clung right away. Team, sleigh, riders—all were swallowed up at once in boiling snow.

Back inside, the phone was ringing. Mother answered. It was the same man. He said he'd done as Father had told him. The hemorrhaging had stopped and his wife was resting quietly. The storm had worsened out his way and he didn't feel Father ought to try to come.

"Mother, let me go after them!" I cried when she told me. "I can still catch them!"

"No!" she was horrified. I was only twelve. It was a blizzard. Where were Ray and Burke? If we waited for them, I pleaded, it would be too late. All the time I was scrambling into my boots, reefer, cap, scarf and mittens. Mother clutched my arm, full of frightened protests. I promised not to go beyond the Larson place. She hesitated. I ran out to the barn to saddle up Snowflake, Mother screaming after me to be careful.

We were off. Wet snow and wind lashed at us. At once the lights of our house were snuffed out in the boiling snow. Snow settled on my cap, my shoulders, my pony's back. Snow had covered all trace of the runners of Father's sleigh. Heading into the open prairie was like diving into ice water. I wound my woolen scarf up over my cap and tied it around my neck good and tight. Just in time. The wind started blowing with terrific velocity and hitting me in the face. The flakes got harder. They hurt. Snow got in my nose and throat. I couldn't breathe and pulled the scarf over my face. Father said if it ever got too bad, to turn and drift along with the wind. The biggest danger was to get overheated and exhausted by trying to buck the wind. I kept going for several miles more.

By then it was roaring; I knew I'd soon have to turn back. Each separate flake became a particle of stabbing ice. Ice formed on my lashes and froze them together. I couldn't see. Snowflake reared, but kept going. I was pretty sure she could keep her bearings, so I gave her her head. It was all I could do. Everything now depended on Snowflake getting us to some kind of shelter . . . It wasn't long before I began to feel as if I'd been riding for a long time and was getting drowsy . . . The wind's high-pitched scream was deafening, like wailing voices all around me . . .

"Jimmy! Jim-m-m-my!" the ghostly wind-voices wailed and shrieked. "Jim-m-my! Jim-m-my!" Somebody was hollering my name. I pulled Snowflake up and hollered back. The answer seemed to come from my right. I dismounted and, hanging tight to the lines, worked my way back, talking to her all the time, until I reached Snowflake's head, just feeling it as I was blinded by the icicles on my lashes. "Jimmy, Jimmy!" I recognized the voice. It was Claus. He kept calling and I kept calling back until, leading the pony, I bumped into him. Then, holding Snowflake with one hand, I gripped a rope around Claus's waist with the other. He reeled in the rope, I hung on for dear life, and Snowflake followed until we reached a barn. Claus rolled open the big door and we went in, leading Snowflake. In a second we were blown out of the shrieking white blindness and into the warmth and quiet of the barn—the smell of animals, leather and hay had never been so good. Claus was cursing me in Norwegian and hugging me all at once . . .

We found the Larsons huddled in their kitchen around a pot-bellied stove. It was all fired up and they'd piled snow on the outside of the house and draped blankets and rugs over the doors and windows. Even so, gusts of wind would hit and billow them. Father was in with his patient. A plump woman with tucked-up sleeves, who was breathing heavily, said it was a miracle the doctor had come when he did, as Larson, sick as he was with flu, had badly strained himself getting his stock into the barn and had a strangulated hernia. Mother had been able to reach the Larsons by telephone, and a grown son had been spelling Claus out on the rope yelling "Jimmy!" as they figured Snowflake would keep to the road. Mrs. Larson kept telling us how they'd managed to sterilize the instruments and how she'd stood over her husband, dripping the ether. She said it was so cold they'd poured boiling water down the pump and when that didn't work, they'd melted snow in a tub in the kitchen for surgery. *"Gud vist!"* she kept exclaiming in Norwegian. "God knows!"

Father filled a pan with snow and made us take off our boots and stockings and rub our hands and feet in it. My toes were already coals of pain from warming up at the stove. The Larson place wasn't sheltered by trees or anything and the floor kept making cracking sounds. If they didn't keep the fire roaring hot, you'd start to feel a deep chill coming in from outside. I was too tired to care and kept nodding off until the wind died a few hours later and we could go home.

In winter in Hunter we had coasting and skating and snowball fights and sometimes a whole crowd from Christian Endeavor would go out in a sleigh filled with straw and sing, "Jingle Bells." If we had a hayrack on a bobsled and too many boys crept over to the girls' side, it would tip right over and dump everybody in the snow. It was always dark by the time school got out at four, and we boys had chores at home, helping Claus milk the cows or feed the horses or remove the ashes and the clinkers from the furnace and shovel some lignite from the bin. We banked the fire at night and stirred it up in the morning. Mother got awful cranky if she came down to a cold kitchen. She liked the fire stoked to a roaring pitch so the house was already warm.

Ground Hog Day would come and go and one day you'd notice the snowman out back had shrunk to something gray and slushy and the wheels of the buggy got all clogged with gumbo. Icicles would start dripping from the eaves, there would be the eerie crackle and glow of northern lights at night, and water would melt under the snowbanks and trickle down the ditches. Mother would start to squawk, "Don't you track in here with those muddy feet! I just scrubbed that floor!" When you're twelve years old, if it's not one thing, it's another. Stand up straight. Say, "Please." Cover your cough. Don't pick your nose. Don't chew with your mouth open. Don't lick your knife. Wait to have it passed. Wash your hands. It was like "Things to Remember" in *McGuffey's Third Reader* the teacher fussed about in school: ". . . When you rise in the morning, remember who kept you from danger during the night . . . Do not eat in a greedy manner, like a pig . . . Do not slam doors . . . Be kind and gentle in your manners . . . Do always as your parents bid you. Obey them with a ready mind, and with a pleasant face." Heck!

At last the day came when it was warm enough to go without a coat. The next week at school everybody would be whooping and coughing. Mother would start spring cleaning and looking over her seed catalogue. The dead grass would have to be raked up and burned, the apple trees blossomed and the day came when we went barefoot on the way home from school, tying our laces together and hanging the shoes around our necks.

And then it was summer, which meant staying outdoors all day, and swinging in the yard, and baseball, and having to wheel the twins around in their wicker perambulator, and people wiping the sweat from their faces and saying, "Is it hot enough for you?" And fixing a stand with Burke and Ray and hollering, "Lemonade, lemonade, made in the shade by an old maid! Five cents, a nickel, half-a-dime, a twentieth of a dollar! Step right up, ladies and gents, get your ice-cold lemonade!"

And swimming. Summer days, we went down to the old coulee about a half mile west of town to what we called Beard's Swimming Hole. Closer to Hunter, the creek was lined with low willows and cattails, all croaking frogs and chiggers and crickets, but out at Beard's it had been dammed up to make a big pond, there was an old cottonwood for shade and big rocks so that you could climb out and dive without muddying your feet. There was also the Gravel Pit, where people went for picnics and you'd see ladies in black stockings hitching up their long flannel skirts to paddle their feet in the water. Out at Beard's there were no girls screeching, "Now you stop splashing water on me! Quit it now! Quee-yut, Jimmy! I'm gonna tell!"

Mother didn't like the swimming hole. She was always going on about how somebody could drown. "Suppose you got the cramps, Jimmy," she'd say. "Then what?"

"Aw, Mom, that ain't nothin'. How'm I gonna learn to swim if you don't let me go?"

"Now, don't start that, Jimmy. Goodness gracious! It's just an old mud-hole. Why, the very idea! You can't go and I don't want to hear one more word about it."

"Ma!"

"Don't you yell at me, young man. Sakes alive, I'm not deaf. Did you cut me some wood like your father told you?"

"Yes, ma'am."

"*All* of it?"

"Well, pret' near all of it."

"Uh. Well, you just march right out and finish. Pronto. And I don't mean maybe."

"Now?"

"Now . . . . Jimmy! JIMMY! You come right back in here and shut that screen door properly. I won't have you boys slamming it like that. I declare,

I don't know what's got into you. Acting so peevish and sassy. Now, run along with you!"

"Holy smoke!" Seemed like every time I wanted to have some fun, Mother would say there was wood to chop or kindling to split. If it wasn't that, it would be "Run over to Mrs. Muir's and see if she has some extra Mason jar lids" or "Run down to Gale and Carr's and get me a spool of white thread, Number Sixty." Don't worry. She'd think of something. That day, as soon as I heard the butter churn get going real good, I dropped the ax and run into the back alley, south to Beard's house and up the cow path behind their place. When I got to Beard's pasture, after making sure to fasten the gate again with a loop of wire, I caught up with some of the gang.

When it was all sweltery and still, and everybody groaned that it wasn't the heat but the humidity, nothing looked so good as that cool water out at Beard's. Mom might call it an old mudhole, but it sure looked blue from the reflection of the sky. Once past the stubble fields, we'd go barefoot. The closer we got, the faster we went, until at last we broke into a dead run. We'd throw off our clothes as quick as we could and either creep out on the slippery rocks, or, with a whoop, slide right down the muddy bank. I'd leap and fling myself into the cold water and dive under and swim on my belly, or roll on my back to float, squeezing my eyes shut. We'd all be snorting and splashing and hollering. When I got into shallower water, there were shoals of little teeny-weeny minnows scuttling away in all directions. A few boys stayed at the water's edge. They couldn't swim or maybe they could just dog-paddle a little and they squealed and crouched and splashed and shot water at each other with the heel of their hands. It got deeper quick. One time, Merland Carr, who couldn't swim, was jumping around in the water and he went down a couple of times before some of the bigger boys grabbed him and pulled him out. He was all right as soon as he got a little water out of him.

Some older boys tried to teach their little brothers by throwing them out into the deep water. You could hear their splashes and sputtering protests and see their hands clawing and their faces all distorted with awful fear, and how they looked once they were safely back on the grass, panting and trembling, teeth chattering, shoulders shivering, scared to death. Better was the way I done, edging out slowly, kicking up your heels and paddling with your hands. You could try it like a dog, or a cow, any old way. I liked to lay on my back and float, or splash, or swim on my face, or on my side, just as I pleased, until I got tired.

Of course there was always somebody gonna try to grab you by the foot or shoulders and duck you. I'd choke and laugh and yell as if they were trying to drown me, all the while squirming and twisting to get away so I could turn around and duck them. We'd wrestle in the water, splashing and panting and trading insults, until one or the other went under. And there was always somebody to cry, "Anybody who can't touch bottom is yellow!" Sometimes the bigger boys used to taunt the ones who couldn't swim, calling them "Sissy!" and "Crybaby!" The *McGuffeys* at school were always telling about boys who got punished—mostly by drowning—if they gave in to the taunts of other boys or disobeyed their parents. There was "The Truant," who played hooky and went out with some boys in a boat that turned over—they got rescued "just in time to save them from a watery grave." If some boys dared you to do something and made fun of you if you didn't, you were supposed to be like George in "True Courage" and tell them, "I will not do that which I think to be wrong, if the whole town should join you in laughing." Shucks! Who's gonna do that?

At first I'd dive down, but I couldn't reach the bottom. Some force seemed to hold me up and bring me back to the surface, where I'd pop into the air like a cork from a bottle, snorting and blowing bubbles. After I learned to swim hand over hand and do the breast stroke and kick, at last I was able to plunge all the way down to where it was cooler and darker and there were reeds and catfish and crawdads in the slimy, liquid mud. When I opened my eyes in the water, I saw something muddy-brown like the prairie sky gets in a real bad dust storm. Some power always brought me bobbing back up.

One time, on a dare to see how long I could hold my breath, I stayed down too long. I let the air out slowly, blowing bubbles, but when I went to kick off to get back up, my feet slipped in the ooze. Panicky, thinking with sudden terror how Merland had kept going down, I clawed at the water, frantic to get to the surface, thrashing away for all I was worth. I got my head out as far as my chin, floundered, sank and swallowed water. At last, coughing and choking, I was able to tread water and breathe deep enough to get my wind back. Worst of all, there were humiliating shouts, asking if I was all right. Thinking fast, I cried in hoarse mock hysteria, "Drowning! I'm drowning!" I flailed my arms like crazy, kicked my legs and made a panicky face to show it was just a joke, ending the performance by slowly sinking under the water. Several members of the audience showed their appreciation with running leaps and cannonballs aimed in my direction. Going home that day, my whistling was nice and loud. Everybody'd been fooled and I guess I hadn't done no harm by it. I knew I was all right now as far as swimming went. But, you know, it was awful dark and scary down there.

Jim

Bang! Bang! BA-R-O-O-O-M! Come dawn of the Fourth of July and the whole town would explode. Father would get an anvil from the blacksmith's shop and he'd go out about five o'clock in the morning and put it out in the middle of the road with gunpowder in an iron ring on top. He'd put another piece of heavy iron on that and he'd take a hot poker and explode the gunpowder . . . W-H-A-A-A-M! It was enough to shatter your eardrums. It scared the daylights out of the twins, who ran bawling in to Mother.

Burke and Ray and I each got from Father a whole pack of firecrackers, the kind with red paper pasted on and printed with a yellow dragon and Chinese writing. And two punks apiece. That had to last out the day. You disentangled the crackers' little tails from the braided fuse and then you'd light one and hold it in your fingers until j-u-u-u-st the last split second when the fuse sputtered and spit. Then you flung it. If we had the "test of courage," you held the cracker in your fingertips way out and squeezed your eyes shut and got all shivery and in a pucker when the fuse started to sputter. And you held on! Burke wouldn't play, saying you could lose a finger.

As soon as the twins were big enough, Father gave them those rolls of red paper for a cap pistol, the kind that made a cracking noise if you put them on the carriage step and hit the place just right with a stone. Mother would come out to put up the flag, see the mess and get mad as a hornet. She'd squawk, "I declare, smells just like sulfur and saltpeter out here. Now, you boys pick up all those scraps of paper. Folks will be driving by to the picnic and I don't want the front lawn looking so slack." It was a losing battle. By the next morning there would be burnt-out punks and sparklers and little red pieces of cherry bombs and Roman candles and serpents and pinwheels and double-headers. If we didn't clean it up pretty quick, she'd have a conniption.

The picnic was where you stood under the trees while everybody talked about "cats and dogs" and "pitchforks" and "good for the crops." When the sun came out, they'd have a ball game and a cracker-eating contest and a potato race, a tug of war and a three-legged race. It sure was funny to see those girls in their fancy white dresses, trying to run and hold onto their hair ribbons at the same time. There'd be all kinds of jumping and races and horseshoe pitching, and they chased around a greased pig and you'd hear the hog callers screeching, "Soooo-eeee! Sooo-eeee!" When I was thirteen, I started playing cornet in the Hunter band. On those Fourth of July picnics, we tooted and tooted so steady, I'd get all winded and red in the cheeks. The real fireworks came at night. After dark, rockets and Roman candles would shoot into the sky over Main Street, exploding in a shower of red, green, white, yellow, orange and purple lights. It seemed like no time before Mother would be calling, "Bedtime!"

"I made you look, you dirty crook! You stole your mother's pocketbook!" That just called for a sock in the arm. "Mama's boy!" or "Crybaby!" were a lot meaner, because that meant you were a sissy. You'd have to clean up on whoever it was or it would look like you were yellow. There was also ordinary name-calling. "I can lick you, you think you're so smart!" "Who says?" "Me, that's who." "Oh, yeah? You'd better shut your trap or I'll shut it for you!" Mostly, I'd pop somebody in the eye and maybe he'd give me a bloody nose, and we'd be friends same as ever. In Hunter, if you really wanted to pick a fight, you talked politics.

"Sixteen rats! Sixteen cats!
Sixteen dirty Democrats!"

Except that Hunter didn't have sixteen Democrats. Just Father, who was for free silver and William Jennings Bryan and Populism, just like Grandfather back in Ohio. Every time there was an election, Ray and I were in for it. I'd shout, "Hooray for Bryan!" and quicker than you could say Cross of Gold, somebody'd haul off and punch me in the jaw, and I'd give him the old one-two, left-right, and knock his cap off, and he'd swing back at me—zip!—his fist just dusted me off, never touched me—and I'd whack him in the ribs, and the other boys would come running, shouting, "Fight! Fight!" And we'd square off with our fists held up like real boxers, until old Burke would step in and stop it. Burke was an awful bully. He just made a point of being bossy and interfering. Like one time he was supposed to be putting some shingles on the barn roof. He told us, "You gotta help me put these shingles on, see? I'll give you each five cents an hour." We knew we'd never see it and said, "We ain't gonna work for no five cents an hour." We turned him down flat. Burke never forgot a birthday spanking, either, with an extra hard one to grow on. He knew how to make them sting.

Some fights, he'd go and tattle on us and the teacher would have us before her desk, me with my shirt torn and nose bleeding and the other boy with his eyes puffy. That teacher knew how to whip a boy proper; if she took a switch to you, you'd be ridgy as a washboard. But she only told us, "You boys have got to learn to respect the political preferences of others." She had to say that, I guess. We Democrats in North Dakota did have some legal rights, though I could see who she was rooting for, all right. They all were. You'd hear people say the only good thing for a Democrat was a rope to hang him. The whole town talked like that. If some old drunken tramp came into town and had too much to drink and staggered down Main Street, they'd all har har and say he must be a Democrat. All the respectable farmers and merchants were Republicans, it seemed, and to hear them tell it, if a Democrat ever got into the White House, crops would fail, prices drop, businesses be ruined and the country would go to hell in a handbasket.

The Republicans wore clean collars and gave jobs to the common herd. They were like the Farmers Land and Loan Company, which owned twenty-two farms around town and loaned money to men from Iowa and Illinois and Indiana so they could buy land and a house and barns and take out a mortgage. If the men couldn't keep up the payments, the company took back the farm. Some sorehead Democrat might grumble about "land sharks," but to Republicans this was just "sound business practice." The Republicans called Father "a Bourbon reactionary," and he called them "the God and morality party." Except for Father, just about all the Democrats I ever saw looked like the "great unwashed" and the "radical protesters" the *Herald* was always warning about. They'd be foreign-born Swedes or Norwegians or Rooshuns, poor farmers or boxcar-riding harvest workers looking for a job. They wore blue work shirts and if they chewed tobacco it was plug.

In Hunter, most farm families didn't turn to the doctor until illness put somebody at death's door or an injury threatened life or limb. When they did come running, any failure to find Father right away could mean it was all over but the burial. Unlike the merchants downtown, Father could never close up shop. What he did do, for two weeks every summer, was to take the whole family on a camping trip. We'd all head West one morning like pioneers. Father had a horse, Burke and Ray had horses, and I had Snowflake. The twins rode with Mother in a covered, four-wheeled surrey and she and the hired girl, who was always a Sioux Indian from Devil's Lake, took turns driving it. Claus drove a covered wagon, a regular old prairie schooner, which carried all the gear—tents, bedding, mosquito nets, food, clothing, cooking utensils, extra harness and a spare horse tied behind for Mother. She liked to ride but got tired after a spell.

We went in July just before threshing season, when Father would get real busy. The Red River Valley was the bed of Lake Agassiz, long extinct, and was flat as a board until you hit the rolling slopes that in prehistoric times were the lake shores. Once out of the valley, you saw only a few log cabins or ruined sod houses, hardly a tree, and just dirt tracks or an old wagon trail. Mostly, we crossed virgin prairie grass. Now and then there were oxen, their heads bent low under creaking yokes, plodding to slowly break the soil. It was a smooth ride across the grass, as hardly anybody had ever been over it before. Once you got a day or two out of Hunter, the prairie looked just like General Custer saw it, "an almost unbroken sea of green, luxuriant, wavering grass."

The trip I remember best was to Spiritwood Lake, about eighty miles west of Hunter, when I was thirteen. Mother talked a good deal about these trips; she liked the adventure. We'd break camp and make an early start when it was still chilly and dew drenched the grass. When the sun came up, you could feel its warmth on your back, and by eight o'clock the dew was gone. Meadowlarks flew across our path; if you whistled at them just right, they'd whistle back. We'd imitate the sparrows, the call of killdeers and plovers, the coo of mourning doves. If you scared up a covey of prairie chickens, they'd flutter up with their soft *boom, boom, boom* and fly off to the hills. And all the time we'd keep an eye out for field mice, gophers and jackrabbits, grasshoppers, crickets and white and yellow butterflies, all buzzing and humming and darting about in the grass. A gopher, startled by us, might dash across our path, stop, freeze, stand up on its haunches, turn its head this way and that, give a quick whistle, flick its tail—that's why they called them flickertails—and be off again down into its hole. Same with the jackrabbits. Or you'd see a hawk flying way, way up high, and it would suddenly stop in the air like it was looking for a gopher, maybe flutter its wings, and shoot like an arrow over our heads and out of sight. There was no telling why it flew off or what it wanted.

The horses jogged along, the buggy rattled, the wagon creaked, and what we saw was always the same—sky, prairie, grass. As it got hotter, the sounds in the grass would hush, the birds fly away, the prairie chickens hide from sight, and about the only living things to be seen were fierce red ants that busied themselves in the dead under-grass. If it got really hot, you might come upon a blackbird or crow perched in the grass, panting with an open beak and outstretched wings, like it was dying of thirst and ready to croak. Sometimes, way off, we'd hear a faint whistle and rumble and just make out a train racing along the horizon. The engine, puffing out thick clouds of black, curling smoke, might be dragging thirty or forty freight cars behind it. "Look at that power," Father would say. "And all from steam." Also far away might be an old cabin or a windmill, looking as lonely as anything could look.

Sometimes I picked dandelions so the twins could blow off the fluff. We kept an eye peeled for arrowheads. Burke found a rusty knife with six notches on the handle and told me its owner, a Sioux brave, had scalped that many white men. To show he didn't scare me none, I put my fingers under my eyes and pulled down and my little fingers in the corners of my mouth and pulled out, while sticking out my tongue. We also came across some buffalo wallows and the white bones, half-buried skulls and horns of long-dead buffalo.

In those days it was wetter on the prairie and we passed many swamps and sloughs. At sunset, the foamy, green stagnant water would come alive with croaking frogs, chirping crickets, darting lightning bugs and buzzing mosquitoes. Big, purple-winged dragonflies skimmed back and forth over the water, and there were coots and ducks; if a mother took her ducklings on shore, they tottered and stumbled after her, cheeping all the while. Back in Hunter's sloughs, you never heard such a quacking and honking as when the ducks and geese came to nest. In the spring, big herds of Canadian ducks and geese would fly north in their long, wavering, V-shaped formations led by an old drake or gander. The ducks stayed in the swamps, living in the water and cattails and thick green reed grass, from September until it got real cold; then they'd fly south and come back in the spring. We had all kinds: mallards, teals, pintails, redheads, bluebills, canvasbacks, baldpates.

Sea gulls, too, flocked in by the thousands if there was a big grasshopper infestation, just like they did when they saved the Mormons. You'd see them soaring and circling and swooping over a newly plowed field to catch all the bugs and worms and grubs, sometimes so dense they looked like a field of snow. We were always hoping to sneak up to a giant whooping crane. But if you got anywhere close, it'd be off running, tall as a man, and go soaring into the sky. A whooping crane, why, you could hear its deep, trumpeting call for miles.

With hardly any trees on the open prairie for shade, we'd eat lunch on a mat spread in the shadow of the wagon. After looking after the horses, we'd munch on our boiled eggs, bread and cucumbers. Afterward we all stretched out and took a little snooze. Sometimes, riding along in all that green grass, I'd see a lake ahead and larrup Snowflake and gallop up only to find that what looked like blue water was just a mirage.

Best were the prairie nights, when you lay back with your head on your arms and took in the whole star-sprinkled sky, immense and limitless out on the plains, like a sky at sea. You might hear the whoop of a crane, a coyote's howl, the hoot of an owl. Or see the aurora borealis, the northern lights. Father said electricity drawn toward the North Pole excited the upper air and made it quiver. They came in shimmering flashes—mainly green, but also yellow, red or purple—rippling across the northern sky like a big gust of wind through a curtain. It was worth living for.

A steamy, sultry night by the campfire. I kept going to the water jug but I couldn't quench my thirst. Ray and Burke went to a slough for water; you could hear the clank of their pails and their voices. The fire cast a flickering halo on the grass; although the moon was shining, everything outside the halo looked dark. The twins were worn out and cranky. Father was out with the horses, who were browsing and snorting nearby. Claus complained his jaw was sore and predicted bad weather. The whole day, we had seen no one, no huts, no trees, no shade.

The moon looked too red, as if it were sick. The prairie mist seemed thicker than usual, layers and layers of hot air. Crickets shrieked in the grass. After supper, Ray picked a fight with Burke out of boredom, but it was too hot for roughhousing. I lay on my stomach, chewing on a straw and wondering what it would be like to smoke one of Claus's black cigars. Lightning began flashing on the horizon. The shadows around the fire, the dark shapes of the wagon and buggy, the restless horses made me feel something was going to come. Father told us to put out the fire and to do it carefully, stirring water into the ashes and not leaving a single spark. He and Claus went to stake out the horses. "Is there going to be thunder, Henry?" called Mother in an anxious voice.

Once we put the campfire out, you could see the prairie and sky much more clearly. Big thunderheads were piling up in the north. Faraway lightning was flashing every minute. The eastern sky was getting blacker too. A hollow, rumbling sound came out of the sky, like somebody shaking a big sheet of steel.

"It's all around," Burke said.

Soon there came a flash so bright it lit up the whole prairie. Everything looked purple and white; it hurt my eyes. There was a distinct, no longer distant, rumble of thunder. A black cloud was swooping down our way; it moved swiftly over our heads, blotting out the moon, the stars. It got terribly dark. The wagon creaked and the buggy gave a piercing scream as Claus and Father drove them into a slight hollow. They unharnessed and staked out the rest of the horses, Father shouting at them and whipping the bays. Mother helped the twins and the Indian girl under the wagon and called to us, "Boys! Take cover here if it rains." All at once, a squall of wind got up and tore over the prairie with such violence it billowed out my shirt and ripped off my cap. As I ran after it, the prairie grass blew this way and that in a frenzy, making such a noise it dulled the sound of the thunder. The wind seemed to blow from the black storm cloud, whirling dust with it; I squinted into the dust but could see little but flashes of lightning.

Father shouted for everyone to get under something. I tore under the wagon, which was closest, chased by an angry clap of thunder, which rolled across the sky and back again. Just as I made it, the blackness in the sky exploded into white fire. There was a huge clap of thunder. Burke and Ray were crouched beside me and I squeezed my eyes tightly shut and made up my mind not to think about the storm any more.

"What's the matter?" Burke said hoarsely. "You a scaredy-cat?"

I was afraid he'd call me a sissy, so I opened my eyes, even if the flashes of lightning were blinding. When I stuck my head out, a big cold drop fell on my nose. The rain at last. Soon it came pelting down. I told Burke to move over and squatted on my boots, trying to keep dry.

Suddenly, exactly right over the wagon, the sky smashed with the most terrible explosion I ever heard. I held my breath and screwed my eyes shut, but the flashing lightning seemed to pierce right into my head. I was convinced lightning had struck the wagon and would kill us all. The thunder, which roared instantly, no longer rumbled but made a crackling noise. It started raining very hard and I could hear a strong wind roaring through the grass, but now it was pitch-dark and neither rain nor grass could be seen. Little streams of water began flowing under the wagon. The rain seemed to blow in from all sides. After some time I could hear voices, though the thunder was rumbling as before and lightning was streaking the sky.

"It thunders and thunders," Mother said. "There's no end to it." Then

Father's deep bass. "It was a good storm all right." When we came out from under the wagon, we boys were soaked to the skin. Our hair was plastered to our heads, our trousers clave to our legs and I could feel water squelching between my toes. Wet and bedraggled as we all were, everybody was in good humor, relieved we'd escaped the worst of it without harm. Father said he was mostly worried about a prairie fire, with so much lightning. There was a thick mat of dead grass under the green, and he said that if a fire got started in it, it could spread to thousands of acres. Even the new, green grass burned, because the flames got so hot. Father said that after a bad prairie fire there was nothing to be seen anywhere but black ashes and bare earth. If we ever got caught in one, he felt our only hope was to gather buggy, wagon, horses and ourselves and light a backfire, covering our faces with wet towels. Even so, you could suffocate in the dense smoke or be blinded by the ashes. In January of 1903, the year after our trip to Spiritwood Lake, a prairie fire swept across two whole counties in North Dakota, killing people, sheep, cattle and horses and destroying farms and crops.

Spiritwood Lake itself was ringed by trees and there was clear, cool water to swim in. Our Indian girl told us that ever since Sitting Bull's death, at Wounded Knee the year after I was born, the Sioux held dances at the lake praying for a return to the time when buffalo were many and no white man had yet been seen. That didn't say much for us, I guess.

It was the coming and going on these trips that stays in my mind. There were times when the heat and monotony of the prairie got to be too much and I'd feel I'd been jolting up and down on Snowflake a very long time. Father would keep lashing his horses, the geniality gone from his face, and with his temples, nose and mustache all covered with dust and sweat, he looked intimidating. At such times, Mother alone would seem to be brooding over something pleasant and nice, as if such thoughts were brought to her mind by the bouncing buggy and heat. It was always Mother who asked, at last, "Well, Henry, how far shall we go today?"

He was such a commanding figure, so tall, such a powerful build and heavy, dark mustache, such a deep, sonorous voice. My impression of Father, I see now, was colored by a boy's idea of heroism. He seemed younger than his more than forty years, the man who, if danger came, took charge. Once, Ray and I took a load of barley downtown to have it ground up fine enough to feed a few pigs we were keeping at a neighbor's farm. Afterward, I climbed up on top of the wagonload to scatter the grain so it would be level enough for the trip back. Ray was holding the horses. One was a wild mustang colt which had stepped over the lines; Ray was trying to unscramble them. Just then, a train came through town. There was a rattling of iron wheels, a hollow rumble as it crossed a bridge, then, just as it got close to us, the son of a bitch blew his whistle. The horses bolted, the wagon rattled after them, I stumbled, lost my footing, fell off the load and landed on the wagon tongue. I held on for dear life, terrified, and somehow managed to straddle it with my legs. Ray ran alongside the horses, shouting, "Whoa, whoa, boy! Steady there, steady!" and trying to stop them. Women screamed, men hollered at me to hold on. Suddenly Father was there, seizing the reins, calming the horses, taking over, in control. It was like he would always be there when you needed him, taking command, bold and assured, overcoming the odds, winning out, making things right.

Seeing him, I thought that to drive about the countryside with fast horses healing sick people was the perfect way to live. It was only looking back years later that I could see the age of the country doctor was even then starting to draw to a close. Every year would make medicine more of an exact science and leave less place for the old-fashioned doctor with his intuitive ability to diagnose born of hard-won experience. Ahead was the specialist, the impersonal laboratory, the clinic and hospital, modern scientific techniques. But how were we to know? So in 1902, seeking to follow Father's footsteps, Ray went off to the University of Minnesota in grand style, with his own buggy and a team of bays. Three years later, I, too, went to study medicine. Nearly six foot, like Father—I was never to be more than five foot eight—Ray became a star guard on the university basketball squad; I played too, but spent more time warming the bench.

Father knew how to relieve suffering, set bones, sew up cuts, deliver babies and open boils. But what else? Only a few therapeutic drugs existed. What he lacked in scientific knowledge, he partly made up in practical experience and in his warm relationships with patients. Father never tired of telling about how, when he first came to Hunter, in 1886, few patients came to see him. People felt he was too young, just twenty-five. One day, he saw a stray mangy mongrel dog downtown limping around with a broken hind leg. Men wanted to shoot it. Father took the dog back to his office and put a splint on the leg. As soon as that dog was running around again, mean and frisky as ever, patients started to come. By the time I was a boy, everybody respected him. People from all over the county came to ask his advice on crops or land disputes or how to invest their money.

From taped 1982 interview with Harry Rasmussen of Hunter:

". . . Dr. Critchfield brought me into this world in 1898. We lived six miles from town and he drove out there with a team. And he didn't spare them. The twenty-fourth of March, a storm, in the snow. Father paid him five dollars for the delivery. You can imagine. Six miles out. My parents often talked about what a wonderful fellow he was, to go that far in a snowstorm for five dollars. My wife, Ella, lived twenty-four miles out and one time when her brother had typhoid, why he came out there. There was nobody else closer . . ."

From Jim:

Father went in for show. Somehow, even if many of his patients paid in a pig, chickens or a sack of potatoes, he managed to build a big, grand house out there on the prairie. It was a sprawling two-story, white frame Victorian mansion with dormers, big bay windows, cupolas, wooden lace under the roof peaks, stained and leaded glass, and all of fourteen rooms. In 1902, he put in central heating and indoor plumbing, which was something in those days. We had a coal furnace in the cellar to heat the whole house by hot air welling up through metal conduits and brass registers. The water system alone cost Father a thousand dollars. Claus pumped water up to two big lead tanks in the attic which were hooked up to the big kitchen range and hot-water spigots in what we called "the laundry."

Over the years, Father kept adding on. In time, an open porch with white columns ran clear around the front of the house, and there were several side and back porches too. Inside, the house had hardwood floors, high orna-mental ceilings, kerosene-lamp chandeliers with cut-glass prisms, Oriental rugs, claw-footed maple sofas and chairs, marble-topped tables, velvet drapes, lace curtains, flowered wallpaper and an enormous painting in a gilded frame, six feet high, of Father's sister Adelaide, who'd died young. Fretwork and urns filled with green ferns adorned a big door between the front parlor and living room, which in turn opened up into the dining room with sliding wooden doors. Facing the long dining table over a mahogany sideboard, a big mirror ran the full length of the room. But the crowning glory of the house, installed in 1902 when the old one was torn out, was a grand oak staircase that rose along the southern and western walls of the living room. From the first landing, built below a stained-glass window, one set of stairs went up and another down into the butler's pantry and kitchen. It was imposing.

The piano from Chicago was in the parlor, as was the Edison with its fluted black horn decorated with blue and pink morning glories and a case of cylinders; you could play Rudolf Friml and Victor Herbert, and the old Irish songs Mother loved—"When Irish Eyes Are Smiling," "Danny Boy," "The Hills of Donegal," so many sung by John McCormack. The parlor table held the family Bible, big and heavy with ornamental letters beginning each chapter. Beside it was a pink conch shell you could hold to your ear to hear the sound of waves and the sea, though Burke said it was just your own blood swishing and gurgling around. And there was Mother's workbasket with her spools of thread, papers and needles and her scissors, which nobody was allowed to touch.

The cellar, with its cistern, furnace room, and bins for hard coal and lignite, was always spooky. Wriggly white sprouts grew out of the potatoes in their bin, and in one corner was dirt where Mother grew celery in the winter. There were shelves of Mason jars, some empty and gathering dust or spoiled so that the lids were ringed with mold, but most of them were a dust-coated green or red or orange and filled with canned fruit and vegetables, pickles, jams and jellies. Grandfather sent three barrels of apples from Ohio every October; one had big red eating apples, another greenings or Wealthies for sauce and pie. The third, MacIntosh Reds, were as hard as bullets; you couldn't eat them until Christmas.

I tore in and out of the cellar; the barn was where I liked to stay. If you opened the door real quick, you could hear mice scrambling to hide and pigeons and swallows flapping their wings in the loft. The barn smelled of hay, oats, horses, dust and old, sweat-stained leather. Sometimes one of the barn cats would rub its back against your legs, purring. I always milked on the run, forcing the cow I was supposed to milk against a stanchion or a wall, dodging her tail, setting the stool on the right-hand side, ramming my head against the cow's belly and squirting two streams of milk into the rising white froth in a bucket. We carried it to the cream shed, where the Indian hired girl would strain it through a cloth into a big bowl, or sometimes just ladle it off with a spoon. If it was my turn, I'd have to run around with a basket looking for eggs. To feed the horses, you climbed up into the haymow, scaring the barn swallows out, and dropped hay down into all the mangers, then carried oats into the stalls. You had to be careful around the horses; Minnie, one of the mares, once kicked Harry in the nose. Behind the barn were Mother's plum, cherry and crab-apple trees, a big clump of willows and the lilac and rose bushes she'd brought from Minneapolis. Back of that was Beard's pasture, where we kept our cows. As boys, this was where we went to throw stones, play catch, fly kites, and look for garter snakes or little toads.

Comment by Bill Battagler of Hunter, recorded in June 1982. He bought the old Critchfield place in 1959 from a family who had bought it from Burke, and tore it down in the seventies, after it had stood derelict and empty, gaining a local reputation as a haunted house, for many years:

". . . Every time I went inside that great big old house I had an uneasy feeling. I never got over it. I'd walk through the cemetery out here any time of night, but I don't think you'd have got me to stay overnight in that house . . . One afternoon, it was getting fairly late though the sun was out, well, it was just as bright as could be in the living room and parlor as far as that goes, the sun reflecting off those big old-fashioned glass chandeliers they had . . . But I got the feeling that somebody was watching me. I don't know, you just feel funny about things once in a while.

"I was working on the wall, just below that stained-glass window on the lower staircase landing, you know. I'd torn away the wooden balustrades or banisters or whatever you call them that ran down the staircase and was ripping plaster and laths off. And somebody took hold of my shoulder. Just like you walk up to someone and lay your hand on their shoulder and you're going to talk to them. I could feel those fingers gripping me. Hard. I looked around, expecting to see someone. But there wasn't anybody there . . . Well, I picked up my tools and I left and I never went back inside that house again. You can ask my wife. After that I took a wrecker and I pulled the house down in sections and salvaged what I could and drug all the rest out to the dump and burned it."

Jim:

Nineteen oh four. A wet day in May. Father came home with a chill, his clothes sodden. He said he had cut across country with the buggy to save time and somehow driven into a slough, probably not more than two or three feet deep. Trying to get out, he headed the horses into a ravine which seemed to lead out to the shoreline. Instead of dry ground, the grass hid several feet of mud, muck and green slime. The horses panicked, rearing and getting stuck deeper in the slimy ooze. He couldn't get them out and had to wade in and unhitch the team. The water was icy and he got drenched. His coat got soaked, his trousers clung to his legs, there was a bitterly cold wind, and when he finally reached the bank of the slough, no farmhouse was in sight. He drove straight home. After he changed into dry clothes, Father went to his consulting room on the north side of the house to receive patients. He examined a boy with a rash, treated an old man with arthritis, and after that, work came with a rush. But he kept feeling achy and feverish. He went to bed early, but he didn't seem able to get warm. Mother put extra quilts on him, but he started trembling all over. His arms and legs twitched; it seemed like his whole inside was shivery. She put on still more covers, but that did no good. His shivering grew worse in the night and he could not get to sleep.

"I'm very ill," he told Mother.

She kept putting her hand to his head and touching his cheek. "You took a bad chill, Henry. Did you give yourself quinine or some other drug?" He didn't say what he had taken.

"Lillie, I think I ought to have something hot. Soup or tea. I was chilly before, but now I feel hot. And I ache all over . . ."

I heard Mother stirring in the kitchen and went down. She told me how ill Father was. "Please God," she murmured under her breath, "he'll be better tomorrow." Burke came down and she told him Father was as hot as fire.

The next few days, he did not get much better. He stayed in bed upstairs and we had to send away his patients. The fever persisted, his mouth stayed dry and sticky; at times he seemed in awful discomfort, and kept asking for water. The smell of food nauseated him and he could not eat. When Mother said she felt we had better take him to Fargo or even to a hospital in Minneapolis, he said in a low, hoarse voice, "I don't know what is best, Lillie." He told her a kind of heaviness was creeping over him and he had to exert his strength to talk. "I'm sorry, dear . . . I'm not well. I've caught a cold . . ."

Mother had given birth to my little sister, Kathryn, four months earlier. Father felt the baby was too young to make the trip to Minneapolis and it was decided that Burke and I would take Father on the passenger train that night. We booked a compartment from Casselton and Father tried to lie down comfortably and go to sleep, but he could not. Wearing slippers and without a cravat, a blanket about his shoulders, he sat motionless in his seat; he seemed exhausted and it made his face look thin and sunken. He did not seem himself, but like someone else entirely, a stranger with a bad fever, who would shiver with cold and then turn hot and trembling.

Ray met us at the station and drove us straight to the hospital. It was pneumonia. Father was put to bed at once. He no longer seemed to know where he was, nor whether daylight had given way to darkness; he talked to us now of present things and then of episodes that happened long ago, as if he'd lost his sense of time and place. We stayed close to his bedside, and on the third day of this delirium, he died.

He was forty-three. There was some confusion at the hospital. Ray, who knew the interns, said there was speculation that Father had overdosed himself with drugs. I never knew if this was true or not. It became one of those strange, clouded stories that grow up in families, that Father's death, once he'd caught a cold and it went to pneumonia, had "something to do with drugs."

It was the biggest funeral Hunter had ever seen. The evening of the day before, after dark, men brought the coffin from the railway depot; it was new and shiny, of glistening mahogany; they set it in the wide archway between the living room and front parlor. Father lay in state there throughout the night, dressed in his best black suit, with his habitual wing collar, cravat and silver tiepin. For some reason, his mustache was gone, and clean-shaven and sunken-cheeked, he looked very young and gentle and remote. Mother, red-eyed and terribly pale, sat beside him, all in black, never taking her eyes off his face. All night, she rested her hands on his body, and like him, she did not move, but remained bent forward and pressed close to the coffin, unstirring in this quiet posture. Her face showed no expression; only the wetness which glistened from time to time showed she was steadily weeping. At long intervals she dabbed at her eyes with a big handkerchief, quickly and silently, as if careful not to disturb the heavy, stifling air and quietude. From time to time somebody would bring coffee and murmur to her in a hushed voice, "Drink this, Lillie. You need something to keep you going."

Upstairs, lying in my bed, long before dawn I could hear the creaking of harness and the hoofbeats and grating wheels outside. These sounds and the hum of muffled voices grew, and when daylight came, I went to the upstairs front window in the big bedroom; the road outside our house, as far as I could see either north or south, was filling up with teams and buggies. I had never seen so many. In the street, people were bustling about. Women in long black dresses wore black gloves and hats adorned with black crepe and black veils; the men wore black too. Soon it was noisy, with a stream of mourners flowing into the house and another coming out, people talking and greeting each other, the horses snorting and munching, children crying out and whimpering. Fresh crowds kept pushing their way up to the gate and milling about the grass; Burke said, with all the crush and confusion he wondered how we'd ever get Father out to the cemetery to bury him. I peered down from the upstairs landing: so many white flowers and the shades all drawn, a shadowy pale green light, the smell of candles and chrysanthemums, mourners filing past the coffin, Mother in the stern still-ness of grief. Down in the kitchen, Uncle Lyman, Father's brother who was a judge in Ohio, was standing about with some cousins, all of them talking and eating and drinking. The undertakers, who had come from Casselton, ran about in a frantic hurry; they seemed agitated and anxious, yet their faces remained in fixed smiles, their voices were genial, their movements poised. They had brought a magnificent hearse, a big, black-painted four-wheeled carriage of carved wood with glass walls and imposing silver kerosene lanterns in the front. It was all decorated with silver curlicues, and the fringed black velvet curtains inside had silver tassels. Once, Burke came in to say the crowd was estimated at between four and five thousand. People crowded around like flies in autumn, waiting for the funeral procession to begin.

Remarks of Beatrice Carr Sayer, widowed farmer's wife in Hunter, taped during interview seventy-eight years later:

". . . We stood in the backyard and watched that long procession of horses and buggies following that black hearse to the burial. Our parents, of course, were all there. And those horses and buggies stretched out for half a mile, maybe even a mile. You know where the cemetery is? Well, they were up to where the half-mile road comes out of town and all along the other side of the railroad track as far as the Presbyterian church. The doctor lived just across the road from the church. We could see the procession from our place because there are a lot of houses and trees that are there now that weren't there then.

"I just loved Dr. Critchfield. He was a peach. He always brought candy when he came to see me. I was only around five or six years old, but I can remember the dark hair and quite a good-sized man. He had a black team and he'd go anyplace, whether it was stormy or not . . . He caught pneumonia, didn't he? I remember my folks telling that he got lost and got sick and got pneumonia and didn't last long."

Jim:

The day after the funeral, Uncle Lyman gathered the family in the parlor. He talked a long time, as judges do, but the gist of it was that from now on we were going to be poor. Father had left us the house, the barn, the orchard and garden, a five-thousand-dollar life-insurance policy, and books showing his patients owed him over thirty-five thousand dollars. It was all in small amounts: two dollars an office call, three dollars a house call, and fifty cents a mile both ways if he drove a team out to the country. Uncle Lyman collected about six thousand dollars before he took the train back to Ohio and left our lives forever. Grandfather was ill and couldn't come to the funeral. He never did come to visit, but every October we could always count on getting three barrels of apples.

We had to let the Indian hired girl and Claus go right away. Faithful old Claus was close to fifty and maybe it was best for him, as he went out to

Montana and staked his own homestead claim so he wasn't a hired man any more. A friend of Mother's, Sarah Denham, who was moving back East, offered to sell us her three-hundred-and-twenty-acre farm at a fair price. The twins were just eight, I was fourteen, Burke was fifteen and Ray eighteen. Mother said it was up to us, but if one of us farmed, it might be the way to get the rest through school. We agreed. At first we tried farming with a hired tenant. We also rented the house in Hunter and moved into an apartment, what they called a tenement in those days, in Minneapolis, taking with us a team, buggy and sled, and a freight-car load of furniture. Ray and I were to finish medical school and Burke to take up economics. Right away, there was trouble with the tenant, and Burke and little Harry went back to farm.

Somehow we managed. Ray earned his degree and came back to North Dakota as a country doctor in 1909, five years after Father died. In Minneapolis he'd married a Swedish nurse, Irene Swenson, who sometimes sang on the radio. Ray set up practice in Galesburg, just north of Hunter. Everybody wanted to come home, and Mother, Kay and the twins were back living in our old house. I was still in medical school.

Most people remember 1910 as the year of Halley's comet. Or, if they come from Hunter, as the year the bear, driven out of Minnesota by forest fires, showed up outside town and had everybody chasing it in automobiles like so many circus clowns.

I remember it for another reason. We were threshing. Sam Richardson and I were grain haulers. That day, we'd just brought in a load to the elevator. It was about noon and so hot and windy we were taking a break in front of the hotel. Not a soul in sight, and then up the road comes one of the new schoolteachers. Slim, pale, pretty as a picture in her high-collared white blouse fastened with a ribbon and a skirt down to her ankles. In spite of a stiff neck and stern frown, she had wonderful brown eyes, so warm and alive you hardly saw the rest of her. Sam said she was a Methodist preacher's daughter from down in Iowa. She looked it, walking so primly erect, her heels tapping on the wooden sidewalk, her face set in a severe, ladylike expression as if she would rather die than take notice of the likes of us. Just as she came by, her skirts flew up in a gust of wind. I grinned and told Sam —loud enough so she'd hear—"Now *she's* got damn good-looking legs." She threw me a disgusted look like I was some sort of low-down harvest tramp. Slam! went the hotel screen door, hard as it would go. Any look was worth it from those eyes.

Anne

There were no more drunken knocks on the door. After two months at the Hunter Hotel, I and two other teachers took rooms in a large white house owned by the widow of a prominent doctor. The lease read: "Half of the house and half of its contents." I used to say I was the only one who got my share.

Lillie Critchfield was a pretty little woman, prematurely white, with a large family. I met Ray, who had just become a doctor, and Burke. Both were married. There was one daughter, Kay, almost seven years old, and the teenage twins, Harry and McLain. Another son was away at college. I was pleased at the arrangement, as the Critchfields were the nicest people I'd met in town. They had been well-to-do, but since the death of the father, had come down in the world. The white-painted clapboard of their rambling old house was scaling, the roof shingles looked ragged, and the splintered wooden sidewalk out in front needed repair. But, across the big, now snowy, lawn, there were lilac and rose bushes, and behind the house, a kitchen garden, orchard and big barn, and many willows, cottonwoods and box elders.

Dr. Critchfield had then been dead over six years, but I found you heard more about him dead than most people alive. He had not only been a good doctor, but a kind of father confessor to most of the people in the town. But he was most renowned as the man who drove horses faster than anybody in the county. He'd kept many trotters—blooded stock—and his fame was secured after he once drove a team over a house in a snowstorm. Mrs. Critchfield's family came from Ireland, but she'd been born in Minnesota the night they'd fired on Fort Sumter. Lace-curtain Irish, when I look back on it, not shanty.

Hunter was typical of the little towns coming into existence as the railroads, new milling processes and machinery, and John Deere's steel plow opened up the northern prairie. The Great Northern Railway tracks divided Hunter's rich, black alluvial soil, called gumbo, which was on the east side of town toward the Red River, from sandier soil on the west. Gumbo stood drought, and sand heavy rain, so Hunter's people said one side of town was sure to get a decent crop, whether the year was dry or wet. The main crops were wheat, potatoes, feed corn, alfalfa, clover, barley and oats. Every farm had its pigs, poultry and milk cows. Many used big, heavy workhorses, Clydesdales or Percherons. Hunter was still a jerkwater town; steam engines stopped to take water from a tank down at the depot. But the town's boomers—mostly railway men and bankers—kept trying to attract as big a commercial and professional class as they could, so property values would go up.

Further comment from Harry Rasmussen, for many years a clerk in Hunter's biggest general store:

". . . You could buy everything in Hunter in those days. We had tailor-made suits. We had furniture. We had crockery. We had everything you can think of. When I first went to work for the Gale-Carr store, in the grocery, I could talk Danish and also understand the Norwegians and Swedes. Most of them spoke English, but they felt more at home in their own language. Farms were all over then. There was a farm on pretty near every half section of land and even some of the quarter sections were just one farm. Everybody'd need a hired man in the spring. They'd come in the store and they'd want shoes, overalls, work clothes. Some were just younger fellows going around the country for a lark, I suppose, but the older men quite often come year after year. All we'd ask is who they were working for. They charged stuff. Never lost a cent on any of 'em. Soon as they got their wages, they'd come in and pay. There was never no question of credit to those men."

From Merland Carr, eighty-one, retired farmer whose father was a partner in the store:

". . . The town hotels might have been nice at one time, but not when I was young. Traveling men and transients would stay. It was tough. They'd work in the woods in Minnesota and then they'd come up here. Well, they'd drink, you know. They'd come bouncing into the hotel and you didn't know where they'd go . . . In those days you didn't have the hygiene that you have now. I asked Doc Baillie—he came after Doc Critchfield died—about George Hayward, who was so dirty he'd just jump out of his clothes at night and jump into them the next morning and they stood right there. How come he was never sick? Well, Doc Baillie answers right up. He says, 'No self-respecting germ would have anything to do with George.' "

Anna Louise:

If Hunter had its rough element, it also had its church ladies. Mrs. Walter Muir, whose father had built Hunter's first house, had been its W.C.T.U. president for twenty-five years. She was a "white-ribboner," as they called those who got a law passed making it illegal to buy liquor in the state. These ladies had also decreed the strictest rules for Hunter's teachers: we were not to marry, keep company with men, go out after eight o'clock at night except to school functions, smoke cigarettes, wear bright colors or dye our hair, get into a carriage or automobile with any man not our father or brother, nor wear any dress shorter than two inches above the ankle or less than two petticoats. The rules were not zealously enforced.

For such a little town, Hunter was up to date. It still had gaslight when I arrived but soon got electricity every night from seven o'clock to midnight, and on Monday and Tuesday mornings so women could do their wash. It also had two hundred wall telephones, the kind with party lines and so many rings that you cranked. There were as many as eighteen on some county lines and a lot of listening in. Some of the farms were very big. In Iowa a family might have forty, sixty, maybe a hundred acres. In Hunter at least a dozen had one to three thousand acres. These were not the famous wheat-growing Bonanza farms around Casselton, where ten-thousand- to sixty-thousand-acre holdings were deeded to some officials of the Northern Pacific Railroad in exchange for their railroad bonds after the crash of 1873; by 1910 most of them were broken up. But they were still big. A Danish farmer, Peter Madsen, was said to have gone home after fifteen years with sixty thousand dollars made from wheat. Hunter's people did remarkably well. One of the Gamble family started a national chain of stores. A Muir became a noted sculptor. One man was to go off and build racing cars and airplanes.

The most distinguished Hunter farmer was David Houston, a Scotsman who had owned three thousand acres and died just four years before I came. His widow spent most of her time in Florida, but when she was in Hunter she played a grand piano and sang, drove a pair of fast Hambletonians and had a parrot which could squawk, "Hey, boys, c'mon in!" Houston invented what became the basic principle of the Kodak camera: rolled film on reels. (The "dak" and "ko" are from Dakota, Hunter's people claimed.) He sold this and other patents to the Eastman Company in New York State. Like Henry Critchfield, buried two years ahead of him, Houston met a tragic and gloomy death. One winter night in 1906, he lost his way while walking home from Hunter in driving snow. He wandered for hours, got badly chilled, never fully recovered and died three months later. An amateur poet, he once had written that when it was "snowing, blowing, growing dark" it would be easy to get "lost on the prairie plain." Bad weather in winter could come terribly fast. One moment there might be nothing, and the next the wind was so strong it rocked the buggy on its springs and wailed so loud you could hardly hear. It scared me to death.

That December, all the Critchfield family was home but one. When he arrived, I had already left for Iowa to spend Christmas with my family. But I heard from this other son. He wrote and wanted to know when I was passing through the Twin Cities. Could he have a date? I couldn't be bothered. Conceited college type, I thought, and then: I'm much *older*. Why, he can't be more than twenty-one! I was a mature twenty-three by this time. That I was still unmarried was not because I hadn't been asked. I was still engaged to Beecher.

That January, Mrs. Critchfield told me her son Jim couldn't afford to go back to medical school. He was going to teach in a country school near Hunter and take up farming in the spring. The first time I saw this son I was out in the kitchen and heard somebody come stamping up on the porch, stopping to knock the snow off and pull off his overshoes. When he came in, his face cold and rosy, and I saw who it was, a hot flush of embarrassment came into my cheeks. So this was the boy in front of the hotel.

Beecher wrote faithfully that spring, but by now I was very busy. There was Dancing Club, for one thing, every two weeks on Friday night. "Pink Lady" was popular. And I always danced the "Rye Waltz" with Leland Lane. "When a body meets a body, comin' through the rye . . ." Three steps each way and then into a waltz. Jim Critchfield always played the piano. I never thought what I wanted out of life; I was so busy living. I bought a lovely rose chiffon dress with cloth-covered buttons all down the back, and a gathered waist, a nine-gored skirt and a three-tiered flounce. When I whirled around dancing, the filmy, ruffled skirt would billow all around me. Tightly laced and with my hair swept up into a pompadour, held in place with pins and tortoiseshell combs, I'd dance the whole evening without pausing for breath—dance until I was ready to drop.

One boyfriend was Asa Sherritt, who danced as lively as a cricket. Sometimes they had an accordion, clarinet and fiddle besides the piano, and they'd play waltzes and polkas. Jim, like the rest of the band, was always in short sleeves and suspenders, and when the fiddler would ask, "Give me C, please," he would raise his shoulders, spread his hands and strum the chord. After they played the first slow steps, they'd pick up the tempo and the dancers would waltz in full swing. When they really got going, the tune didn't matter so much as the rhythm.

Once in a while, if it was a barn dance or a basket social, Jim might call off a square dance. Leland or Asa or some other partner would be teetering around, first on one foot, then the other, just about tearing themselves apart with twists and fancy steps, their feet tramping so hard and fast to the rhythm it raised dust from the cracks in the floor. Jim would be calling, "Choose your partners! Allemande right! Do-si-do! Promenade left!" When it came to "Swing your partners!" the I.O.O.F. Hall would fairly shake as hands joined and came apart, skirts billowed and ballooned, petticoats rustled, and couples whirled this way and that. Afterwards, if it was a waltz, Jim might get somebody to spell him at the piano and take a turn dancing himself. He'd take me firmly by the waist, offer his shoulder for my hand, and whirl me away. We'd waltz right through the crowd in time to the music. Jim was so swift and light on his feet he could swing me around fast enough so that even my starched petticoats flew out. Afterwards I'd feel quite giddy.

Often, after the midnight supper, Jim ended up walking me home. As we headed across the tracks from Main Street, I'd say, "Well, I really had a good time tonight." He'd grin and say something like, "I was hoping you did, Miss Williams. Every time I happened to look at you during the square dance, your face was all scrunched up like you didn't quite hear the last call. I kept hollering louder until I got hoarse." I knew he was teasing.

He could be serious. "I don't know if dancing affects other people the way it does me," he said one night, "but as I'm sitting there playing and watching everybody flinging themselves around, I really enjoy it. Nobody seems to be giving a thought to feeding the stock or who's going to haul water in the morning or what happens if the barn catches fire. The only trouble is my face gets so cramped up from grinning all the time, I have to hightail it out back every so often to have a slug of hootch." He wasn't joking. I'd learned by now that Jim, like so many men, felt a human being needed a drink before he could fully relax and enjoy himself. I always stayed perfectly sober and had fun. Maybe men were different.

That Easter, Beecher came to visit. He seemed his old earnest, handsome self. He stayed at the hotel, brought his Kodak and took lots of photographs. One day, he rented a buggy and we drove out to the Critchfield farm, two-and-a-half miles from town. When we got there, Jim was breaking in a new mustang stallion. The horse was in the corral chute, its saddle tightly cinched and bridle adjusted and Jim was up, calling to his hired man, "Let him go, Jack!" As quick as lightning, the stallion plunged from the chute, and kicking, bucking, twisting and turning, his back humped and his legs stiff, he tried to throw Jim off. Sitting easily in the saddle, Jim waited until the horse, stretching his body full length, plunged furiously across the prairie. We watched as Jim gave the mustang his head until the horse, panting, his nostrils distended, his sides heaving, came back to the starting point, well under control.

Jim apologized for not being able to spend more time with us. "This horse can strike, bite and kick all at the same time," he told Beecher. "You just have to win these mustangs with patience, kindness and some judicious feeding. Right now I've been trying to get a halter on this one. With any luck, in a couple of days I can hitch him up with an old reliable. In a few more days, Mr. Beal, if you don't have a runaway, you can have a well-broke horse." Photographs were taken of Jim and the new stallion. Somehow Beecher seemed to fade in the fierce North Dakota sunlight.

I wrote Beecher a letter soon after he returned home, breaking off the engagement. I told myself, "I would never marry a schoolteacher. Beecher's gotten so darn conceited. All the teachers and kids play up to him." Beecher quit the teaching profession later and entered a bank. He still continued to write now and then.

I began to see more of Jim. Nothing serious. He was rather wild, and there were stories of drunken sprees and amatory adventures. He was good at all sports—baseball, basketball, he always won the bowling tournaments. Once, he bowled a game with ten straight strikes. He got a split on the eleventh frame. The score was 298 out of 300. Two pins. All but one had been strikes. Then, with one ball left, the two pins left standing were too far apart to hit both. He hit one. It was the closest I ever saw anybody I knew get to a perfect score.

In those days, every little town had its band and baseball team; in Hunter, Jim led the one and pitched for the other. Every Saturday night after it turned warm enough, we'd go to a band concert downtown, to hear the rousing music and slap mosquitoes. The Hunter band played Sousa's "Washington Post March" and "Stars and Stripes Forever," the "Poet and Peasant Overture," the march from *Tannhäuser* and the "William Tell Overture," as well as selections from *Madame Butterfly* and *Faust,* and a new song, "Take Me Out to the Ball Game." The bandstand was on the grass of a small park beside the depot. During a concert, automobiles and buggies would park in a semicircle around it. Everybody in town came. One old drunken fellow was always coming up to say, "Shay, Jim, play 'Home on the Range,' will you? Thassa good feller. Much obliged."

On the Fourth of July and other holidays, the band would parade. Jim always looked so soldierly in his maroon uniform with its matching braided cap as he came marching by, head up, with a proper band leader's swagger. There were glittering brass instruments, and some men in front carried flags. Besides leading the band, Jim played the solo cornet parts. When he pitched the highest notes, he scowled, and making the sound by vibrations of his lips, he drew his breath through the corners of his mouth; resting, he'd rub his lips with his forefinger, while looking at the audience with his humorous eyes; sometimes he'd grin at me or give me a wink. As leader, he just stood there and waved his baton, while the other players blew themselves purple and the drummers pounded away: *"Tucket-a-brum-brum, tucket-a-brum-brum.* Or instead of hitting the drumhead, they might click their sticks together, *"Rat-a-tat-tat, rat-a-tat-tat . . ."*

During baseball season, Jim would come home after sundown every night with his hair wet with sweat and sticking to his forehead and his uniform streaked dark gray down the back. He'd be tired, but he never seemed to mind changing and going out to do the chores. I thought: he'd be an easy man to live with, he's got such a good disposition. He loved baseball. As boys, he and Ray would go out to Beard's pasture and hit for hours, he said. They'd hit a beat-up old ball as far as it would go and then they'd chase it down and throw it around. As soon as they were old enough, they started playing team ball, first Ray, who always pitched, and a couple of years later, Jim, who either pitched or played shortstop. Jim felt that, brother or no brother, Ray was a marvelous pitcher. He'd brag on Ray's behalf, "He was just as good as anybody they had at Minnesota." He said Ray was a good hitter and a good catcher, too. Jim said he never saw Ray lunge for the ball or take a strike away from the pitcher the way some catchers did; he made catching look real easy.

Jim sometimes told this story:

"Ray really taught me to pitch. We got along fine. One time, there was a game against Blanchard and I was just starting to pitch some. Ray happened to be in Hunter that afternoon and he agreed at the last minute to fill in for the catcher; the regular man had fallen off a hayrack. So there was Ray, giving me signs, the little old one-two-three for fast ball, curve and straight change-up. I kept shaking him off; I wanted to try throwing my roundhouse curve, something a little bit like Christy Mathewson's fade-away. Well, Ray got tired of squatting there and having his kid brother keep shaking him off, so finally he hollers, 'Throw any damn thing you please, you son of a bitch.'

"Boy, did that get my back up! I wanted to powder that ball by him quicker than hell would scorch a feather. So I kicked the mound around a little bit, pulled my cap down tight on my head, and wham!—I fired Ray a reverse curve—as good a one as I ever threw, I swear—and he just reached down so easy and caught it backhanded with that mitt of his. It kept on that way. I'd be throwing the best outshoots and drops I had and he catching them so soft and easy. Well, we went through the whole ball game that way. And there's Emil Moen, standing out at shortstop, wondering what the hell is going on—he's not seeing any signs!

"I held Blanchard to two hits, fanning fourteen, and when it's over everybody's coming over to hit me on the back or shake my hand. All except Ray. 'Listen, you bastard,' he says, 'you pitched a pretty good ball game. But if you'd listened to me, you'd've pitched air-tight ball!' " At this point, Jim would burst into laughter. "Boy, that was Ray all right," he said. I think he always kind of hero-worshiped Ray, just like he did his father; they were the ones Jim wanted to be like.

Hunter just had a little country ball park; the diamond was on Fred Williams's farm. There was no fence or anything, and the bleachers were just crude wooden boards and pretty rickety. Yet the whole town turned out for games; people drove in from farms, mostly in buggies and horse carts, but a few in Model T's. Because he had a teaching job out in the country, Jim was just a relief pitcher and didn't play all the time. When he did play, he loosened up fast. It looked to me as if he forgot everything the minute he walked across to the mound and had a look around. He'd throw the ball at whoever was at bat just as hard as he could, what he called trying to powder it so fast the batter couldn't hardly see it.

From interview with Emil Moen, in his late eighties, a retired implement dealer:

". . . Oh, that baseball, that was serious business. One time, we were playing Arthur. It was right across the tracks north of the elevators on Fred Williams's place. Well, Fred lost a lot of money betting on the game and he says, 'They're not going to play on my land any more,' and he went home and plowed the diamond up . . ."

Anna Louise:

That summer, Mama and I took a journey back East. The folks had moved to the town of Sumner in the fall of 1910. Dad's previous pastorates had three or four churches, and he traveled to them by horse and buggy. Sumner was what the Methodists called a "station," just the one church, and the parsonage had no stable. Father sold his team and buggy for two hundred dollars and gave Mother half the money, saying she could either buy a new sewing machine or take a trip back East. "If I was you, I'd take the trip." Dad became a great walker after that. You didn't hire a livery horse very often for a dollar a time on a preacher's salary. But in 1876, when he was twenty-two, Father had worked as a township census taker just before the Centennial. He'd used the money earned to go back to New York State to see his Quaker relatives and felt it was the sort of once-in-a-lifetime trip Mama should get too. She took me along.

It was a "Circle Tour" which began in Chicago and included a boat trip on the Great Lakes and rail travel along the Hudson River to New York City. We also visited Philadelphia, Boston, Niagara Falls, Montreal and Toronto. Mama wanted to meet all the relatives, and we visited Reeds, Owens, Williamses, Hadwens and Browns. In New York City we went out to Coney Island, joined by my Quaker cousin from Whittier, Catherine Williams, who was also visiting back East. We were strolling down the boardwalk by the beach when, to our great surprise, a gaudily dressed carnival barker came up to Katie and introduced himself. The folks had always talked about the trainloads of "New York orphans" shipped out to the Midwest in an earlier day. Uncle Aaron and Grandfather Williams each took a boy. After he grew up, the one at Grandma's went back East, and here he was, a barker at Coney Island. He and Katie had a good old gab fest and he gave us a tour of all the shows and rides, and so many souvenir stands and eating-places. We also heard our first radio—a public one with a loudspeaker outside a building.

I went back to Hunter in the fall to teach a second year. Again I saw a lot of Jim. He was very likable, a kind of leader in the community. When the Presbyterians had a membership drive, what did Jim do but go down and meet the trains when they came in. He'd approach the newcomers, talk sports with them—he knew batting averages going back twenty-five years—and after making friendships, bring them to church with him. His team won hands down. Jim had so much life to him, he could talk your arm off, was forever making jokes, and played the piano like nobody's business. Still, he was always tearing around with older fellows, six to eight years older than he was and some of them real roughnecks. I wasn't thrilled to pieces when I saw him several times with the wilder sort of girl, all rouge and wriggles and jingling bracelets. One of them, Jim said, he might have married if she hadn't talked so much. I think he was just teasing. And once while I was staying at the Critchfields' he'd come home hopelessly drunk, his knees and chest all covered with dust and straw and reeking of beer and cigar smoke. I liked quiet walks, poetry, reading, dancing. He liked fireworks, hunting, baseball, pounding on a piano, marching with a band, hats-in-the-air excitement. Jim rode a lot, and was an omnivorous reader, though not the classics or poetry. And he wasn't much of a churchgoer, not at all like my Dad.

At the end of two years, despite everything, I decided to return home to Iowa. I felt I'd had enough of North Dakota prairie life . . .

From a letter of recommendation, Hunter High School principal:
". . . She is splendidly equipped, uses a great deal of tact in the schoolroom and gets along well with the pupils . . . Miss Williams has a winning personality and splendid health . . . I feel I cannot be too emphatic in my praise . . ."

From Beatrice Carr Sayer, a former student in Hunter, sixty-one years later:
". . . One time, we were doing chalk work of autumn flowers and scenes and she was helping me. And she said, 'You'd rather be making pies and cakes, wouldn't you?' And I said, 'Yes, I would.' Was she stern? I'll say. You had to mind . . ."

Anna Louise:
I went back to school, this time at Upper Iowa again in Fayette. Here I met Forrest. He was everything Jim had not been. Tall, handsome, unathletic. We went to summer school and a romance blossomed. We might have settled down to a quiet, pleasant life in Fayette, where Forrest had been promised a very good job with the local bank. My story almost ended differently.

Forrest Claxton, though twice married and twice widowed, remained remarkably faithful. In a letter to Anne in September 1979, when they were both ninety-two and he was dying, he wrote:
"Ever since the days of Junior Society and on through that summer at Upper Iowa and to 1913 and beyond . . . I have loved you—always have —always will—so good-bye—I love you—Forrest."

From Peggy, younger daughter of Anna Louise, seventy-three years later:
". . . Mother talked more about Forrest than Beecher, because he stayed part of our lives. I can remember Forrest all during my childhood, because we'd go through Fayette on the bus coming and going to Iowa and we'd stop there and get out. And Forrest always met the bus. This tall, elegant, gray-

haired man. And this one time, just as I got off the bus, I threw up. I was always carsick about the time we got to Fayette. I was wearing a sunsuit, remember them? Gathered pants and a little bib top? Poor Forrest. Here's Mother's old beau and her little girl is carsick and vomiting . . ."

Jim

Further comment from Emil Moen, seventy-two years later:

". . . Jim farmed six or seven years, all the time he stayed out of medical school. As far as I know, he liked it. One time when Jim was on the farm he had us all out for a friendly poker game. Had a barrel of beer. The Critchfields were Presbyterians, but Jim wasn't much on church. They'd have beer parties after the baseball games and he'd get a little tight. In those days you could get beer at what we called a "blind pig." Right on Main Street between the livery barn and the lumberyard. It wasn't legal, but everybody looked the other way . . . Oh, I think Jim was well satisfied farming . . ."

Jim:

After Miss Williams went back home to Iowa for good, intending never to come back, I badly missed her. I'd grown so used to having her around. But I can't say I blamed her for deciding not to come back to Hunter to teach any more. We'd had plenty of good times together, wonderful times, but I had no prospects to offer her. Out on the farm, how could I support a wife like that? She was educated and refined, used to living in town, and other girls her age—she would be twenty-five in December—had many of them long ago married and had children. The farm was not very big, the land sandy and I could be "hailed out," "dried out," "blown out" or "starved out" at any time. I thought that if my life in Hunter could have been represented in a picture, all that was hard and rough—the heavy physical labor, shivering in winter, sweating in summer, the thistles, the mud, the wind, the loneliness—these would have been true, while my dreams of a life with Anna Louise Williams would have stood out from the whole as something false, as out of the drawing; and I thought, too, that it was too late to dream of such things, that everything was over for me, that it was impossible to go back to the kind of promising future I'd seen ahead when Father was alive. At twenty-one, my hopes of becoming a doctor were dead.

I expected to stay a farmer the rest of my life, and with grit and gumption and luck, hoped to make a go of it. Times were hard for the family. Farm prices were down. Mother rented rooms to the teachers and did what she could, but Father's death had been very hard on her. Since then, her hair had turned completely white and her health was poor. Ray was struggling to get his practice started up in the next little town of Galesburg. I guess he was doing okay. One time during a delivery he sterilized two strings just in case he dropped one on the floor. Out popped twins. Ray said his reputation was made after that.

Everything in North Dakota depended on wheat. The "Better Farming" people from the railroads and the Agricultural College professors in Fargo urged diversified farming. What they were really talking about was the dairy cow. I figured that was fine in a humid, densely populated state like Iowa; North Dakota was too empty and too dry. The experts advocated many good things—better seed, summer fallow, crop rotation—but when it came to dairy cattle, I stuck with wheat.

I'd soon found nothing protects a farmer from changes in prices. In the old days, when a man lived in a sod hut and plowed up virgin soil, he worried about prairie fires and Sioux on the warpath. Now he worried about money. We were stuck with a grain market in Minneapolis run by millers and elevator companies and railroads. Farming was already a high-risk, low-profit enterprise, and these businessmen naturally liked to pass their losses on to the farmer. "It's just a goldarn highway robbery from start to finish," you'd hear some old-timer say. We wanted our own terminal elevators in St. Paul. But until we got them, farmers would go on plowing their land and trying to get a wheat crop out of it. The elevators and railroads still ran the Dakota farmer.

Weather was the other worry. North Dakota averaged just seventeen inches of rainfall a year. It was so dry that just about all that saved the wheat crop, aside from the coldest climate in all forty-eight states, was that three fourths of the rain fell during the wheat-growing season, most of it in thundershowers. Even an inch or two at the right moment could make the difference between crop failure and a bumper harvest. The extremes of temperature could be so great that the year Miss Williams left—1912—it went up to 124 degrees Fahrenheit and dropped to 52 below—think of that. Sometimes the prairie wind got to be just like a living presence; it could blow tumbleweed as fast as a horse could gallop, rolling it over and over.

There is nothing so forlorn as a lone tumbleweed blowing across an empty prairie.

The worst was a dry winter when you had light snow and blowing dirt combined; then you came in from chores looking like Rastus in a minstrel show. Except in a wet blizzard, the snow wasn't often deep; our precipitation was too low. In winter the fields were white but swept almost bare, with big drifts on the lee side of barns and houses, shelterbelts and fences. A summer day in Hunter could be beautiful or a hell of blasting wind—the "hot southerly"—blowing dust and sweltering heat. But it was the northern winter, with its endless months of short days and bitterly cold weather, that made farm life what it was. Some said you didn't feel it so much, because it was a dry cold, or that it killed off germs. People did seem healthier on the prairie.

But the snow, the unchanging blackness and whiteness of it, the bitter cold, the ceaseless wind—it could give you a really bad case of "cabin fever" if you let it. Father used to tell about finding patients in remote farmhouses, most of them women, who'd made themselves ill with depression and loneliness over the long winter. All the early settlers had tales of women on isolated homesteads going mad. Even our farm, just a half mile south and two miles west of Hunter, could get pretty lonely. In the dead of night the sound of a coyote—three short yelps and a long howling wail—can be just about the most desolate sound there is.

"Batching it" at the farm, either alone or with Harry, I got so I didn't take much notice of the landscape. Then, maybe riding home from town some evening, after a beer or two and feeling in good spirits, all of a sudden I'd be struck by the sky, maybe filled with row after row of great big cumulus clouds, just going on and on, such as you commonly get in the big northern sky. Or if it was dusty enough, one of those blood-red prairie sunsets. And always that feeling of space, so much horizon, so much empty prairie. At unexpected moments in North Dakota, nature just sort of seized you in its grip and made you gasp at its splendor; even the heavens seemed new.

To go back to 1911, I was farming the half section we'd bought from the Denhams five years before. One time, I discovered in the county clerk's plat book that Father had owned the whole section next to it in 1890. I was surprised; it was the first I'd heard of it. I reckoned he must have sold it to get the money to build the big Hunter house and barn. The Denhams had been the land's original settlers, and their simple white frame house had a parlor, dining room and kitchen below and three small bedrooms upstairs. No basement; they'd just laid two-by-twelves flat on the ground. Every stud and beam was hickory, shipped in by rail from Minnesota. The barn was old and painted red and there was no silo or anything, just a lot of rusted old farm implements lying about. They'd planted a few cottonwoods and box elders, but there was no windbreak at all. So the first thing we'd done after we bought the place in 1905 was to bring four hundred willow cuttings from our orchard in town and plant them in two rows west of the homestead. Within five years they were already starting to become big, lofty trees. There was an artesian well with brackish water by the windmill. It was all right to fill the cattle tank, but I put in a new, fifteen-foot well and hand pump, the kind you had to prime, for us to use. The water had plenty of minerals in it, but it tasted good.

Sometimes Harry, who helped me out a lot, and I made a little home brew, while keeping one eye peeled for the sheriff. What you did, you took half a bushel of barley or wheat and mixed it with an equal amount of water. Then you added your cakes of yeast and let her spin. It bubbled up and made a froth on top. When it quieted down, you knew that was all you were going to get out of it. But it packed a wallop.

We had a regular blizzard my first March, but in April we got warm days, if freezing nights, and the muddy fields were flooded with water from melted snow. Flocks of wild ducks settled everywhere. I'd get up at five to plow, splashing some water on my face in the kitchen basin and drying on a roller towel. I just shaved if I went to town, which I did a good deal until Miss Williams went home to Iowa. After washing and a drink from the dipper, I'd go down to the barn to clean out the stalls and drop fresh hay from the mow for the horses and fill their water buckets and give them oats. Then I'd pitch hay to the cows and milk every last one of them.

That first spring, after a good breakfast, I'd hitch four horses to one plow and Harry three to another and we'd head out to the fields. My pride were two pairs of dappled gray Percherons, perfectly matched. Harry was always anxious to be at work by seven o'clock. Latecomers took a lot of razzing from the neighbors. In 1911 Harry was just sixteen, but he worked as hard as any man. Burke came up from Fargo sometimes, but he didn't do much but stand around and get his two cents in. If he got too bossy, I'd have to tell him off: "To hell with that, Burke! *You* go do it."

All morning, I'd go back and forth across a field, riding on a steel seat behind sixteen plodding hooves. When it turned too hot, I'd rest the Percherons every other mile, trying to do ten miles in the morning and ten in the afternoon. Five acres was a good day's work with a gang plow.

Sometimes a big thistle caught, plugging up the plow with clods of dirt; it was a job cleaning it out. One time, I had an Indian boy working with me who'd played football with Jim Thorpe; he was so strong he could tip the plow to one side and hold it there with one hand while he cleaned the blade off with the other. Then he'd be on his way again. I couldn't do it. Some of those Russian thistles weighed damn near as much as I did. The stickers pierced right through your overalls. The blacker soil on the other side of town plugged up even faster. We'd say, "You've got twenty minutes to plow that gumbo."

At noon we unhitched the horses, just taking off the bridles, putting them in a stall and watering and feeding them before we ate. At night we did the same thing, only the harnesses came off too. Sometimes we'd turn the horses loose in the pasture overnight; they liked to run. So did I. After chores were done, I'd often ride into Hunter to bowl or play baseball or basketball or go to band practice. When school was on and Miss Williams was still there, I always played piano for the Friday Night Club. That second summer I farmed—1912—she wrote that she was going to summer school and planned to stay on in Iowa and continue at college in the fall. I wrote back and told her she'd be missed. I couldn't imagine what life in Hunter was going to be like without her.

In the meantime, I worked hard. We plowed. We harrowed to make the land level enough for planting, using a four-horse seeder for wheat, barley and oats. So it went, day in and day out, seven days a week. All the time, the cows had to be milked morning and night, the eggs gathered, the cream separated. That was another big job. At home we'd just put the milk in bowls and skim the cream off the top with a ladle. Out on the farm we used a separator, which meant Harry or I washed it every night, all thirty-two discs, the two spouts and all the floats and fillings. Each morning, we'd put it back together and start turning the separator's hand crank—sixty revolutions per minute. It whirred until a bell rang it was ready and we'd turn the valve and let the milk flow from the bowl into the float. After we'd run it all through, we'd pour the warm cream into a can and tag it to take into town. Then we'd lower the cream and the five-gallon tin milk cans into the well to keep them cool. Cream, like eggs and butter, which we churned once a week, was our main source of cash income. A farmer, of course, needed a wife and family . . .

From an interview with Rose Rasmussen of Hunter, a farmer's widow in her eighties, June 1982:

". . . We grew wheat and barley, flax, corn and oats. We milked cows and sold the cream. Separated the milk twice a day, morning and night. He'd come in from the field and help milk and we did the same thing, morning and night. We never could go anyplace. We had to come home early, you know. Do the chores. I suppose it'd take a half an hour to separate the cream. To get all that done. It wasn't so hard. Of course, every day that separator had to be taken apart and washed. I don't know. I washed clothes by hand those first years, rubbed on a washboard.

"I used to raise chickens and then we'd set a hen on some eggs and hatch out the chickens. That was a big chore, you know, watching all those setting hens. Raising those little chicks, all that. All summer long, you know. As soon as the kids were five, six years old they could have chores to do. Little chores. I don't know if it was a case of want to; they *had* to help. We had three boys, you see. The oldest boy, he didn't stay home so long. He went down to his uncle's in Minnesota and worked in the packing plant. He wasn't home much. Then Jerome, he got away too. He went into the Army. It was the youngest one, Harold, that really farmed. He took to it more and helped his dad. After sixteen, Harold could have farmed by himself. He could. He took more to it.

"In the winter we had to use horses lots of the time. When the roads were so full of snow. We haven't had that kind of deep snow for many years, you know. We had a kind of old sled with runners on it, and we'd hitch the horses to it. One year, Dad bought a buggy with a top on, a regular buggy, and we got a horse from Mr. Collins, and the boys drove themselves to Hunter to school. One day they came home, just before Christmas and terribly cold, and they were both sick with measles, mind you. Here they drove home from town, both sick and three miles in the cold weather—I've thought of that lots of times. We never had the doctor. They had measles and you put 'em in bed and kept 'em warm and they stayed home for a few days and they were all right.

"I was never afraid of snow or loneliness on the farm. We knew how to cope with it, you know. When I was a kid, we danced all the time. We'd go to a farmer's house and dance. I danced ever since I was ten years old. In Hunter I wasn't allowed to go to the Friday Night Club. Those were the higher set, you know. I stayed pretty well at home . . ."

Jim:

Out west of town there was a stretch of virgin prairie that belonged to the school; everybody called it Hayland. For a small fee you could go out and make hay there. So when the time came, we took our mower and rack out.

Hay had to be mowed, raked and turned over once, then loaded on the rack and hauled back to the farm to be cured and stacked, some in the barn loft and the rest in the fields to be winter fodder. Harry drove the team while I worked on the back of the hayrack, pitching it onto a high pile. Alfalfa wasn't so bad, but the wild prairie hay was slippery. Back at the farm, Harry would go up in the loft while I forked it up to him. It was a tough job for Harry, keeping out of the way of the tines of my pitchfork, sweating in the heat and choking in that sweet pungent smell and all the dust and chaff. But he never complained. Harry was good-natured and we had a lot of fun while we worked, racing when we hoed potatoes or picked corn to see who was the fastest. With the corn, we stacked it in shocks and gave it time to cure before chopping it into silage.

I was getting concerned about Harry. He'd managed to finish his junior year of high school, but only by going just eighty-five days. Even on days when he was in school he helped with the chores. I didn't know how I could manage without him. Even so, I was relieved when he got a chance to enroll in the Agricultural College in Fargo the fall of 1912. What happened was that Harry grew some Early Ohio seed potatoes on a ten-acre plot I set aside for him and he was able to sell a carload of them—six hundred bushels—to the college. The professor who made the sale was so impressed he invited Harry to come down and earn credit for both his senior year of high school and his freshman year of college at the same time. It got Harry off to a flying start, though he kept coming back to work on the farm so much it was going to take him twelve years to earn his bachelor's degree. Aside from myself, Harry was the only one in the family who really took to farming. Mac, his twin, had won a music scholarship to the university in Grand Forks; though Mac was a long-distance runner, and ran many miles a day around town, he hardly ever came out to the farm.

The wheat harvest began in August. In North Dakota it was a gigantic task, with the fields gradually turning into a great sea of shocks curing in the sun, and later large numbers of horses and men coming in with the threshing rigs. With wheat, you cut it, shocked it into bundles, pitched the bundles on a hayrack and took them to a threshing machine. When the wheat was ripe, I'd oil our old reaper-binder, put on a new ball of twine and trundle it out to the corner of the field we'd planted first. Then I'd lower the blade and start cutting swaths. The blade would slice the dry stems and rotating wooden wings sweep up the wheat as the spool of twine turned and tied up the bundles. The team drew the binder counterclockwise around a steadily smaller field of uncut wheat. We shocked by hand, Harry and I, going up the rows of bundles, taking a couple at a time, stacking twelve to fifteen into a

THE NORTH DAKOTA BOY

shock, all sloped upward to stay upright and with the grain heads on top to dry in the sun. I was always glad to get it done. As long as the wheat was ripe and standing, rain or hail or a high wind could knock it over and break the heads off.

John Wergin, a neighbor, always brought his threshing machine, a thirty-eight-inch separator, as well as a separator man, fireman and engineer, all Hunter people who went home at night. It took eight horse-drawn wagons to keep Wergin's rig supplied with bundles. Harry and I hauled the threshed grain into the elevator. There were a few itinerant workers, but most of Wergin's crew were local boys with their own teams and wagons. Threshing was a big undertaking; it could last until snowfall, and it needed strong arms and backs. But once you got going, it went fast. The bundle pitchers had to work steadily, going to and from the shocked fields in their wagons, to keep the rig's chute full. Chaff blew in the air, and the straw blasted out in dusty clouds and settled into a big, light-colored stack. A stream of grain poured down to make a brownish-yellowish cone on the wooden floor of the grain hauler's wagon. Most crews threshed by the bushel if the crop was good, by the hour if it was poor.

The big worry hauling grain was that the road might get so muddy the wheels would sink in and get stuck. On a rainy day it was common to see five or six men, all rolling on the wheels, pushing some wagon, trying to get it going again. That and runaways, when you'd have to run like hell after your frightened horses. Once the cold weather set in, if a team heard the wheels rattling on the frozen ground, they could get skittish. If you were still threshing, those were the long days, starting and ending in the dark, and if it was snowing, getting the tiny, hard, stinging flakes in your face. I can't think of a rougher ride than in an empty grain wagon on frozen ground, nor any place colder than inside a bin shoveling grain when it's below zero.

Once threshing was over, I turned the cattle, hogs and sheep out to graze in the stubble fields. I usually left them out by themselves until it got too snowy. As soon as the horses' coats got thick and brushy, I'd let them run loose too. Running free in groups, especially on days when fog shrouded the snow-covered fields, those horses were a sight to see.

That winter, the lumberyard downtown got in a shipment of eight Model T's. The tops, fenders and running boards weren't assembled yet; they were all piled in the center of a boxcar. Henry Ford advertised they came "in any color you choose as long as it's black." Ford was saying that the market for such low-priced cars was "unlimited" and that a light-weight tractor was going to replace workhorses. A Ford wasn't fancy enough for Burke. He bought an EMF—Every Morning Fixit, Harry and I called it. It was a light blue roadster and came equipped with pneumatic tires, isinglass curtains and Prest-O-Lites—you lit them with a match and they would only shine about fifteen feet out front. That EMF was a snazzy car, though, with brass head lamps in front of the radiator and brass side lamps over the fenders. Tufted upholstery, a red dashboard and spare tire behind. There was a white canvas top and side curtains in case of rain. Burke was so proud of it he fretted like an old hen. He was forever stopping to feel the hubs of the wheels and the differential to see if they were getting hot.

Ray had bought the first car in our family, a Reo, the year before. A one-lunged Reo, Ray called it. It had a crank on the side and a chain drive to the axel. Everybody was getting the automobile craze. Our trouble was that all we had were dirt roads. In gumbo, if it got wet and muddy, the cars would bottom up. The wheels would clog and stop turning. You'd have to stop and jack it up to get it going again. A Model T had close to a two-foot clearance underneath, but even it couldn't match a buggy's narrower wheels and no fender when it came to mud. So, come October, up went all the cars on blocks and the fluid got drained out of their radiators. Then it was back to buggies and bobsleds like the rest of us until the roads thawed and dried out in the spring. Even in the summer, those early tires were bad and got an awful lot of punctures. Out on the farm, I stuck with horses.

Anne and Jim

Anna Louise:

On the next presidential election day, I found myself back in North Dakota, this time in Casselton with a brand-new job. Banners and signs for
Theodore Roosevelt were all over, with a few for Woodrow Wilson, too.
There was already a fall chill and the days were shortening into winter. I
was to teach fourth grade. The people of Casselton were an even rougher
bunch than my first days in Hunter. Such devils, I thought of my students.
They're terrors to snakes. I met the superintendent, a grave man who
handed me a rubber hose. I was aghast. But, the first day of school, I licked
three boys with it. Some got drunk, others used "snoose." Casselton was
plainly a tough railroad town.

I'd been enrolled as a sophomore at Upper Iowa and thought I was
perfectly content. I'd gone to classes for two months and was seeing a lot of
Forrest. One day, a telegram came from Andrew Love; there was an unexpected opening in Casselton; did I want it? Reading it, the yellowish strips
of paper pasted on the telegraph blank blurred; I had tears in my eyes. I
didn't think twice. I cabled him yes and caught the first train.

Soon discipline was less of a problem. Much was demanded of my pupils
—most had chores before and after school—and these little prairie towns
were bleak. Small towns in Iowa, too, owed their existence to the railroad,
but most had come into being by the Civil War and their shade trees had
had time to grow; it made the towns look older. The Casselton park had just
a few elms, cottonwoods and box elders, but after the prairie it was like a
woods. That fall, even on rainy days, I took my classes there for walks; how
the children would squeal when the trees, stirred by gusts of wind, dropped

sudden showers down. I'd say, "Let's see if we can find some crunchy leaves to walk through." Or I'd ask, "Did you hear that sound? What's that?"

"The wind." "Blowing the leaves."

"Now look all around, above, over your heads." I'd drop my voice. "Don't say anything. But if you see one fall, raise your hand. I haven't seen one fall. Listen . . ." Wide-eyed and holding their breaths, the children would turn their heads up, looking this way and that, until another gust of wind shook a black branch, dripping rain, and a whole cascade of yellow leaves came fluttering down and we gathered them up to take back to school. The prairie had a kindlier look about it this time; I had no desire to dream, homesick, of Iowa.

I wrote Mrs. Critchfield I was in Casselton and she invited me to Hunter to spend Thanksgiving. By then there was frost, the branches were bare and the first snow had fallen. In Hunter, people were using their bobsleds and it was good to see the familiar flat white land with its snowdrifts and smoke rising from its chimneys. I felt scared and shy to see Jim, and when he came to pick me up at the depot I stood rigid, blushing and going pale by turns. Then I saw the beaming smile on his face and, except for the moist film that came over my eyes, was able to greet him quite calmly, "What a long time it has been!" We sat side by side at the dinner, with its steaming turkey on a silver platter, the best glass and china, white damask tablecloth, fruit center-piece, and all the trimmings, hardly taking part in the general family con-versation. After washing up, in the late afternoon we went for a walk. It was clear and frosty. The snow lay deep on the ground, and on the path it crunched under our feet. Icicles hung from the gutters of the houses, and the wooden fence posts were capped with ice. In the orchard, the snow lay much deeper in drifts, and Jim remarked that the fruit trees had been just as old and gnarled when he had been a child and his father was alive; the orchard had changed hardly at all. We turned into Beard's pasture and followed the tracks of sleighs down the road that led to the old swimming hole, now a pure-white expanse of snow. Here, too, every corner seemed to recall the faraway past to Jim, when life had seemed very good. In his boyhood, he said, the winter sun looked the same through these sparse trees, hoarfrost on their leafless branches. I felt so happy and so confused by my feelings; hearing him talk so sadly and seeing how much weight he'd lost in farming, I also thought I might break down and burst into tears. For a time we followed the traces of the runners in the snow without speaking.

"You've grown thinner, Jim. Have you been ill?"

"No. Just trying to make a go of it on the farm."

"You look worn out. It makes you look older."

From Jim:

The steady and serious gaze of those wonderful brown eyes, her voice, her step, her smile that was like a gift, showed me how much had gone out of my life, had been badly missed, and now quite unexpectedly had come back into it again. We would talk for a long time, and for a long time surrender to silences, each thinking his own thoughts. At last, overwhelmed by her shy, happy smile and her radiant eyes, I suddenly embraced her and kissed her on the lips. She responded, then, cautious, she looked around—had anybody seen us? Beard's pasture was empty; not a soul but ourselves. I felt dazed with happiness, and when we got back to the house, where I played for her on the piano, I kept looking up at her lovely eyes. She looked at me with a smile that never wavered.

I rode over to see her in Casselton two weeks later. Mother invited her to spend Christmas with us instead of going home to her family in Iowa. After that, every weekend I rode my horse down to Casselton or she came up to Hunter by train.

One Sunday in early March we drove out to the farm in my horse cart. There had been a spell of good weather and the road was dry and the sun was warm for the time of year. Only a patch of slush or mud or gray heaps of dirty snow in the windbreaks were reminders winter wasn't over yet. Anne was wearing her light gray dress, a shawl and a straw hat. I was depressed. I had nothing to offer her and felt a sense of terror that she might leave my life again. Would I be left alone—without her? Sitting beside her in the cart I could see nothing of attraction in the flocks of blackbirds flying over puddles—puddles from melted snow as large as lakes—you always had blackbirds flocking in every spring to feed on your grain. Geese, too, were settling, seeking roots and insects in the stubble fields and freshly turned earth. To me there was nothing to hold her in the whole desolate scene toward which the horses' heads plunged so dumbly.

For two years I'd been a farmer, and during the course of these two years I'd been over this road a thousand times: to haul grain, fetch supplies, market cream and eggs, go to the blacksmith, the harness shop, the livery barn, the lumberyard, so that the times of jolting along in these same old ruts were past counting. And whether it was spring, as it seemed to promise that day, or a rainy fall afternoon, or winter, it had all become the same to me, and I always longed for just one thing: to get where I was going as quickly as possible. But where was I going? Nowhere. Nothing was ahead of me but a future of long, cold, winter prairie nights and long, hot, summer days, some of them terribly long.

I told Anne how I'd given up the idea of ever going back to medical school. Mother wasn't well. The twins were still in high school and there was little Kay to look after. Somehow, farming, I could never get ahead. When I started out I had hopes of getting the farm finally all paid for. But as soon as I'd get some stock or machinery in the clear, I'd go in debt for something else. Anne just listened, hugging her knees to keep her skirts from blowing. I told her all my troubles. Somehow it all just poured out, unstoppable. Maybe I'd held it up inside me too long. How it sometimes seemed like I didn't leave a single clod in the whole three hundred and twenty acres unturned. Except for Harry's help, I plowed, sowed and reaped it all myself. I felt I could plow a straight furrow, break a horse, cut hay, drive a team, shuck corn, slop hogs, handle an ax, scythe weeds, or build a crib as well as the next man. Yet hail, wind and unexpected weather, falls in market prices, one damn thing after another, kept me from getting a foot-hold. My body ached, I'd started falling asleep sitting up, but I saw no way out. Oats were bringing just thirty-two cents a bushel, potatoes sixty, barley around forty, wheat less than a dollar. A farmer had to take what he was offered. I couldn't afford to even think of getting married. God knows if I could ever afford it. I was happy enough with the physical side of farm work. I liked using my hands. I just couldn't make it pay. I was trapped, my life futile.

Anne just kept listening, not saying a word, but gazing at me seriously with her truthful eyes. I kept right on talking, slowing the pace of the horses. Here, I told her, I found myself beside a young woman such as I'd never known before. Over these past few months she'd become Anne to me, not Miss Anna Louise Williams, the prim Iowa schoolteacher who'd boarded at my mother's, but my own Anne, a being that was closer to me than anybody I'd ever known or ever would know. A silence followed. Anne's eyes shone with a soft light, and looking into them, I felt a growing tension of happiness, for in her eyes I saw all that I needed to know.

Anne:

I walked into the Casselton principal's office. He smiled and said, "I'm happy to tell you, Louise, that you've been reappointed with a raise in salary for next year."

"I'm not coming back. I came to tell you I'm leaving the first of April."

"But, Louise, you've done so well. You've tamed the lions."

"I'm getting married."

Further comments from Merland Carr, seventy years later:

"Jim was clean-shaven and slender in those days. Perhaps a bit chunkier and broader-shouldered than the other boys. He was a good athlete and a good mixer . . . Anne was a fine-looking lady. I remember that. And very sincere in her work . . . I think she got stronger as she was here, you know. I first noticed it when they were out at the farm . . ."

From a taped interview with Kathryn Garrett, former Hunter housewife now in her eighties:

"Anne was just a lovely person, the kind that can accept anything. If she didn't like something, she didn't show it, that's for sure. We all thought she and Jim were a happy couple, exemplary. You wanted your own marriage to be like that. Later on, we felt so sorry for them . . ."

From a taped interview with Sarah W., an Iowa relative:

". . . How many years was it this spring that they were married? Seventy years, wasn't it? Well, now, I'll tell you. For seventy years I have had the superiority of that family rammed down my throat. From *all* of them. Louie became a Critchfield when she married him . . . And I have never been able to understand it. Our people weren't ragged immigrants when they came out here from New York. I have silverware and linen tablecloths that are a hundred and thirty, a hundred and forty years old. They *had* things . . ."

Anne:

After our wedding and we came back to North Dakota, I knew from the start it would not be easy. It was never going to be. Life is only given to us once and I wanted to live it boldly. In those early days out on the farm, Jim was always trying to make things easier for me. I'd come down to make breakfast and find him and Harry swallowing the last of their coffee, standing, caps on, in the yellow lamplight, as the spring wind softly fluttered the curtains at the open windows. They'd be out to harness the horses by sunrise. After that, Jim milked. He said it was not a proper job for a woman.

Harry soon left for college, though he was to spend much time with us at the farm. At seventeen, he was at that awkward age, all's Adam's apple, red cheeks and chin, unruly black hair. He was cheerful company, eager to help gather eggs or hitch up the horses, and was forever getting all excited about schemes to make a killing in hogs or sheep or potatoes. Mac, his twin, was as much of a loner as Harry was gregarious, as blond as he was dark. Mac liked to run miles and miles along the country roads. Though all the Critchfields sang and played the piano, he was the best musician. Mother Critchfield came out to the farm a lot, once I was there, but in spite of her many years in Hunter she was still a city woman, who fussed about with her hats, gloves and scent. Once, out in the barn when a ewe was bleating while giving birth, she said, "I didn't know animals had trouble like that." Harry said, "Mom, how do you figure they'd do it, then? They have to push 'em out the same as people do." Many times, she brought little Kay, a real sweetie, out with her.

From Jim's sister, Kathryn:

". . . I never lived out on the farm with them, but I loved to visit. Even when I was just a little girl, I used to go out and butt into everything they did. If they went for a ride, I had to be right in the middle. One time, Anne's mother came from Iowa, Jessie Williams. Do you know what a dowager is? Oh, I don't mean she was at heart. She dressed that way, erect and ladylike, with long skirts . . . Out on the farm, I can remember being on the hay-rack and riding along, but I never did anything. Jim and Harry worked awfully hard and sort of associated more with farm people. I always thought Jim and I were alike. We got along the best. I just loved him. Oh, Burke always saw to it that Mother had some money. I've got to hand that to him . . ."

Anne:

I soon learned to do the housekeeping in no time flat so I could spend the time outdoors caring for the chickens, pigs and a big garden. The house had been neglected, and a dripping faucet, a kitchen drawer that stuck and a chair with a cracked seat that pinched all needed to be put to rights. I got new shades for the kerosene lamps, cleaned out the rain barrel and replaced the old kitchen calendar with a 1913 one. Jim emptied the shed off the kitchen and we moved the churn and the washtub and boiler out there, and I cleaned the woodbox, filling it with logs and kindling, scrubbed the sink and hung the carpets out on the clothesline, taking the rugbeater to them.

The worn, grassless farmyard, with rusted old machinery standing about, and quack grass and dandelions everywhere, was soon transformed by a green lawn and flowerbeds. But the dingy old-fashioned farmhouse, no matter what I did, seemed to keep its grubby air; burning lignite left a lot of grit. I wallpapered the rooms and laid down new linoleum and covered the overstuffed chairs with cretonne slipcovers and crocheted white lace antimacassars. We bought a secondhand piano for Jim, and I made rag rugs to cover up the worn places in the parlor carpet. I hand-painted a china water pitcher and some vases with pale yellow and pink roses. In the parlor I hung a pastel I'd done years before in Hardin to illustrate Gray's "Elegy Written in a Country Church-Yard." ". . . The lowing herd wind slowly o'er the lea . . ." I'd copied it from a calendar and it was brown and misty with cattle going home in the moonlight. Somehow my pale yellow moon wasn't quite round; for years it never failed to disquiet anybody who looked at it long enough. They'd say, "Isn't there something wrong with that moon?" I ordered a gilt frame from the Sears catalogue for it.

At milking time, as Jim went back and forth from the barn to the milk house, buckets of white froth in hand, I'd help separate the cream. I also churned butter, gathered eggs and tended the chickens, some of them newly hatched and all yellow fluff. I was forever hauling manure in a wheelbarrow to my garden. By early summer I was able to pull new carrots and green onions and radishes and string beans; later on we had peas, cucumbers, dill, spinach, beets, potatoes, sweet corn, turnips, squash, lettuce, cabbage and pumpkins. My pride were my tomatoes, first planted in a seed flat and then put out, tied to pieces of lath, weeded, and given plenty of water. That first year on the farm, I canned close to three hundred quarts of vegetables and fruit, meat, jellies and jams.

So the summer went. Twice a day, at dinner and supper, I spread the oilcloth on the kitchen table with solid, rib-sticking meals: roasts of pork or beef, fried chicken, a steaming bowl of gravy, lettuce salad, hot buttered rolls, green peas, new potatoes, roasting ears, strawberry shortcake, rhubarb and blueberry pies, devil's food cake with chocolate frosting . . . And every meal began with grace. I'd bow my head, saying in a firm voice, "God is good and God is great. We thank You for our food. Amen." Jim joined in, not always too audibly.

He respected my religious views but never shared them. Sundays, to please me he'd put on his best suit and drive me in to church. We took our Saturday-night baths in a big tub in the shed off the kitchen after heating several pails of hot water on the stove. You stood in it and poured warm soapy water over your shoulders. Driving in on Sunday mornings, as I sat high up on the buggy seat all powdered, perfumed and corseted, I could tell from the way Jim snapped the reins that it had been worth all the trouble. He enjoyed the sociability of it all.

If anything was needed from town, Jim usually rode in, coming back with a tow sack full of supplies behind the saddle. Sometimes I could smell liquor on his breath. But I was determined not to be conquered by my father's misgivings. It was just a weakness for a dram too much now and then. Only once, about three months after our wedding, did Jim come home really swaying from side to side. He went straight into the bedroom, ashamed, and without undressing fell on the bed, rolled over, and in a minute was snoring. I slept on the couch. In the morning, he was penitent and seemed so nauseated, I thought he had been punished enough. I felt like sticking up for him to Papa more than ever. Why, a man like Jim sometimes needed to stop for a drink with his old companions; that much was plain.

And so that first summer passed. The long days of mowing and haying and threshing, but ball games and band concerts and dances, too. In June, prairie roses blossomed on the edges of the fields; in August, they were gone and there was yellow mustard and the whitened plumes of goldenrod gone to seed. It went too fast, and the afternoons came when, if it was as hot as ever in the sun, the shade seemed cool, the nights downright chilly. The hay was put in the mow and stacks, the harvest came and went, the hogs were butchered and Jim cured ham and bacon in the smokehouse, and in the storeroom the shelves were stocked with canned goods, salt pork, sausage and lard; nuts were drying on the henhouse roof and Jim said that when he saw the ripening pumpkins, all he could think of was pie. When he went around the farm now, his boots clumping in the beaten dust, or heavy with clay and mud, wearing a thick woolen sweater I'd knitted him myself, I could hear him whistling, a distinctly satisfied sound. Soon the sky was leaden, and V-shaped wedges of geese flew south day after day, the air smelled of dust and drying leaves, and by November the ground was hard and you could hear the hoofbeats of horses on bare frozen ground. We put on storm windows, dug potatoes, laid in a coal supply and banked around the house's foundation with dirt and hay bales. Jim said that now that winter was coming and the field work had eased up, he thought he'd start playing basketball with the Hunter home team.

One evening, as I was getting ready to bake pies and was kneading and folding the dough on my flour-sprinkled breadboard, Jim came in from the barn and washed up in the kitchen basin, drying on a roller towel and combing his wet, slicked-back hair in the cupboard mirror. Then, his collar wet, he sat down to clean his shotgun, clicking the hammer and squinting down the barrel. When he finished, I gave him some coffee and he sat looking at the funny papers. He read aloud about the Katzenjammer Kids. Hans and Fritz were lighting a cannon cracker under the Captain's chair. Jim turned to the *Herald*'s editorial, reading, with a grin, "The woman at the washtub is a much better asset for the country than the painted society lady who struts and swaggers in a feminine way . . . ." Jim thought it was funny. "You just wait until we get the vote," I told him. "You'll see."

What a "woman at the washtub" I'd become! Carrying all that water from the well, unless I could catch enough rain in a barrel with moss on the inside. Jim had seen me all perspiring, my hair damp with steam, stirring the clothes in the big copper boiler, scrubbing with a washboard out in the shed. For months I hadn't been anywhere to shop, only to Hunter. Even then it was easier just to mail in an order to Sears, Roebuck or Ward's. With Harry gone, we could hardly ever leave the farm, since there was nobody to do the chores or look after the stock. I sliced off the dough and kneaded it into the shape of a pie, a good deal more vigorously than I needed. Paderewski was coming to Fargo. Why not take the train in, go to the concert and do some shopping? High time I was a painted society lady. Jim look chagrined when I told him my idea as I filled another pan, punched down the dough, wiped my floury hands on my apron and began to slice some apples.

He brightened as soon as the pies were in the oven and he could smell them baking. "How are they coming?" he kept asking. "Hold your horses," I'd say. "They're just beginning to brown." He loved hot apple pie.

When I got back, Jim was waiting for me at the depot. When I saw his stubbled chin, the bits of straw on his earflaps, the mud on his boots and his tired face, I felt a little guilty about my holiday. Back home, in time to help with the chores and with my apron on again, as I rinsed the supper dishes— I'd cooked a roast—I told him of my impressions in Fargo: about the Waldorf Hotel, where I'd stayed, getting about on the electric trolley lines, how crowded and hot the Orpheum vaudeville theater had been, my seat on the aisle in the fourteenth row, what pieces of Tchaikovsky, Chopin and Beethoven were played, and how the audience applauded Paderewski and shouted encore. It seemed far away as I poured boiling water over the stacked dishes and pans in a hiss of steam. I'd gone into the Stone Music Store to see how much a Victrola would cost. I wanted Jim to hear Paderewski, too. His music had risen to a feeling so lofty, so far beyond the reach of our little world of furrows to be plowed, stock to be tended, chores to be done, meals to be cooked and frustrated hopes to be overcome.

Anne

Entry by Jessie in the family journal, New Year's Day, 1914:

"Once again I will write in this old book. I see it is a good many years since I have written anything. Life has been so busy we never found time to write it down. April 19 Louie was married to Ralph James Critchfield, who is farming, and went to Hunter, North Dakota, to live. That was the first break in our family. Two weeks later, Hadwen, Jr., sailed for the Philippine Islands to work for the Govt. teaching for two years. Two weeks from that day, Mary was taken sick with peritonitis and for days her life hung in the balance with little hope of recovery . . . Now she is almost well, plump and rosy . . . After Conference, we moved here to Plymouth.

"The day after Christmas, Louie came home for a visit and now, this first night of 1914, we are all here except our boy . . . We are beginning to feel we are not as young as we used to be. Hadwen still looks quite young and handsome, but I—I am wrinkled, gray, 'sans eyes, sans hair, sans teeth, sans everything.' But thankful after this hard year that we are in as good a shape as we are."

Extracts from letters home by Hadwen, Jr., journeying to the Philippines; this one, dated June 1913, is postmarked aboard the S. S. Governor Forbes:

"This is the fortieth day since I left home . . . At Frisco we were at the Saint Francis Hotel for two days. Big automobiles, beautiful women, plenty of booze and steep hills. There's nothing slow about San Francisco—not even the horse cart that runs down to the ferry . . . Twenty hours at Honolulu. Saw a precipice from which King Kamehameha once drove 700 Natives by cannon fire to death below . . .

"Japan is very thickly populated, beautiful and odorous—very . . . We took in Kyoto and Kamakura with its temple and bronze Daibutsu, fifty-three feet high and the largest Buddha in Japan; and Fujiyama, the sacred mountain (which appears on so many Japanese fans) up to the snow line, a trip of two days walking and on horseback among Natives who couldn't speak a word of English . . . Two days through the Inland Sea, and then Nagasaki, a fortified post, where no Kodaks could be taken ashore, and about 20 Japanese soldiers were aboard all the time to see that the order was enforced. As soon as the whistle blew for departure, and the little brown soldiers got aboard their steam launches, more Kodaks were visible than before, and nearly everyone got a picture of the forts and soldiers drilling as we passed down the Bay. Everyone out here is talking war with Japan. Uncle Sam has an extra-large amount of supplies and ammunition at Corregidor, the fort at the entrance of Manila Bay . . .

"In China we anchored at the mouth of the Yangtze River at Woosung and took a tender up the river to Shanghai. A few days before, pirates captured a French boat about 100 miles up the river and sixty thousand Mexican silver dollars were taken. Pirates captured another ship a few hours out in the China Sea and took all the treasure aboard and set fire to the ship. Two hundred Chinese passengers drowned or burned to death . . . I notice the pirates don't touch any English ships. For a warship would probably go out and blow them to pieces . . . We were two days in Hong Kong, ordered white suits and sun helmets, rode in sedan chairs and left on the King's birthday. The English flag looked mighty good . . .

Mailed from Bacolod, Philippines, April 1914:

". . . War at last! So the papers say that I saw at the Club tonight. I hope the United States gives Mexico a good drubbing and annexes a few North Mexico states . . . There are too many Countries that snap their fingers at Americans. I believe in Teddy's Big Stick . . . We seem to lead a very lazy life, with our siestas and servants, but all White Men come to it sooner or later in the tropics or die . . ."

From Jessie, Methodist Hospital, Des Moines, where, lacking drugs to fight bacteria, they are trying to drain the infection from Mary's abdomen, to Hadwen in Sumner:

". . . They took out the last of the stitches this morning. The main incision is nearly healed. The odor is not what it was, by any means. It seems to me plenty strong yet. When she has not been dressed for a while. But Dr. Ruth says it is 'peaches and cream' compared to what it was . . . Will go now and chase up a girl and get Mary's temperature. It has run a little higher this last 24 hours. I asked the nurse about it. She says when it drains well the temp goes lower & it had not drained quite so well yesterday, but that Mary is doing very well indeed . . ."

Meanwhile, Hadwen, wifeless back at the Sumner parsonage, fusses and frets about Jessie coming home:

". . . I don't wish to appear to act in undue haste, but Conference is one month from today. I cannot make much headway with my work under present conditions. Cleaned the parlor and kitchen yesterday. The doors were so sooty and greasy with coal and gasoline smoke it takes a half hour to wash one door . . . Used hot rain water with Gold Dust and Ivory soap on the floor. It looks fine and clean. Shook the parlor rug. Swept. Dusted. Will put sitting room and dining room into shape and put up Mary's bed. I have not been so tired all summer . . . As planned now I expect to be in Des Moines Tuesday evening. Then we can come home the first train out if Mary is ready to come. Good-bye, Papa."

Anne:

When I didn't marry Forrest, as Dad and Mother wanted, the same estrangement grew up with Haddie. It was as if I'd rejected him, too. He was entirely different when he came back from the Philippines; we were never very close again. With Mama, it was different. When our first child was born out on the farm in Hunter our second November there, Mama came up for the confinement and got to know Jim much better than the rest of my family. Poor Jim. He watched the coming birth with something like terror and rushed off to get Dr. Baillie hours too early. Mama said Jim wandered around so frightened and strained and acted like he didn't know what was going on at all. She'd take his hand and tell him, as gently as she could, not to worry. All the neighbor women and his mother and everybody tried to get him to eat something. Dr. Baillie even offered him some drops to calm him down. Once, Mama said, when he heard my cries and moans, he grabbed her by the shoulders and demanded, "What is it? Oh, my God, what's the matter?" She told him, "Jim! Calm yourself. Everything is going just fine."

At last, of course, the moaning stopped and Jim heard the slap of Dr. Baillie's hand on the baby's backside and a loud, protesting wail that announced our little girl's appearance. We named her Elizabeth Hadwen. Soon, as little Betty would be bawling or suckling or sleeping in her crib, or Mama would be wrapping her in swaddling clothes, or giving her a bath and applying talcum powder, Jim kept coming in to stare at the wriggly little red thing in amazement. He looked at her so carefully, as if to make sure that the little wrinkled-up nose and half-closed eyes and tiny lips, and all those wee, squirmy red toes and fingers were really all there. He kept saying, though Betty looked quite wizened and ugly those first few days, "What a beautiful baby!"

After the baby came, Jim brooded more about farm prices. The oats went to feed the stock, but Jim sold all the wheat and potatoes and some of the corn and barley. All the farmers felt they were too dependent on Twin City grain traders, banks and railroad men. Even in Hunter, when Jim took his grain in he never knew when the miller might dock him ten cents a bushel for supposed smut, or the elevator man refuse to grade wheat Number One, saying the protein content was too light.

The Nonpartisan League was just getting going that year, and Jim said all you heard at Hunter's barber shop, livery stable or on the street corners was League, League, League. Jim agreed that state ownership might be needed to bring about a fair deal for wheat farmers, but he found the League's leaders "an outlaw bunch of guys." Their organizers went from farm to farm preaching against "Big Biz." Jim said they went too far. "It's too much to swallow that Emil Moen's dad down at the implement store or Gale at the lumberyard are tools of eastern interests." Those against the League called its members "Reds" or "soreheads" and said those who paid dues were "six-dollar suckers." But it showed a lot of farmers were in revolt.

That summer, a hailstorm struck. It was a muggy, sweltering day, too quiet. Jim was out oiling the binder so he could start cutting a forty-acre stand of ripe oats the next day. It had stayed so hot all week, I was using an outside shed as a summer kitchen to avoid heating up the house any worse than it was. Flies buzzed outside the screen door, the baby was asleep in her crib and about three o'clock the whole eastern horizon began turning a dull greenish purple. There were deep rumbles of thunder. I didn't like the looks of it one bit and ran to take in the washing. A gusty wind came up and shook the tops of the trees. After that, dark rain clouds started to gather so fast, Jim and Harry rushed in to get their rubber boots. As they ran about rounding up the stock, the animals seemed to know a bad storm was coming: the sheep baaed and bleated, the horses whinnied and reared, even the cows were mooing anxiously.

The house got darker as heavy black clouds moved in from the prairie. The curtains were swelling and billowing and I ran upstairs to shut the windows. No sooner did I get downstairs again than the clouds were split from end to end by a shattering burst of lightning. Something like a cloudburst struck the house with battering force. It shook the windows and the roof with violent fury. There was a pelting, deafening, drumming sound. It was hail, not rain. It sounded like somebody was dropping hundreds of rocks on the roof, faster and louder . . . crash, smash! The hail beat down violently. I looked up the stairwell to the second-floor ceiling, hoping the roof could stand such a pounding. Betty, awakened, began to scream. Afraid the hail might smash the windowpanes, I snatched her up, cradling her body close in my arms to protect her. It was one of the worst storms I ever saw, though the hail didn't last long.

When I heard Jim and Harry at the back, I ran to let them in. They stood just outside the door, water pouring from their jackets, their heads dripping, their trousers sopping wet, water squelching in their rubber boots. Jim's hair was plastered to his head. Water ran down his face, which looked more tense and strained than I'd ever seen it. He roared at Harry, a white line around his mouth, "Goddamnit, why are you just standing there? Go take off those wet clothes before you get a chill!" He told me a swath of slushy white ice cut right across the farm.

A cold wind had come up and there were more flashes of lightning and deep, rolling thunder, as if we were on the edge of a tornado. Jim rode out over the white hailstones to see what damage there was. Water poured from the gutters and overflowing rain barrels. I put Betty in her high chair in the kitchen and went out to wade through the hail, picking up dead chickens which had been caught out in the open. Jim came back to say that the wheat on the west side of the farm had been spared. But all that was left of the oats were the spears of stems, some of them six inches long, some a foot or so. He figured he'd lost three thousand bushels of oats in that one field. All the crops suffered some damage. So much hard work for nothing. It'd all happened in one fell swoop.

We ate supper. Jim was wet, his shirt sticking to his back, and he was tired and horribly depressed. I saw to it that he and Harry ate well, knowing all the work they'd have to do in the morning. We soon learned we'd escaped the worst of it. The hail did even more damage farther east. Our neighbor there, an old German, came over to say he'd lost almost everything. The hail had destroyed every crop he had. When he told us, he broke out crying, the tears streaming down his bearded face. *"Ach, Gott im Himmel!"* he cursed bitterly, recovering. *"Ja,* all that work to get the farm paid for and now it is nothing. *Das ist nicht recht!"* Mother Critch came out by buggy. She said it had hailed so badly in town, she was afraid our oats would be lost. And now she'd seen the oats and, sure enough, they were lost.

That hailstorm was, I think, a turning point for Jim. He kept farming but never seemed to quite get back his old zest for it. In spite of the storm, he managed to harvest much of the wheat. But North Dakota had a record wheat crop that year and the price fell off so sharply that when Jim went to sell our crop it was down to twenty-five cents a bushel. It turned out the hail had badly damaged the farmhouse roof. We moved into the big house in Hunter while it was being repaired, and when Jim's mother wanted to take Kay, now eleven, and spend the winter in Ohio and Minnesota, we agreed to stay on, keeping an eye on the twins. But I'd never seen Jim's spirits fall so low. It scared me.

Well, as Mama used to say, you can't get blood out of a turnip. Somehow, we had to make money. One night, I was darning Jim's socks and I rolled them up and said to him, "Let's open a hotel." His mother's house had seven upstairs bedrooms. We were just two blocks from the depot. There had once been central heating. I could cook. The old hotel had finally closed down and Hunter had been without either hotel or restaurant for some time. We could count on everybody boosting it. Jim went right out, then and there, and painted a sign. He stuck it up in front of the house by the carriage step.

"ANN INN"

I had to laugh when I saw it and teased him that he didn't know how his wife spelled her name. But it stayed that way the two years we ran the hotel. The old house and its grounds had been badly neglected with just Mother Critch, Kay and McLain living there alone. "God almighty," Jim said, "you'd think Mac could take a paintbrush in hand once in a while and clean up that litter in the barn." All the horses were gone now, and the old barn was full of broken furniture, a rusted plow, old horse collars and ragged harness, rotting lumber and cobwebs all over. Paint was even peeling off the sides of the house, the roof needed shingling, grass grew in the chinks between the front steps—everything had a ramshackle look. The whole indoor plumbing and hot-water system had broken down, but it turned out to be too expensive to repair. Jim fixed up the old three-holer out back with ashes and quicklime; it would have to do.

He put new shingles where they were most needed, and we gave the house a fresh coat of white paint. We knew we could never restore it to the way it used to be, but by October it was habitable again. So we decided to go ahead and Jim placed an advertisement in the *Herald*. It said: "ANN INN, R. J. Critchfield, Prop., Board and Room by Day or Week, Board $5 Per Week, We Solicit Your Patronage, Sunday Dinners a Specialty."

From the Hunter Herald, *Jan. 16, 1916:*

"The local fire boys gave their annual banquet on Monday evening at hotel Ann Inn. They gathered at about seven o'clock and were taken into the large dining room of the hotel where they sat down to a fine six-course banquet, which was daintily served by the Messrs. Jim and Harry Critchfield. And right there we wish to say that the boys sure did ample justice to this swell meal prepared by Mrs. Critchfield . . ." *The menu, the* Herald *reported, included grape cocktail, oyster soup, apple salad, Saratoga wafers, olives, roast turkey, pork dressing, gravy, hot buttered rolls, mashed potatoes, macaroni and cheese, cranberries, ice cream, cake, coffee, nuts and candy. After supper, the firemen gathered round the piano to sing while Jim played, one fireman gave his imitation of the "one-armed fluter," another "The Hunter's Pantomime," and several performed "acrobatic feats."*

Anne:

It was easier in town. We got a hired man to stay overnight on the farm with the stock. With more free time, Jim organized a minstrel show with blackface and songs and Tambo and Bones jokes. We hunted for ducks and prairie chickens with Jim's two old retrievers, Bob and Doc. Once, for a charity bazaar at the I.O.O.F. Hall, Jim and Ray put up a tent and got Harry to paint himself with potassium permanganate so he looked real brown. They dressed him in an old wolfskin; Harry wanted to leave part of his chest bare, which was very risqué at the time. Jim stood outside the tent as the barker and cried, "Step right up, ladies and gents, and see the ferocious Wild Man of Borneo!" Harry made a face like a gorilla by putting his tongue up under his upper lip. When the girls would enter the darkened tent, all nervous and jumpy, all of a sudden Jim would flash the lamp and Harry leap out at them, growling, "AAR-R-R-GH!" When the girls rushed out shrieking, of course the rest of them would have to go in and see what was going on.

Hunter got its first picture show that year, mostly one- or two-reelers with titles like "The New Housekeeper" and "Girl Across the Hall," or a Keystone Kops comedy. Later in the year came feature-length films like the nine-reel *The Spoilers,* from the Rex Beach novel, or *The Prisoner of Zenda* and *Tarzan of the Apes.* Soon everybody was learning the names of Gloria Swanson, Harold Lloyd, Fatty Arbuckle, Douglas Fairbanks, Mary Pickford and Charlie Chaplin. Even Mama was becoming a movie fan. She wrote she'd seen *The Tramp* and was so disgusted with herself because she couldn't help laughing at Charlie Chaplin and his mashed mustache. She thought the way he hitched up his baggy pants, tipped his bowler, shrugged his shoulders and flapped down the block, twirling his cane, was so *silly*.

Chautauquas, too, were still popular. When Dr. Russell H. Conwell came to Fargo to give his famous lecture, "Acres of Diamonds," Jim and I took the train down. Dr. Conwell told about Al Hafed, an Arab who looked in vain for wealth all over the world while the biggest diamond mine in history was found on the land he left behind. He said, "If Al Hafed had just stayed at home and dug in his own garden, instead of suffering wretchedness, starvation, poverty and death in strange foreign lands, he would have found 'acres of diamonds,' for every acre, yes, every shovelful of that old farm afterwards revealed the gems that have since decorated the crowns of monarchs . . ."

The chautauqua tent's plain benches, its portable stage under a red marquee and the string of naked light bulbs at night, like the smell of dust and the sunbaked wood, reminded me of Papa's tent meetings. Even Dr. Conwell's lecture was like the "inspirational message" you heard at revival meetings. Jim said, "You can bet that if a talk at a chautauqua isn't about the brave Salvation Army girl who meets a gang of hoodlums in the slums of a strange city, it will be about the soldier fallen among the heathen in the far-off Philippines." I laughed and said, "What about the famous gambler lying at the point of death, or the silver-haired mother of five daughters who once asked the speaker this question?" He wasn't so smart. I could do it too. I wasn't a preacher's kid for nothing.

It was really the Great War in Europe that saved us. In the spring of 1916, Jim planted twenty acres of potatoes, getting a yield of close to a hundred bushels an acre. In early October, potatoes started selling at eighty cents a bushel. By November, they were a dollar fifty. We held our breaths. By March, potatoes topped two dollars and fifty cents. We sold a carload for two thousand dollars. It was the same with wheat, going over two dollars a bushel for the first time ever in October, then over three dollars, until the government set a ceiling price for Number One Northern wheat at two dollars and twenty cents in Chicago. Harry made five thousand dollars from the sale of hogs alone, half that much from lambs. When a tornado wrecked the barn, Harry rebuilt it and added a silo, paying for it with his own money. He was eager to take over the farm.

For, at last, Jim could go back to medical school. Between the hotel and farming, we'd saved eighteen hundred dollars in cash. Jim and Harry worked out what compensation was coming from the farm; there were more cows now, more feed in storage, Jim agreed to come back to help shock and thresh each year. They worked it out that Jim could draw checks on the farm's bank account in Hunter. Harry was generous; he said, "Now, Jim, don't you get in a position where you don't have anything to go on. You just write a check." When we got into the war, the next year, Jim enlisted in the Student Army Training Corps. With what he got from that, and later as an intern, he had to draw out only three thousand four hundred dollars from the farm account to finish medical school. Before leaving Hunter, we moved back out to the farm for a time, and there, in January 1917, our second child, Jimmy, was born. Once again, Mama came up from Iowa. When we joined Jim in Minneapolis, our apartment at Oak and Fulton, near the university, was filled with drying diapers and milky-clean baby smell; Jimmy was just six months old. He was still in long, ruffled dresses, and I used a trunk for a playpen while I cooked and ironed. Betty, now going on three, was getting to be quite a handful. My sister Mary, who was now working for a mail-order house in Minneapolis, stayed with us on and off.

In May 1917, a month after President Wilson declared war, McLain enlisted in the Navy. He had always been crazy about flying machines, and after training in aerial photography at Harvard, he was assigned as an observer on an airplane looking for U-boats in the Atlantic and Caribbean. My own brother, Haddie, caught in Europe while coming home from the Philippines, was arrested and accused of being a German spy while trying to make his way to Paris from Spain on foot; Dad and Mama were relieved when he got home at last.

Once President Wilson said, "The world must be made safe for democracy . . . the right is more precious than peace," people started to become terribly patriotic. We'd never seen anything like it. That Fourth of July, Jim led the biggest celebration Hunter had ever seen; the whole town was festooned with red, white and blue bunting. Even Mama was swept up in the war fever . . .

From letter by Jessie to Anne, September 1917:

". . . This week we are having a Y.M.C.A. drive. Hadwen is one of the canvassers, and while they are not nearly done they have $1,368. They will possibly make their $2,000. Though there are many Germans here. Some of them not very loyal to the U.S.

"Saturday there will be a Red Cross sale in the street—from which we are hoping great things. We are all knitting and serving, trying to do our bit in this big fight to make the world a place where women and children can be protected . . ."

Anne

From the Hunter Herald, *summer of 1918:*
June 20:

"ARE WE IN BACK OF OUR BOYS 'OVER THERE'?

"Latest reports from Washington are that there are nearly 900,000 soldiers in France. Nearly one million American boys are facing the Hun. Are we going to back them up? You bet. To the absolute limit. How are we going to do it in Hunter? We are going to grow more food . . ."

June 27:

"FOOD WILL WIN THE WAR . . . BREAD WILL WIN THE WAR . . . EVERY ACRE IS AN ARSENAL . . ."

July 20:

"Do you people at home feel at times that this war has made your life pretty hard? Read what an American correspondent writes about one of our boys who has been doing his duty:

"In a little field hospital west of Montdidier I stopped at the bedside of an American boy, one of those victims of the German mustard gas, with which the Huns are making all their present gains. His eyes were mattered with yellow pus and he could not see. His face was terribly burned. His lips were swollen and purple. His whole body had been turned the color of an Indian and portions of it looked like melted flesh . . . I said to this soldier, 'The boys are getting their revenge for you fellows tonight.' He smiled through his seared lips and in a voice so faint I had to bend down and listen, he gasped, 'God! I wish I was back there with 'em!' DO YOU STILL THINK YOU HAVE A HARD LIFE?"

Movie advertisement:

"THE MAN WITHOUT A COUNTRY"

"The story of a man who cursed his country, then blessed it . . . This movie is A WARNING TO SLACKERS . . . A MESSAGE TO PATRI-OTS . . . A play that will enthrall you—thrill you with patriotic fever—make you happy you're an American . . ."

Sept. 5, excerpt from talk by evangelist Billy Sunday at Liberty Bond rally:

". . . What a mountain of crime God has on his books against that Horde of Hellish Huns. What grave is deep enough for this thousand-armed, thousand-fanged pirate of the air, assassin of the seas, despoiler of the earth and ambassador of Hell! . . . We will never stop until Germany dips her blood-stained rag to the Stars and Stripes . . ."

Advertisement:

"PROTECT YOUR HOME AND YOUR FARM, YOUR WIFE AND YOUR CHILDREN AND ALL YOU HOLD DEAR—BUY LIBERTY BONDS!"

Same paper:

"WHAT WOMEN CAN DO TO WIN THE WAR—

WOMEN OF AMERICA, WAKE UP!"

Anne:

That summer, Harry came down with typhoid fever. Jim was in school. There was nobody to farm. Yet we all depended on it. At once, I took the children down to Iowa and left them with Mama and headed for Hunter. The trains were crowded with soldiers in wool uniforms and puttees. They kept singing songs like "Tipperary," "Keep the Home Fires Burning," "Pack Up Your Troubles in Your Old Kit Bag and Smile, Smile, Smile." I found even in Hunter the drumbeat of war fever never let up. Older boys were let out of school to do farm work. All the younger children could recite, "In Flanders Fields the poppies blow . . ." The *Herald* published letters from Hunter boys telling how they marched through mud and rain, dug trenches, laid barbed wire, slept in barns, ducked artillery fire, went over the top or got gassed or shot or blown up. Everybody said we must Give Till It Hurts. There were no farm workers to be had. Even horses were in short supply; people said the French and English had lost so many, they were trying to buy any they could get.

By now, people were used to hearing about farmerettes, part of the Wom-an's Land Army, so nobody paid much attention when I put on a pair of

Jim's overalls and went to work. I milked twice a day, separated the cream, fed and watered the stock, drove the hay rake, shocked corn and oats and did just about the work of a man. It seemed that if I wasn't out in the fields, I was either carrying buckets of water or skim milk up to the barn, or buckets of milk and baskets of eggs back. Or pushing wheelbarrows full of manure to the compost heap. Or going to hoe weeds in the garden. My hands got so callous and blistered, even with gloves, I despaired of them.

Harry had seeded fifteen acres of potatoes before he got sick. Now I found the plants covered with bright yellow eggs and tiny larvae which hatched into red-spotted black-and-yellow bugs in no time. On the advice of the neighbors, I mixed some flour and Paris green, London Purple and copper arsenate, filled a barrel with it, used a board to walk it up onto the horse cart and found a pump, spray can and nozzle out in the barn. I sprayed all the plants. It didn't work. So I went to town and hired two of my former pupils and we went over every single potato plant again, this time picking off the bugs, eggs and larvae with our fingers. We put them into a two-gallon can; once we'd filled it, we'd pour into it some kerosene and drop a match in. I'd forgotten how to be ladylike and squeamish. As Mama said, better to wear out than rust out.

Harry was better by haying time and he came back to drive our small Fordson four-cylinder, twenty-horsepower tractor while I rode the mower. He and Jim had bought the tractor the year before but just used it for plowing, as the drills and binder were set for horses. One day, Harry had a narrow escape . . .

From Harry Critchfield, interviewed sixty-five years later, now retired in California's Napa Valley:

". . . We were going to go out and cut hay. So we hooked the mower to that Fordson tractor. Anne was riding the mower. If we came to a gopher hole or something, she'd push down on a lever with her foot and raise the bar up so we could get over the uneven place. It was a five-foot mower and we were going along, cutting hay, when I think something started to plug up the sickle bar—the bar that goes back and forth with the cutting blades. This shows how crude some of that old machinery was. That steering wheel was fastened onto the steering column with a burr on top. And somehow that burr fell off. And while I was leaning over, looking at the mower with my hand on the steering wheel, all of a sudden it went right up in the air and I tumbled off. Just fell right off. Right in front of the sickle bar. The only thing I could see to do quick enough was to leapfrog right over those cutting blades. That's what I did.

"Anne was on the mower but there wasn't anything she could do. Afterwards she said, 'You had a look on your face like a caged beast.' You see, it could have cut my legs off. Cut me to pieces. After I got over typhoid fever, Anne and I worked some weeks together out in the fields on the farm. Jim wasn't there at all. He was at school in Minneapolis. Anne was a darling woman. I loved her.

"I visited her people in Iowa one time. I was down at Ames and I really stopped to visit Mary. She was a lovely girl and one summer she came up and spent some time on the farm. She'd bring cold drinks and cookies and cakes out to the fields where I was shocking wheat. I visited the Williams family for a day in Jesup and then went on. Reverend Williams was kind of very quiet and conservative. I don't think he thought much of me . . ."

Anne:

Jim was able to come home for the harvest. Men and women from town came out to shock, even Dr. Baillie. We had John Wergin's threshing rig as usual, but the younger men were gone, and merchants from downtown volunteered as bundle haulers and spike pitchers. My job was cooking, which meant making huge cans of coffee, and plenty of cookies, cakes or gingerbread, with cheese, jelly and roast beef sandwiches, to send out by buggy in the morning. Threshers could eat you out of house and home and at noon we set a long table outdoors with roasted beef or pork or stewed or fried chicken, mashed potatoes and gravy, corn or peas or fresh cabbage, or carrots and tomatoes, maybe coleslaw or pickled beets or baked beans. I also made stewed dried fruit—prunes or apples—and always pie: apple, raisin, lemon, chocolate or custard. A neighbor girl helped catch the chickens with a long, hooked stick; she'd grab one and put its head down on the block and take an ax and—pop! When she'd throw it, the chicken would run around with its head cut off; that's where the expression comes from, of course. I didn't like to do it. We put them in steaming water before we plucked them; we also had big tubs of hot water for corn on the cob and potatoes; we didn't peel them, just stirred them in steaming water with an ax handle.

After Jim went back to school, Harry and I picked potatoes. Harry drove a four-horse digger, and I and some neighbor women came behind and picked the potatoes up. It was hard on the back, but in those days it was the only way it could be done. Each of us tied ten or fifteen gunny sacks around her waist with a rope; a woman could carry about half a bushel at one time. Though it left us aching, the work went quickly with so much gossip and laughter. Afterward, Harry hauled a carload of sacked potatoes into town.

It was October before I left to pick up Betty and Jimmy and go back to

Minneapolis. By then, Jim had entered the Army from the Student Army Training Corps. He received a commission but was allowed to continue his medical training. Once Harry joined me on the farm, his company was a relief. It was terribly lonely otherwise, all those hot summer nights when the Milky Way was as bright as anything in the prairie sky, so many stars would fall, and sounds would carry on the flat plain so I'd hear a dinner bell, or the hum of a binder, or the clatter of buggy wheels on a wooden bridge way, way off. Worst were the thunderstorms when the whole house shook; sometimes it sounded like it would crack into pieces and all the windows would suddenly flash white with lightning and there was nowhere to run. Once, a neighbor warned, "Country's full of tramps, Anne. Don't you have nothing to do with them." Only one ever came to the door. He said, "I spent my last dime to wash out this shirt." I believed him and gave him a meal.

You had to take people on trust. One of the most awful things since the Russian Revolution, the year before, had been the anti-Red hysteria; Nonpartisan League organizers had been attacked. But anti-German hysteria was even worse. About a quarter of Hunter's people were either born in Germany or their parents were; many still spoke with accents. These farmers and shopkeepers were the neighbors, just as much a part of our lives as their wives' recipes for *Apfelstrudel* and *Kaffeekuchen*. What did they have to do with Boches in spiked helmets who cut off the hands of Belgian children? Every time somebody tried to get a German charged with sedition, the case would be thrown out of a North Dakota court, the judge explaining that refusing to buy a Liberty Bond, or give to the Red Cross, or put up Old Glory, however lacking it might be in patriotism, was simply not a crime in America.

The war was such a big and unexpected change for us. As a child growing up, I could recall no fears about the future at all. There were no wars, nobody went into the Army or Navy. Europe was a long way off. I suppose we were isolationist. We were not expecting wars. If anybody had ever told me that young men I knew would be fighting in France or Germany in a few more years, I'd hardly have believed it. Now all you had to do was to pick up the *Herald*.

Extracts of letters from local boys overseas published in the Hunter Herald *during 1918:*
From Asa Sherritt, Anne's old partner at the Friday Dancing Club, to his mother from "Somewhere in France," dated July 18:

". . . They are about 100 years behind the times. France has a lot of nice springs, running water, hedges and pretty places, but it can't compare with North Dakota . . ."

From Lieutenant William Cowrie, "Somewhere in France":

". . . Well, Mother, they got me at last . . . Not at all serious but the wounds will keep me out of action for several weeks . . ."

More than one Hunter youth found the French decadent and deplored their sanitary habits:

". . . They take care of nature's needs anywhere they happen to be—on the street, anyplace. Kids smoke pipes and cigarettes. Production of wine and liquor seems to be the chief industry. Everybody rides a bicycle—a whole family comes along, each one on a bicycle. They also ride in big heavy trucks on two wheels, like a cart, heavy as a lumber wagon. I guess they're milk wagons. There are women driving and the little burrow has bells on, like Santa Claus's reindeer wear in America . . ."

George Hogenson finds England snooty and class-conscious:

". . . I noticed while traveling by rail from Plymouth that they have three classes of cars. But they make as good time in 3rd Class as they do in 1st. Only, the seats are not quite so pretty. The English government makes all soldiers and sailors ride 3rd Class, no sleepers. Only the officers are allowed to go 1st Class. But wait till we get back to the United States. Our government believes in seeing the uniformed men go before others. I will be enjoying American sun and air. All it does in England is rain and stay cold . . ."

Writer only identified as "Ray" to his father in rural Hunter, from "Somewhere in France":

". . . Picture lines of uncouth tanks, big and small, creeping over acres of barbed wire, spitting fire from machine guns, one-pounders or three-inch guns and one trench after another. Lines of artillery banging away in front, the big ones in the rear. New lines forming as the tanks and infantry advance and open up. Flocks of aeroplanes overhead and red-hot scraps in the air with machine guns. Usually someone coming down like a fiery comet. It's odd to watch them at night with their unceasing bullets. Ever so many bullets leave a streak of fire and you can watch their course in the air . . . It's more strenuous than the County Fair . . . We were all night in mud and rain but just at daybreak the weather broke. It was some daybreak. You know how the wind howls and whines in late fall and winter in Hunter?

Well, you'll see me duck when I hear that sound again. I'll expect a crash and whang at the end of it . . .

"I wore blisters on my hands digging a trench deeper and three of us piled in with two German shelter-halves and a couple of blankets. German blankets have too many fleas in them, and when you put that on top of cooties, a kind of lice, it's too much of a good thing . . . I have a Boche mess gear which I manage to take a bath in. I captured Boche ammunition and once I had a peach of a German rifle but I couldn't carry it away . . . Fritz's bread tastes mighty good when you're hungry. It's black and sour, heavy but nourishing. His hardtack is like soup crackers and excellent. He uses burnt barley as a coffee substitute and it's got Postum backed clear off the map . . .

"Can you picture those women and children and old men who have been prisoners under that iron hand for four long years and the reception we got and the jolt Fritz got? Some places the beer steins and mugs were sitting on the tables out under the trees just as they left them the night before . . . Things certainly look bright. But Fritz is putting up a game fight. It's a long way to Berlin yet . . . We know we Marines will go where it's hottest as Marines always have gone . . . Gee, Dad, I'd like to have a ride in that new Dodge . . ."

Hunter's boys were widely scattered. One, Lieutenant Chris Anders, writes from the Allied Expeditionary Force in Harbin, Manchuria, October 13:
". . . We have had trains of British, French, Japanese and Chinese troops here. The Russians are making an effort to reorganize an army to liberate the country from the Bolsheviks. I will do all I can and hope they make a go of it . . . The turnips are somewhat like our rutabaga, only larger and of a dark red color. The onions are as good as those we grow in Hunter . . ."

From Herbert Knudtson, October 20; he writes his parents he hopes to be home by Christmas. He has just spent six days in Paris:
". . . It's a beautiful city. Was in Napoleon's tomb and saw the flag he carried into battle. I've been over here six months, but it doesn't seem that long. Expect you're thinking about winter. I hope you have enough coal . . ."

From Louis Geleke to his parents in Hunter, mailed in Paris November 12:
". . . Did you notice the Armistice was signed on the 11th hour of the 11th day of the 11th month? I tell you there was a happy bunch of French people last night. The streets were so crowded it was hard to get through. It sure makes a difference here in Paris when they turned the lights back on

again. Before, you couldn't see your way around. We are only about ten miles from Paris so it doesn't take us long to get there on the subway, which is only three blocks from the barracks . . . I am getting so I can talk French pretty good. I'm feeling fine, Mother. I don't believe anybody could feel better than I do. We have some good times here. It sure is a great place . . . I am feeling just fine and dandy . . ."

From the popular song, 1919:

> ". . . They'll never want to see a rake or plow
> And who the deuce can parley-vous a cow?
> How ya' gonna keep 'em down on the farm
> After they've seen Paree?"

Hadwen

From Jessie, Postville, Iowa, to Anne in Minneapolis, October 28, 1918:

". . . Hope you and the children got there safely. Helen got ill just after you left. It seems to be a recurrence. She had it awfully hard last year. I'm keeping her out of school. So far the rest of us have been spared. We keep hearing wild rumors. One is that some doctors and nurses at Camp Dodge outside Des Moines were caught injecting flu germs into patients and were court-martialed and shot. Another is that fifty black soldiers who died of flu were buried in a mass grave behind the hospital. Who can be believed? Dad says none of it's true but that so many of the young boys who got drafted and are down at Camp Dodge are sick and going overseas. One of the fellows we knew died of flu on his way to France and had to be buried at sea.

"Liquor is outlawed here, but the police will issue medicinal whiskey permits if Doc Schmidt signs them. No more than a quart and the man is watched. Doc Schmidt got hold of what he calls 'pneumonia serum.' He told Papa, 'I don't know if it's any good, but c'mon over and I'll give you a shot.' So he went. I tried a new medicine, 'Vick's Vaporub,' with Helen. Folks have been trying just about anything—onions, kerosene, Hicks tablets, mustard poultices, lemon juice, turpentine, linament. Papa had me make up some little cheesecloth breath strainers. But there's plenty of quackery . . ."

From Jim, Minneapolis, to his mother in Hunter, November 4:

". . . The streets are full of funerals all day and ambulances all night . . . We're putting in fifteen-hour days tending the soldiers at Fort Snelling. Before that, the S.A.T.C. boys all went through it. I've never been so dog tired . . . You mentioned people in Hunter are going around in white masks. This is crazy. How can a few layers of gauze keep out the flu bugs, like a screen keeps flies off the front porch? These germs are carried in the air by very small droplets of mucus, from coughing, spitting, even just talking. They can travel in dust . . . If Harry or Kay or Mac gets sick, put them to bed right away. Clear the room. You'll need a wash basin, pitcher, slop bowl, soap and towel at hand. They're likely to cough up a lot of mucus. *Burn everything* it gets on . . . Don't fuss too much, Mother. Let them sleep and rest . . ."

Anonymous poem published in the Hunter Herald *November 16:*

". . . And you're doggone sure that you're going to die,
But you're skeered you won't and afraid you will,
Just drag to bed and have your chill,
And pray the Lord to see you thru,
For you've got the Flu, boy, you've got the Flu . . ."

Emil Moen of Hunter, interviewed sixty-four years later:

". . . I was a medical corpsman at the Seventh Regiment Headquarters at Camp Perry on the Great Lakes, where the flu first broke out in this country. About nine o'clock one night we had ten guys come into sick bay. Before morning, we had hundreds and within three days we had whole drill halls full. Corpsmen worked until they passed away. We'd be on duty two or three days and nights at a time. We had liquor to keep going and prevent us from catching the flu. If we started walking into walls, they knew it was time to take us off duty. You can tell people about it and they'll hardly believe it. That's right. Nobody wanted to see stretchers or ambulances, because if they took you to the hospital, you almost never came back . . ."

Edwin Anderson, retired farmer, also interviewed sixty-four years later:

". . . It got you so weak and chilled all over, you know. I know my cousin, he got sick, and he told his wife, 'Well, I shouldn't go out, but I've got to get this rye seeded.' So he laid on the drill, just think of that, he laid down on his drill and he worked when he was so sick with flu. Next day, why in the morning, he couldn't get up and six o'clock that evening he died . . ."

Further comment from Harry Critchfield, 1983:

". . . In the family I think it was just me. And mine only lasted four or five days. I give credit to the stove in the depot. The agent kept that stove red hot all day and all night. And I'd turn one side and then I'd turn the other side . . ."

Anne, 1959 interview:

". . . Father, though no longer a doctor, was still in demand as one. Finally he had to get rid of his medical equipment . . . Then in the flu epidemic, when he was already an old man and hadn't practiced for years, he went back to his old profession. Doctors were exhausted, people were dying at enormous rates and there was little to be done for them. It was routine treatment. He cared for them until they died, then held the funeral service as their pastor . . ."

Widely reported statement by Rev. Algernon Crapsey, Methodist minister, Rochester, New York:

"We are living today in the midst of a great dissolution. We are standing by the deathbed of a great religion, Christianity!"

Fragment of a sermon, "The Coming Kingdom," delivered by Hadwen November 30:

". . . The only progress we have ever made is along the lines laid down by Christ: The Golden Rule; the Law of the Neighbor; the Loving our Enemies and doing good to them . . . The worker for the coming Kingdom of God, loves God and shows it in every act and manner of his life. He loves his fellowmen—*all* of them, even the humblest. He loves his enemies— every one of them—even after four years of the Great War against the Germans, four years of wounds and deaths, disease and destruction, mud and blood, typhus and poison gas, all the terrible losses and suffering. For the true Christian can only overcome evil with good. He will willingly be crucified with Christ. He will willingly die to save men . . ."

From a letter by Jessie, Postville, to Anne in Minneapolis, Jan. 17, 1919:

". . . I'm just worried sick about Papa. In early November, after about five weeks of it, the worst of the flu seemed over. Now a second wave has struck that is just devastating. Every day, carts with bodies are brought into town for burial. The hearse keeps going to the depot. No church services. The families just go to the graveside.

Papa keeps going off to that rugged hill country of Allamakee County near the Yellow River where it's all timber and bottomland. Caring for the sick and dying. He leaves home two or three days at a time mostly just going by foot. What can I do? We've been married thirty-five years by now and I know Papa will do what he's set his mind on. Whole families are bedfast. One family, the woman is dying, the man is down sick and nobody even to wash her face. So often there's two or three deaths in one family—one child will see another die and in a day or so, go too. Papa will go down and tidy them up, bathing the sick and changing filthy beds, trying to get help to feed and care for them. But he comes home looking so beaten down and exhausted . . ."

Hadwen:

As I walked up to the Bauer place, I was struck by two things: the house was too still and the barn was too noisy. You could hear bleating sheep, whinnying horses, bawling cows; only unfed or thirsty animals make their kind of uproar. The Bauers were German immigrants on newly cleared backwoods land; much of it was still in timber. None of the family had been seen for days. There'd been some ugly anti-German incidents up in these parts and I didn't like the way none of the neighbors had looked in. Just now the evilly inclined and depraved Germans were in the limelight, but the percentage of them that was truly bad was small even if those were the most insistent on what they wanted. The great mass of people anywhere always have their hearts right. If only they would assert themselves after the manner of Christ on the side of right just as much as evil men do on the side of wrong! A thick, wet snow was slowly whirling down, but I was warmly dressed in my old fur cap and big old buffalo coat and was wearing leggings and thick Norwegian socks. I'd given my newer buffalo coat to Louie to take to North Dakota. The one I had left was wearing out, but so was I and I hoped it would last as long as I did.

The Bauers' house looked well maintained, the usual white frame; this one had two stories and a big open back porch. As soon as I'd taken a look in the barn, I went up to the back door and knocked, not seeing a soul around the place. When nobody came, I just opened the door and went in. The kitchen was filled with such a deep chill the floor boards gave out a cracking sound when I stepped on them. Pails of ashes and garbage stood about. A closed door opened into a small living room, which was heated. A mattress and bedding had been dragged close to a pot-bellied stove, but the bulging iron sides no longer gave off a glow. It looked like the fire had burned way down and would need tending right away. On the mattress, bundled up in blankets and a feather tick, two sick young women lay motionless. But they were alive, and from time to time one of them sighed.

"Are you all right? Do you hear me? I've come. I've come to help you."

One of them stirred. She raised herself and leaned on one elbow on the mattress, her back bent and her head hanging low so that her blond hair fell across her face. She spoke with an effort but extremely distinctly and managed to tell me that she had coughed up some bloody froth and that her nose was bleeding from time to time. She did not raise her head, but only looked up, her eyes trying to reach my face. Both she and her sister, she said, had high fevers. They became dizzy and nauseated when they tried to get up and move.

"You are a doctor, aren't you?" she asked slowly, pausing between the words. When I said I'd once been one, she said, "Yes," in a slow tone of relief, and then, "Thank God!" and she muttered a heavy sigh. She described the familiar symptoms: first the chill, then fever, and a headache and backache, the running nose and weeping eyes, muscular pain, and now, the stage of spitting mucus streaked with blood and pus. Her eyes looked badly congested. Her sister lay with closed eyes, but the muscles of her forehead twitched now and then as if she were listening.

Over the next twenty-four hours I managed to piece their story together. The whole family had come down with flu five days before, probably having picked it up in town where they sold their cream. After two days, the old grandfather, who owned the farm and had lived there ever since he came from Hesse, had been the first to die. The two girls, between them, had managed to drag and carry his body into a small unheated shed off the kitchen, where I found it, white with frost and frozen stiff. Somehow the two of them had kept the wood stove burning. A stovepipe, swelling overhead into a drum, gave off a little heat upstairs. They'd shut off the kitchen to save fuel. There was enough drinking water. The girls kept the family fed with hot oatmeal. One of them would cook a kettleful on the stove and the other would take it upstairs and dish out a helping to each of the family members. The girls also took turns bringing in wood and water and tending the fire. After each effort they had crept back into their warm bedding. At last, after the younger sister became delirious, the other had carried on alone.

On the fourth night, their mother, a widow, had died in her bedroom upstairs. She was still there. She had developed pneumonia and, delirious, began to speak only German, which her daughters found hard to follow. Their eldest brother, twenty-four, had nursed the mother as long as he could. He seemed to be dying now and had coughed up a lot of yellowish-greenish pus. I found him in his bed. In a third bedroom were the hired man and an eighteen-year-old boy. All five survivors were gravely ill.

Through five terrible days, no neighbor had come to see if they were all right, or to wash them or clean the dishes, to remove the foul bedding or air out the rooms. The house was pestilential, filthy. I knelt, feeling, as I always did, that forearming prayer was absolutely necessary. Our Lord's victory was won in the garden. The trial, mocking, scourging and crucifixion were all triumphant in Gethsemane. At once I set to work, feeding and watering the stock, bringing in more wood, stoking up the fire, heating water, washing dishes and bedding and clothing and taking it outside to freeze stiff and dry. I cleaned the kitchen and prepared hot oatmeal and rice; I also heated up some stewed fruit, found some crackers, made coffee and boiled some eggs. Around the family members I wore a gauze mask Jessie had made me.

The younger of the two girls seemed better the next day. She was still mentally confused, but her fever went down and she spent most of her time in a quiet sleep. I was more worried about her older sister; she'd borne the brunt of it. But she said her appetite and strength were returning. She thanked me with tears in her eyes. The illusion of recovery didn't last long. In the afternoon she developed the flu's deadliest complications: bronchitis and pneumonia. Soon she was in awful agony; she coughed, her arms and legs were twitching, her whole inside was shivering. Her suffering just about crushed any glimmer of hope I had left.

I sat up with her all night, staring at the stove, its reddish glow encircled with shadows and blurs. Time wore on; a piece of wood would collapse in the stove or the clock would tick loudly. I was exhausted from mental strain but feared to go to sleep. I thought of the time I was a boy in Whittier and how the doctors then knew little but bloodletting, blistering and purging. And how they had taught us at the university that infectious disease was caused by microorganisms. And what a revolution since! Thanks to antisepsis and anesthesia, they now performed operations long thought impossible. We knew the causes of typhoid, malaria, tuberculosis, diphtheria, tetanus, pneumonia, whooping cough, plague, dysentery—so many diseases. And what about the theory of heredity, the discoveries of Pasteur and Koch, the treatment of pellagra and rickets with vitamins? Well, what about it? I asked myself how any of it could save this dying girl. There was all that science, but the essence of a doctor's work stayed the same. Illness and suffering and death stayed the same.

Toward the morning, she sighed and opened her eyes. I thought she might speak, but the shivering grew more acute, her breathing became jerky; I could tell her heart was laboring to beat. She sank deeper into a heavy lethargy, no longer moving except for her hot breath going in and out.

I knelt by her side, and spoke aloud to God: "Lord, I saw plainly from the start that this wasn't a case for scientific medicine or anything a doctor could do. It called for help on high. And I'm going to be real plain spoken with You, Lord. Just real plain. Lord, you've got to do something for this girl. Facing death, she carried her burden, her and her sister, for five days alone. She's as brave and worthy as anyone I've ever known."

I stopped, feeling the closeness and mystery of death all about me. "Take my life instead, Lord. I'm an old man. But do something. Save her. I don't care what it is, so long as it be Thy will." I got up from my knees, sure that I'd been heard. The girl had that fixed smile they get. She was dead. After a short, exhausted sleep, I roused myself and removed all three bodies—the girl, her mother and the grandfather—and dragged them over the snow. The surviving sister, like the men upstairs, was curled up in her blankets, in a deep, delirious sleep and mercifully unaware of what was going on. The sun was blinding on the snow. I found a spade in the barn. In a pine grove out behind the house I found some ground soft enough to dig. "I am the resurrection and the life; he that believeth in Me, though he were dead, yet shall he live . . ." Through the turmoil of my tired brain, I think it was in my mind to bury the three Bauers right there. "I know that my Redeemer liveth, and that he shall stand at the latter day of the earth: and though after my skin worms destroy this body, yet in my flesh shall I see God . . ." I kept seeing the face of the dead girl, to whom I gave the place of a saint, mingled with the menacing and trembling shapes of the whole influenza epidemic, those shapes which appear in our worst nightmares and which rested men can never afterwards remember; grief weighed heavily, heavily . . .

I guess that's where they found me, some of the neighbors, belatedly concerned. That trip back to Postville was just a blur of blowing snow and the scrape of bobsled runners, clattering wheels, whistles, shouts, people running, bells clanging, doors slamming, I was too tired to pay any attention. I do remember how it felt to wake up in a soft, warm, clean, comfortable bed, a pitcher of cold water to quench my thirst; Jessie was there, gently smiling down at me, resting her hand on my head, her eyes full of concern. And Doc Schmidt, gruff and cantankerous and fussing about; it was a good tonic. But my voice sounded peculiar, too weak and dry.

Daylight soon gave way to darkness and I slept and slept. When I awoke, sunlight streamed through the window and I could hear wagon wheels rattling; the street was cleared of snow. I looked at the shafts of sunlight, misty with specks of dust, and at the clean white pillows and the familiar patchwork quilt. All of a sudden I had a strong desire to talk to people, to see things moving. God's world, even in the narrow space of the bedroom, was great; He was in human history and bringing order out of chaos. God knew what He was doing. I fell back to sleep. When I woke up, Jessie was there.

"Well, Mama, what was the matter with me?"

"Just all worn out. You came home utterly exhausted. Tell me all about it." And then what happened at the Bauer farm came back to me.

The worst was soon over and the flu faded away as swiftly as it came. Everybody was talking about Versailles and the League of Nations and how our soldiers had sacrificed to bring about a better order of things. In time, of course, we saw it didn't quite work out that way, just as in time the Spanish Influenza left its own grim legacy. Fully a third of the flu victims who survived came to suffer from cardiac problems, tuberculosis, nephritis or other diseases. More than 548,000 Americans died of flu, far more than the 125,000 troops killed in the war. Worldwide, something like 20 to 40 million people died of the flu. Just think of that.

I'd gotten off easy, or so I thought. It was a year later that I noticed while shaving that one of the glands beside my left jawbone was swollen. At first I didn't think much about it, but after I saw a couple of local doctors and it got worse, I went over to Des Moines to consult a surgeon who'd been a classmate of mine at medical school thirty-eight years before. He suspected a malignancy of the lymph glands, or Hodgkin's disease, which was fatal. But though they took out a few small tumors, it was never positively diagnosed. Radiation therapy was prescribed. They gave me thirty-minute X-ray treatments every three weeks all summer. Of course within a few years the maximum X ray considered safe would be down to a couple of minutes. It was brand-new, you see.

One evening, Jessie and I were sitting in the parlor. I was reading from the Book of Psalms and she was sitting close by, mending by the same lamp. I was past sixty-five and was going to ask for retirement at Conference that fall, and it seemed like a good time to talk it over with Jessie. She didn't seem too surprised. I put down my Bible and said, "I'm getting along in years now, Mama, and they want younger men. Men more in tune with the times. We can go home to Mount Vernon. Thank the Lord we've got our own house to go to. Maybe we can take in boarders from the college. That should help out a little. I may have been an unprofitable servant, but I hope to have gathered in a few sheaves for the Lord . . . It won't be long now, dear."

So we had borne the burden and the heat of the day and now we could take our rest. You know, somehow those X rays affected my metabolism. Any day I didn't go out and chop wood or otherwise work up a good sweat, I just didn't feel healthy.

Anne

Jim always said he wouldn't go to a small or Scandinavian town. Maddock had six hundred people and was 99 percent Norwegian. Only two families weren't eligible for the Sons of Norway, the Irish barber and us. Jim went first in March. I followed with Betty and Jimmy in June. I'd gone down to Iowa to teach for a year to help pay expenses. Jim had just finished medical school and bought a new Model T Ford to start his practice.

We had to wait about ten days for our house and stayed in a little country hotel, the kind where the office had a big stove and if the proprietor left a lantern on the table when he went to bed at night, it meant there was an available room upstairs. If you left early in the morning, you put the lantern back, left fifty cents under it and that was that.

So I was glad to get into our own house. The first night, Jim twisted and wriggled and squirmed. Bedbugs! I woke up in the morning and saw them crawling up the wall. It was a new house and the former occupants had left their beds. There was no exterminator in town. A dentist who had followed these same people into another house knew of a solution which you sprayed behind doors. It killed the bedbugs but turned my fingernails black. I was invited to welcoming functions and people wondered if it was some new style the city slickers were wearing.

Maddock had advertised an opening for a doctor. There was only one other doctor, an old Norwegian, who terribly resented the competition. At first I found answering the telephone was difficult because all the Norwegian names sounded alike. Dilleruuds, Gilleruuds, Almonruds, Aanderunds. The town owned its own electric plant and, by custom, the lights always went out from one o'clock to six o'clock in the morning. We always had to dash madly home from parties before the lights went out. Betty was a chubby, blue-eyed girl of seven now, with long, curly blond hair, and Jimmy, who was towheaded, was five. Our friends included the druggist, banker, two men from the department store and the dentist, Vince Bousquet. He and Jim shared the same office.

It was a perfectly flat prairie town way out in the middle of North Dakota. Only one well, at the railway station, for the entire town. The train came up in the morning and went back at night. It went up just as far as Esmond, what we called "Russian Territory." Most of the people there were Germans whose families had gone to live in Russia at the time of Catherine the Great and Alexander I; they had begun migrating to North Dakota in the 1880s. All the people in Maddock had big square cisterns in their basements with triple filters against rats and cats. That water made the best coffee you ever tasted in your life. There were also some poplar trees, very bleak-looking streets, white clapboard houses and gardens with zinnias and hollyhocks. There were a few roses but they didn't winter well in the harsh climate. The town was arranged on a main "T" street. Every way you looked, the open bare prairie, with hardly a tree, was always in sight. We were to live in Maddock three years.

We hadn't been there long before Jim discovered he had a shirttail relation living in town, a man named Hartley Shaffer, who farmed on a coulee ten miles southeast of Maddock. It turned out he was the long-lost younger brother of Jim's grandmother back in Ohio who'd died when a gas stove exploded in 1895. That same year, Hartley, the black sheep, had "gone West." "There's one in every family," people used to say. That was the last heard of Hartley, Jim said, except for tales he'd become a horse thief and safecracker and spent some time in the penitentiary—not, if one counts Amos Whitfield, the first ex-convict in the family. So it came as a great surprise to find that in 1922 he was farming in Maddock. He'd homesteaded there years before and by then was a man in his fifties; while respectable enough, he was still a character.

From George T., 1984 interview:

". . . I remember Grandpa Shaffer—that's what all us kids called him. He was just a nice old man then. Oh, he was still a crack shot with a rifle or pistol. You heard stories that he'd been part of a gang that stole horses in Montana and brought them back to the Maddock area. Years before, you know. There was hearsay they'd come back with big herds of horses, and it was assumed they were stolen. The story was that they had this holding place for the horses way out in the country and they'd go up and sit in a cupola in the barn with a bottle of whiskey and take a shot if anybody got too close. To scare 'em away. They didn't shoot to wound or kill. Just dusted 'em off . . . When hog-butchering time came, he'd have his rifle slung loose in his arm and he'd ask, 'What hogs shall we butcher?' He'd just shoot from the hip, he was such a crack shot, and kind of a showoff, old Grandpa Shaffer was . . ."

Anne:

Jim was very patriotic. He felt the town should have some kind of Fourth of July celebration. Until then, they'd just celebrated Norway's national day on May 17. Jim was elected commander of the local American Legion and decided to organize a bang-up celebration. He fired the anvil at four o'clock in the morning, hitting gunpowder on it. Three pregnant mothers all delivered that morning. Whether this had any effect . . . Jim was also the band leader. It was a busy day. Three deliveries. Leading the band. Running the celebration. The band marched, schoolchildren decorated bicycles, each store had something in the window, kids dressed up in funny clothes, there was a pie-eating contest, catching a greased pig, climbing a greased pole, fireworks in the evening. There was no other celebration like it for a hundred miles around. All the farmers in the region were Norwegian. In those days, everyone was well off. They always paid cash . . .

From the Maddock Standard, *front page, July 5, 1923, under the eight-column banner, FOURTH WAS GREAT DAY IN MADDOCK; the* Standard *has a new young editor, Jim Lowell, who has also just come from Minneapolis:*

"It started off with an industrial parade, led by a cavalry squad. Every business had a float. In the afternoon ball games, Flora defeated Minnewaukan three to two and Fessenden beat Maddock two to nothing. During the games, the returns from the Dempsey-Gibbons fight came in by radio, announced round by round. After dark there was a fireworks display and a big dance at the Opera House. It was a good-natured, orderly crowd. There was little evidence of 'tanglefoot,' and specially appointed police had no trouble in maintaining order at all times. It was a glorious Fourth of July . . ."

Hadwen, Jr., back again teaching in the Philippines, writes Anne about the celebration there:

". . . We went to the Fourth of July parade this morning in Manila. It was all-American, and the cheering by the natives, what there was of it, was very feeble. No independence for them, and they can't see why. Old Glory looked very nice as the boys went marching by with all their cannons, searchlight motor-cars, etc. Good thing to get the troops out once in a while and let 'em see what real fighting men look like in comparison with their own runty selves . . ."

From interviews with Mabel Swanson, who lived with the Critchfields as their hired girl while she attended high school the entire three years they lived in Maddock; now—more than sixty years later—a retired farmer's widow and well-known activist in statewide senior-citizen groups in her seventies:

". . . It was Dr. Critchfield who got me in the band. He was the bandleader and he needed a French-horn player. And he said to me, 'Mabel, I know you can play piano by ear—if I get you a few lessons, will you play in the band?' And I said, 'I sure would.' So he got Ed Bell from Oberon to give me ten lessons. And I played in that band for four years. Once I got married, a farmwife, you know, she can't be running to town, practicing for band, band, band . . . But golly, it was fun . . ."

From Agnetha Nielsen Bergsgaard, interviewed on her farm in South Norway, near Maddock, 1982:

". . . The most fun I ever had was when I was young and went to dances. In winter I lived with families in Maddock. Got paid seven dollars a week. Threshers got five dollars a day, but men got more money, you know. Mrs. Critchfield had lots of beautiful party dresses, I remember that. In her clothes closet. Sometimes Dr. Critchfield played the piano at dances . . . waltzing, one-step and two-step, the polka and the schottische . . . I went to a lot of dances. Then when I got married, my husband, he didn't dance. He used to say, 'I'll stand still and you dance around me.' But he never learned. That was the end of my dancing days . . ."

From Edwin Anderson, retired farmer, Maddock, in his eighties; during 1920s, clerk in a confectionery:

"Doc Critchfield? He'd treat 'em for anything. Common cold to typhoid. He kept his horses in the livery barn and if he wanted to see a patient, he'd just notify them to hitch 'em up. He was the leader of the town band and he was also one of the first golfers I ever saw. Doc was the founder of our golf club . . ."

Anne:

Jim had taken up golf in Minneapolis, and in Maddock he wanted to get a course started. At first everybody said the game was just something for city slickers who could afford such luxuries. But, within a few months, Jim had recruited thirty-five members. They even went out on their improvised greens and played Christmas Day. In March, a golf club was formally inaugurated with Jim as president. That spring, he and Vince Bousquet and some of the others burned and raked some fields and got nine greens in shape. By summer, they were ready to play against nearby towns like Fessenden and Devil's Lake. I took up golf myself, wondering what my folks in Iowa would say. At first, there were some signs of resentment of golf in Maddock. One night, somebody knocked down all our signs and poles and scattered the gravel piles. Another time, some automobiles drove over the greens, knocking down signs. But golf was gaining in popularity all over the country. Soon nobody scoffed at Jim's plus fours. Besides, Maddock was getting used to having an athletic doctor. Patients might find him crouched over a crystal set with earphones, trying to hear a ball game or boxing match through the static.

From the Standard, *February 21, 1924, story headlined "CRITCHFIELD AND FELLAND STAR—Comedy Prevails Throughout Basketball Game." Teachers at Maddock's Agricultural High School had bet the men downtown a box of La Pollina cigars that neither side could score. Jim Lowell wrote:*

". . . 'Twas the most wonderful constellation of stars and meteors that the people of Maddock beheld last Monday night . . . It was a dreadful melee . . ."

Anne:

Mother Critchfield, Harry and Kay used to drive over from Hunter a lot. A terrible thing had happened to McLain. During the war, he'd crashed in the Caribbean. The observer plane he was in went into a tailspin. He'd bailed out and seemed to be not badly hurt at the time, but now the doctors suspected a brain injury. He had become terribly on edge and jumpy. Mother Critchfield, Jim and Harry wanted to keep him at home. He turned paranoic and Ray and Burke took him down to a veterans hospital in Knoxville, Iowa, where they treated shell-shock cases . . ."

Comments on the mental illness of McLain from family members and Hunter neighbors sixty years later:
Merland Carr:

". . . After the war, he took a room downtown. He had a chest, a sort of strongbox, made up for him, metal-bound and everything, that he could lock. He kept some food in that. He was afraid somebody was going to poison him. Oh, McLain was never violent, nothing like that. He was just leery of other people, liked to stay by himself. They say he could've come home from that hospital any time, but he didn't want to. Just stayed and played the piano all day long. Did that for over fifty years . . ."

Ella Rasmussen:

". . . I was an operator in the telephone exchange, you know, the kind where people would call into Central and you'd work the switchboard and say, 'Number, please.' One time, somebody gave us girls a box of apples for Christmas and McLain came in and sat down and I said, 'Wouldn't you like an apple?' And he said, 'Thanks. I love apples.' So I gave him one from the top, but he said, 'No, I'll go over to the box and get one.' Shortly after that, they took him to the hospital, didn't they? I couldn't pass any judgment on him. I think he used to come in and visit me a lot because I was alone and he knew nobody else would bother us there. He knew I wouldn't harm him in any way, you see. He felt free with me. I never knew the rest of the family at all . . ."

Beatrice Sayer:

". . . I heard he went bugs over music. One time, I sang in a music contest in Grand Forks, and when I came out, McLain grabbed me and said, 'You're a coloratura soprano!' And I looked at him and thought: What in the world are you talking about? That's the last time I saw him . . ."

Kathryn Garrett:

". . . McLain was just the most wonderful fellow you can imagine. Blond hair, good-looking. He lost his mind while he was going with Laura Dixon, a friend of mine. They were a lovely couple. We thought the world of them. It was after the war, when he came back from the Caribbean and lived all alone in that great big house . . . I don't know what went wrong with that family. The father died young. She was sharp. She'd always had servants . . . When that happens, a mother's got to have a pretty strong character to hold the family together. Maybe I'm wrong about it. That's my version. But I loved the Critchfields . . ."

Betty, daughter of Anne and Jim:

". . . Once in Maddock when I was about nine, Uncle McLain showed up from nowhere. I walked home with him. He was shadowy. You were always finding him and losing him . . ."

Kay, Jim's only sister:

". . . He crashed off the coast of Florida. They'd go looking for German submarines. And they crashed. I don't know if that's what caused his trouble. Nobody really knows that . . . He was blond and handsome and had this wonderful tenor voice. I can still hear him singing 'Danny Boy.' He could play anything on the piano, from classical pieces to ragtime. He could have left the hospital and gone back to Hunter, but he didn't want to go. He was too mixed up. It was too confusing for him at home. There wasn't anybody to say to him, 'Well, you have to do this or that now.' I'd married and gone away . . . Many times, I thought of going home. But I knew I couldn't go back there. I didn't have the money to go back there and start anything. I could have made an inn out of it, I suppose. Like Anne and Jim did. But I didn't know how to start anything . . . All of us played the piano and sang. But McLain could play and sing the best . . ."

Anne:

Early the fall of that first year, Jim had his first baby call. It was past twelve o'clock. Jim had just gone to bed and hated terribly to get up. I went along that night and from then on to every baby case he had . . .

Jim:

"I couldn't have done it without her. Any doctor who has practiced obstetrics knows you can expect almost any kind of emotion from your patients. It wasn't long in Maddock before we were called out to a remote farmhouse and I asked the woman who was about to give birth to pull back the bedclothes. "No, no," she protested. "I never did that with my other babies!" I was amazed. "You mean to say you want me to deliver the baby under these blankets?" Anne made her see reason.

Another time during a delivery, the husband said he would give the ether while I turned the baby. Anne was going to take the baby after it was born. I'd urged the woman to go into the hospital in Harvey, as the pelvis was so flat labor would be difficult. But she'd insisted on staying at home. Ether came in a can and you put a gauze mask over the patient's mouth and nose and just dripped the ether on. The husband, a big man with large wrists and hands, seemed to be doing very well at it. We'd reached the stage of unconsciousness and immobility, but not yet of deep, surgical anesthesia. Anne had gone out of the room for something. The mother looked fearful in her strained distortion and the moans underneath the mask. I happened to look up and saw the husband's face had an expression of utmost horror. He looked green and started to gag. He put his hand to his mouth and got out of the room fast. I could hear him vomiting. I shouted to Anne, but the delivery could not stop. So, falling on my knees and stretching out my left hand as far as it would go to keep the drops of ether coming, I delivered the baby with my right. After that, Anne gave the anesthetic.

Bringing new human beings into the world was a doctor's most rewarding work. With all the babies I delivered, it still seemed incomprehensible to me.

Where did they come from, not existing one moment and the next so marvelously alive? I think my greastest fear as a doctor was losing a baby or a
mother. That first year in Maddock I used to have a recurring nightmare:
I'd dream that I'd just delivered a fine, healthy baby when a stream of blood
hit my surgical gown. A bad hemorrhage. My training told me what to do.
The packing was within arm's reach. But I couldn't move. I just sat there,
paralyzed. People were yelling, "You're letting her die!" "No, no," I'd protest, and then Anne would be shaking me and trying to get me to wake up,
saying it was just a bad dream . . ."

Further comment from Mabel Swanson:
"She was like a second mother to me, and he a father. I never saw him
lose his temper. We used to play horseshoes, the doctor and I. Well, Betty
and Jimmy, they wanted their father to beat me. And a couple of times I
beat him. And they sat right down and cried. How we laughed about it!
They loved their dad that much . . .

"You know what I always thought? I made up my mind that if I could
only have a home like that, I'd be happy. They never had a fight, not that I
heard. They were very close. I can remember his hands would get so
chapped in winter and she'd sit and rub cold cream on them. And she
washed his hair and she combed it into place. You bet your life. She waited
on him hand and foot. And he appreciated it. He worked so hard.

"He had some patients that made me wonder why anybody would want
to be a doctor. One was Danielson. He had a burst appendix. He was
terribly sick and he died. But it took a week to die. And there was the
Carlson girl. She'd been roller-skating and she fell and hurt her knee and it
got infected. And Dr. Critchfield read books. And he called Minneapolis
and asked other doctors, 'What should I do? What should I do?' He never
had to amputate in all the time I knew him. Gladys Carlson was in a
wheelchair for a long time and then on crutches. But afterwards, she didn't
have to use them. I know he saved that leg.

"People came to the office or they'd telephone him to have him come out
to the farms. I know one girl—she's Con Beck's wife now—and this boy
wanted to go with her and she didn't want to go with him. And he had a
buggy and he wanted her to get in and go riding with him and she wouldn't
do it. He pulled out his revolver and shot—he said he shot at the carriage
step. But it ricocheted and went into her ankle. And he picked her up—she
was a Togstad—and he rushed to Dr. Critchfield's office with her. And he
took the bullet out. That boy was a real outlaw . . ."

Take me out to the ball game. (Clay County Historical Society)

Batter up. (Wells County Historical Society)

Jim and Anne, wedding picture, 1913.

The members of the wedding, Methodist parsonage, Sumner, Iowa, 1913. Front row from left: little Helen, Jim, Anne, Hadwen, Jr. Second row: Jessie, Catherine Williams (a Quaker cousin from Whittier), Mary, Reverend Williams. The four young women on the upper steps either taught or went to school with Anne.

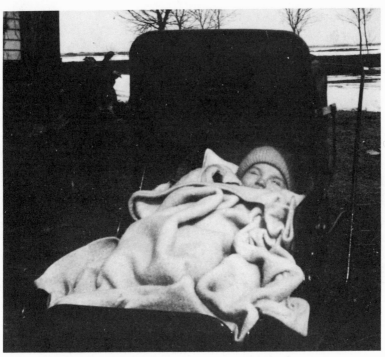

Betty sleeping in her buggy on the Hunter farm, 1915.

"Welcome to Hunter!"—Jim leads the band, 1915.

Main Street in Hunter, 1910, the year Anne arrived.

The Hunter Hotel.

The North Dakota prairie. (State Historical Society of North Dakota)

Shocking. (Fred Hultstrand Collection)

Threshing. (Fred Hultstrand Collection)

Spike pitching. (Fred
Hultstrand Collection)

Haying. (Fred Hultstrand Collection)

The house in Hunter, "Ann Inn," 1915.

Jim, Anne and Betty on front porch of the Hunter house, 1915.

Anne, Jimmy and Betty, 1920, in Minneapolis.

Jimmy and Betty in Maddock, 1922.

From the Standard, *November 22, 1923:*

"Doc Critchfield handed us a great big fat seegar yesterday. 'What's the idea—is this your birthday?' we asked. 'Nope,' was the reply. 'My son's.' He had just received word from Minneapolis that he was the daddy of another boy, who's been named Billy."

Jim

From a 1982 taped interview with the late G. C. Olson, retired jeweler in Maddock, then ninety-six:

". . . Well, I'll tell you. Doctors back in those days, they worked a little too hard, you know. They didn't get the hours. They'd come in and have to go way out again to Wellsburg or someplace. That's six hours by sleigh. Just to see one patient. That's a long, cold ride over the prairie in winter. You bet. They went into the country. Kitchen surgery and childbirth, you know. They didn't bring 'em into town like they do now . . ."

Jim:

When I think of those three years in Maddock, I see a Model T Ford bumping along rutted country roads, or, if winter, plunging horses and a bouncing buggy chased by yelping dogs. The Model T cost $635 brand-new. It was open to weather; most people still thought a closed car was for city slickers—you know, the profiteer in his limousine. If it was rainy and windy and I'd set off for a country call, those old-timers who always hung around downtown would cheeringly predict I'd never make it. Somebody would call, "All hell won't stop Doc, but, by God, that's where he may end up tonight." And they'd all have a good chuckle. To them, the good old days were the days of horses.

I loved that Model T. To go anywhere, I'd climb in and set the spark and throttle levers in position and jump out and crank. I'd pull the loop of wire that controlled the choke, spin the crank as hard as I could and, if the engine roared, I'd leap on the running board and set back the spark and throttle, but you had to be fast before the engine sputtered out. Patients would come in with fractured wrists and broken arms from cranking. One man in town, Nels Markusan, trying to get a tractor going, even broke a leg.

What happened was that the crank stuck and wouldn't budge and Nels climbed up and jumped down on it with both feet, trying to turn it over. It was a damn foolish thing to do. The crank slipped out of its socket and threw Nels down with a bad fracture. I could sympathize with him. It could be frustrating, especially on a cold morning. Many a time, I'd have to holler to Anne or Mabel or one of the kids to come out and sit in the driver's seat and pull that spark lever down before the engine died.

Once I was finally sitting at the wheel with the engine roaring full blast, I'd release the emergency hand brake, shove my left foot against the low-speed pedal, and as the car chugged into the street making a terrific racket, I'd release my foot, let the car in high gear, and with a shuddering jolt, be off. All I had to watch out for, aside from hitting somebody, was a long slope that you could burn your brake on. If you had good sense, you drove about fifteen miles in the outskirts of Maddock, ten miles downtown, and five miles around curves. It was so high and top-heavy, it didn't take all that much to tip a Model T over in loose gravel.

You bet your life. One time, right downtown, a careless twist of a steering wheel bumped a Model T against the hitching rail and overturned it. Two men were thrown out on the dirt. I saw it from my office window and came running. One man was unconscious, with a large, bleeding scalp wound, a nasty fracture in his right leg, and various cuts and abrasions. The other man got up on his feet right away and said he was unhurt. They were salesmen from Valley City. He and I drove in my Ford to the Harvey hospital with the unconscious man. My companion was so worried, he came to the operating room to watch the repair surgery. After a while, he said the sight of blood made him feel faint. He went outside to the reception room, where they found him lying on the floor, dead. An autopsy revealed a ruptured liver and massive internal bleeding. The other man was up and around in three months.

Cars went too slow in those days to cause many bad accidents, unless they hit somebody. One farmer outside town was badly injured when a Model T drove into his team during threshing. Since the driver, a young man, had hit another Model T and wrecked it just two months earlier, I was damn mad. But we didn't have traffic laws yet. In St. Paul just a few months before, for the first time, they found an automobile driver guilty of third-degree murder after he hit and killed a pedestrian. A lot of cars upset and had to be righted, but it took speed before we started getting the really bad collisions.

Somehow I found car breakdowns more aggravating than trouble with a team and buggy. Not Anne. A car meant she could go places. As soon as I bought the Ford, she couldn't wait until I'd teach her how to drive it. After that, I let her take it a week or two every summer so she could drive down to Iowa to see her folks. She'd pack the whole kit and caboodle of them—Betty, Jimmy, the new baby, Billy, even our dog, Brit—into that Model T. It must have been quite a sight. Three kids, a woman and a dog. The kids all glued to the window. Betty claimed that, once, a man cried, "Oh, look!" and went off into a ditch.

From a letter by Anne to Jim, mailed from Mount Vernon, Iowa, June 1924:

". . . We left Hunter in a pattering rain. Rain most of the day—mud splattered all over the windshield. Ran into gumbo mud by Casselton and Amenia and got stuck for a while there. By then we'd gone an average speed of five miles an hour. We had to detour two miles east of Amenia over a sod road so we could get through. Finally I pulled out the new lunch basket and put it in the least-muddy place we could find and the kids filled up. We all felt better and plugged on again, the baby sleeping, Brit, too. Just out of Amenia we headed east to avoid more mud and got lost. We plunged into sod only to get stuck. Nothing to do but pull out the rope you rigged up for us, hang it on the rear of the car and start the rescue work. After unloading suitcases, dog, kids and other items, I got enough rocks under the wheels to pull out. We plowed on nine miles more until we reached the old Red River Valley Trail north of Fargo. Landed at the Waldorf Hotel at ten-thirty Thursday night. The next day, while the kids played, I removed about a ton of mud from the Ford.

"In Minnesota stuck twice more in deep ruts but no serious trouble. After that graveled roads, extremely rutted, unmerciful shaking. The roads were rapidly drying and I took off the chains. Too soon. It rained again and back on went the chains. I kept driving and stepping on the gas and wondering why it wouldn't go any faster. I think you're right. Model T's are built for comfort, not for speed. A lovely graded road after Pelican Rapids. Stopped at a bakery to buy cinnamon rolls for the kids. Have been averaging 17.8 miles to the gallon. Gas has cost 27 to 33 cents a gallon. I expect I can do the whole trip on $15. I've used one quart of oil. No engine trouble at all. The cylinder didn't miss a stroke and haven't touched the spark plugs. It's a lot more strenuous than the train. But what a good way to see the country! . . ."

Jim:

Anne had great affection for that Model T. She said it always got you there and brought you back, even if your teeth got shaken loose on the way. If the tires failed when you were way out in the country, you could just take them off and make the trip back to town on the rims.

We still took the overnight train to the Twin Cities. If it was just me, I rode in the smoker to save the expense of a Pullman berth, and you could always count on getting a good poker game going. When Anne and the kids were along, we'd go Pullman.

The Model T went up on blocks in the woodshed from October until the roads dried up in the spring, and then it was back to a team and buggy if I could, getting Jim Pritchard or one of the boys at the livery stable where I kept my horses to go with me. I used to tell Anne one of my mares, Nellie, must've had some of her Quaker blood. As soon as Nellie was hitched, and harnessed, she'd balk and stubbornly refuse to go until the spirit moved her. If the night was overcast, it could get as black as pitch out on the prairie. Then you might have to get your directions from the railroad tracks. On clear nights, you could always get your bearings from the North Star. Barking dogs usually let you know when a house was coming up. I think some dogs just lived to chase and torment horses. Also, a few teams were terrified of trains and might try to beat one to a crossing.

Teams were afraid of dogs, but they could be calmed down after you went down the road. What really filled them with holy terror was a strange car. They'd rear, plunge, almost upset the buggy, back up and try to kick their way loose. The worst were headlights. You could see them a long way off at night, and when I did, I'd drive into the first farmyard or even a field and wait until the terrifying apparition went past. Still, it was a pain in the neck sitting there in the dark while some old Model T took its own sweet time slowly wheezing by. In time, most of the horses around Maddock got so used to cars they'd let them pass in the daytime. Never after dark.

In those days, horses and tractors were kept on together on most farms. At first, mostly all the farmers around Maddock just got tractors for plowing; they did their seeding and harvesting with horses. Even so, so much new machinery was coming in, I found a lot of a country doctor's practice had to do with trauma. A big threshing rig was getting all those belts and pulleys and levers and cranks. Or somebody could run a pitchfork through his hand. Or slip under the cleated iron wheels of the tractor he was driving. Or maybe a tractor would start up unexpectedly when he was fixing a disc or harrow, and the farmer could fall beneath the knives or teeth and be sliced into the dirt. It happened. I was also to see men get caught in the tines of hayloaders, get snagged and hoisted up by a haylift rope or get dropped, fall into a well or fall off the roof of a house or barn or from a windmill ladder.

Further comment from G. C. Olson:

". . . When I was maybe eight, nine years old, back in Wisconsin nearly ninety years ago, they threshed with twelve horses running around in a circle. My grandparents came over from Norway and I suppose it was the old way . . . I seen the first binder that come out too. A Champion grain binder, they called it. I was just a little shaver and I stood on a box and cut the bands off the bundles. And this fellow with the threshing crew, he says to me, 'Kid, you be careful, now. Don't cut my hands or I'll put you right in the threshing machine.' Boy, he scared the life out of me . . ."

Further comment from Emil Moen, of Hunter:

". . . My dad started the implement business here in 1894—back in the old horse-and-buggy days—and I went into business with him when I got out of the Navy in 1919. I'd say tractors didn't get into full force until World War I. Afterwards, everybody around here started getting tractors, a lot of them caterpillar and steel-wheeled, a few of them steam-powered. There were no rubber-tired tractors then. Of course, everybody still kept on their horses . . ."

Norman Borlaug:

". . . The first functional tractor we had was a little Fordson in 1926 or 1927. Oh, we still had horses, kept them right through World War II. I had a bachelor uncle, Oscar, he was a damn good mechanic, and he bought some of those old very first tractors. No tires. Just on steel. They never were any damn good. He bought a Waterloo Boy and he bought an Avery. They'd been junked someplace. And he had 'em out in the woods. For enjoyment, he'd just be out there on Sunday afternoons, trying to beat those things into shape and they'd be completely hopeless . . ."

Jim:

My very first patient in Maddock, Herman Smith, had been brought in from his farm twelve miles out with a badly lacerated hand. He'd been driving a new tractor and decided it needed some adjustment near the fly-wheel. While he was tending it, he got too close and his hand caught and was jammed against the hot fender. The palm was badly burned and torn, with several tendons severed. My second patient, a young Norwegian farmer, like so many of them were going to be, Chris Tvetan, came in with a broken forearm. He'd fallen off the hay load.

There were a lot of tractor accidents. One time, Jim Pritchard came in looking like the wreck of the Hesperus. His face was all cut and bloody. Jim's story was that he was working out at B. B. Gustjolen's farm and he wanted to drive a tractor into a field, but it meant taking down a barbed-wire gate. He hadn't intended to stay but just a few minutes, so he left it down. Along came Gustjolen himself, who saw the wire down and looped it back up in place. Pritchard crashed smack into it, the barbed wire ripped his clothing and cut a few deep gashes in his neck. I told him one just missed his jugular vein. "Doc," he said, "I'm just glad to be alive after such a close shave."

From Knut D., a retired farmer in his seventies:

". . . One time I was a spike pitcher on a threshing rig. So I pitched off every damn load that came up to the machine, you know. And my brother was hauling bundles. I don't know whether I slipped or what, but we were pitching and—you see, you face each other, you swing the old fork and you throw bundles in the feeder. And for some reason or other, his hand got in the way. Just when he swung, I swung, and the tine of my fork went right through his fingers. Way up in his hand here. And Doc Critchfield—we took him in there because I was afraid of tetanus or blood poisoning or something, you know—but that fork was so nice and shiny and clean, he said, there were no germs on that. But he run a swab down in that hole and it hurt pretty bad. He didn't use any anesthetic or anything. So we asked him if we could go pitching again, you know, go ahead and finish the day. He laughed and said, 'Sure can. It won't hurt me a bit.'

"He was tough, but he could be gentle, too. One of those old-fashioned country doctors. You don't find 'em like that any more. One time, another of my brothers had a runaway with a five-horse gang plow and broke his leg. Doc, he came out and wanted to take him to Minot, so a bone specialist could work on the leg. He asked if we had some whiskey. All we had was a pint of Four Roses, about three-quarters full yet. He told my brother to drink it all right down. Took him a little while to drink it, but, boy, did he pass out! It was the anesthetic to get him up to the hospital, you see . . ."

Jim:

Maddock is where I learned to be a doctor. A country practice quickly taught you to diagnose. Mistake pneumonia for appendicitis and it might cost your patient his life. So, when you got the Model T going or the horses calmed down or whatever, and finally got to that remote farmhouse, the first thing was to make a diagnosis. A blood count could be made. Sometimes I could do it right away; other times, if surgery was involved, it could take an hour or more. If the patient was too scared, I tried not to operate; at school, they'd taught us that you can literally frighten people to death.

I'd spent two years as an intern at Northwestern Hospital in Minneapolis and been offered a post at the Mayo Clinic in Rochester. Anne, I think, would have liked me to take it, but she left it up to me. Ray argued it was too soon to specialize and wanted me to come back to North Dakota. I looked around, convinced there was a Hunter somewhere just waiting to welcome me with open arms. I guess the truth was that I was still trying to follow in Father's footsteps.

If I decided on surgery, I'd get the woman of the house to put my instruments on the kitchen stove to boil, along with her wash boiler half full of water and a teakettle or two. In my black instrument bag, I usually carried enough clean linen to cover two tables, a clean sheet for the patient, and surgical gowns for myself and maybe Anne or a nurse. We used sponges and rubber gloves. Some doctors were using chloroform, but I stuck to ether and the drop method, getting Anne to do it when I could. The sterilized instruments were laid out on a sheet. In a real emergency, you had to make do.

You had to shave the patient. Among the German-Russians the men might be bearded, with no razor in the house. In that case, I'd clip the hair with scissors and scrub the stubble with home-made lye soap. When you came to dress a wound after the operation, you always had to figure that if a patient complained of pain from the sutures—as a good many did twelve to twenty-four hours after an operation—some darn fool might remove the dressing. If they did, the wound could burst open and I'd have to scramble like hell to get out there to put somebody's guts back inside.

You never knew what to expect next. The most common surgery was taking out tonsils. I usually just did it with a local anesthetic while the patient sat in a chair in my office. Most of them got up and walked home. But you never knew when someone might start hemorrhaging. Then you'd have the nerve-wracking job of placing sutures in a blood-filled throat. Or there was always the chance you might drop something. It happened once when I was taking out an appendix. The patient unexpectedly moved and I dropped my knife. His wife had gone out and left me alone. I was able to twist the catgut until it broke, but for a minute I was sweating.

In a country practice, you also ran into a lot of phobias. Oh, people in town bandied about Freudian theory real casually. A pain was just "psychosomatic," so-and-so had "an Oedipus complex" or "an inferiority complex" or "should overcome his inhibitions." Mostly Maddock just had its chronic female complainers. If one of these ladies came to me about her stomach, did I tell her there was nothing wrong? No, not if I wanted to live in peace. Many a night, I'd go home for supper and tell Anne, "I had one lady come in today and there wasn't anything wrong with her that I could find. But she was awful sick."

The phobias you didn't belittle were among the country people. Norwegians, Danes, German-Russians, they were closer to one another. A measles epidemic might start in a country school and pretty soon a whole neighborhood of farms would be affected. Generally, they didn't call me, but put whoever was sick to bed and kept them warm. This usually worked unless the bedclothes in some of those cold farmhouses got disarranged. Then I might find children with bronchitis or pneumonia. As in Hunter, most farmers around Maddock didn't call the doctor unless somebody was gravely ill or badly hurt.

But the loneliness of the North Dakota prairie was a great breeder of anxiety and worry. Sometimes it seemed like the more remote the farm, the more likely you were to find a mentally distressed patient waiting for you. It could be aggravating to make a long trip only to find a hysterical male or female with an imaginary illness at the other end. But to a sufferer way out on a farm somewhere, such an illness could be terrifyingly real. About all I could do was show sympathy and patiently repeat all the negative findings. One farmer's wife way out in the country who had a big brood of children took poison after she failed to menstruate. It turned out in the autopsy she wasn't pregnant at all.

Another not uncommon problem I had in Maddock was an old-school doctor's resentment of a newly graduated one. Dr. Moeller had earned his medical degree at the University of Christiania in Norway in 1892, over thirty years before. We had to cooperate some, as he was city health officer. He dealt with dogs suspected of rabies, made sure people put their "Small Pox" and "Scarlet Fever" signs up; a couple times we operated together, and we examined all the county's babies together in the spring. But, for a long time, Dr. Moeller kept his distance.

From the late Myrtle Legreid Olson, then a farmer's widow near Maddock, interviewed on tape sixty years later:
". . . We lived next door to the Critchfields in the wintertime. In the spring, we'd move back to the farm. My brother, Noralf, who was Betty's age, got sick and we called Dr. Moeller and he said Noralf had an acute appendicitis and he was going to have to operate on him at home. You see, it was December and storming so. The trains were blocked. In the blizzard there wasn't any way to get Noralf to a hospital. And Dr. Critchfield, he wanted to help. But the old doctor said, 'No, I'll do it myself.' He was an old man and kind of stubborn that way. But he needed a nurse for the anesthesia. Somebody took a team and brought one from Oberon, over twenty miles away. It was already four in the morning. And this nurse was

so chilled, she couldn't do anything for a while. And then they operated on Noralf. And he died."

Jim:

As time went by, I learned that though Dr. Moeller was sometimes pretty helpless when it came to recent medical advances, he stuck to his task. It was the faithfulness of such old doctors that endeared them to their patients. Dr. Moeller was a man of few words, because there were no words. He did his best. I learned how to earn the trust of patients from him. In time, we made our peace.

Further comment from Edwin Anderson:

". . . I'll tell you, I was sick. Couldn't swallow for nothing. I couldn't even drink water. Just think of that. And I did my chores and sat on a plow for a week. My father, he said at last, 'You better ride into town with me.' He had a load of grain and I had to sit on that. It was cold in late fall. I should've been dead a long while ago.

"Old Dr. Moeller, he took a culture and put it under his armpit and it grew in the warmth. And he says—he had this strong Norwegian accent, you know—'These are the healthiest diphtheria germs I've ever seen.' He gave me antitoxin. Then the ride back home on this wagon and they put me to bed. The whole family got antitoxin and they quarantined the place.

"Dr. Moeller says, 'I'm putting you on just a gargling water, because there's no other medicine I can give you.' I laid there a whole week. I couldn't swallow. I couldn't breathe. Dr. Moeller came out in his Model T Ford every day. One morning, my throat started to bleed. My mother was just about frantic. Then Dr. Moeller came and he says, 'Well, now we got it just about licked. You just keep gargling every day.' After I got well, my voice completely changed. It affected the vocal cords, you see. But old Dr. Moeller, he drove out to our farm every single day . . ."

Jim

One of the worst blizzards in memory struck Maddock our first winter there, in February 1923. There had been a cold snap and then it had warmed up again. I went out to Wellsburg that morning and remember it well. The air had that same moistness it used to have just before bad storms in Hunter. In town, there was no longer any frost. The day before, snow was melting on the roofs and water dripping from the gutters. I was on my way home that afternoon when the mist turned to drizzling rain, the rain to snow and I wondered if we were going to be in for it. Big wet flakes started whirling around. I was anxious to get back to town.

Soon the horses' backs were white with snow. My face was wet with it. The air grew colder, the wind came up. When I passed a windbreak, I could hear the storm shaking the trees. The snowflakes got harder as the temperature fell. They started blowing over the road in angry sheets. The wind picked up steadily. It was starting to shriek. I bent forward. Within fifteen minutes, I couldn't see a thing, just the team and buggy and snow. I couldn't tell what was thirty feet ahead. It was that rushing combination of wind and snow even horses can't face very long. The snow found its way through every crack. My team soon had a mind of their own. At every crossroad and driveway, they'd try to turn and make a bolt for it. I had to hold the reins tight to keep them headed toward Maddock. The fiercer the wind, the more frantic the horses got. Once, with a terrifying jolt, the buggy went off the road, tipping on two wheels in the ditch. Instantly I was thrust back as those scared horses fled on. It wasn't long before we entered an area with dark shapes just visible on either side. Then I saw a tree, a house. I'd made it to the edge of town.

It was going to be a real storm and I didn't envy those in isolated farms way out on the prairie. If you got caught outside, the natural urge was to run for it, to try to reach the nearest house. The danger was, you might never find it, as I almost didn't that time in Hunter when I rode after Father and Claus in the snowstorm as a boy. People got lost ten, fifteen feet from their own doors. What you had to do was go with the drift of the wind or wait until it lifted. The cold didn't become intense until the wind went down, so there was little danger of freezing unless you got overheated. Blizzards kept claiming lives. Just the year before, a party of children returning from a spelling bee froze to death. A whole family died when their house caught fire during a storm. The only one found alive was a small boy who'd crawled into a straw pile with a lot of pigs; the warmth of their bodies saved him from freezing.

All night the storm howled outside. It was nice and cozy in our house, and before they went to bed, Betty and Jimmy sat with their faces pressed to the window as great flakes of snow, flashing white, darted against the glass, clung to it a second, and then were whirled away by the storm. Frost formed on the glass, and when they scratched away a place with their fingernails, Mabel told them not to put it in their mouths, as it would taste like dirt. Of course they had to find out for themselves, and sure enough, it did.

The next morning was clear and thirty below. Everything—houses, barns, horses, sleighs, trees—was white with snow. The telegraph clerk down at the depot said train service throughout North Dakota was at a standstill. The wires were down. He expected the trains to be blocked for several days until the main Soo line was cleared. There were reports of mountain-sized drifts of hard-packed snow that would have to be tunneled through in places. People coming into Maddock in sleighs told of circling huge drifts and seeing cows feeding from the tops of haystacks. There were tales of sheep smothering as they huddled for warmth. The biggest drift downtown was higher than a one-story building and so hard I could easily walk on the crust without breaking through. The kids were going to have a grand time coasting on their sleds and toboggans and sliding down on their homemade wooden skis. The hotel was full of stranded "drummers," salesmen who normally would have caught the morning train. Down at the *Standard* office, Jim Lowell said he was worried about Henry Liudahl, whose farm was about a mile from town. He'd set out by foot when the storm started, saying there was nobody at home to look after his stock.

That afternoon, a phone call came from a man who farmed six miles northeast of town. One of his neighbors, a Mrs. Erickson, was missing. Her children were in bad shape. Could I come out right away? I had them saddle up a horse and took along wire cutters to cut barbed wire so I could head straight across open country and save time. The roads were so badly drifted I knew nobody would mind. Farmers just repaired their fences, knowing they were helping out a sick neighbor. Carl Erickson was a familiar figure downtown; he'd only rented that farm and moved his family out there the previous summer. The neighbor said Carl had been stranded at the Louis Warberg farm, about a half mile west of his own, where he'd sat out the storm. When he'd returned home this morning, he found his three children huddled in bed under a feather tick, trying to keep warm. The fire had gone out. The oldest child, seven, had said his mother had become frantic worrying about Carl and had gone out to look for him. She'd never come back. I rode as fast as I could and hoped like hell she'd found some kind of shelter.

Long before I reached them, just before dark, I could see the huddle of little black figures, practically lost in that empty expanse of white. They were standing by a fence not too far from the Warberg place, which was off in the distance. At first, as I rode up and dismounted, it looked as if they were grouped around an unfinished work of white sculpture, though they'd done their best to brush away as much caked snow from her head and shoulders as they could. She was in a kneeling position, her head and body plastered all over with snow, and she seemed to be crouched with one hand held up to her face, as if she were trying to shield her eyes while she tried to see ahead into that boiling snow. Closer up, I saw her arms and head and shoulders had naturally slumped down in death and that it was the barbed wires of the fence that had caught her coat, holding her arm and body up in what looked like a searching posture. The fence must have stopped her. Her face was frosted white all over too. The poor thing's eyes were open as if she'd died while staring ahead in a fixed, concentrated gaze; you could feel her sense of horror. Judging by the direction of the wind during the storm, which must have decided the direction she took, she couldn't have missed the Warberg house by very much, maybe just a couple of dozen yards. She must have been trying to find her way home, maybe going in circles. Staggering around so close in the blinding snow. God almighty!

The children needed urgent medical attention. The youngest, the baby, had a severe case of frostbite; the yellow urine on his diapers was frozen stiff. The seven-year-old boy told us, "Mama said, 'I'm coming back right away. You kids get into bed and keep warm. Do you hear?' " Carl Erickson said he thought Chris Sabbe, who owned the farm, would have come out to see to his stock.

What prompted Mrs. Erickson to take such a desperate chance? She must have been beside herself worrying about him. It was easy enough to imagine her, a young woman used to living in town, with the wind and snow shriek-

ing and screaming and wrapping the house in blackness. Loneliness was
what you had to fear most on the prairie. How often had I left a farmhouse,
with human company and warmth behind me, and gone into the cold and
dark again, and felt that hush of solitary places where the wind howls and
nothing else is heard. Emptiness all around and that terrible sense of futility
and fright. Poor Mrs. Erickson! Stiff as a board and dressed so poorly. We
had to bring a horse tank into the house and fill it with water to thaw her
out enough to straighten her . . .

From the Standard, *February 15:*
"THURSDAY, 11:30 A.M. THE BODY OF MRS. C. B. ERICKSON
HAS JUST BEEN FOUND. MEMBERS OF THE SEARCH PARTY LO-
CATED THE BODY LYING ALONGSIDE A FENCE ABOUT A
HALF MILE EAST OF THE LOUIS WARBERG HOUSE . . . SHE
COULD NOT HAVE MISSED THE HOUSE BY MORE THAN A FEW
FEET . . . She became frantic over the welfare of her husband, started out
to search for him and got lost in the blinding storm . . . She was thirty-
five, the children eight months to seven years . . ."

Further comments taken fifty-nine years later:
Myrtle Olson:
". . . Our farm was just a quarter mile from where she was found. Frozen stiff. They had to thaw her out, you know . . . Her husband didn't
come home. Some said he was drinking and playing cards . . ."

Agnetha Bergsgaard:
". . . She didn't have any business going out and leaving the children
either, as far as that goes . . . I guess she must have waited and waited for
him and she didn't have any coal or wood in the house and three small
children and she knew where he was . . . But out in a blizzard, you know,
you can lose your direction in a hurry . . ."

Mabel Swanson:
". . . My father was in the search party. About six neighbors found her.
She'd wandered into the coulee and come up against a barbed-wire fence.
And there she set, kneeling, with her hand up like she was trying to see
through the snow. Dr. Critchfield was called out. They couldn't straighten
her out, so they brought the horse tank right into the kitchen and filled it up
with water and put her in that. Golly, it was thirty below. She was froze
solid. The baby's diapers froze right to his seat. Yes, when he come home,
that's what Erickson found. He had to leave town. They would have tarred
and feathered him . . . The manager of the creamery and his wife took the

one boy and raised and educated him. They would have taken them all, but her sister from Minnesota come up and wanted all the others. That boy is well situated now. Of course, he's a man in his sixties and a grandfather . . . Mrs. Erickson was the doctor's most tragic case in Maddock. Unless you'd say it was that young man from Wisconsin. But that was kept pretty secret . . ."

Jim:

For ten years or so, David W.—not his real name—had been coming out every summer to work on his uncle's farm. His family were big landowners in southern Wisconsin, but one figured David just liked to get away from home. The year before, around threshing time, I'd seen him around town, at ball games or shows at the Crescent Theatre. He was tall and husky, maybe in his mid-twenties. So that it came as a shock when his uncle, an elderly man, called me out to his farm and took me into David's bedroom that day. Instead of the big, healthy fellow I expected, he was so wasted and emaciated I hardly recognized him. His muscular arms still had some strength, but his face had the sunken cheeks and darkened eyes of a much older man. There was something so crushed and humiliated in his weak smile, I could hardly look him in the eyes. I did an examination and found partial paralysis in the limbs and a general paresis setting in. The germs had invaded organs and tissues all over his body. It was the worst case of neurosyphilis I'd ever seen.

The initial infection evidently went back to his teens. From the start, the family had kept it secret. I found out that when symptoms first appeared, his parents had sent David to Milwaukee, where he was given a Wassermann test. After a positive diagnosis, he was treated with bismuth salts and arsenic. This appeared to arrest the disease.

Then, a couple of years before, he'd started getting spells of irritability; he'd get tired easily, become forgetful. At first, David thought nothing of it, then his behavior become more erratic. He'd go from extreme elation to deep depression for no reason. Often, he was confused, he forgot things, sometimes his judgment seemed impaired. Then came periodic seizures and the onset of general paresis. Aside from paralysis of his arms and legs, its most devastating effects were on his mind. It was a common cause of insanity.

His family, evidently fearing the social stigma, didn't want him home. They sent him out to his aunt and uncle on the farm. Now, as his condition rapidly worsened, the old couple didn't know what to do. I told them no hospital would accept him. The only facility that took neurosyphilis cases was the Insane Asylum in Jamestown. David was paralyzed enough to be helpless, and though often manic, he was still rational much of the time. He needed medical attention, but I was damned if I was going to send him off to die in a madhouse.

I told the family I'd see what I could do, maybe find somebody equipped and prepared to give David the nursing care he needed. I wanted to talk to Anne. Until I could find somebody, it would really be up to her. At the back of our house, just off the pantry, there was a small bedroom intended for the hired girl. Mabel had her room upstairs with us, so it stood empty. It might do for the time being. The seizures were getting so frequent, I suspected David might not have all that much time left. If so, the main thing was to make his days as restful as possible. There was some question whether late syphilis was infectious. Taking no chances, I decided that everything that came in contact with his body—towels, bedding, brushes, comb, razor, soap, cups, glasses, knives, forks, spoons, plates—would have to be disinfected with alcohol or destroyed. Anne responded as I knew she would. I gave strict orders to Mabel and the children not to go anywhere near David's room, not even into the pantry. Nor was anything to be said to the neighbors about his presence in our house; attitudes toward victims of venereal disease weren't always humane and there was no sense in scaring people.

They brought him there that night. We carried him into the little room and put him to bed. He could look out on the backyard. Luckily, we were having a warm fall and heating was no problem. David told me of the intense pain he felt in his legs and his back, a chill, heavy pain. I gave him some drugs.

In the next few days, I got to know him. David's once muscular legs had slowly become shriveled and immovable. His arms, now fixed to his sides, were also emaciated and limp, and his ribs and shoulder blades stood out unnaturally from his shrunken chest. He could hardly move his head without suffering pain. It seemed there was no part of his body, no limb, that did not ache and cause him agony. Yet David was somehow still a gracious human being. I attended him many times a day, and almost every time I did during those first few days, he'd struggle to tell me not to "bother." He could still speak, articulating with difficulty, and once he said, "Doc, I want to die. I'm only a burden to you and there's no hope for me. Why don't God just let me go?" I think his wish for death was genuine; what was happening to him was making him look on it as the fulfillment of his desires. I hoped fate would mercifully grant him his wish quickly.

He hung on. A couple of weeks went by. David could hardly move his hands or head at all. He lay with his eyes closed, listening, he let me know, to the sounds of life that reached him through the walls: Mabel calling the children, Anne rattling pans in the kitchen, Betty and Jimmy playing, the baby crying. David in all his weariness would listen and drift in and out of sleep until, at last, the door would open and I'd be back again.

Further comment from Mabel Swanson:

". . . David W. was in that little room for about two, three weeks, maybe a little longer. I saw him just the once, the night they carried him in. He was terribly thin and white. There was a bad smell. I think he had open sores. Dr. Critchfield kept his dishes and bedclothes in the pantry and he washed it all out there with alcohol. He kept disinfecting his hands. When the doctor wasn't with him, David stayed there alone. He was paralyzed and couldn't move his legs. I know the doctor had to put diapers on him and took them out and burned them. The doctor worried about him. He worried too much about his patients. David's folks back in Wisconsin were well-to-do people, I heard the doctor say. I don't remember any of them came to the house, though. If they did, I didn't know about it . . ."

Jim:

Then David caught pneumonia and I knew it was just a matter of time. When I slipped the ear tubes of the stethoscope in place, his eyes had an intense, reproachful look. I examined his chest and found the lungs were thickening. My expression must have shown something, for there was a faint stir and his clammy lips moved, forming the words quite distinctly, "I can't, I can't . . . die." From then on, he seemed to be fighting for every breath. Before daybreak the next day, when dying patients often go, I got up and went down to sit beside him. I didn't want him to be alone at the end.

With the paralysis of most of his body, his brain so damaged its reasoning power now came and went, his vision fading from atrophy of the optic nerve, David had little to live for. He looked paler and more wasted by the hour; sometime during the night he seemed to have aged; his face was more emaciated, his eyes more intense. He could only move his lips a little now, breathing painfully, but somehow he was able to let me know that everything "at home"—I suppose he meant back with his family in Wisconsin—was going far, far away from him and it would never go on again or be repeated. I rested my hand on his burning forehead and tried to get him to say something more, but while he kept his moist eyes on me, he didn't utter a word. Soon I surmised he could no longer understand anything. When the sun came up, it got warm, almost as warm as a summer day. It was so quiet in that little room that a fly that had flown in when I'd opened the door could distinctly be heard buzzing at the window screen. I got the swatter and killed it. In mid-morning I was called out on an emergency. I hated to go, but David now seemed to have slipped into a coma. Anne said I was not to worry, that she would take a look at David every so often and keep a close eye on him. She would phone me if need be. When I got back, she said he was still alive but his eyes were closed.

"I'll let him sleep . . . what's the use . . . it's not good . . . a coma . . ." I couldn't express myself, but Anne understood anyway. Night came on and passed slowly. There was a hush about the house which even the children seemed to feel; they were subdued. Tired as I was, I couldn't sleep. I tossed and turned, and towards morning I went down to the patient's room. Sometime after that I came out and told Anne that David has just breathed his last.

That night, I wanted her company, so I asked Anne to leave the kids with Mabel and come along while I made my evening calls in town. The first was a look in on a little boy who'd been burned when he'd held a celluloid pinwheel over a fire on the kitchen stove, thinking the heat would make it twirl. It had exploded, burning his neck and chest. Now any touch on the angry, deep burns was painful. It's hard to be stoic when you're only seven and he whimpered and cried as I gave him a hypodermic sedative to see him through the night. The second call was to lance two abscesses on a man's swollen purple arm and put on a new dressing. The third was to a little old Norwegian man dying of cancer; normally brave, that night his courage had left him and he kept saying, "I'm frightened, Doc, I'm frightened." The last was a straightforward case of senile dementia. The patient was a ninety-two-year-old woman who would peacefully lie in her bed for weeks on end in calm acceptance of her state. Then, all of a sudden, for a day or two she'd get all excited. That night, she was deeply agitated about a fight with somebody who'd been dead for forty years. Just coming up to the house, we could hear her voice rising in a querulous outburst. I gave her a sedative so she and her family could get some sleep.

As we walked home, I asked Anne, "Why so quiet tonight, honey?"

"It's nothing . . . Oh, Jim, I know somebody has to look after all these people. But you enter into things so, feel with people. That young man such a long time and all this pain tonight. It makes you liked by your patients. But I know it's taking an emotional toll on you too. You worry about them so much. Sometimes I wonder . . . Oh, I don't know. You were happy on the farm . . ."

"Anne . . . This is what I want to do."

I thought her mood had changed, until, just outside our house, she burst out again.

"Oh, Jim, are you going to give your whole life to fighting pain and death? I'm afraid for you."

Jim

Whenever freight trains came through town, migrant workers would be riding on the boxcar roofs. The country's farm economy had never recovered from the collapse of 1920, when the wheat price dropped from almost two dollars and a half a bushel down to a dollar. A migrant army was on the move. Many were just farm boys from Minnesota, Wisconsin and Iowa, out to see the country and earn some money. Others were just aimless hoboes and tramps. But there were growing numbers of lone wanderers who'd lost a factory job or been evicted as a southern sharecropper. A good many were tenant farmers who'd been "tractored off" their land by an owner who wanted to consolidate two or three farms and run them with machinery.

Some of these men had been on the road for years—jumping freights, hitchhiking, panhandling, shunting back and forth across the country in hopes of a job. They slept in haylofts or bunkhouses, with the crudest of stoves, cots and water buckets, nomads nobody wanted to see except in the August-to-October threshing season. I got them as patients—or bodies to examine. One time, a young man hanged himself from a viaduct just outside town. The first thing I noticed were the burns around his mouth. I did an autopsy, which confirmed he'd drunk carbolic acid first. Terrible. Inside his overalls was a billfold and the address of his parents. A farm in Kansas.

Among this wandering army was Elihugh Johnston, Jessie's only surviving brother. A man now in his sixties and the family ne'er-do-well, Elihugh had gone off as a youth to follow the railroads West, laying ties. After he hadn't been heard from for years, a rare postcard arrived for Anne, postmarked Tulsa, Oklahoma:

"My Dear Niece—. . . Times are very dull here. No work and no money in circulation. The town is full of idle men and I don't see it getting better. I am selling a pretty good can opener but I have to work hard to make a living . . ."

A letter to Jessie from their father, Eli Johnston, dated forty years earlier, perhaps suggests how some lives go wrong:

". . . Got a card from Elihugh this evening postmarked Red Cloud, Neb. He wanted to borrow $200 for a year . . . Of course I did not let him have it. If he should write to you anytime during the winter to borrow any money, don't let him have any. He would be better off without. Unless he should get sick or be in distress I will not give him a cent. I want him to learn something about the value of money. If he'd come home to Linn Grove I'd have helped him raise cows as we have both hay and grass now. He chose not to and thinks his way is best. I told him in the card I sent that he had made a mistake and time would tell which had the better judgment . . ."

Riding the rails was dangerous. Another time, we found the body of a youngster literally torn apart. Arms and legs severed, torso badly ripped up and the head completely crushed. As far as we could tell, he'd either fallen off the roof of a boxcar or from the draw rods below the body of the cars, right above the track, the most dangerous way to hop a freight. It was how so many of them rode. The wheels must have gone right over him. It turned out that Gunder Legreid, a farmer in town, was able to identify the boy. He'd been working for him a few weeks earlier and left to go to Canada. The boy's folks had a farm in Minnesota and Gunder figured he was on his way home.

One of our own boys, from a place called Munich near Devil's Lake, joined the wandering migrant army and got arrested down in Florida for what they claimed was "fighting his way onto a freight train." He was sentenced to three months on a chain gang and sent to work in a lumber camp owned by a Wisconsin company. It was a real hellhole, and the boy, Martin Tabert, was flogged by a guard named Walter Higginbotham, notorious in the camp as the "whipping boss." Tabert died four days later. The American Legion in North Dakota raised a big outcry, and people all over the state, and finally the whole country, donated money. Ultimately, the lash was outlawed in Florida, the sheriff who arrested Tabert was punished and the judge who sentenced him was kicked out of office. Higginbotham was given twenty years for manslaughter, though another Florida judge a year later reversed the sentence and set him free. Tabert could have been anybody's boy. The case brought home how vulnerable any migratory worker could be.

Sometimes Maddock's labor market got completely glutted. Wages were low or not to be had, and the migrants, broke and with nowhere to go, would squat in a hobo jungle along the tracks out east of town or they'd sleep on hay in the stockyards. I'd see plenty of them downtown, begging and hanging around the poolroom or the cafe, hunched like so many ragged black scarecrows on the hitching rails, spitting their tobacco juice and talking in low voices. They scared Mabel, who said nice girls couldn't hardly venture down Main Street any more. Some of the migrants took the meager wages and all the humiliations bitterly. They talked of striking, and sometimes, while on a threshing crew, they struck.

Everytime they did, you had a real panic in Maddock. There'd be anti-strike ordinances, sometimes armed deputies would go out and knock down their pitiful camps, some hotheads around town even talked of violence. The trouble was that few people in town saw the migrants as a doctor who had to treat them naturally did—most of them just ordinary men down on their luck. Instead they were commonly seen as dirty, ignorant outsiders, misfits, failures, dupes for Red agitators, potentially dangerous criminals. Maddock's solution was to keep this sad army moving.

From the Standard, *July 26, 1923:*

"DONE GONE—Two gentlemen of color have returned to parts unknown after a three-week visit to Maddock . . . The cop was moved to inform them that the stockyards were not a tourist camp and he would be pleased if they would spend their vacation elsewhere . . ."

Jim:

Not everybody was so unsympathetic. Here and there I heard of instances of real hospitality and kindness toward the migrants. One time out in Hamberg, when I went out to pick up a worker with pneumonia and take him into Harvey hospital, the local farmers passed the hat to pay the bill. Some people were decent.

Edwin Anderson:

". . . You know, the train would come in and there'd be anywhere from ten to thirty, forty men lined up along the roof of a car, sitting there. When you had so many, the railroads had to let them ride . . . Some of them were really nice. One man who came back to thresh year after year, name of Tuttle, why, he was a prince of a fellow. One time, I asked him, 'Why are you out working with a threshing crew?' And he said, 'Have you ever heard of John Barleycorn?' He was battling with liquor, you see. Another time, my brother asked a good worker if he wanted to stay on as our hired man.

'Oh,' he says, 'I gotta get back to my job.' My brother asks, 'What kind of job have *you* got?' 'Oh,' he says, 'I'm a professor of English at De La Salle University in Kansas City, Missouri.' We had all kinds. There was an author, writing a book, you know, and one time, there was a detective, working undercover to try and find out who set fire to an elevator in Esmond . . ."

Jim:

It was the time of the Red Scare and the way some people in town talked you'd have thought every migrant worker was a Wobbly or a bearded agitator with a smoking bomb in hand. Maddock even had its Ku Klux Klan. Oh, nobody in town ever got lynched or tarred and feathered or kidnapped and beaten up. But we read in the papers about the Klan doing those things in other places. They had picnics, those men would parade in white hoods, there'd be a few burning crosses and everybody'd wonder, "What are they really up to?" One time, when I was leading the Maddock band, they asked us to play for a picnic and I tried to figure out why such ordinary people would join. Maybe the white hood and robe, the fiery crosses, the secrecy and hocus-pocus appealed to folks who found a North Dakota prairie town pretty drab and dull and wanted a little excitement.

From the Standard, *August 12, 1923:*

"Maddock's best, biggest, and in fact, only band has been hired to play at the August 23 picnic on the Sheyenne River of the Ku Klux Klan. Klansmen should fill the lunch basket full, pile the Mrs. and the kids into the old Tin Lizzie and head for . . ."

September 25:

"KU KLUX KLAN SPEAKER . . . Reverend August Deming of Fargo spoke to a capacity crowd at the Opera House Tuesday night on 'One Hundred Percent Americanism.' He got into a hot argument when he attacked parochial schools . . ."

Edwin Anderson:

". . . They were all over North Dakota. Certain people, they all of a sudden discriminated against. You could just as well be white to the Ku Klux Klan as you could be colored. They burned four or five crosses in Maddock, right down on Central Avenue. They'd saturate them with petroleum, I suppose. They'd burn a cross against Catholics, foreigners, anything. I remember seeing them march through town in their white hoods. Nobody knew who they were. Oh, not very many of them. Twenty or thirty was all . . ."

Jim:

A few of our local hoodlums took advantage of the Klan's existence. I was called out to the Hofstrand farm to treat their son Magnus, after a gang of boys had driven up when he was home alone and attacked and beaten him. It was just a school feud, but one of the boys chalked "K.K.K." on the side of the house.

It was hard times. For a little while, when the Great War brought a big demand for wheat and tractors came in, it began to look like North Dakota had a great future. A new power era was going to revolutionize agriculture. Cars and radios and electricity suggested modern factory methods could work in farming, too. The bandwagon of Coolidge prosperity didn't lack for riders in the cities. But Maddock's boom had fizzled out by the early 1920s. Now rainfall was poor and high interest rates, high taxes and high prices on tractors and machinery were bringing real hardship to my rural patients.

It was the same story back in Hunter. In the harsh cost-price squeeze, Harry couldn't keep up his mortgage payments and our farm was soon taken over, in 1925, by the bank in a sheriff's seizure. Like so many others, Harry left farming for good, becoming a county agent down in South Dakota. The war and the end of homestead land at first pushed land values up too high. Maddock's farmers were caught between heavy debts, high costs and low prices. Now, as land values fell, a good many were losing savings in a wave of small bank failures.

How to solve the farm problem? We'd tried our socialist experiment with the Nonpartisan League. After six stormy years in power in North Dakota, it was judged a failure. Even Theodore Roosevelt had turned against the League's leaders, calling them "vicious Bolsheviks." The nearest it all came to blowing up in Maddock was in 1924. That summer, the Industrial Workers of the World in Chicago called for a general strike during the wheat harvest. An IWW manifesto said the Wobbly in "the rattletrap barns of North Dakota" had little to cover "his freezing body," but whatever "soggy comforter or stinking horse blanket" the farmer, "in the greatness of his heart," chose to supply "the 'harvest bum.'" There was a certain truth to this. I always said that good meals, a place at the family table, and a bed with clean sheets would convert any Wobbly.

Instead, the county passed a new law; anybody the sheriff deemed a "vagrant" could be fined a hundred dollars and jailed for thirty days. In July, farmers all around Maddock met to work out a plan "to keep the profits at home." They wanted to hold down a thresher's pay to thirty-five cents an hour. While this was going on, the migrants started begging more aggressively. They'd put the arm on you downtown, saying, "I say, buddy, could you stake me to a feed? I haven't eaten in two days."

From IWW pamphlet given Maddock's harvesters:

". . . The jails of North Dakota are small and the harvest is ripening fast. The farmers must give way . . . This is raising a stench all over the country . . ."

From an editorial in the Standard, *August 28:*

". . . The boys in their 'flivvers' from Minnesota, Wisconsin and Iowa have gone out to farms and asked for work and proved the most desirable help. The Wobbly who expects the farmer to come to town and beg him to work for him is out of luck. No, Maddock isn't afraid of the IWW . . ."

The Standard, *September 4:*

"MADDOCK CITIZENS WILL BE ON GUARD . . . More than 40 men have signed up as volunteer night watchmen from midnight to 4 A.M. With the community on the alert and armed with businesslike shotguns, it is likely the lawless gangs that have preyed upon banks and stores of smaller towns in the state the past few weeks will confine their attacks to communities where the citizens are asleep at the switch . . ."

Same edition:

". . . There were at least half a dozen IWW organizers in Maddock this week. Fellows who never do a lick of work but bully harvest hands into paying tribute to them . . ."

Edwin Anderson:

". . . That collector of the Wobblies, he'd come up to each man and he had a little red book. And red stamps he sold for ten cents a stamp. The membership was three dollars. So he'd sell a man thirty of them stamps and he'd paste that into the book. They'd come out and thresh in the morning and if they figured they should have a little more money, they'd strike. They go up to the owner or whoever had the threshing machine and say, 'We won't go out this morning until we get five cents more an hour.' Or ten cents more. It didn't matter to them whether it might be going to rain or anything like that. These weren't real farmers, see. It happened lots of times. Some people got scared there was going to be violence. It never came to nothing, though . . ."

Jimmy

From James Critchfield, eldest son of Anne and Jim, interviewed at Bannock-burn Farm, his home in Oakton, Virginia, thirty-five years later:

My first memory of Father is when I was six years old in Maddock. One spring after the snow had melted, I can remember . . . H-m-m-m, I remember going out in back of our house, there was a field there and—yes, it was after a rain ended, not snow—and we had sort of a gravel pit back there where kids used to play. I had forgotten to come home for supper. I had been told to come home at a certain time and I forgot. I saw Father coming through the dusk across the field and I hid behind a shock of grain. Actually, I pushed some grain aside and sat in the middle of a shock. I saw Father coming and somehow he knew just where to go and he came straight to where I was. He walked right across that field of grain to where I was sitting. I looked through a crack in the grain at his feet standing there and knew the jig was up. Father spoke.

"All right, Jimmy, hold out your hand."

I did and he slapped it. It was the only time in my life that Father ever laid a hand on me. It was Sunday evening.

With Mother, I can't remember a time when I couldn't remember her. She has not only been the central figure in my life but in the lives of all of us . . . In Maddock all the kids spoke Norwegian. And Jens Nielsen, a wonderful old Dane, lived on the farm in back of us. Father and Jens liked to play cards and we'd go out to see him in a bobsled filled with hay and blankets on those brilliant, cold North Dakota nights. The Nielsens lived about a mile from us, out in the country.

From Edith Nielsen Bjelde, retired teacher, Fargo, sixty years later:

". . . Dr. Critchfield had a shock of curly hair and he was stocky. In fact, we thought he and Anne looked alike, more like brother and sister. He was just a real happy, smiley person. He and my dad played cards a lot . . ."

Agnetha Nielsen Bergsgaard:

". . . They played whist and poker. Dad was always a gambler. Anything he'd do, it had to have a little gambling in it. Same way they played cards. They never did it just for the fun of it. It wasn't big money, but there was always gambling. Another thing: there was always liquor in our home. Us kids never touched it, never thought of touching it. If they were playing cards, why, then there had to be liquor. That was the way with all the Danes. It came from Denmark, I suppose, that habit. But in all that time I was a kid, I never saw anybody drunk. Women, of course, never touched it. And my brother, Chris, he was twenty-three years old before he ever took a drink. It was just something for grown-ups . . ."

Jimmy:

When I was eight, the circus came to town. They posted gorgeous bills all around Maddock. A man with his head in a lion's mouth. Jugglers defying the law of gravity. The daring young man on the flying trapeze. We'd seen a lot of movies, but never a circus. Down at the Crescent Theatre they showed Harold Lloyd in *Grandmother's Boy* and *I am the Law* and Douglas Fairbanks in *The Mark of Zorro* and *Robin Hood.* Or there'd be one kids couldn't go to, like *Human Wreckage*, about the evils of the dope habit. The Crescent always smelled of kerosene and damp crepe paper and somebody sat pumping a player piano so it would play "The Herd Girl's Dream" or "Hungarian Rhapsody Number Five" real fast—*jingle ping tink-tink*—like that. And Tom Mix or Hoot Gibson or William S. Hart or whoever was leading the posse would chase the robbers over the range. Betty was always going to those stinky society pictures like *Why Girls Leave Home, Ashamed of His Parents, The Woman He Chose, Silk Husbands and Calico Wives* ("Do you charm your husband or do you wait for another to do it?"). She went to see Rudolph Valentino in *The Sheik* five times ("Eight Reels Aglow with the Wine of Life"). Heck! Sometimes on Wednesday night you had to sit through all that mushy stuff to see the serial like *The Lost City* ("Deep into the Mysterious Jungles in Darkest Africa went the daring company of players, braving the very jaws of death to picture the terrifying dangers of those strange lands, uncivilized savages of the Dark Continent and ferocious beasts . . . WILL THRILL AND STARTLE THE WORLD . . .").

Betty said the morning the circus train came in she was going to sneak down early to the station to watch it. I wanted to go too.

"No. I know you, Jimmy, you go and tattle everything to Mabel. Well, you promise you won't go and blab it out. Cross your heart and hope to die? I guess you can come. But we've got to get up real early and sneak out." Mabel was always threatening to give us a licking if we didn't mind better, but we'd learned by now it would be just little love taps.

Mabel Swanson:

". . . I tell you, those kids liked to make candy. Candy, candy, candy. One time, I'd just cleaned the house up spick-and-span and they got into the kitchen and started to make taffy. And they were pulling taffy—well, I guess maybe I cooked it for them and they were pulling it. And chasing each other and getting it on all the doorknobs and everywhere. Everything was getting sticky. And I hollered, 'You kids bring that into the kitchen!' Betty says, 'I don't have to!' I says, 'As long as you've got taffy on your hands, you've got to stay in the kitchen.' She wasn't going to and I spanked her. And she says, 'I'll tell my folks.' 'Oh, boy,' I thought, 'now I'll be fired.' I didn't have any authority to spank. So I sat down and cried, because I thought I shouldn't have done it. I was wiping off sugar all over the house, every doorknob was sticky.

"She never told her mother. Neither did Jimmy. But one time, at the dinner table, we were talking about somebody crying, and Jimmy piped up and said, 'I saw Mabel cry.' And Mrs. Critchfield said, 'Oh, Jimmy, Mabel doesn't cry.' I thought: 'Oh, oh, now here it comes.' But Jimmy never told why. And Betty, she never said a word. She was nine or ten and Jimmy two years younger. Oh, we had a lot of fun . . ."

Jimmy:

That morning, it was still dark when Betty and I went tiptoe down the stairs and out the door. Brit, our dog, wanted to come along, but Betty made me put him back inside the screen door and he whined and whimpered so much we had to run till we got past the livery stable. When we got to the depot platform, it was so early only old Alfred Larson, the station agent, was around. He knew all us kids, because sometimes when we'd hear the round, flat bell at the railroad crossing on Central Avenue start to clang back and forth, we'd tear down to the tracks to count the cars and wave to the people as they rushed by. There were boxcars from the Southern Pacific, Great Northern, Milwaukee, Chesapeake and Ohio, Union Pacific, all different railroads. You could see sheep and cattle through the slats on the stock cars and sometimes Fords and Chevies tied down on the flat cars and big round oil tanks on special tank cars. And there'd always be hoboes or tramps or maybe harvest workers riding the rails or sitting up on top of the cars. They'd be moving by so fast, *clickety clackety,* and the cars crashing and bumping and grating like they might tip over and it seemed like it'd never end when—wham!—the train was gone and all you could do was wave at the brakeman with his lantern on the open platform of the caboose.

The depot platform, that early in the morning, seemed sorta scary. Our footfalls on the gritty brick sounded so loud, Betty said maybe somebody was chasing us. I turned around in the dark to see who it was. All I could see was the empty tracks and freight yard. Inside the depot you could hear the clicking of the telegraph. Pretty soon that stopped and Albert Larson came out and went down the tracks, swinging his lantern. It got all quiet again. I felt like going home. Betty said, Don't be a crybaby, we'd just have to sit on the bench and be patient. She said maybe someday when she grew up she might be in a circus. She knew just what it would be like, too. "Listen, Jimmy," she said, "when that show came to Maddock, everybody would ask, 'Who is that bareback rider in the white silk tights with all the spangles and the pink satin sash and long golden curls who is standing so brave on top of that big white horse?' And another horse would come running around the ring and when the ringmaster cracked his whip, I'd somersault from one to the other. And everybody'd shout, 'It's Betty! Hooray!' If you behaved, you could come too."

Well, I couldn't see Betty doing anything like *that,* but it still sounded good. When Mabel heard we'd joined a circus, she'd be sorry for the way she'd tormented us, squawking about a little taffy on doorknobs. Mabel would find out how lonesome it was, with nobody to bang the screen door and wipe dishes and swat flies for her and spill the gravy bowl on her nice clean tablecloth and lean too far back and break the chair.

After what seemed like an awful long time, the light turned grayish pink, pigeons on the station roof started to coo and birds in the green summer leaves of the trees woke up and started chirruping. At last, just when even Betty was about to give up, the red bell at the crossing started a terrible clanging like it always did just before a train came in sight. Alfred Larson came hurrying back to let down the road gates. Way down the track, we could hear the engine whistle. He said it was the circus train. Once the bell started clanging, it wasn't long before other kids came running.

When it came, the engine rushed by so fast I could just catch a glimpse of the engineer as he waved at us kids. As it slowed down, some mailbags were thrown off the red baggage car. The train pulled in. There were a lot of wooden cars with windows and more freight cars, all with YANKEE ROBINSON CIRCUS painted in big red, black and yellow letters on the sides. We didn't see any people getting off. Then the engine hissed, letting off its earsplitting steam, and some men in dirty work clothes stepped down from one of the cars. They were swarthy and shifty-eyed and looked about as frowsy and unshaven and unwashed as the bums in the hobo jungle on the other side of the railroad yard. They stared up and down the platform, rubbing the sleep out of their eyes and scratching their heads and looking cross and mean. "Jesus, what a hick town!" one called to another. "Hey, Jack, where the hell are we?"

"Be goddammed if I know!"

We went home, disgusted. Mabel was just setting the breakfast table. After toast and jam and oatmeal we revived enough to go back to watch the circus parade. Seemed like everybody in Benson County had the same idea. A whole line of buggies stood empty outside the livery stable, the shafts down. Down on Central Avenue, the board sidewalks were packed and people were pushing and shoving you had to walk on the grass. All the spots along the hitching posts were taken up by Model T's or by whinnying country horses, switching their tails at flies. It seemed like every dog in Maddock was running around downtown, barking at nothing and scaring little kids.

The parade began with the blare of brass and the crash of drums coming down the street. The circus had a big bandwagon, and the players were seated way up on a high deck so they could be seen by the crowds. Painted in gaudy, weatherworn colors on its sides were scenes of horses and elephants, some standing on their hind legs and some even wearing clothes. A real, live elephant, higher than the bandwagon, with a swaying howdah and red silk canopy on its back, lumbered by, and it seemed the earth was gonna shake under the elephant's giant feet. Betty said it was king of all the beasts, the largest living four-legged creature on earth. There were some smaller elephants and camels and cages with striped tigers, monkeys, bears and giraffes. In one there was a lion and a man in spangled tights with a whip. There was a tooting calliope, a kind of boiler on a wagon with whistles, followed by swarms of boys as it played, over and over, "Daisy, Daisy, give me your answer, do . . ." Some painted and gilded wagons, dusty-looking and faded, creaked by and the farmers around me talked about the way the circus men handled their horses. Almost all the farm kids in town for the parade were "Scandahoovians" or "Rooshans," freckled little girls with sun-bleached, braided hair and tow-headed brothers who were a lot grubbier-looking than their sisters. Most wore bib overalls and straw hats and some were barefoot, while us town boys generally wore shoes and had to run around in itchy old knickers and caps. The parade was over in no time. Last of all came a sad, white-faced clown in baggy old hobo pants, rattling along in his donkey cart; with his big drooping red mouth, he looked so miserable you had to laugh.

The big white circus tent was pitched along the railroad tracks west of town, and for three days it stayed there, with colored flags flapping near the center poles and guy ropes. Right next to the big top were the sideshows, with their own painted-canvas banners billowing in and out with the wind: the Fat Lady, the Snake Charmer, the Siamese Twins and the India Rubber Man. The day Dad took us, there were hawkers selling lemonade and popcorn balls and slices of red, dripping watermelon, and we climbed way up to an upper tier of seats to get a good look at the horsemanship and tumbling feats in the sawdust rings. Acrobats did hair-raising somersaults from one trapeze to another. There were giddy tightrope acts and three men who, all at once, rode a bicycle across a high wire fifty feet up. Girls in spangled tights slowly came down ropes with just one leg twined around. The whole time, the band blared out stirring marches.

When the clowns came on, they drove old flivvers and had funny little white dogs and turned backflips and walked on stilts. One was a Drunkard with a chalk-white face and a big red nose and a torn black top hat. He had a big bottle marked XXX. Another was the Drunkard's Wife, and she wore a baggy calico dress with bright yellow ruffles at the neck and hem, and her eyes were all black and blue. It was awful funny, as she'd chase him with a rolling pin and wallop him with it and stub her toe and they kept bumping into each other and his pants were falling down and her bustle ran away.

I remember we lived in two houses in Maddock. In the first there were bagged potatoes stored in the basement. There must have been hundreds of bags. I climbed up on the bags one day and, to my surprise, I found a box with a toy train in it. It was just before Christmas. Saturdays, teams from the country were tied and blanketed all along Central Avenue and all the Norwegian farmers would greet each other, *"Glade Jul, Glade Jul!"* They brought a big silver spruce from Minnesota which had been cut in four sections to make it easier to ship. When they wired it back together again and put it up on Central Avenue, with red and green streamers, tinsel and colored lights, it was the biggest tree I'd ever seen.

From the Standard *front page, December 18, 1924:*

"North Pole

"Dear Boys and Girls,

"You know, Kiddies, the Community Christmas Tree will be Monday evening, December 24. I'll be there, sure as shootin'.

Loves of Love,

S. Claus"

Mabel said that Santa Claus lived at the North Pole with his wife and helpers, *troll*, elves, and that when he came down to Maddock in his sleigh he already knew who was good or not. She said, "If he finds you don't mind when I tell you to let the cat alone or wipe your nose, Jimmy, he'll put old, rotten potatoes and lumps of coal in your stocking."

Around Christmastime, the kitchen was always warm, with pleasant cooking smells. Sometimes a young man named Claus would be there. He was stuck on Mabel and would ride into town on his horse. Father said you could tell Claus was a farmer because he had that long, loping walk you got from going down too many furrows behind a plow. Dad was always teasing Mabel. He'd say, "Is Claus coming tonight?" And she'd say, "I don't know . . . If he comes, can I have the evening off, Doctor?" And he'd say, "Nope, you can't have the evening off." But if Claus came, she always did. Dad teased Claus, too. He used to sing, "The Cannibal King with the big brass ring fell in love with a Zulu maid . . ."

Mabel always went home to spend Christmas out on the farm with her folks. They'd have a big Norwegian feast, with *lutefisk* and *lefse* and meatballs and fruit soup and *julekake*. Before going, Mabel would take Betty and me to the Lutheran church to hear Reverend Orwoll's Christmas message. He was the one who'd fixed it up for her to stay with us so she could go to high school in town. None of the country schools went past eighth grade. Mostly, Mabel just kept an eye on Betty and me and washed the dishes and did the ironing. "All those white coats," she'd say, because Father, being a doctor, wore one or two clean ones every day.

From a Christmas message by S. M. Orwoll, published in the Standard, *December 18, 1924:*

". . . We sinful mortals, doomed forever to outer darkness . . . to us Christ comes again and proclaims salvation from sin, death and the power of the Devil . . . No other day is so widely advertised as Christmas. It is talked about and symbolized and sung the world over . . . But, oh, how it has been abased and abused. The amusement world offers its brand of Christmas joy. It, too, promises a merry time for all. At no other season does the world appeal more boldly and brazenly to the flesh. Through revelry and dissipation and shamelessly suggestive shows and open immorality and vice, the world and the Devil offer us a merry Christmas. And so, thousands and tens of thousands keep Christmas. They become the children of the Devil! . . ."

From the Standard's *"Local News" column:*

"Odin Cleveland, while trying to get Europe on his one-tube radio set the other evening, tuned into a strange station, but he heard a voice over the headphones that was curiously familiar. And throwing a bit more juice into the amplifier, he heard none other than our old friend, S. Claus, announcing that if there was any sleighing at all, he would be down this way that evening, with candy and nuts for all good boys and girls."

Jimmy:

One night Mr. Lowell, the editor of the *Standard,* came over to our house all upset and I overheard him telling Dad, "Doc, it burns me up the way some of the old-timers downtown won't give money for candy and nuts. Why, when they had that Kickapoo Indian Medicine Show at the Opera House, those invalids clamored to buy Rocky Mountain Tea at a dollar a bottle. It's no skin off our nose how people spend their money, but I do feel rather put out when some of the American Legion boys get turned down on the Community Christmas Tree proposition by people saying it's 'all foolishness.' "

Father said, "They've always had the tree at the Lutheran church before. It's like the Fourth of July and the Seventeenth of May. Some people in town like to stick to the old ways. Why, old Lars, who's driving my sleigh this winter, hardly speaks ten words of English."

"You know as well as I do, Doc, that better roads and the automobile are going to kill a lot of small towns. Just as sure as the Day of Judgment, Maddock is going to have to step lively to keep up its reputation as an up-to-date place to live in."

The last day of school, we had a tableau with Mary and Joseph and the shepherds and wise men and a doll in swaddling clothes. A sixth-grader read from the Gospel according to St. Luke: "And it came to pass in those days, that there went out a decree from Caesar Augustus, that all the world should be taxed . . ." And when she got to the part about ". . . peace on earth, good will toward men," out came Betty looking all flushed and solemn to sing "It Came upon the Midnight Clear." At home we put up the tree, and Mom kept us busy stringing popcorn and cranberries. She was making up baskets for all the neighbors, with cookies, and candied orange peels and popcorn balls wrapped in waxed paper.

From the Standard, *headlined "We Are Proud of Our Tree," December 25, 1924:*

"New York, Milwaukee, Chicago and Minneapolis have their Community Christmas trees. They have nothing on Maddock . . . The good roads and beautiful weather Christmas Eve made it possible for people to come from farms all around. Fully five hundred children were there . . . The 34-foot tree, richly adorned with trimmings and blazing with colored lights, was lit with due pomp . . . The Midnight Owl Quartette, led by Doc Critchfield, sang 'O Holy Night,' followed by carols in which the crowd took part . . .

"All this time, the little tots were asking, 'When will Santa come?' Suddenly, around eight o'clock, way off in the distance, a bugle call was heard. You could have heard a pin drop. The bugle call came closer. Someone gave the cry, 'Santa is coming!' Words cannot describe the screams of delight that came from the children when they saw that dear old duffer coming down the track in his sleigh. He was clad in a red suit, red stocking cap and black boots, his belly fat as ever, white whiskers blowing in the wind, and bent down by a monstrous sack full of candy and nuts . . . *'Ho-ho-ho'* . . ."

Jimmy, sixty years later:

It was a perfectly clear night. Father would find the note on his pitch pipe and we'd sing, "O Come, All Ye Faithful" and "Joy to the World." They kept bringing messages from Alfred Larson at the station. They'd telegraphed from Esmond, the next stop on the Great Northern spur. Santa had just left. And, sure enough, it wasn't long before we could hear the jingle of bells and a large bobsled painted green and white and very well maintained, came up, looking for all the world like a favorite four-span I knew. Even then I had the suspicion that Santa Claus was Jens Nielsen . . .

Jessie

The trial of John T. Scopes in Dayton, Tennessee, in July 1925, for teaching Darwinism, was personally troubling to the now mortally ill Reverend Williams. When Clarence Darrow, self-proclaimed agnostic known for his recent defense of Leopold and Loeb, questioned William Jennings Bryan about his literal interpretation of the Bible, Hadwen, like most fundamentalists, felt his beliefs were under fire too. In the most dramatic session, Bryan was trapped into affirming his belief that the world was created in 4004 B.C., that a "big fish" swallowed Jonah and that the Tower of Babel was responsible for the world's diversity of languages. Darrow said his purpose was "to show up fundamentalism . . ." Bryan, jumping up, his face purple and shaking a fist at Darrow, said his own purpose was "to protect the word of God against the biggest atheist and agnostic in the United States!" Five days after the trial, Bryan died in his sleep. That year and in 1926 Bruce Barton's The Man Nobody Knows, which called Jesus "the most popular dinner guest in Jerusalem" and "a great executive" who "picked up twelve men from the bottom ranks of business and forged them into an organization that conquered the world . . ." was America's Number One nonfiction bestseller. In ads for his new biblical epic, Cecil B. De Mille listed among his "THE TEN COMMANDMENTS OF SUCCESS": "have a hobby" and "keep smiling."

From letters by Jessie in Mount Vernon, Iowa, 1926:
To Anne, March 18:

". . . Breakfast is just over and while some visiting missionary ladies have the kitchen, I'll write you a bit. Papa says he really feels better this morning than for a good while. He has been just about the same all this time. But he has a little different feel this A.M. As though he'd been sick and was getting better. I hope so. But a week or two ago he would walk alone, and now he holds on to me and doesn't try to walk alone.

"Our ladies expect to go the last of next week. Friday or Saturday. I'm going to clean house as soon as they're gone. Pronto . . . Well, bye, bye. Better write occasionally. Will be glad when we can drive, but since the snow melted the roads are too muddy . . ."

To Hadwen, a patient at St. Luke's Hospital, Cedar Rapids, leukemia diagnosed, possibly caused by protracted X-ray exposure in 1920; he is now seventy-two, Jessie sixty-three; dated April 28:
"Dear Daddy,

I believe I brought the checkbook home & maybe you're broke so I'd better send you a bit. I hope you are feeling better today. I'm going to clean off the garden today and try to plant some radishes and lettuce. I'm also washing your undies. Suppose I'll be up to see you again in a day or two.

Love, Jessie."

To Anne, May 9:
". . . We are home again after Papa's six weeks in the hospital and my peripateting—is there such a word?—there and back. The doctors felt they had done all they could. And of course we know that after a certain time in any illness a hospital ceases to be the best place to be.

"Papa wanted to come home. And came to find the big old pear tree in the back yard a huge white bouquet, the old sprawling apple tree another. And the little peach trees all dressed in their pink blossoms. But he has not been able to get out to the garden. He sees it from the window of his bedroom. His color seems a little better, but his body is too thin. He has such a strong will to live . . ." *Soon after receiving this letter, Anne and Jim drove down to Mount Vernon, bringing Betty, Jimmy and Billy with them. Jim returned to North Dakota right away, leaving Betty in Hunter, but Anne stayed on six weeks with the two boys until it was time to start school. She had left by the time Hadwen slipped into a coma one day at the start of October.*

Anne:
"I told Lena, the hired girl of the time, that I was going down to play bridge with Jess Oser. Lena didn't call when the telegram came. Jim was taking out tonsils that morning. It was the only bleeder we ever had. Poor Lena was scared to death. I just had time to pack and catch the 107 for Minneapolis. I took Billy, now almost three . . ."

October 5 entry in the diary of Betty, who had just been reading Peg O' My Heart:

> *"O tempora, O mores,* Grandfather died today."

From Jimmy, nine years old in 1926, interview forty years later:

". . . He used to call me 'Buster.' I can remember riding the interurban from Cedar Rapids with him. And also coming into his garage at night after being out in his Model T and the headlights shining on the far end. And cutting down dead trees. Grandfather Williams was a very thin, lean, almost pathetic old man, but strong, too. He spent all his spare time cutting down old trees with a big crosscut saw and an axe . . ."

From Helen Collins, 1985 interview:

". . . Evidently those X-ray treatments completely wrecked his metabolism. He had to work hard and sweat each day or he felt miserable. He'd always walked a great deal, but in Mount Vernon he rented ground to raise a large garden and several pens of chickens. There were many big old trees dying and needing to come down all over town. Father removed many of them. He used ropes and pulleys to take them down safely in small sections. I suppose people all over town got used to seeing him around every day. At the time of his death, everybody from the railroad section boss to the wife of the president of Cornell College came to call. There were flowers from people we hardly knew. During those last years, he preached many times. His final sermon, in January the year he died, was out at the country Presbyterian church in Linn Grove, Mother's old home, where both her parents were buried in the churchyard.

One time, when we knew there wouldn't be much time left, Father said, 'You know, I tried to live my life the way I thought the Lord would want me to, but He had other plans. I can see that He knew best. I wouldn't change one thing, if I could, in my life.' I tell my children anyone who comes to the end and feels that way has lived a successful life . . . He loved people. And they felt it . . ."

From the Mount Vernon Hawkeye, *October 8, 1926:*

". . . A native of New York state, he came to Iowa with his Quaker parents in 1859. They located on a farm near the village of Whittier. Here he grew to manhood. His father died young. But that godly Quakeress mother instilled into his heart the principle of obedience to constituted authority; reverence for God and religious things; faith in the Bible . . ."

From the Official Records of the Upper Iowa Annual Conference of the Methodist Episcopal Church, 1927:

". . . Brother Williams had a rich ministry during the thirty-one years of his active service. He and Sister Williams served the following charges: New Hampton, Volga, Ridgeway, Kenwood Park, Elwood, Le Claire, Monona, McGregor, Lime Springs, Sumner, Plymouth, Jesup and Postville. Brother Williams retired in 1920 and moved to Mt. Vernon. He was always helpful to the pastor of the local church, loyal to Christ, and a spiritual force in the town. During his last illness, which was long and somewhat tedious to him, he said one day as the pastor called upon him, 'Well, Brother Ellis, one of these mornings you will hear that Hadwen is gone, but I hope that you will know where he has gone.' I assured him that there would be no guessing as to where he could be found. He died in great peace . . ."

Further letters from Jessie:

To Anne, 1926, undated; Jessie's widowed sister, Allie, has moved in to stay with her in Mount Vernon from Eli Johnston's old farm in Linn Grove; Anne wants her to come and visit North Dakota:

". . . A few minutes ago your package came, Louie. The blue dress. And it's very pretty. Now I have more clothes than I have places to wear them. So all of you must quit bothering about me.

"Allie & I have been cleaning the yard today. It goes slow. Everything goes slow, I guess. The business we were trying to get done, to get Papa's estate in order, seems to be at a standstill. Mr. Stucksleger says, 'If there is any more delay, just let me know.' He seems like an oasis in the desert of words which seems to surround us when Mr. Wilson is around. I suppose it will all get over sooner or later.

"I wrote Hadwen, Jr., today to lay off as far as Cleora is concerned. I told him if he really wants the book, I'll pay to buy a new one, as it was Papa's and I had no right to lend it to her. I thought Cleora was as safe as a church —then. But all in all we have to stand things and what peace there is between the two families mustn't be disturbed. Not after so many years. Aunt Mary is still addressing her letters to me in what she calls the Quaker Style. Like no other anywhere . . .

"Allie went down to the cellar a while ago. And thought she'd break up a chunk or two of coal. Now she is setting with her foot on a cushion tenderly caring for a sore toe. It's swollen. But I'm hoping it is nothing serious. Well, my ideas seem to be dwindling, so I'd better quit. When it gets warm enough to let the furnace fire go out, you'll see your Ma walking in most any time. Write. Love, Mother . . ."

To Helen Collins, October 24, 1927. Jessie is writing from Fessenden, North Dakota, where Anne and Jim moved in February 1925. It is a little bigger

*than Maddock, with about seven hundred people, and is the county seat of
neighboring Wells County.*

". . . It owes what prosperity it has, like Maddock, to the surrounding
wheatland. But there's also a courthouse and that always brings in a lot of
people. It's right on the Minneapolis, St. Paul and Sault Ste. Marie Railway,
what everybody calls the Soo Line. The folks live over a bank, a big wooden
building right downtown on Main Street. Jim has his surgery and waiting
room out front, but for living they just have two rooms, two great big
rooms. Well, Louie can fix anything up, you know. There's a shortage of
houses in Fessenden right now. Louie's divided the one room into bedroom
and kitchen and the other's the living room. Then there's a wide hallway
and she has a row of cots out there—that's where I sleep. Betty, Jimmy and
Billy are all out there too, but it still is enough to scare me to death when
one of those harvest workers comes up the stairs to see Jim.

"We shop at Quarves', a big two-story brick building, where they have
everything, groceries, hardware, clothes . . . It's like a city emporium.
They have those whirring wire baskets that swing from moving cables over
the counters. They carry money and receipts back to the cashier, old Mr.
Quarve, who sits on a dais in the middle of the store. The sales clerk yanks
on a wooden-handled rope pull to bring the baskets down and pulls another
one to get them back up. The store is really something, way out here on the
prairie. There's a fancy brick hotel, too . . .

"Jim is crazier than ever about golf, since he was Number Two in the
whole state two years ago. Louie plays a little too. I have to admit I was a
little taken aback my first Sunday morning when the rest of us were dressed
to go to church and out came Jim in knickerbockers, red-and-green stockings, a checkered cap and a bag of golf clubs over his shoulder. All these
grown men spending their time knocking a little white ball around. Louie
plays bridge and mah jong. They are all on the run. Everybody plays in the
band, Betty the clarinet and Jimmy the cornet. Just before I came, Jim and
Louie drove down to Fargo to see Charles Lindbergh do an exhibition flight.
They say the crowds practically fought for a chance to get near Lindy. With
so much crime and scandal these past few years, it's a pleasant change to see
such a brave, heroic young man . . ."

From Betty:

"Grandmother Williams was just real sweet and nice. She wore long
dresses and had grayish-white hair and a pink-and-white complexion. She
had only spent a short time in college and read a lot to compensate. She
wrote wonderful papers for the local club. 'Philippine Folk Lore.' Billy kept

her busy all the time reading the Bible to him. There was a little fat lady in one of the illustrations. He thought it was Mrs. Muir, a Hunter personality. They had peach trees in their backyard at home and Grandma made the most wonderful peach pies. One time in Mount Vernon all the people next door broke out in diphtheria. We were taken to Cedar Rapids for shots. Huge needles. Grandpa also had us take swimming lessons at Cornell College.

"Sometimes Grandma took us to see Harriet Varner Johnston, her step-mother. She also lived in Mount Vernon and was little and real old. There was lots of furniture in the living room and big overstuffed chairs. Great-Grandma Johnston was senile and was talking about the Apostle Peter. 'Oh, I always liked Peter,' she said. 'Peter, Peter, Pumpkin Eater.' She had a mechanical Santa Claus that wriggled around the top of the table. Also a puzzle map of the United States. Each state was a separate piece. She had a passion for puzzles. There were little cloth bags all over the house, full of jigsaw pieces. Once she asked Jimmy, 'Where's Colorado?' He had to slip out and ask Grandma, 'What's a Colorado?'

"Both grandmothers vied for my favor and they each gave me dresses. Grandma Critchfield switched me once and I never forgave her. She was very jealous and she'd always ask me the same question. 'Who makes the best rolls, Betty, Grandmother Williams or me?' I'd look her right in the eye and say, 'Grandmother Williams.' I carried that right to her dying day. I really sassed Grandma Critchfield. She made me work, made me help make dinner, help set table because I was a girl. She was little and could be ornery as sin. She was always making gravy from fried bacon and apple sauce. When Mother stayed in Iowa the summer Grandpa died, I had to go to Hunter. Grandma Critchfield had a gorgeous complete bathroom with marble fixtures. But it never worked. We always had to use the outhouse. That summer, I'd just finished fifth grade. Grandma bought some bright blue calcimine and said, 'Why don't you go outside and paint the toilet, Betty?' It was Robin's Egg Blue. I waited until Grandma went up to take her nap and then I painted the inside of the toilet, then the outside, then some nearby wooden stumps, then the wooden walk, then the pump. Grandma was furious."

From Jessie to Anne's sisters, Mary and Helen, in Viola, Iowa, November 14, 1927. Henry Ford's new Model A—with its Niagara Blue roadsters and Arabian Sand phaetons—was about to be revealed. Since the war, the number of cars in America had quadrupled to almost twenty-eight million, or two out of three families. The age of horses was dying with the decade.

". . . I'm sitting here waiting for the psychological moment to arrive when we can wash up the breakfast dishes, Louie's little kitchen being too small for me to work in when she does something else. I want to get home before Christmas. I'm planning now that I'll leave here just after Thanksgiving and get to Mount Vernon Saturday evening. It's certainly getting wintry here, snowing a little this morning, and pretty cold with that prevailing northwest wind blowing straight down from Canada. But there is a good janitor, and this apartment is kept nice and warm.

"I'm having a nice time, and as you know, there's always plenty doing in Louie's home. Betty had her thirteenth birthday last week. She had her long blond hair all done in sausage curls and wore a white frock starched as stiff as a milk pail with a wide blue sash. She looked very sweet. There is a Chet Parsons lurking around who gives her books, boxes of flowers, etc. Last evening it was a book.

"Did you hear any more about the new Fords? Since Henry Ford scrapped the Model T last spring, we've certainly been living in a state of suspense. It will surely be a shame if you have to take the train, Mary, when you and Fay go on your vacation trip next year. But I would not advise getting a Chevrolet yet, but waiting to see what Henry Ford comes up with . . . Write. It's nice to get letters when one is away from home. Love, Mother"

From Peggy, younger daughter of Anne and Jim, fifty-two years later:

". . . Grandfather Williams always sounded admirable, but Jessie fun and warm. She wasn't a terrific housekeeper, had a good sense of humor. Mother said she did things like putting the dirty dishes in the oven if company came unexpectedly. She always told Mother, 'Take your adventurous spirit with you.' "

Anne, thirty-two years later:

". . . It was the day before Thanksgiving. That morning, Mama didn't feel too well. She'd been so lonesome with Papa gone. In the afternoon Mrs. Tanner came by. I'd always said Mrs. Tanner could kill anybody with her conversation. That night around bedtime, Jimmy and Billy were already asleep and Betty was out on her bed in the hall reading *Treasure Island.* Mama was resting on the living room davenport, taking a little nap. She was wearing Jim's warm flannel robe. I was sewing. Mama stirred, opened her eyes and told me, 'You know, Louie, every time we moved, Dad always went ahead to fix up the house for me. I just feel now that Dad's gone ahead.'

"After a while Jim stuck his head in from the office and took Mama's blood pressure. Then he went into the kitchen. Mama looked at me. 'That's funny, Louie,' she said. 'He didn't tell me what it was.' I went out and asked him. He said it was two-sixty over one-eighty. He was worried. Jim said he was going to run down to the drugstore and get her something to take.

"He'd just gone down the stairs. All of a sudden Mama sat up and said, 'Oh, I'm so . . .' She took three deep breaths, with long intervals in between then she was perfectly still. Cheyne-Stokes breathing. I ran out of the office, threw up the window and screamed to Jim. He ran all the way back and up the stairs and shot adrenalin into her heart. She took those three breaths and died . . .

"I took her home to Mount Vernon the next day. Mary, Helen and their husbands were there, and Hadwen, who was teaching at a college in Texas since his return from the Philippines, arrived right away . . .

Jimmy, fifty-six years later:

"I remember it well. At seven the next morning, Mother came to wake me. And in the first moment of consciousness, I asked, 'How is Grandma?' because Mother was crying, and I'd never seen her cry before . . ."

From the family journal, entry by Jessie, May 1, 1927:

"So many years have passed since anyone has written in this old book. Years of happiness, work, anxiety and sorrow. All of which goes into the making of an average life, I suppose.

"As far as I know, this may be the last entry in this book. It was to be the chronicle of our married life. And while for forty-two years we walked through life hand in hand, now it is ended and I am alone. On October 5, 1926, he went to what must have been a wonderful reward. For his life was so devoid of self, and so gladly given to the work of his Master that it could not be otherwise. We laid his poor worn tired body in the cemetery here, a beautiful spot to lay his castoff garment. As someone said, 'An inn on the way to Jerusalem.' But, from earth into the beauty of Heaven was to him but a step.

"And now I am alone . . ."

It was indeed the final entry in the journal.

Betty

Everybody liked Daddy because he was real fun. He was the great American of our family. A good athlete, not very intellectual. Loved to play the piano, an extrovert, fun to be with, good company. He liked things like *True Detective* and read only for escape. He and Mom were real popular, the country-club set. A little drinking, slightly wild, but all innocuous and fun, no promiscuity.

From the Fargo Forum, *August 7, 1925, a story on the North Dakota State Golf Championship matches:*

". . . Yesterday's play developed a full-grown dark horse, 'Doc' Critchfield. This Fessenden bird swooped down upon the course yesterday and counted out two of Fargo's best comers, Dell Owen and W. P. Chestnut . . . He is straight down the course, shot after shot, none of them spectacularly long or brilliant, but he always lobs up serenely on the green, a smile behind his moustache and a good healthy putt in his bag . . . Critchfield proved to be one of those grim reapers who bang, bang, bang right down the course . . ."

From the late Fred Mietz, then eighty-seven, retired grocer at Quarves' store, 1982 interview:

". . . Jim was Number Two in the whole state that year. It was just a few months after he came to Fessenden from Maddock. They called it runner-up. Jimmy Barrett from Devil's Lake beat him. Barrett was just like a pro and did a lot of golfing. Jim was a very good golfer, but as a doctor he often had to drop everything to go out on a call. But Jim never got mad. He had a very good disposition. I never saw him mad, and I played so much golf with him and all the minstrel shows we did and everything . . . Yep, Barrett took the final match ten up and eight to go. Jim's runner-up trophy, a big silver loving cup engraved with a citation, was in the window of Fisher's Drugstore for some time. The shafts of the clubs were wood in those days. The long-distance clubs were called the driver, the mashie and the spoon, and the driving iron was called a cleek. It'd be a Number One today. Many of us got by with just a driver, one or two irons and the putter. We played every evening in the summer after supper until it got dark and on Sundays . . ."

Jimmy:

". . . Father practiced his golf very hard. I'd go out in the mornings with him, just before noon. And he'd take a bucket of golf balls and practice driving. He'd tell me to go down to about the two-hundred-and-fifty-yard mark to shag balls. I took an empty bucket down. And he would hit. If I couldn't pick it up in the sun or something, he'd point right or left or straight ahead with his driver to signal to me. Father really enjoyed playing golf out there. There's no question about it. He played very actively . . ."

Irving Clark, retired garage owner, in his sixties, interviewed in Arizona:

". . . Doc could hit off bare ground even better than from grass. That's unusual in golfing. I used to go caddying for him. He was always friendly. One time, he took out my dad's tonsils in a chair in his office and Dad got up and walked home. Caddying, I'd make a buck on Sunday. Four rounds, twenty-five cents a round. Most of them wore soft caps, golf shoes, long fancy socks and golf knickers . . ."

From the Wells County Free Press, *July 28, 1927, under headline, "GOLF-ERS BEAT BASEBALL TEAM":*

"Yes, Willie, that bunch of disgruntled and angry-looking gentlemen you saw on the streets last Thursday were the Fessenden Baseball Team. Why were they mad? Well, you see it was this way. The golfers challenged the ball team to a game and the ball team lost. It was some game. Those decrepit golf players set down our regular league team 2–1 last Thursday evening at the Fairgrounds in a five-inning contest. It was a bitter pill for the baseball stars to swallow for they had confidently boasted it would be just a little practice for them . . . In the Fifth, Winterfield socked one towards third, Weiss knocked it down, and Critchfield at shortstop backed him up, and made a nice throw to first to get the runner out . . ."

From Rees Price, then eighty-two, a Fessenden farmer, 1984 interview:

". . . They used to have baseball games out at the Fairgrounds. The grandstand was so far away, spectators would park their cars—mostly

Model T's—right around the diamond. They pulled the windshields down so the fly balls wouldn't hit 'em and they'd take the cushion out of the car and put that on the windshield so a ball wouldn't come down and break it. It was hard telling where a foul would go sometimes. Home base was right where they have the free acts at the County Fair now and third base was right off where they saddle horses. Home plate wasn't very far off from where they've got the judges' stand. And those Model T's would be parked all around in a semicircle . . ."

From the late Ben Oser, Fessenden's only Jew and the owner of clothing and grocery stores in several little towns around; interviewed fifty-five years later, when he was ninety:

". . . We had a lot a fun hunting, too. One time we were down by Hurds-field. We'd leave town before daybreak and build a fire in the stove of a country schoolhouse way down on Fifty-two South. Jim always made break-fast. One time Jim wrote on the blackboard, 'Go into Ben Oser's store in Fessenden. He has a box of candy for you. '. . . We'd go out and sit under the bushes and shoot the ducks as they flew over. Sometimes we'd be back by noon with a wonderful bag of fine big Mallards. Jim would grin and say, 'Just give me twenty minutes or so and I'll quit with my limit.' I've still got that stuff in the attic—boots, wooden duck decoys, my old repeating shot-gun, lunch boxes, boxes of old shells with brass caps . . . Once fall came and the fields and sloughs were full of ducks and pheasants and quail, why, Jim would come over, raring to go . . ."

From Jess Oser, his wife:

". . . Our bridge foursome met every Thursday. Golf was fun, but bridge was more serious. Auction, mostly. Contract was just coming in. One time, we played all night. Just for the fun of it. We met at my house and I said, 'What'll I fix to eat?' And they said, 'Vegetable soup.' So we shuffled and reshuffled and doubled and redoubled each other's bids and blinked and nodded and all you'd hear was 'One spade.' 'Pass.' 'Two hearts.' 'Three diamonds.'—and we'd go out and get some more soup. Once, Anne made a small slam after bidding two spades and taking four overtricks."

From Lois Pritchard, mid-nineties, fifty-five years later:

". . . We always wore long party dresses for our bridge club. Oh, yes, that was a real dress-up affair. Every two weeks. Fessenden used to dress up. Now I haven't had a hat on . . . Well, I can't tell you for how many years . . ."

From Betty, interviewed at length in 1959–60, also occasionally over the next twenty years:

In Fessenden, since we lived right behind Daddy's office, Mom usually gave the anesthetic while he did the operating. If there were children, I took them for walks. If there was a delivery, I sometimes helped give the babies their first oil rub. Daddy said I was quite a capable little nurse. My bed in the front hall was just a little way past the door to Daddy's waiting room. One Saturday while I was lying on my bed in a new red corduroy bathrobe, a man came upstairs carrying a lady. He dropped her on my bed. He just got her there. No time to undress her or anything. The baby was born then and there.

One time, a little girl was brought in with a severed toe. Blood dripped all over the steps. Mom was home alone and they had to send for Daddy, who was way off somewhere. Later the toe was thrown in the garbage can and I went to the back alley and rummaged through the garbage looking for it. I was curious to see what a severed toe looked like. Another time, two shrieking women and a wailing boy came running up the stairs. They said the boy had swallowed a penny. "Don't worry," Billy piped up, "you'll get your money back." We all started to laugh hysterically . . . Billy was always sorry for the children who came for operations, he gave almost all his toys away, including a long-treasured Nigger Doll.

Rees Price:

". . . One time, my dad was out here on the farm cleaning grain and he fell against the granary and cut a big gash in his head. We threw a pail of water on him and revived him and I took him to town. Doc Critchfield was sewing him up and Billy happened to be around and I guess Doc wanted to take my dad's mind off the sewing. Anyway, he says to Billy, 'Sing that dirty song to Mr. Price, Billy.' And Billy sang, 'When the wind blows a girl's skirt high, dirt gets in the bad man's eye . . .' I guess it served its purpose, as Dad didn't flinch. But we never could figure that song out . . ."

Helen Collins:

". . . Betty was a hellion when she was little. She had long Shirley Temple worm curls, brushed around a finger when damp. She wasn't about to have that hair combed very often. In Postville I'd be left to look after her and I couldn't do anything with her. I'd have to chase her around the yard, the neighbors watching, and I'd be so ashamed . . ."

Betty:

Jimmy was eating dirt all the time and he always had a runny nose. Later, after Pat was born, he ate bugs *and* dirt. One time when he was little, I pinched Jimmy in his crib to see if he would cry. We were visiting Postville and I had to spend the afternoon in bed because I'd been naughty. So I pinched Jimmy, then ran down to the kitchen, "Oh, Mama, Mama, Jimmy hurt himself!" When he got bigger, Jimmy was real rough-and-tumble. Once, he chased me with a butcher knife after I squeezed his mumps. In Fessenden, we had to do the dishes every night and we'd set the clock for ten minutes and race through. So we could go outside and play. Later, when Peggy and Pat came and they were old enough to do the dishes, they did them lingeringly, singing, gossiping or playing "I'm Thinking of Something" ("Animal, vegetable or mineral?").

One of our favorite places to play was the icehouse. All winter long they'd cut ice from the James River and move it into the warehouse with a block and tackle. In the summertime a man named Schroeder took it around to all the houses in town in a horse-drawn wagon. We'd holler, "Here comes old Schroeder!" and all the kids would try to snitch slivers of ice to suck from the wagon while he took a block of it into somebody's house.

In 1927, when I was in the seventh grade and Jimmy in the fifth, we had a Valentine's party. Jimmy wanted a party for his birthday, January 30, and I wanted one for Valentine's. At school, each room was making a red-paper-covered valentine box with a slot in the top and we were all going to bring our valentines. One night we were sitting at the supper table and talking about it when Daddy joked, "Why don't you hire the Legion Hall? Then you could have both parties at once." "Oh, Daddy, could we?" we cried. Mom said he was "hoist with his own petar." We invited the fifth, sixth and seventh grades, about seventy-five kids. Mom fixed a huge table which she covered with white sheets and red hearts and cotton and mirrors and little marshmallow figures she made. They were skating and skiing and everything. The party was seven-thirty to ten. It was real cold in winter.

Fessenden could be terribly cold. We used to go sledding on Hope's Hill. After they flooded the rink and we went skating, we had to keep going into a little warming house with a stove and benches. Our two-story, red-brick school, with a bell housing on its roof peak, was just across the tracks and two blocks north of where we lived on Main Street. One time, Billy froze his nose just waiting for the passenger train to pass so he could cross the tracks on his way home from school. He was all bundled up, too. I had to run and get some snow and Daddy rubbed it on Billy's face. As soon as Billy said he felt a burning sensation in his nose, Daddy knew he'd frozen it for sure.

One time in the seventh grade, Mother found a flat fifty of Lucky Strikes under my bed. Auntie Kay was a real flapper and I guess she was sort of a bad influence. I used to smoke a cigarette at night down in the alley. Or in

Hunter, I'd go behind the outhouse or in back of the lilac bushes. Another glamorous relative was Uncle Hadwen, who'd been chased by pirates in China and was always having narrow escapes.

From a letter to Anne from Hadwen, Jr., now teaching at the American Academy in Guatemala:

". . . We heard that a revolution had started about 75 miles west of here at Totonicapán, but it was only the annual protest of the Indians there against paying the land tax. Government sent 1,100 soldiers and we heard no more about it . . . Last Sunday we took in a bullfight. Indians danced in the plaza, wearing fancy dress and masks. We had a great time. Bull got out of the ring & hundreds of us ran toward the church where it turned around & went the other way. Threw several men into the air as it went & I think one was killed. But I doubt if it was as dangerous as driving on Iowa's Lincoln Highway on a Sunday afternoon . . ."

About this time, Helen Hope and a few other girls and I formed a "Secret Story Club," publicly known just as the SSC. Mother made gold-black-and-red sealing-wax pendants and we wore them around our necks. The club spent most of its time writing stories—"The SSC at the Seashore," "The SSC at the Mountains." When Helen started to tear around with some tough girls in town, the SSC told her to drop them. About this time, a new book, *The President's Daughter,* came out, in which the author, Nan Britton, claimed to have had an illegitimate baby with President Harding, I was thrilled to learn she was a third or fourth cousin of the Critchfields in Ohio. I went around bragging about it. There were juicy love scenes in hotels, the Senate Office Building and White House cloakroom. We read parts of it out loud at the SSC ("He died of a broken heart . . ."). At home, it was forbidden reading, along with *Flynn's Detective Fiction Weekly* and a book called *Sixty Seconds,* about a man dying in the electric chair who sees his whole life flashing by. I'd wait until Mom and Daddy were out on the golf course and sit by the window keeping an eye out for their return.

They were strict. When Chet Parsons gave me a gorgeous silver vanity case with semiprecious stones and a mirror, Mom and Dad said I couldn't keep it. Grandmother Williams was there on her last visit and she made them let me. In the eighth grade, Chet gave me my first box of candy. I gave him a long golden curl. Later I bobbed my hair.

At home somebody was always playing the piano and singing. I sang in the Lutheran, Congregational and German Baptist choirs. Daddy loved to play romantic, schmaltzy stuff. Ragtime and songs from Broadway musicals. "When Day Is Done." Shubert's "Song of Love," as adapted by

Sigmund Romberg in *Blossom Time,* was his favorite. Daddy and I used to sing it as a duet and I'd have to hit high C.

> "You are my song of love, melody immortal,
>   Echo of Paradise, heard through Heaven's
>   portal . . ."

At an American Legion show in 1927, the wives put on a review and Mom made fun of Dad singing it. She parodied the words: "Let me chew your chewing gum . . ." Daddy got back at her a year later when the men burlesqued their wives in a skit, "Us Wimmin." Daddy pretended to be Mother playing "Flower Song" on the piano. All her life Mother almost never played. Then, once in a blue moon, she'd sit down and play just that one song. She'd sit real stiffly, arms outstretched, and she'd play in such a stately and ladylike fashion, it took you back to Longfellow, hearts-and-flowers and turn-of-the-century days. Not Daddy. He really pounded the keys. He'd launch into "On Wisconsin" or "Minnesota, Hats Off to Thee" and let her rip.

Alfalfa Day was one of the main traditions of Fessenden. It was always on St. Patrick's Day in March. A seed train came up from the Agricultural College in Fargo. A queen was elected. Since the number of votes cast depended on how many acres of alfalfa you grew, some of the queens were real doozies. The first one was in 1928 and they went on for fifteen years. That first year, Mom made me a lovely yellow taffeta dress. It was on sale and must have been cheap material because it split pretty quick. Mom always had an eye for a bargain. She painted green and gold roses on the taffeta and I wore it for the first time on Alfalfa Day. I wanted to go bare-legged, but Mom said it was too cold, so I had to pull on long black stockings. She wouldn't even let me roll them. She fixed up a garter belt with rubber knobs and hooks and I had to fasten them on to that. It was awful.

The whole town pitched in. They had all kinds of committees and people went around and told everybody how we were going to show that Fessenden had plenty of get-up-and-go. They told Daddy, "We expect a pretty generous donation from you, Doc. Anybody with such a big practice ought to show his appreciation of the town. Of course, we'll take anything you're in a mind to give. Anything comes in handy for prizes." To merchants like Ben Oser, they'd say, "What we need most, Ben, is ready cash, but, good Lord, anybody who does the business you do will make it all back and more, too. We calculate there'll be, at the very least, four thousand people in town that day. It's just naturally bound to be that some of them will want to do their trading." Not everybody gave. Daddy said a couple of the store owners downtown, you'd be lucky to get five cents out of them. The prizes were exhibited in the window of Fisher's Drugstore, each with a card showing the name of the donor. There was a grass seeder, two hundred pounds of sugar, a hundred pounds of Dakota Maid flour, ten pounds of coffee, an emery wheel, a Big Ben alarm clock, a pair of halters, a pair of workshoes, five gallons of motor oil and a crate of apples. In the middle of Main Street a grandstand was put up, wooden tiers of seats rising from each curb. The street was rolled and swept and they hung a great big banner across from Quarves' Store to the Fessenden Cafe:

"ALFALFA DAY MARCH 15
WELCOME TO FESSENDEN"

From Mac Solberg, eighties, retired grocer, master of ceremonies, first Alfalfa Day, 1928, fifty-four years later:

". . . Well, we didn't know we were going to have an Alfalfa Day, in fact. Pasture was short and the county agents and Agricultural College were promoting alfalfa. The railroad companies used to bring out seed trains and they'd been over to Sykeston. So some of the businessmen in town here decided to get them over and tie it in with a little celebration. It went over pretty big. A queen was crowned and we had three dances going at once that night. I'd judge we had four or five thousand people here. We hired one good band that cost a little money—the figure I remember is a hundred and thirty-five dollars—and a couple of local bands.

"As Emcee, I'd get out there on the stage of the Auditorium and give them a hearty welcome, or the best I could. You had to have a good strong voice, as we didn't use a microphone in those days. Then I'd introduce the mayor. When he was through speaking, we'd put on the acts, musical numbers. That first year, two little kids put on a miniature prize fight; they'd get in there and they'd just slug hell out of each other with these big, pillow-like gloves. They were just as cute as the dickens. Then there were two trombonists and couldn't either of 'em play anything. We had a couple of real musicians backstage that really did the playing, you see. It was quite a joke. As Emcee, I wore a top hat and tails.

"The Queen gave a little speech. And it would be pretty hard for a girl sixteen, seventeen years old from out in the sticks to get up and speak to all those people. Then she went to all three dances and kept busy. She wore a crown, a homemade one, golden paper, most likely. We always gave her a wrist watch. One year, Ben Oser presented the gifts to the Queen and her attendants and they all hugged Ben and messed his hair up. There was a lot of horseplay in those days . . ."

From a letter to the Wells County Free Press, *March 8, 1928:*
"Dear Mr. Free Press,

Fore the past ten weaks yure valyble journil has bin filed with glowing akounts of the Alfalfy Day wich is going to be pulled awf in Fessindin March 15. Yew tell us plenty bout the Kween wich is going to be krownded but I notis that yew don't say a werd bout an Alfalfy King . . . If yew going to have wun I wish to aplie fer the job. Yure kween is going to be a good-looker and I wood make a fust-rate king. My wife sez she wud lik to crown me wunce a day. I want to get my appearance on erlie bekuz Bill Jakle and sum other boys down this way are hankering fer the chans.

"Aniway if I don't get it I won't be sore but yew'll find me doing the cirkul tew-step at the dans and if yew don't kno me jest ask fer,

William Watertank

P.S. I'm komin to the dans but I'll have to bring me wife."

From the Free Press, *March 17:*
". . . In spite of several inches of snow, farmers from all over the country poured into town Thursday for Alfalfa Day . . . The Coronation Ceremonies were the big event . . . The Queen, Mildred Zumpf of Hamberg, and her retinue of Flower Girls, Train Bearers, Attendants and Warriors, took the stage. Alvin Lyness, the first Alfalfa grower in the county, was chosen to crown the Queen and after a few fitting remarks placed the diadem on her head . . ."

Betty:
The maidens to the Queen wore knee-length, airily cut gowns of green and pink cheesecloth, which gave the effect of flowing garments. Somebody in a false beard wearing a bathrobe and carrying a scythe was Father Time. During the Coronation Ceremony, each of the Queen's attendants rose, one by one, and identified herself:
"I am good seedbed. The farmer plants me."
"I am fertility."
"I am the plow and the harrow."
"I help the hired man."
It was always terribly funny. After the program, there was a band concert before the Grand March and dances; I always played clarinet. That first year, I was just thirteen and a little young to be dancing. But I went anyway

and at one dance up at Anderson's Hall, a boy held me out of the second-story window and kissed me.

From Alvin Mohr, late sixties, retired banker, interviewed in Palm Desert, California, fifty-four years later:

". . . When Alfalfa Day came around, we'd have our dances all picked out. We'd just go to a girl ahead of time and say, 'How about the second dance?' And she might say, 'Well, I've got it, but how about the third?' I used to do the Charleston. I just loved it. I danced the Charleston with Betty and Marion Fahey and Judy Thornton and Grace Bietz. The Charleston was real fast and real hard and the older people wouldn't even think of trying it. It was more fun.

"I think the first drink I ever took was on Alfalfa Day. I must have been a junior in high school and somebody had a mickey, or a half pint, and we'd take a swig out of that. The country boys were going to dances and taking drinks long before we did. Those guys out on farms near Hamberg and Sykeston, they kinda grew up a little bit quicker. They could drive. They had to drive to get to school. In the summer they had bowery dances out at the Fairgrounds. A bowery was a big, circular wooden floor with a canvas roof in case it rained. In those days they used to erect them all the time for outdoor gatherings and dances. It was great in the summertime with a breeze blowing through and when we'd keep liquor in the car. You could sneak over for a drink.

"I don't remember any fights at dances, but some boys would come and never dance, just hang around outside and drink. One time when I was a sophomore in high school, two of us boys drove to Sykeston for a dance one night. They said Sykeston was a rough town and we didn't have dates or anything. I had a derby on. In those days you always got dressed up. So, I had a hat on and was just buying a ticket when one of the bullies from Sykeston, he just took my hat off and sailed it down the hall, you know, just like that. Now, I had a buddy named Harold Pellet—in fact he still lives in town, his son is sheriff—and Harold, he wanted a chance to rough somebody up, you know. So he come up and said to the kid, 'Now, you go back and pick up that hat. And then you come back and you put it right on his head just the way you took it off.' Harold was a lot bigger, so the kid did what he said. And Harold said, 'If I ever catch you monkeying around again with anybody from Fessenden, I'll kick your butt right up your shoulders
. . .'"

Betty:

In mid-winter there was a big AOUW dance. Whole families went. Fathers danced with their little girls. It was the first time you really danced. I can still remember Daddy's stomach when I danced with him. In 1928 we also had a Play Day Parade. I was a Blue Geranium. I wore a costume of blue crepe paper and blue stockings over long underwear. It was a chilly day and I almost froze. Mother made all my brassieres until I was out of high school. You didn't buy them in those days. You had to be very careful about your underwear. Boys peeked through the wall into the Girls' Locker Room. Some of the girls had tons of runs in their rayon pants.

There were no school buses, so kids from farms had to stay in town, often in rooms with hot plates. I was sorry for some of the girls and I'd charge groceries and fix meals for them. I was always dragging somebody home. Once, when Auntie Kay came, Daddy laid down the law. He said, "There will be no company while Kay is here, Betty. There's no room." That night, when he and Mother came home, they found two easy chairs pushed together in the living room and the two McCain girls sleeping away. School was hard for some of the farm kids . . .

From Chester Zumpf, retired implement dealer who grew up on a farm near Hamberg, 1982 interview:

". . . Goodness gracious, when we got home from school at four-thirty, boy, it was 'Clean the barn, fill the racks with hay, put feed in the feed boxes, get ready for the men coming in with the horses from plowing.' By that time it'd be time to get the cows in and milk, see. And feed the pigs and chickens and collect the eggs and chop kindling and carry water and get ready for evening. When Dad and my oldest brother that was home would be doing the fieldwork in the spring, why, the rest of us were busy right up till suppertime . . . Sundays when I was small I'd walk to church barefoot, carrying my good patent leather shoes, and I'd sit down and put them on just before I went inside to Sunday School. Those shoes passed down, brother to brother. You're darn tootin' . . ."

Betty:

That summer, we got Vitaphone synchronized talkies at the Auditorium. Bert Southard and Hugh Parsons, who were running the theater at the time, went to Minneapolis and bought two Ultraphone machines. So we saw *and* heard *Broadway Babies, Hot Stuff, Syncopation, Younger Generation, House of Horror . . .*

From Jim Parsons, seventy, retired from the Post Office, interviewed in Fargo, 1983:

". . . They had a turntable underneath the projection booth. The show would start and you'd set the needle on the record disc while you were watching the screen. I had to do it for my dad lots of times. It was hard to get the sound so that it matched the movement of the lips just right. You'd get it too fast, or maybe they wouldn't talk at all, the sound wouldn't come, and the crowd in the Auditorium would start whistling and hollering. The worst were the sea battle and chariot race in *Ben Hur* . . . We used to have to go around and peddle handbills house to house advertising the movie, too. Us kids, you see. Then, on Saturday night, when the picture was about to start, we had a cow bell, and Irving Clark or Jimmy or me would walk up and down Main Street ringing that bell and shouting, 'Show's about to start!' . . ."

Jimmy:

". . . The same year we got talkies in Fessenden, I spent the early part of the summer down in Iowa with Aunt Mary and Uncle Fay. They had a radio technically good enough so we could all sit around and listen to the national conventions. Hoover and Curtis. We listened to them for hours every day. Aunt Mary had a great interest in everything and was fun to be with.

"It was either that year or the next that a big airplane flew over town. Everybody said it was supposed to be figuring out the best route for airmail service between Fargo and Minot. Dad said, 'If it comes our way, maybe it will put Fessenden on the map.'

"I well remember our first radio set in Fessenden. It was a Crosley, a very early one, and it had ear sets and three or four dials on it. You had to tune them all just right in order to get a station, and reception was just terrible . . . On Saturday afternoons, Father would be sitting there in a haze of cigar smoke, trying to hear something like the World Series or maybe Graham McNamee shouting through the static, '. . . *And* he did it! Yes, sir, he did it! It's a touchdown! Boy, I want to tell you this is one of the finest games . . .' Father was a great sports fan. Some years, he'd go all the way to the Twin Cities just to see the big Minnesota-Iowa football game."

Betty

We had a grandstand box at the County Fair in 1929. Grandma, Uncle Harry and Kay had come over from Hunter, and Daddy reserved the best seats right across from the judges' stand. It was the tenth of July—I remember the date, because the phone rang and Uncle Harry answered. Uncle Ray was speaking from St. Paul. He thought he had Daddy on the line and said, "Congratulations! You are the father of a nine-pound daughter!" Uncle Harry was really flabbergasted; he wasn't married yet.

Mom was forty-one and had the baby in Minneapolis, as the doctor feared complications. In June, we'd taken her down to St. Paul; after ten years practicing in little towns in North Dakota, Uncle Ray had gone back to school in Chicago to specialize in pediatrics. Now he was very successful and lived in a great big old-fashioned house just across the street from Macalester College in St. Paul and not far from Summit Avenue. Isabelle, Ray's oldest daughter, was my age, and we both wore bobbed hair, rolled stockings, short skirts and swinging beads, like John Held, Jr., girls. We had fun; one time, we went out and bought a lot of forbidden goodies like French pastries, dill pickles and pickled pigs feet. We slept on an upstairs porch overlooking the backyard and we hid our things for a planned midnight spread. A thunderstorm came up and drenched our beds, blankets and the food, and Aunt Irene discovered us.

After we waited and waited but Mom didn't have her baby, Uncle Ray put me on the train home, the Soo Railroad. Daddy came racing over to meet me at the station. It was hot back in Fessenden. June had been one of the driest Junes on record. Now, in July, searing winds were drying up the crops. When Daddy drove us to the fairgrounds, I saw they'd put up the lathing and siding on the new Baptist church; when I'd gone away, they'd just laid the cornerstone.

The County Fair was Fessenden's pride and joy. The Fairgrounds, with its freshly painted white buildings, shade trees, tents and flags flying from the bleachers and grandstand, was just south of town. Daddy said the gate on opening day was over seven thousand people, a new record. He parked his Buick and we all piled out. The July heat, even in early evening, was terrible and there were dust clouds from so many people stamping around. Inside the gate, men were selling squawking toys and rubber balloons on sticks, and Kewpie dolls and little wind-up clowns with canes. From the grandstand, somebody was shouting through a megaphone, "Ladies and Gentlemen, tonight you will witness one of the greatest death-defying feats ever attempted in these United States!" Down the midway, painted banners billowed in and out in the wind and promised "The Snake Charmer," "The Alligator Wrestler," "The Fattest Woman in the World." Barkers were yelling outside the sideshows—"Twelve United States Cavalry swords are going to be thrust through a box while this little lady is inside . . ."—and we could hear the clanking machinery of the rides and see the two Ferris wheels and then the merry-go-round with its calliope blaring away. Concessionaires were shouting, "Come and eat! Ain't you hungry! Roasted peanuts! Hot dogs! Ice-cold lemonade! Hamburgers! Popcorn!" With so much noise and confusion on the midway, you hardly heard the bleating and whinnying and bawling coming from the stock barns, or noticed everybody pushing and shoving and stepping on your toes.

Daddy carried his black bag right to the fair, as somebody was always getting hurt in the races, or injured in a fight, or falling off a ride, or fainting from heat exhaustion. The whole family trooped into the grandstand after him. The seats above us were packed. Everybody was all dressed up, the women in white and yellow summer dresses, the men wearing white shirts, ties and suspenders, holding their coats, and with derbies or straw boaters on their heads. There was a smell of perspiration, starched cotton and wooden bleachers. More vendors were climbing up and down the aisles, hollering. About a hundred cars were parked in three big half-circles behind the platform and judges' stand, facing the track. Most of them were open roadsters and windowless, canvas-roofed Model T's, but there were plenty of Model A's with steel roofs, side curtains and isinglass windows, too. The grandest car in town, a 1922 Lincoln, was driven by G. L. Hope, who owned the Ford garage. With its jump seats, it rode seven people crowded in.

Our box had twelve seats in it, but, knowing Daddy, we knew they'd soon fill up. "I hope they'll clear those boys off the rail," Grandma complained. "I can't see the track. They're right in our way."

Uncle Harry called to them. "Hey, boys! Do you think we can see through you? Yes, I mean you. Don't you smart me!" Some boys and men were sitting right on the edge of the track itself. Fair officials kept coming by to shoo them off. Daddy said, "You tell people, 'Don't walk here,' and that's where they'll walk." Daddy waved to his friends. "Hello, Ben! Where's Jess? C'mon and join us." Before long we had the Osers, the Southards, the Netchers and the Pritchards in our box and Daddy was sending for extra chairs. "Move over a little there, Billy. Can't you squeeze him in with you, Betty?" The Harvey Band started up in a blare of brass and drums. They were to play tonight. "Thank God it's not us," Daddy said. "I'm getting so I hum 'Stars and Stripes Forever' in my sleep." In Fessenden, a Victor Picco, who had once played with John Philip Sousa himself, led the band, though Daddy sometimes filled in for him.

Jim Parsons:

". . . It was a community band. Everybody played, all ages . . . My dad, my brother Chet and I, Jess Oser, Lois Pritchard, Betty, Jimmy, Doc Critchfield . . . Once, we started out to play at a Lions convention in Minot. In every town we came to—Harvey, Drake, Anamoose—we'd always stop and get out of the school bus and make a big circle right out in the middle of the main street and we'd play two or three tunes: Schubert's *'Marche Militaire'* or Sousa's *'El Capitan,'* *'Semper Fidelis,'* 'Washington Post March,' 'Stars and Stripes Forever.' They called them 'booster bands' . . ."

Betty:

One of the high school teachers came up to talk to Auntie Kay. I guessed he was going to try to get her to go with him to the bowery dance after the races. He was goofy about her. She was wearing a tightly fitted white cloche hat and a short, long-waisted, transparent-looking chiffon dress, with rolled silk stockings. I knew she'd stashed her Lucky Strikes in her purse. I wished Mother would let me wear light, high-heeled slippers like that. Auntie Kay was a real flapper. One time in Bowbells she lost her teaching job after she crossed over into Canada and was seen having a drink at a roadhouse. Daddy wore a white linen suit to the fair, but he refused to wear a boater. He said, "They're hot as hell. The air don't go through them at all." Instead he had on one of his checked golfing caps.

Out on the track, the drivers were starting to jockey for position. There was plenty to watch at the races, the trotters walking around in their dusters, with eyeholes bound in red braid, and the drivers of the sulkies looking over their two-wheeled carts and limbering up their horses. Some of them came a month ahead of time, so the horses and trainers could practice on the track. The pacers ran on two right feet and two left, while the trotters trotted. Just before the races, it always seemed like some bewildered old farmer would drive his wagon onto the track about the time the heat was to start. Everybody in the stands would start shouting and laughing at him.

The bell rang so many times for them to come back, I was always caught off guard when, all of a sudden, there was a pistol shot and a big roar and people jumped to their feet, shouting and screaming and clapping their hands. "They're off! THEY'RE OFF!" "Why can't people sit down? Boys . . . hey . . . here they come now! Zoooo-o-o-m! Come on!"

"Come on! COME ON, BOY!" The crowd broke into a roar.

"ATTABOY! GO, GO!"

"That horse can run and I don't mean maybe! GO, YOU DEVIL, GO!"

"What's the time?"

One rider, Harold Jakle, had to climb up on his horse and grab the bit after one line of the reins broke. That brought the whole crowd to its feet again, roaring and shouting. "Harold can ride like nobody's business, even if he walks kinda funny," Daddy said. "One of his uncles said Harold couldn't turn around in a wagon box if his life depended on it." Daddy smelled a little of whiskey. I bet he was carrying a flask in his black bag. When he saw a young farmer friend of his, Rees Price, leading a short-horn bull out onto the track, Daddy shouted, so loud everybody around us could hear him, "Here comes an Angus and that's Price on the front end!" That got a big laugh.

Daddy seemed to know half the people at the fair. Sometimes he couldn't place a face. "Now, who the hell is that?" Then, before you knew it, it would come to him and he'd go over to the man grinning and sticking out his hand. And the other would look at him confused for a minute, when all of a sudden he'd grab Daddy's hand as if he were going to jerk his arm right out of its socket. And the friend would shout, "Well, by God, HELLO, DOC! Well, for Ker-risst sake! Hold still a minute and let me look at you. Gol darn your hide, where have you been so long? Well, how the hell ARE you? Long time, no see. Hey, let me introduce the little woman, or should I say 'my ball and chain'? Heh, heh . . . Maude, this is . . ." And *she'd* start in.

"Now, don't tell me, honey. Let me guess . . . Why, Jim Critchfield! Well, what a sight for sore eyes! Why, how you've changed! Honest, I wouldn't have known you." More exclamations, questions, recollections.

And it would turn out that she was a girl in his class way back in high school in Hunter or something. "Do you remember the time we went sleigh riding, the whole gang of us, and we tipped over down there in the coulee?" And then Daddy would start in on "Do you remember?" and they'd chew the fat about old school days and who married who and who moved out to California and how Mrs. Houston went to Florida but she came back to visit her husband's grave in 1925. And how somebody died of cancer. And who got killed in the war. And that boy who used to always be on the go, well, he went on to study law at the university in Grand Forks and got to be a county attorney, but he started hitting the bottle—well, you know how politics are. What a shame! Um-huh, Daddy would agree solemnly, a crying shame. Listening to the fate of their old classmates, life started to seem pretty grim. Then Daddy would tell a funny story and they'd all start laughing again.

I'd never seen so many flivvers. Uncle Harry spotted a few Maxwells, a Dort, some Chevies and Studebakers, but they all looked like Fords to me. The Harvey band played a very oompah oompah-pah style, I thought. In between heats, they had platform acts. Some came back every year. The Flying Fishers performed somersaults on a precarious high wire with their heads in gunnysacks. Maria Le Flors, the Flexibility Girl, balanced on a high single steel pole and made you hold your breath. There were Zipp-Bang-Whiz, pantomimic acrobats, and the Six Avalons, who did a teeter-totter act, and the Florence Four, who did a strong-jaw trick without a net, and Ardoth Maxine Schneider, a former North Dakota girl in a white riding habit whose white horses walked on their hind legs. The most popular act that year were the Gold Dust twins, two black brothers from Chicago, who sang and played ukuleles and harmonicas and danced and put on a comic boxing match. Daddy said they put on a special show at night, after the races, where they told dirty stories and all; there was a "blind pig" under the grandstand that sold beer illegally. The sheriff looked the other way.

That night, a man from the Flying Behees did a shallow dive. It was awful to see. He was wearing a black, sleeveless, one-piece bathing suit and he bowed and started to climb a very high ladder fixed to a pole. Way up on top—Daddy said ninety-two feet up—was a little platform. Uncle Harry said he'd heard about divers getting killed this way if it was at all windy. I looked back up at the flags at the top of the grandstand to see if they were hanging limp; they were perfectly still. There was a drum roll as the man got ready to dive. *Ta-rum, ta-rum, ta-rum* . . . He fell backwards and came down head first. I screamed and shut my eyes. It was horrible. When I opened them, he was climbing out of the tank, sopping wet. He came forward to take a bow as the crowd cheered and applauded. He had bulging, muscular thighs and muscles like ropes on his shoulders. Even so, he looked scared. I told Daddy, "I was afraid, and the diver was afraid too."

When the horse races resumed, everybody was excited and shouting again. "They're off! Which horse broke? Go, go! GO, YOU DEVIL!" There was that second when they were going under the wire and the horse I favored was about a nose behind and I was jumping up and down and shrieking for all I was worth. Then a horse Harold Jakle was driving became frightened. As soon as the horse got scared, Harold made a flying leap from the seat of the sulky and rode him. He kept going. The crowd went wild. But, in the next race, Harold was thrown right off his cart. Daddy ran down to look at him and said he'd just got bruised. Everybody said it was one of the best races in years. One of the trotters, running a heat in two minutes and ten seconds, broke the track record by half a second.

What I liked was the Ford race, all old Model T's. Each driver had to circle the track from a dead start. Then he had to pick up a pig from a pen near the judges' stand, crank up the flivver again, make a second round, and put the pig back in its pen. I nearly died laughing when Louie Kunkel, a boy at school, tried to crank up his engine with the pig under his arm and it wouldn't go. Everybody was yelling, "Hey, Louie!" "Attaboy, Louie!"

The races went on and on. Free-for-alls and Shetland ponies, horse chariots, mule chariots, hurdle jumping, relays, with the jockeys bouncing up and down so easily, knees held high . . . When I saw Helen Hope, we snuck out to explore the midway. We had soda pop at one of the new "vending machines," and got some gooey red cotton candy. Helen dragged me past more banners for the freak show—the Thin Man, the Bearded Lady, the Mermaid—into a tent showing "The De Milos—Poses Plastiques—Living Statuary." It was the same old girlie show we had every year. A couple of fat peroxide blondes with untidy hair in sequined pink satin bathing suits— they looked as flabby as boiled turnips. All the farm boys were goggle-eyed. A barker said all women had to go outside, even wives who came with their husbands. Any man could stay, if he paid twenty-five cents more. Helen said she heard they took everything off.

Out on the midway we ran into Bud St. Jacque and some boys from school. They'd been inside the "Wrestling Tent." Bud said three or four men traveled with the sideshows and if you paid a dollar you could challenge them to a match. If you beat them, you won twenty-five dollars. Nobody hardly ever did, Bud said. "These old carnival guys, they wrestle for blood. They ain't about to lose twenty-five bucks."

*From Helen Hope Graves, now a retired psychiatric nurse; interviewed in
Seattle fifty-five years later:*

". . . Betty and Bud St. Jacque were a duo for a very long time. They say
Mrs. Critchfield broke it up because Bud was part Indian. I don't think
that's true. I think Betty recognized that Bud was just not husband material,
as I did with his brother Speed. Grandpa St. Jacque was a full-blooded
Sioux. They were Catholic. And Phil, Bud's father, who ran the pool hall,
was an alcoholic and froze to death on the steps of the drugstore in 1926. It
was just awful. Right on Main Street. He got drunk and sat down in the
doorway. After he made the All-State Football Squad in 1930, everybody
said Bud was the 'greatest gridiron warrior' Fessenden had ever had. But
there were those three strikes against him in the eyes of our mothers. The St.
Jacques were a star-crossed family . . .

"I think Betty and I smoked by the summer of 1929. Oh, there was a little
sin in those days too. We used to smoke in the car because it was the safest
place. Mother wouldn't permit it at home. Dad would have been in orbit
. . . One time, when we were sophomores, we heard about a new bootlegger by the cemetery. About six of us piled in my brother's car one night and
we went out to get some beer. The man said the beer wasn't quite ready. We
wanted to look at it. I remember my brother and Betty and I going upstairs
in this farmhouse. And I tell you, I think it turned me off home brew
forever. If you've never seen the setup, they had this big crock, with cheesecloth over the top and a light bulb to keep it warm. And there were flies,
bottles, cans of malt and mash, it was dirty and smelly . . . yuk!

"There were places in town where you could go and get a drink. When
the man who ran the funeral parlor got jailed for bootlegging, my dad tried
to stop the *Free Press* from printing it. Dad said it didn't do the town any
good. It hurt the children. It hurt the family. Fred Zuber, the editor, said,
'But it's news.' . . . The first drink of alcohol I ever had in my whole life
was in Dr. Critchfield's office. Ninety percent grain alcohol. He had access
to it as a physician. Dad used to buy bootleg Canadian beer, and when he
made a good sale on a Ford or a Lincoln, he'd bring the customer over to
our house and go to the basement and they'd seal the deal with a bottle of
beer. But my impression is Dr. Critchfield drank more than beer . . .

"You didn't think about Betty being pretty or not pretty. She was so
vivacious and outgoing. She was attractive. Auntie Kay was the real dish.
She'd come and visit and she was full of life and went to all the dances.
She'd started smoking when she was only fourteen years old . . . The
whole aura of the Fessenden years I got from Betty when she was older was
one of total rosy, romantic, marvelous, loving living . . . I couldn't buy

that. Because it was *not* like that. There were tons of things going on all the time. Covering up was very much part of the ethic of that town. My mother would get so angry at me if I told her I saw so-and-so with so-and-so. She'd say, 'That's something we don't talk about, Helen.' . . ."

Further comment from Kathryn Critchfield Edwards, interviewed in Livermore, California, age eighty-one; she still has something of the air of a twenties flapper and has been smoking a pack of cigarettes a day for sixty-seven years:

". . . I'd come over to the County Fair. There'd be a big dance and Jim would meet me at the train. One time, I got acquainted with these people on the train who wanted booze so bad, I sent on word to Jim. He came with a couple of bottles. They were going on somewhere. Jim and Anne lived right downtown. So he could catch the patients, you know. And I think it was probably the only place available. But it was nice. Jim had a couple of office rooms up front and the rest was fixed up nice. A great big living room and a bedroom right beside the kitchen. In the hallway, we just had the beds lined up like a dormitory. It was kinda crowded, but everybody was happy and contented . . . Anne was so much fun . . ."

Betty:

Helen and I took a quick look at everything before going back to the races. At the barns, where wagons and rigs stood about and big farm horses like Clydesdales were staked out, dairymen were standing around arguing about how to get the most butterfat. The poultry exhibition was all cackling and crowing and barnyard smells. In the farm exhibits, they had super-long ears of corn and giant potatoes and a new kind of wheat, Ceres, that you were supposed to grow instead of the old Kota or Marquise varieties. One sign showed income per head per year in North Dakota was just $375 compared to the national average of $703, and that almost a hundred rural banks had gone broke that year. The 4-H Exhibit had a display saying that Rugby, North Dakota—just fifty-nine miles from us—was the geographical center of all North America. I guess that made us pretty close, too. They also showed you how to trap a fox and how to avoid lightning or getting smothered if you fell into a grain bin. Next door, at the Old Settler's Cabin, with its flintlock rifle and quilt hanging over the door, an old lady showed us how to put sourdough into a kettle and cover it up with hot coals.

The Women's Hall, a big, white-washed, flimsy wooden building, had great heaps of vegetables and all kinds of flowers. Mom usually won prizes for her cinnamon rolls and fancywork. They had all kinds of pies and we tried to guess which ones had nice, flaky crusts. Mom had taught me how to

trim the edge off the top crust and pinch it into scallops and draw a couple
of leaves in it with a sharp knife, and get the oven temperature just right, so
you could bake it at 350 degrees for forty minutes like Fanny Farmer said.
In the Fine Arts Hall, we found quilts and embroidery and hooked rugs and
cut work and cross stitching and tatting . . .

Instead of a clown, a man named Rube Liebman came back to the Fair
year after year. He was real tall and skinny and had a fake white goatee and
a star-spangled suit and a top hat so he looked like Uncle Sam. He'd bellow
in his bull-like voice things like he'd never seen such a good county fair or
"Lord, it's hard to be humble when you're perfect in every way."

Back at the grandstand, the races had gone on a long time and it was
close to nine and starting to get dark. Grandma was complaining, "It's got
so the horses whiz by so fast I'm getting a crick in my neck." Even Uncle
Harry was getting restless. "I don't give a hoot myself," he said, "but these
wooden seats must be getting awfully hard for you girls. Why you don't get
splinters with those skimpy little skirts, I don't know." Kay was anxious to
be off. A jazz band was going to play at a bowery dance until three and
everybody would park real close so they could sneak out to drink or
smooch.

Rube was crying through his megaphone, "Modern times are here to stay,
folks. Yes, sir-ee. How many of you ever heard of a radio five years ago? Or
saw an aeroplane ten years ago? Or owned an automobile fifteen years ago?
But thank God we still get our babies in the old-fashioned way. You bet
your life! . . . Yup! That's right, ladies. The stork brings 'em! . . . And I'm
happy to announce that Doc Critchfield right up in front here is the proud
father of a new baby girl born in Minneapolis today!"

Well, I never heard such applause. Everyone in the grandstand stood up
and clapped and cheered. It took Daddy by surprise. He looked real stunned
for a minute, then he grinned from ear to ear. That is how I'd like to
remember him, so happy and easy. Later, looking back, it seemed it was
about the time that Peggy was born that he began drinking so much. That
October, the stock market crashed and it wasn't long before a lot of people
stopped paying their bills—he had so many more worries. There were no
scenes when he came home drunk. He'd sneak in quietly and go to bed.
Mother kept up the façade of the happy family very well.

Betty

One hot August day during the dry spell, the temperature reached one hundred and ten degrees. Rev. Christian Dippel went into the basement of his new German Baptist church to burn wood chips left by the carpenters on the concrete floor. He lit a match. Spontaneous combustion suddenly enflamed the church. Reverend Dippel found himself in a fiery inferno and fled up the stairs, pursued by dense black smoke. He dashed from the burning building, his hair and eyebrows singed.

Within the hour, the roofs of seventeen houses in the neighborhood would catch fire. It was very windy. As soon as we heard Daddy shout that the Baptist church was on fire, Jimmy and I tore down the back stairs and across the alley to ring the fire bell. The fire station was right behind us and we pulled on the bell rope out front for all we were worth. Doors were being flung open and windows raised. All over town, people came rushing out to stand on their porches and look for the smoke. "Fire, fire!" went up the cry.

The whole town went to a fire. The firemen, all volunteers, dropped whatever they were doing in the fields or farmyards or in town and headed for the station as soon as they heard the bell. Somebody scared up a team along the way. At the station, one of them climbed in a back window and stumbled around until he found the latch to the big door. The horses would be trotted up and hitched to the truck, the firemen donned their faded red helmets, and they were off—making a mad dash to the fire. Often, if no horses were handy and the fire was right in town, the first firemen to arrive just pulled the fire cart themselves. It had a sixteen-foot extension ladder, a hundred feet of coiled hose, buckets, axes, hooks and a lead container with hydrochloric acid to give pressure to the hose.

The hand pump may have been old and the hose leaky, but the bell on the fire cart was in excellent condition. It clanged with every turn of the wheels. The faster the cart went, the faster the bell clanged. So when the apparatus came by, firemen pushing or pulling it, or a team of horses hitched on, the bell would be clanging madly as the striking gear on the rear axle was engaged by the cam. *Clang-clang-clang-clang!* If horses were hitched, they always looked frantic to get to the fire. Most probably they were scared to death of that clanging bell and were running to get away from it.

That afternoon, you could hear it and the fire-station bell all over town. Everybody came running to help put out the fire and to form bucket brigades to the nearest wells. Soon half of the lines were passing buckets full of water to the firemen and the rest passing the empties back to get refilled. The burning church, going up like an enormous bonfire, itself could be seen for miles. The fast passenger train from Minneapolis to Seattle chose that exact moment to come through town. People forking up salad in the dining car could look out and see an awesome sight.

Flames and thick black smoke from the flax insulation poured from the arched windows. Gusts of wind blew hot, acrid smoke right in the bystanders' faces. Soon a line of helmeted firemen formed in the street, holding a hose and bending their necks, cowering before the fierce heat. Other firemen ran about, panting and trembling with so much excitement they could hardly speak. The fire already had a clean sweep of the church. The steeple rose from a mass of fire and sparks; it was completely charred, but the bells were still hanging, and it was difficult to see what was holding them up. Tongues of fire slithered up and down and licked the blackened sides of the building with a crackle. Clouds of sparks flew up into the sky. The heavy black smoke made it impossible to fight the fire from inside. Dick Engbrecht, the fire chief, ordered chemicals sprayed, but they made no impression. The dry, new lumber burned too freely in the stiff breeze and generated a terrific heat. The fire cart's hose, squirting its single jet of water, was too puny for these flames.

"Where's Harvey?" went up the cry. Somebody had phoned and Harvey's brand new motorized truck was on its way. Now fluttering great puffs of flame—*phoom! phoom!*—burst from the blaze and you could hear a steady popping and crackle from inside, just like a popper full of popcorn. Firemen rushed back and forth in the terrible heat, their faces streaked with soot and sweat. I heard shouts, "Pour water over him! Take him over to Doc!" and saw Daddy, all flushed and sweating too, bandaging the hand of a man in a helmet. Many people were in chains passing water buckets, while some just stared at the fire, unbelieving and jostling about, not knowing what to do.

I'd just thrown on a flowered chiffon smock and noticed most people seemed to have grabbed the first thing at hand to wear.

"I'll bet you it was tramps," somebody in the crowd said. "They get in an empty building and smoke cigarettes . . ."

"I don't know about any tramps. All I saw was Reverend Dippel high-tailing it outta the church like the Devil himself was after him . . ."

"Stop that whining! I told you to go back home with your ma and that's the end of it. This ain't no place for kids."

Firemen were shouting. "This hose is too short to reach the hydrant! Somebody run back and get that other reel!" A column of flame burst from the roof, scattering sparks in all directions. The burning church was now just spotty red lines around the spaces where the walls had been. Thick, black smoke was pouring out. A cry went up as Dick Engbrecht staggered out of the smoke and fell forward on the charred grass; other firemen rushed over to drag him back to safety. Daddy came and was kneeling over him. Somebody said the chief had tried to go inside to make sure nobody was trapped or anything. He was back on his feet and running around and shouting orders again in no time.

There was nothing to save now. By the time the Harvey truck got there, in a roar of bells and sirens, the church was a dead loss. They'd made the twenty-four miles from Harvey to Fessenden in twenty-five minutes, the fastest time ever. Crash! The few surviving beams gave way and the roof of fire dropped into the main part of the church, the frame of the steeple toppling sideways with it. All at once the whole blaze burst into new life and the crackling grew much louder. Sparks were flying everywhere. Somebody shouted—yellow flames had shot up from the roof of the St. Jacque barn. The hot wind had also shifted toward the Baptist parsonage.

"Hook one of those Harvey hoses up to that hydrant!"

"Where's that ladder?"

"Girls, get water! Shake a leg, girls! Make it snappy!" As flames were sighted on one rooftop after another, everybody rushed about, running into houses with wells or cisterns and hauling buckets of water back. Firemen pumped water, hoses hissed, Dick Engbrecht directed the jet now at the parsonage roof, now at the St. Jacque barn. He held the hose with one hand and controlled the stream with the fingers of the other, making it hiss all the more sharply. Other firemen ran into the parsonage and were carrying out its dark, heavy furniture and everything else they could lay their hands on. Soon, piled right out in the street, were the Dippels' round dining-room pedestal table with three casters gone from its claw feet, and the Reverend's organ with a deep scratch on the side and the top lid hanging from a single hinge where the firemen in their rush had caught it on the door. These were surrounded by a Hoosier kitchen cabinet with the sugar and flour bins missing, a washboard, a bag of clothespins, an oak taboret with the potted fern gone, a hall mirror with four double coathooks and a winter sheepskin jacket draped on one, a hamper of soiled laundry, a pile of Mrs. Dippel's dresses, a heap of Reverend Dippel's bound sermon collections and Biblical commentaries, and many other family possessions, all sitting around in total disarray, including their daughter Alma's piano music. "Angel Eyes," "Follow the Swallow" and "Put Away a Little Ray of Golden Sunshine (for a Rainy Day)" were blowing down the street. These were retrieved by Mrs. Dippel, looking faint and mingling tears with coffee prepared by the Baptist women's circle. Reverend Dippel, his head and hands wrapped by Daddy in white bandages, and patting his wife's forehead with a damp cloth, looked as woebegone as only a preacher can look who has just burned down his brand-new church.

A fireman in the Dippels' second story was rescuing more property from possible flames. A narrow, high walnut chiffonier, with a mirror attached, was handed down the ladder, miraculously reaching the grass undamaged. But its lace dresser scarf snagged on an eave and waved from there.

"It's in the attic!" Bud was shouting. He and some of the other football players came running with another ladder; flaming embers had ignited the roof of the St. Jacque house. Two firemen came running with axes and we quickly formed a bucket brigade to pass full and empty buckets up and down the ladder. "Look at that roof steam! Christ almighty, it was hot!" The blaze was soon put out, with just smoke and water damage. "O-o-o-h!" A general indrawn breath announced a new spectacle. "Flames are coming from the Bohnet roof!" A minute later it was "Now it's the Dix roof!" "The Lutheran Church!" The wind kept shifting. No house in town was safe. The Harvey truck roared off, first one way, then another, part of the crowd running behind it. Others dashed to their houses to soak roofs with what water could be hauled up from wells and cisterns. The sparks would blow over to another roof and set fire to it and people would run and put that out and then they'd all come running back to something else. Firemen, several with bandaged hands and arms, kept hurrying to soak down new walls. My smock smelled like a firebrand. The taste of smoke was in my mouth. I was drenched to the skin. I'd been burned on my neck where an ember flew against it. My eyes were streaming and ash clung to my hair. It was thrilling . . .

Jim Parsons:

". . . I was working on a threshing rig outside town that day. The harvest was going full blast, with binders and threshing machines at work everywhere. We came in when we heard the bell and there were fires all over Fessenden. Smoke sifted just like fog over the town. The wind was blowing and it was hot and dry. I think they had sixteen or seventeen fires going. Everybody was running around trying to put out fires. It was an exciting time . . ."

Rees Price:

". . . All they had was that little fire cart. And a bunch of ladders so they could climb up and knock more holes in the roof to give the fire a better draft. The expression was, 'It's not the fire that worries me, it's the firemen.' They were all volunteers and half of 'em didn't know what they were doing. But they could get there quicker than hell. You bet. The bucket brigade. It was the biggest excitement around at that time . . ."

Betty:

A month later that summer, there was a burning barn in which eleven horses died. Arson was suspected. It was the Albes farm, just west of town, and the whole sky was red and men were leading horses out of the burning barn. They put blindfolds on them so they wouldn't turn around and run back into the fire. They saved a lot of horses. That same night, the Fessenden Cafe, right downtown, went up in flames . . .

Jim Parsons:

". . . When I heard the fire bell ringing, I jumped up and got dressed and ran up to Main Street. It was empty and I stood there all by myself. Here flames were shooting out the cafe's front window. The glass exploded and everything. Pretty soon a couple of firemen came round the corner, pulling that darn hose and ladder cart. They saw me standing there and hollered, 'Hey, Jim! C'mon down here and lend us a hand!' So I had to go down and help pull that darn hose wagon up the street so they could hook it into the fire hydrant. The cafe was gutted. My dad was Postmaster and we moved everything out of the post office for fear it was going to go too—one of those old high, ink-spattered tables, even the partition with its little windows of mailboxes. And we all had to help Mac Solberg carry his grocery stock outside to save that, too . . ."

Betty:

That was the end of it. The Baptist church was insured and by December was rebuilt and rededicated, Reverend Dippel had been treated for ulcers, and Fessenden had a new Model A Ford fire truck with chemical apparatus, hose rack, hooks, a thirty-foot extension ladder and a three-hundred-gallon-per-minute power pump. When the firemen kept roaring up and down Main Street, bell and siren going full blast, Daddy said that Dick Engbrecht must believe in Santa Claus, because he got a shiny new red truck for Christmas.

Those were my tomboy days. At the Girl Scouts grand windup program for parents, we did a skit about an overnight camping trip we'd taken at Wood Lake, where a carload of drunks came by after midnight and hollered at us. I played Mrs. DeVries, our very proper assistant counselor, repeating what she'd said: "Now, you four girls get in the front row. You littler girls back here. Everybody get their sticks. Now, girls, if they come at you the best thing you can do is kick them in the groin. That's where it will do the most good." Mr. DeVries, who was very proper, was also in the audience. They later became missionaries.

Another time, I got kicked out of science class for rolling up my stocking in front of the teacher. Once, we put plaster in all the school locks. On Halloween, once we'd outgrown ducking for apples and carving pumpkins into jack-o'-lanterns and drawing witches riding on broomsticks, we'd always tip over outdoor toilets. Daddy said a Hunter boy once fell into Grandma's that way and Mom told about how one time, when she was a girl in Le Claire, a man was inside when the outhouse was tipped over. It landed on the door and he had to holler for help.

Once, I went swimming, and afterwards Mom asked, "What did you wear for a suit, Betty? Yours was at home." I said, "Oh, I borrowed one," and told her the girl's name. Mother sighed. It was somebody Dad was treating for a venereal disease at the time. Then, after the Crash, the bank downstairs failed and a pool hall came in. There was a hole over one of the pool tables where plumbing had gone through and Jimmy and I used to spend hours lying on the floor listening to the racy conversation of Windy Bill Pellet, a horse trader.

But Daddy was strict. Bud's mother, Mrs. St. Jacque, gave the most wonderful parties. Daddy always made Jimmy and me come home an hour earlier than anybody else. I think Daddy was afraid Jimmy would be a sissy, a mama's boy, if he didn't treat him roughly, but Jimmy was starting to resent his authority. For parties I had a brown velvet dress Auntie Kay gave me, also a blue velveteen, which came down in points, peaked; you wore it with high boots. Nobody ever fancied me up. One time, I wore Daddy's golf knickers.

The most excitement at school came every year when the freshman and senior classes fought the sophomores and juniors, from twelve noon one day to sunset the next. When I was a sophomore they roped us and led us downtown. Bud St. Jacque broke away and snatched the flag, so the freshmen had to have an initiation and all the hazing that went with it. The flag was in a bell tower by the telephone company and it was always a fight to see who captured it. Once, some tough older boys said they were going to throw Jimmy in the Russian thistle patch outside town and I was clawing them. There were signs on cars, "Hurry Up! Hell Ain't Half Full!"

Jimmy:

". . . There was kind of an innocence to it. If you could put up the flag and keep it up for a day, you won. You kept guards posted. It was a free-for-all. The losers got marched down Main Street in chains as prisoners. It would go on for hours, like a scene out of Hades . . . At the big fire, I'd say we were observers. Oh, Betty probably managed to insinuate herself into an active role. Maybe deputy fire chief or something [laughter] . . ."

Jim

Alvin Mohr:

". . . Doc's office was up over the pool hall. You used the front staircase, though there was another out back. Oh, I was up there. The office was small and, uh, very humble. A typical country doctor's office. White enamel trays loaded with little bottles. His black bag with surgical instruments, you know, obstetrical forceps, things like that. Syringes. Boric acid. A can of ether. A white enamel chair with a headrest where he did tonsillectomies and all. His medical certificate on the wall. Medical books in one of those bookcases with glass doors that swung up and slid in.

"There were a couple of stools. That you'd sit on and he'd sit at the same level, you know, and look at you or give you a shot or whatever he was going to do. I remember those stools. They swiveled. And Doc had a little mustache. He'd start out, 'What seems to be the trouble, Alvin?' He seemed to know how afraid you were of illness. And very friendly. He never wanted to hurt you, you know. You had that feeling.

"His stethoscope lay on the desk in a litter of bottles, jars and papers. There was a blood-pressure gauge there too. I think he used an alcohol lamp to sterilize needles. And a basin, maybe to soak your hands or feet. And a scale to weigh yourself. There was a big old-fashioned rolltop desk, I remember that, and a humidor with panatela cigars. Green roll-up shades at the windows. Doc himself wore a white coat with a towel tied around his waist.

"He was a very different man up in his consulting room from out on the golf course or when he led the band. He'd straddle that stool and you'd open your mouth and he'd look in your throat and you'd say, 'Ah-h-h-h-h . . .' when he had that thing on your tongue. It was a metal tongue depressor with a little mirror at the end. He'd stick that thing in and press your tongue down. Then he'd put it into one of those white porcelain trays. He'd take your blood pressure, look in your eyes and ears, take your temperature, and feel your diaphragm and stomach, pressing in different places and asking, 'Does it hurt?' "

Mary Carter, widow, ninety:

". . . We thought a lot of Dr. Critchfield. My brother Martin's wife had a sister, Esther, and she was out with Martin to visit and got the flu and was real sick by evening. It was that quick flu. And Dr. Critchfield came home on the midnight train from the East and my brother Martin picked him up at the station and took him out to the farm. And the doctor stayed with her all night and she died in the morning. That flu was terrible. He couldn't save her.

"So when Martin got the flu too, Dr. Critchfield said, 'Martin, I think we'd better go down to the hospital in Fargo.' Martin says, 'No, Doc, I know you'll do all that can be done.' It was the same flu infection, head flu, they called it. Martin's eye was swelled shut. It looked like a risky business. And Dr. Critchfield told me what to do.

" 'Keep hot packs on it, Mary. Keep hot packs on it. Maybe the pus will come out through the ears or the nose.' And I put hot packs on. I kept two pans of hot water agoing all the time on the old range, you know. And I put hot packs on and I put hot packs on. And the pus came out his nose. He had an awful gathering in his head from the flu. And he got well. I remember Dr. Critchfield by that, you know."

Mrs. Carter had once astonished Fessenden:

". . . I was fifty-nine and I suppose everybody thought I was an old maid. Then I married Lloyd Carter of Minot, of all things. I pretty near knocked everybody down, it was such a surprise. He'd lost a good wife and needed a companion. I felt sorry for him and he said, 'Mary, wouldn't it be better for you to marry? It's no good for you to be alone now that your folks are gone and I sure don't like to be alone.' Well, I finally went. And we went thousands of miles. He had an old Cadillac car and the first nine years we were married, we went to California six times. He had a sister at St. Helens in Oregon, not too far from that mountain that erupted. Yes, I said I didn't know I married a traveling man, but he did like to drive. That old Cadillac rode so easy . . ."

Dan Ehni, of Fessenden:

". . . Doc saved my brother's life. It was out on the farm and my brother was two years old. He was blowing bubbles and backing up. My sister had a tub of boiling water she'd just taken off the kitchen stove. She was going to wash the floor. The water was too hot, so she'd taken a pail to the well to get some water.

"The baby backed into the tub and fell in the water. My father was frantic. He couldn't get transportation. He ran first next door and the man was drunk. Finally he waved to a school bus. The driver put the kids out right there and drove Father into town. Doc Critchfield came right out in his car. He greased some flannel blankets with Vaseline. We were terribly scared. When my mother went to take the baby's clothes off, the skin came off. After that, Doc came every day. We didn't need no graft or nothing. My brother healed without a scar and now he lives out in Oregon and has got grandchildren. And we owe that to Doc . . ."

Helen Litke Musha, of Harvey, interviewed at her home on the golf course:
". . . My dad wasn't feeling good and he went to Dr. Critchfield and said, 'Doc, I don't know but there's something wrong. Feel this growth I got on my neck.' Doc wouldn't tell him. They were such good friends. They'd always swear at each other. And Dad said, 'Doc, you damn fool, you don't know what you're doing. Now, I don't feel good and there must be something wrong!' Well, Dr. Critchfield came out to the farm and he told my mother, 'Mary, I haven't got the heart to tell Steve. But he's got leukemia. It's fatal.' Doc felt terrible; he was crying and everything. Eight more years my dad lived with it. Determination. He and Doc always went hunting together. Dad got so he could hardly get his clothes on, he was getting so weak from the transfusions. Anyway, Doc kept telling Mother, 'Don't tell Steve just yet. There's no cure for it. There's no hope for him.' At last Doc sent him to the Mayo Clinic in Rochester and they told him there. After he knew, it really bothered him. Oh, he didn't give up. He lasted another three years. But Doc was right not to tell him . . ."

Rees Price:
". . . Doc used to go out to Steve's farm a lot. They hunted together. One time, there was a party at the lumberyard one Saturday night. Harve Cook, who ran the lumberyard, was a pretty physical guy and he'd been a ballplayer. Anyway, when the party ended, why Doc and Steve Litke had gone home, as far as I was aware of. And Harve came back from outside, slapped his hands together and said, 'Well, I've just cleaned Steve Litke's clock.' And, of course, we were all surprised, the few that was left there. What was he cleaning his clock about? There was no friction, you know. It turned out it was just one of old Harve's whoppers. They hadn't even exchanged words. When Doc heard about it, he put tape and bandages all over

Steve and they paraded him back and forth in front of old Harve's place. They had quite a joke about that . . ."

Jimmy:

". . . I think being a country doctor in those years must have been very traumatic. Sometimes Father would come back from some farmhouse after being up all night and he'd tell me to go out and bring the 'tools' in. And I'd go out and there in the back of the Buick there was a kind of little flat deck. And there would be all his surgical instruments, sometimes wrapped up in newspapers and all bloody . . .

"In the years in Maddock and the early years in Fessenden, I'd describe Father as very athletic. I remember seeing him play baseball when he was in his late thirties and thinking: isn't that incredible that an old man like that can still play? Later on, we had a garden. Or *he* had a garden; it was strictly his. It was maybe three, four blocks from us along the railroad track in Fessenden. He'd deal with patients in the morning and then he'd take a break and go down to his garden and work there for an hour or an hour and a half . . .

"Some of the cases were terrible. Like one time this lady arrived at his office with this shiny, gray, blood-streaked, kind of shiny gray skull sticking out and the hair and everything over the back of her shoulders. A real mess. Father was down at the drugstore or some place on Main Street and Betty kind of took this woman in hand and got her down and got everybody calmed down. I don't know who went after Father. I guess maybe I did. More likely I was fainting or vomiting about that time, because it was really something. It was night and they were riding in a car and this car had steel arches that went across the ceiling and then the roof was made of some kind of canvas fabric. And this lady was in the back seat and they hit something and she went up in the air and the steel bar hit her head and made an absolutely neat line just at her hairline and folded her—she had heavy hair —and folded the whole thing back.

"Then Father came up and cleaned it all up and put it back down and he stitched right across the hairline and the lady hardly had scars afterwards. He didn't seem nervous. He was a good doctor. No doubt about it. He was a *real* doctor . . ."

Jim:

The patient, Mrs. William Zabel, had quite literally been scalped. They brought her to my office that evening with the scalp cut evenly along the forehead and around each side to a point back of the ears. The scalp had practically been torn from her head. Art Davis, who brought her in, said he was at the wheel with six people in the car when the brakes failed to hold at a turn and before he knew it the car went off the road and was bumping violently along in a ditch. I quickly sewed the scalp back on and when she'd recovered from the shock, I had her come back and we stitched it a second time to minimize any scars. To my amazement and Mrs. Zabel's good fortune, she completely recovered.

More and more terrible injuries from farm machinery and automobiles were coming in. One morning in the summer of 1929, there was a gruesome freak accident at the railway crossing just below my office window. August Wiese, a man in his fifties and well known about town, was waiting in his Ford at the next crossing for a freight train to go by. After the last car passed, Wiese started to drive across the tracks, never thinking that the fast Soo Line Passenger Number 105 might be right behind the freight. The flyer struck August's car at a terrific speed and picked it up on its cowcatcher, either carrying or dragging it a full block past the depot before throwing it off again. The Ford touring car was a total loss, and August was covered with blood. I found he'd suffered severe cuts about the face, a broken hip and internal injuries. Some months later, just when it looked like he was going to be all right, he got a bad cold, developed pneumonia and died.

We'd started warning car owners and anybody running a gas engine not to do it in a closed area. There had been a few deaths from carbon monoxide, usually young couples who left the heater running while they idled the motor. It didn't take exhaust fumes long to fill a closed car with deadly gas.

There were still broken arms from people trying to crank balky Fords; a few weeks with an arm in a sling fixed them up. And more tractor accidents all the time, a few of them fatal. One farmer outside town was using his tractor as power for a grain elevator, when his seven-year-old son climbed up into the seat and accidentally shifted the tractor into gear. The man tried to jump aside, stumbled, and the rear wheels went over his body. I took him to the Harvey hospital right away, but he died the next morning.

The worst farm accidents still mostly came during threshing, when so many men, horses, wagons and big steam rigs were at work such long hours every day in the fields. Herman Sayles, just twenty-four years old, was working as a spike pitcher on a rig at the Grimes place south of town. He left his place to clean off some loose grain from the top of the separator and somehow lost his balance and slipped. One foot went into the trapdoor at the top of the machine, right over the cylinder. Sayles tried to yank his foot back, but his leather boot stuck. The cylinder teeth tore his leg off just below the kneecap. I must say, he had guts. He got another member of the crew to take a strip of rawhide belt lacing and apply it as a tourniquet to stop the bleeding. That probably saved his life. They rushed him into my office, I dressed the wound and we drove him to the Carrington hospital. The doctors there had to amputate just above the knee. Sayles was weak from shock and loss of blood, but I never saw anybody with so much stamina. When I left him, he said, "I'll be ready to fight Dempsey in two weeks, Doc."

The same thing almost happened to Anton Anthonson, a powerful Norwegian blacksmith in Fessenden. He was repairing the tractor hitch on a binder when his overalls somehow got tangled in the power shaft which went from the tractor to the binder. Anthonson tried to shut off the power, but he was caught and couldn't reach the throttle. What saved him was sheer muscle. He seized a fender and held on for dear life while the shaft tore all the clothes from his body, ripping everything right off but his shoes and socks. A man of ordinary strength would have been drawn into the shaft. A couple days later, Anthonson came into my office. He complained his arms were stiff. "My God, Anton," I told him, "do you realize what a terrible strain that was?"

As horses grew fewer, so did injuries from them. But patients still came in with severe gashes or ugly wounds from being kicked—needing stitches to close and dangerous if it was near the eye. Many young boys helped to farm; they were more likely than the men to be thrown from a gang plow or get a leg caught in a wheel or fall off a wagon and get stepped on by a horse. Every so often, a team hitched to a grain wagon at one of the elevators in Fessenden would get frightened when a train blew its whistle. One time, a team swung around the corner of Main Street and the lumberyard toward the crossing just as the train was still passing. The lead horse swung off right away. But the momentum was so great that the pole horse was thrown against the train. It was badly hurt and we had to shoot it.

With cattle, a few farmers got injured when they stampeded going into the barn. The big danger was getting gored by a bull. The only fatality during our time in Fessenden was a pioneer settler, Lars Natland. His bull had always been gentle. One night, Lars heard some cattle creating a disturbance in the pasture by his house and he went out to drive them off a little. When he didn't come back, a son went out but he couldn't find his father in the dark and nobody answered his shouts. The son aroused a neighbor, they drove out on the field in a Ford and found Natland's body, badly gored and trampled, not far from the house. It looked as if the bull had struck him from behind without warning and one horn pierced his heart. It must have been instant death. Another Fessenden farmer, Albert Broschat, had a narrow escape. His bull broke out of the barn, he caught it and was going to lead it back. The bull refused to budge, lowered its head and charged.

Broschat ran for the barn, got into a stall and rolled under the manger, the bull right after him. He couldn't gore or trample his victim, but he did keep butting his head against Broschat's exposed side, reducing it to a mass of bruises. Broschat called his dogs, which rushed up furiously barking, and the bull left the barn to pursue them. In the meantime, Mrs. Broschat had phoned the neighbors. Her husband managed to climb up to the hayloft, where he was still lying when I arrived. Nothing was broken, but he found it painful to move for some days.

The farm accidents I dreaded most involved small children. We managed to save the Ehni baby, but I lost a one-year-old boy, scalded to death when his father lost his hold while lifting a big tin of boiling water off the stove. They were butchering hogs. You needed boiling-hot water for so many things on a farm. We also lost a couple of boys in gun accidents, trying to load their fathers' rifles. The hardest deaths to explain were those of apparently healthy men, like the hired man at the Soren Sorenson farm, a big Norwegian, who just slumped over at the supper table one night, dead of a heart attack. The most senseless deaths were the suicides. One farm boy, just twenty-one, threatened a girl who rejected his attentions with a shotgun, fired it, wounding her in an arm and called, "Now what am I going to do?" He drove home, got out of his car, pointed the barrel into his stomach and fired; he was dead within minutes.

A doctor accepted pain and grief as part of his daily lot. Still, some days, after signing two death certificates since morning and wondering if there was going to be another by nightfall, I'd get so I needed a shot of whiskey. I don't know. Maybe I was trying to brace myself against the failure that might be waiting for me with the next patient. In Fessenden, I always kept a bottle of medical whiskey in the black dresser in our bedroom. As a doctor, during Prohibition, I was allowed twelve gallons of alcohol a year. I suppose you could say that being a doctor out on the North Dakota prairie was hard work, wrecked your sleep and aged a man early. It's funny, I never minded the physical wear and tear. What was getting to me since the Crash was the fear, the endless anxiety. It wasn't just me, it was everybody. I saw it in my patients. Big-fisted, healthy-looking farmers whose stomachs had happily survived all those early years of sowbelly and beans were now getting ulcers and other stomach ailments from nervous strain. In 1929 we'd had one of the poorest crop years in memory. Out on calls in the country I saw a few wheat fields that yielded only two bushels an acre.

All of a sudden nobody had any money. Yet it was the poorest who needed the doctor most. The malnourished baby in convulsions. The confinement of the anemic, overworked farmwife. Illness for country people was always an emergency, the doctor's call an unplanned expense. They were hard put to scrape up the money for it. "Besides," they might well say, "look at his Buick and his bridge-playing wife. Look at him out on the golf course." I didn't blame them, but the more I thought about how to feed and clothe and educate the kids, pay the due insurance premium, fix the car, buy the medical book, the more anxious I was getting.

Anne:

". . . After the Crash, when the banks went broke and there was a bank holiday, nobody paid their bills. Sometimes they gave chickens or produce instead. Jim never turned down a call. One man owed for two babies, two tonsillectomies and one appendectomy. We never got a penny from him. By the time he had money, he'd lost all inclination to pay . . . This same man had a seventeen-year-old daughter, and one time when the Nazarenes held a revival meeting in Fessenden, the girl went and became emotionally involved. She repented her sins, and in a loud voice shouted out the names of all the high school boys with whom she'd been intimate. Everyone was scared he'd be named next . . ."

Jimmy:

". . . Father could never stay grim for long. He had a good deal of humor. One time, the county medical meeting was held in the American Legion Hall, right behind our apartment. Mother gave a dinner for all the doctors the night it ended. She and Father noticed at the last minute that it was the first of April. I can remember them going to frantic efforts. Mother hurried to make doughnuts with powdered sugar on them and he had some little rubber things that were exactly the shape of a doughnut and they put them in the dough and dipped them in powdered sugar. They thought this was very funny. They could hardly stop laughing, carrying on like a couple of kids . . ."

Jess Oser:

". . . One time I was over at their apartment and Jim called, 'Come in here, Jess. I want to show you something.' He took me into his office and a horrible, slimy thing was in the sink. 'That's Mrs. So-and-so's kidney,' he said. He was doing an autopsy and knew I was squeamish. Good Lord, you never saw somebody streak out of a room so fast in your life . . ."

Jim:

So many of the problems brought to me could be traced to people trying to reconcile their biological instincts with the stiff and self-righteous surface morality of the small town. Every doctor faced this in abortion. In Fessenden, an illegitimate pregnancy could ruin a girl's life. Yet abortion was a crime and could ruin the doctor. Again and again a young girl would come into my office, fumble with her handkerchief, her eyes filled with tears, as she struggled to say, "I don't know how to tell you, doctor . . . ," when she already had. What did you say to a lovely, intelligent young girl with her whole life before her? Where did a doctor's true responsibility lie? Immigrant families were the most vulnerable. Many of the rural people around Fessenden were foreign-born, most of them Norwegians and German-Russians, but some Swedes, Danes, Irish and Welsh, too. The older people might speak little or no English. When you went out to call on some of the farms, it was like going to a desert island, so cut off was it from the society around it by custom, language, distance and bad roads. These people were full of gratitude for the smallest kindnesses. If they got into trouble, you felt sympathy and shame that these foreigners, so much less confident than us, should be in such a predicament. My closest friends had always been immigrant farmers, like Jens Nielsen and Steve Litke, and not my fellow Yankees in the towns. I don't know why . . .

She was young, small and blond. I guessed Norwegian. The boy who'd brought her left before I had a chance to speak to him. I just went out into the waiting room and there she was, sitting all alone, trembling, wrapped in an old blanket. Her white face was streaked with rouge and her eyes were brimming with tears. These and the way she shuddered and shivered, and the cringing way she sat, told me she was young and unmarried and that she was very sick and very scared.

"Your name?"

"Norma. Norma Thorson."

"You live in Fessenden?"

She nodded.

"Who is the boy?"

She looked at me, but didn't answer.

"I asked, 'Who is the boy?' "

"I'm not going to say."

"What about the baby?"

"I got rid of it."

I saw from her pallor and the way she gasped for breath that she was faint. The blanket, I discovered, was to hide she was bleeding. At once, I gathered her up in my arms and carried her into the surgery. I examined her and found the placenta had not been expelled. I knew I was going to have to complete the abortion. I wanted to call Anne for help, but remembered she had gone out to play bridge. The girl's pulse was running. So was mine. She couldn't have been more than a year or two older than Betty. I explained everything that I was doing as I went ahead. There would be time to question her later. I was really sweating, but once I had my hands on the instruments, my panic ceased and I worked professionally. I used curettement to scrape away and remove the rest of the placenta and then packed the uterus with the aid of a head mirror. When it was over and the girl lay back with her eyes closed, I washed up and poured myself a drink. I needed it.

I left her to rest and when Anne came home and I told her about the girl, she went in to talk to her. For some time I could hear their low, urgent voices. When Anne came back to the living room she said, "Jim, I want to keep her with us for a few days. She's afraid to go home." That solved my problem. I'd been weighing the risk of trying to drive the girl to the Harvey hospital for a blood transfusion. It was a big risk. I'd never seen death from external hemorrhage in any case where the blood flow was checked. I had seen deaths from internal hemorrhage of even small amounts of blood. So often, it was hidden. There the danger came from the trauma of absorbing blood through the peritoneum. When it came to external bleeding, I felt everything depended on the sense of whoever cared for the patient after the doctor had done what he could. Anne had decided for me. There was no one better to whom I could entrust a patient.

Anne knew the girl and her family. The father worked at a lumberyard in town. I knew him to speak to. He was easygoing, drank some, chased around a little. The mother was churchgoing, a good Lutheran. It was a big family, five or six children, most of them musical and talented. The Thorsons had moved to town a year after we did. Anne wanted to talk to the mother. Norma had concealed her pregnancy, and there might not be any need to tell the father at all. She had a lovely soprano voice, Anne said, and sometimes she sang at church and school. Betty knew her. Anne said she seemed to have grown up suddenly the past year, bobbed her hair, plucked her eyebrows, worn bright red lipstick. She'd been running around with boys, smoking and doing all sorts of things her parents disapproved of. The abortion had been done by an old woman in Anamoose. Somehow it had gone wrong and Norma became terrified and made the boy bring her to a doctor. Norma Thorson. Now I recognized her. Not this desperate creature with her trembling mouth and tear-streaked face, but an innocent little Norwegian girl wearing a starched white apron, her hair in pigtails, singing like an angel.

So Anne nursed Norma back to health. She recovered from the abortion
with no other aid than frequent small sips of water. Anne prepared a bed for
her next to Betty's in the hall. She also met Mrs. Thorson, who had brought
Norma up simply and strictly and still saw her as well-behaved and good. It
was just since they'd moved to Fessenden, Mrs. Thorson said, that Norma
had become so flirtatious and showy, like one of those flappers you heard so
much about. "They get it from the movies," she said. Anne had glimpsed
the room Norma shared with her sisters—chintz-covered cots and the walls
covered with the photographs of film stars—Betty Compson and Clara Bow.

One sensed this aura of make-believe, what I came to think of as her
Flaming Youth pose, about Norma from the start. As she recovered, she
spent the whole day lying on her bed in the hall, reading a cheap novel or
one of those true-confession magazines they sold down at Fisher's Drugstore. Her own story was that since her family had moved to Fessenden,
she'd become popular with boys and started going out to parties, having fun.
She was mad about jazz songs from Broadway musicals and Hollywood
films and loved to dance. She'd promised her folks she'd finish school first,
but someday she wanted to be a professional singer. The trouble, she said,
was that the crowd of boys she'd got mixed up with were a little wilder than
she liked. They drank a good deal and smoked and liked to hug and kiss and
they all had only one idea. Then she'd gone with this boy who could get his
father's car—no, she'd die before she'd tell his name—and, well, usually
they'd just petted or necked but this once they'd gone all the way. When she
found she was going to have a baby, she wanted to turn on the gas. But the
boy knew this old woman in Anamoose. At this point in her story, Norma
burst into hysterical sobs.

Going about my calls in the countryside, I thought about Norma and
how she was just a schoolgirl, doing homework at night like Betty. I
thought about how sick and frightened she had been when I found her in
my waiting room—I wondered how often in her young life already she had
found herself alone. Sixteen, seventeen, wasn't she? Full of adolescent fantasies, her face clumsily daubed with powder and rouge, a pretty little schoolgirl probably trying to be like the flappers and coquettes in movies she saw.
With her mischievous eyes, her shy smile and her slender and delicate
throat, there was something about the girl.

A day or so before Norma was to move home, I'd gone hunting with Ben
Oser up on the Sheyenne River, leaving just before daybreak. It was late
afternoon when I got back with a brace of pheasants. Norma, who was the

only one home, looked at the green heads and gleaming reddish-brown feathers and said I must be a terrific shot. I was windburnt, with a spurious ruddy glow, and after washing and changing clothes I went into the Legion Hall to play the piano. I'd just swung into "Minnesota, Hats Off to Thee," when Norma came in. She wanted me to play something from *Blossom Time*. So, spreading my hands on the keys with a flourish and striking a chord, I sang in mock Broadway style:

> "Once on a time in a kingdom by the sea
> Lived a young prince sad and lonely . . ."

"C'mon, you sing the part of Mimi," I told Norma. She had a great voice.

> "Under enchantment of magic mystery . . ."

I was singing the part of Schubert:

> "To be set free by one only."

She sang:

> ". . . Weary he waited while years sped along,
> Came then a maid pure and holy . . ."

And I:

> "Love broke the spell so the storybooks tell . . ."

And Norma:

> "And he laid at my feet this song."

We both sang the chorus:

> "You are my song of love, melody immortal . . ."

It had never sounded so good. I think we were both moved by Schubert's melody and the lyrics. It broke the ice and Norma sat down on the piano bench beside me and looked through a book of Romberg songs. She picked one of her favorites from *New Moon*.

> "I remember ev'ry little thing you used to do,
> I'm so lonely . . ."

When one song ended, she'd name something else and I'd depress the pedal and put my hands back on the keys, beginning slowly and picking out the notes. Gaining confidence as I'd play it through, I kept adding chords. After *New Moon*, we did pieces from *Maytime*. She knew them all. I kept thinking: why does this weak, unhappy girl possess such magic when she sings?

As if she'd read my thoughts, she stopped singing and turned away. Her back was shaking with sobs. All of a sudden she was crying. I took my hands off the keys. It was time to stop. The songs had upset her. "What's the matter?" I asked. "Come on, now. Tell me about it." She turned around and I saw she was crying like a child, unmindful of how she looked.

"I'm scared to death," she managed to say, choking and sobbing. "Nobody ever told me what life was like. They just said, 'Don't.'" She was terrified her father would find out about the abortion. "Oh, God!" she cried. "Now the whole town will know. How can I stay here?" She began to talk of her fears and spoke some time with feeling. I listened to her with pity, but not without a little irritation at her naïve, self-pitying tone. Common sense told me that I was a married man past forty going gray and paunchy and that for all her remorse she was a reckless and stubborn girl who was already in trouble for trying to wring from life more than it could give. But when her face crumpled up like a child's and she started sobbing again, I didn't care. I felt only compassion for her. She was so small and frail and alone. How could I help her?

"I don't understand," I said as gently as I could. "What is it you want?" Still sobbing, she put her head on my shoulder. "Believe me, believe me, what I have done is hateful to me," she said. "I didn't know what I was doing. What will people say? That I'm bad?"

"Don't talk like that. Maybe nobody will ever know." But I knew in a town this size you could never keep anything hidden. Right then, I suppose, I should have gotten up and ended it. I meant to, glad Anne or one of the kids hadn't come bursting in. I was half off the bench when Norma had a fresh outburst of crying. I took her by the shoulders, which were warm and heaving, and looked into her frightened, tear-streaked face, trying to speak kindly and calm her hysteria. At last, losing patience, I tightened my grasp. I may have meant to shake her. Instead, we found ourselves in a kiss and for a moment neither of us took our lips away. I pulled myself together first. "No, Norma, no." I drew back, slid off the bench and this time I did manage to get to my feet. "I've got to get up to my office . . ." On the way, Norma stopped at a mirror in the hall to fix her face. Slowly she began to smile, and to sigh, and in the end she laughed out loud, called herself an idiot, and ran off.

That was how it began. Norma moved home, but Anne asked her to come in on Saturdays to help with the housework and ironing. Anne said Norma needed the money to buy clothes for school. Often we gathered around the piano afterward and played and sang. Anne encouraged Norma to feel part of the family. A pleasant, cordial intimacy seemed to develop between us, fatherly enough on my part, except for that one time, I thought. A year or so later, after Norma graduated and my office girl left, it seemed natural to offer the opening to her. Soon I grew accustomed to hearing her voice, calling out in the waiting room, "Who else hasn't registered? Come and put your name down." From my office I could hear her hum, peck at the keys of her typewriter, sing snatches of songs, bang drawers and go about her business. I got used to the eau de cologne she wore and the funny face she'd make into the mirror of her big compact when she put lipstick on or powdered her nose, I even got used to her short skirts and rolled stockings and the way she held her finger out when she drank coffee. Sometimes there were patients with venereal diseases, hemorrhages or terrible injuries, but Norma did what was expected of her with an air of showing she could handle the work.

When we were alone, she talked mostly about herself, complaining about her life at home or that she'd been sleeping badly. She tortured herself with fears that she had a bad reputation in town. They were justified. Gossip about the abortion faded away, but all Norma had to do was go dancing with some boy to get the women's tongues wagging all over town. As far as I knew, though, her father had been kept in the dark. Since her mother knew about everything, I wasn't too surprised when Norma announced that her parents had somehow scraped together enough to send her to teachers college in Mayville. The day she came to say good-bye, she was an eyeful in a skimpy little red chiffon dress with a red cloche hat over her blond curls. Where on earth did she get those clothes? Once she was gone, I told myself it was over, just another episode in my life, and thank God for that.

Months went by, and in the course of those months it would seem to me as if I'd forgotten what Norma looked like. And then one day I'd hear she was back in town. Going down Main Street I'd catch myself walking faster than usual and looking around, as if I might get a glimpse of her. When at last I did, she always looked just as I'd imagined she would: the same slim, long-legged figure, waved blond hair, a coat draped carelessly over her shoulders, the same old big blue eyes.

Did I really miss her? I was happily married to Anne, the mother of my children and my wife. To think of Norma was crazy. And yet I sensed, I guessed . . . no, I was certain that I needed Norma's presence in my life as much as I needed a shot of whiskey from that hidden bottle in my desk drawer or the time I had to myself on the golf course or the air I breathed . . . I simply could not get her out of my mind. . . .

Anne

Barbara Dunn, a niece, from a 1984 interview; one of a series of comments and conjectures concerning the Norma Thorson affair the winter and spring of 1930–31:

". . . I don't remember where I heard this or when. It's all sort of a vague memory. I think my mother told me. It was one of those times when she was telling me how great Aunt Anne was and what she had to put up with. It was something about how this girl was pregnant and had an abortion and she had hemorrhaged. And . . . I can distinctly hear my mother saying, 'And they took her into their home and gave her medical care and Anne was the one that had to wash all the bloody sheets and towels and keep her clean and comfortable.' And that's as much as I can tell you. I think I assumed the girl was . . . well, the implication was that she was a friend of Uncle Jim. The reason the implication is there is because my mother was telling me how much Anne had to put up with. If it had been some unknown person it wouldn't have had the dramatic effect of . . . this particular person. Now, I may be way off . . . My memory of Uncle Jim himself is that he was nice to children. Some adults couldn't care less whether kids are around, but he was kind and pleasant and friendly to us, and talked to us . . ."

Elsie Engbrecht Kieper, retired farmer's widow in Fessenden; fifty-two years earlier a nurse who assisted Jim in deliveries:

". . . I do remember something about that abortion. Norma told some girls at school she'd seen the baby. She must have been pregnant at least several months before the abortion. There was an old woman, way out in the country near Anamoose, who performed abortions; maybe she went out to her. Most likely, she did it herself. I'm certain Dr. Critchfield didn't do it.

He was too good a doctor. He wouldn't have made a mess of it. She couldn't have bled so badly that Mrs. Critchfield had to look after her for some days. Most likely, she came in hemorrhaging and Dr. Critchfield fixed up what had been wrongly done.

"You almost never heard of abortions in those days. I know when I was in nurses' training we had four of them come into this one ward. All girls who started an abortion at home and of course the doctors had to finish it because they were bleeding. I have no idea how they did it, those girls. But the doctor wouldn't let you die, that's for sure. Though I think there were a lot of them that *did* die on the way to the doctor. I just remember those four cases. They were all in this one ward and they were discussing why they had to abort their babies. They had the stupidest reasons . . .

"I just knew Dr. Critchfield professionally and there you don't do a lot of joking. I could always depend on him when I went out on a case. He was the doctor. I wasn't afraid to ask him about things and he was real good, you know, about helping. I never saw him lose his temper . . . I only worked when he needed me. Dr. Critchfield would call and pick me up in his car. Sometimes I gave the anesthetic. You put a mask on the patient and dropped drops of ether or chloroform. We finally got an antitoxin for diphtheria. For flu, we gave sponge baths and nursing care. For scarlet fever, chicken pox and whooping cough, we put them in quarantine. But we didn't have all those staph infections so common today . . .

"Mostly, I helped Dr. Critchfield with deliveries. He was very good with his patients, real friendly. And people liked him. I remember one case. Jim McBain. He had mumps and his mumps went down and he was very sick and Doc Critchfield took me out to stay with him. The weather turned bad and he couldn't get back to town, so he stayed all night. He and old Mr. McBain, they just visited all night. They seemed real compatible and they talked about farming and a lot of things. Of course I was busy with my patient, because he was real sick . . ."

The late Jennie Miller Anderson, retired nurse, interviewed at a Harvey nursing home, 1983:

". . . If you worked with Dr. Critchfield as his nurse, he was soft-spoken, gentle, but stern; no foolishness . . . He helped me get into nurses' training at Northwestern Hospital in Minneapolis . . . And Mrs. Critchfield, she was a great lady . . ."

From an editorial in the Wells County Free Press, *June 7, 1926, four and a half years earlier:*

". . . We heard the other day of two men recently pursuing two budding young girls of school age. The little girls, God help 'em, were thrilled over the influence they had over older men. The older men, scoundrels if ever there were, were merely staging another hunt in the quest for gullible young girls. Just how far they will go with their prey we do not know . . . but the subject is such that it seriously deserves the thought of the better citizens of Fessenden . . ."

Nora S., at the time a Fessenden schoolgirl; interviewed in Mesa, Arizona, fifty-two years later:

". . . The Critchfields moved away during the Depression, but it was more than that. There was some trouble. With a high school girl—Norma Thorson. It was a big scandal in a little town like Fessenden . . .

"Everybody sympathized with Mrs. Critchfield. She was such a strong woman. Kept going on as if nothing had happened. Why, she was president of the Mothers' Club! And all those children. People used to think Dr. and Mrs. Critchfield looked alike, more like brother and sister. He was kind and gentle, a very likable man. Once, Mama took me to him and there was whiskey on his breath. Mama said, 'Nora, you won't have to go back there again!' So, next time, we went to Dr. Matthaei. But he was so gruff. Once everybody knew about his affair with such a young girl, Dr. Critchfield started losing patients. He was a wonderful doctor. Even Mama used to say that.

"The Thorsons were like the Critchfields—lots of talented, active children and a father with a reputation for running around and drinking. There, too, the mother was the staunch figure. Norma herself was blond, small, attractive though not beautiful, and she always had a lot of boyfriends. She used to come to our house on Saturdays to iron clothes and clean. She had to buy her own clothes and things for school, as the Thorsons were poor and had so many children. Mama was once criticized for hiring somebody with Norma's fast reputation, but Mama said it didn't matter to her . . . I remember the abortion. She was sick and Mrs. Critchfield nursed her back to health. But that was much earlier. Right away, the affair was a big scandal. It's so long ago I doubt there's anyone left in town who really knows the story . . . After they left, once in a department store in Fargo Billy came up and at first I didn't recognize him. He said, 'Don't you remember little boys?' "

Jess Oser, Anne's close friend:

". . . Sweetpea, that's what I heard him call her, his little sweetpea . . . She was why they went away. It was all her doing . . ."

Lois Pritchard, another close friend:

". . . Jim was a perfectly charming man and a pretty fine doctor, I'll tell you. Never let anybody tell you any different. I never believed what they said about him. Never, never . . ."

Helen Litke Musha, daughter of Steve Litke, Jim's best friend at the time:

". . . Well, I know my dad had no use for Norma. He and Dr. Critchfield would sit at the kitchen table arguing for hours and my dad would say, 'Doc, you're the biggest damn fool in the country. You've got a lovely wife and family and you do something like this.' They'd swear and bawl each other out, but they were very good friends. Dad really got after him about Norma. He'd send me out of the room but I could hear, because they cussed at each other so loud.

"Norma was a nice-looking girl, blond. She was from a poor family and she worked for the Critchfields, ironing at first. I think Mrs. Critchfield, she really took Norma in, maybe treated her more as a daughter than a hired girl. Later she was Doc's office girl. I remember that because Doc and my dad had the biggest fight of their life over that. They shoved me out of the room, but I could hear Dad shouting, 'You're putting her in the office now! You son of a bitch, are you crazy?'

"I think Jimmy was hurt. His dad was always so strict with him. Norma was not all that much older, three, four years. And that, maybe, really hurt him when he heard about it. It probably hurt him because he was that age. You know what I mean . . . Doc was very, very well thought of. He didn't drink more than anyone else. Oh, he might have been more open about it. Some drank more, but they sneaked it, covered it up with Sen-Sen and all that crap . . . Betty was bitter, very bitter . . ."

Betty:

". . . She was dumb. She could sing. A tough babe. She had had an abortion in high school. Rather like Mildred in *Of Human Bondage.* It started in Fessenden when she was our maid, the hired girl. Once, Mom went to Iowa for six weeks and I was staying home with Daddy. One day I went to a picnic at New Rockford. When I got home and went upstairs, I found her wearing my bathrobe . . .

"She was small, blond and homely. Cheap, sharp features, sang a little, was vulgar. An appealing waif. All she wanted was a meal ticket . . ."

Jim's sister, Kathryn:

". . . How do I explain Norma? His age. He'd turned forty. And she worked on him, worked her spell, you know. She was a pretty little Norwegian girl. And she'd come to the folks' apartment, help Anne with the housework. And then Anne would tell her to go in and play the piano and we'd all sing. Anne wasn't the jealous type or anything. Anne didn't worry. We never thought anything about it. We never dreamed they would have an affair . . ."

Helen Hope Graves, Betty's high school friend:

". . . I think it must be the same in every town that's small enough. Everybody knows everybody. And things go on all the time. You have to pretend you don't know about them, because otherwise you couldn't all live together peacefully. Fessenden was like Spoon River. You could start out with each family and go down the list. People knew what was going on and it titillated them. But there were rules. Things weren't done at the front gate, so to speak. They didn't carry the onus of another woman disrupting a family. Or of a middle-aged man going with a young girl.

"So it *was* a scandal. In Fessenden, you didn't tear up your family. You had your fun on the side. Once Dr. Critchfield and Norma were so flagrant, it was a tragedy for everybody involved.

"My strongest recollection of him is as a physician who fit the name of physician. He knew all the secrets and he never told. He could relate to people. That's absolutely essential in a doctor. He was a good-looking man. He could sing. He put on the minstrel show. People expected him to direct it and perform in it. They enjoyed seeing him. You know, 'Moonlight and Roses' . . .

"Norma was young and impressionable. I'm sure she was terribly flattered to have attention from Dr. Critchfield. But wild? What's wild? She was no wholesome and angelic virgin, what we called a *nice* girl. And she was no waif, that's for sure. But she was no vampire-like, man-destroying femme fatale either. Crafty, conniving, scheming, yes. I don't know what fantasies she had. But, you know, so have a million other girls. Without being wicked or floozies or vamps or hard or tough or any of those things. Pathetic, she may have been. All of the Thorsons were frail-looking, so blond and pale, not dynamic, not aggressive like some of us. I guess you could really say she was sort of an 'It' girl, a little like Clara Bow, full of sex appeal, vivacious. She was a good singer. I mean she was no Galli-Curci, but she had a pleasantly clear soprano voice.

"It was so tragic for Norma, just tragic, for her to get involved that way. Those were the crucial years for her. And what in the hell was Dr. Critchfield doing? He wasn't helpless in all this. She didn't throw a lasso around him, making him do it. Let's put some of the responsibility where it lies . . .

"The old woman in Anamoose was known to everybody as where girls went if they got in trouble. Word doesn't get around so definitely about what to do and where to go and all that without there being some business . . . What I'm getting at is that Norma wasn't the only one to be struggling with that kind of a problem, and to call her tough, as Betty did, strikes me as blatantly unfair . . .

"One of the things I've thought about is the incredible way in which those women in Fessenden supported each other. My mother, Mrs. Critchfield, Mrs. Quarve, Mrs. Thornton—the way they held each other up and covered up for their erring husbands and children is really fascinating . . . I have good memories of Anne. She liked children. We were always welcome at her house. I remember you went up those stairs to this long hall—dark, dingy, a bad smell of ether and alcohol from the doctor's office, beds along the side, it was always a mess. The rooms were on the left and the Legion Hall was in the back. It was grim, but I thought it was an incredibly romantic place. There was a certain aura about Anne. She was a handsome woman. Very capable. She knew how to cook like practically nobody, you know. She was good at so many things. She fit in with Jess Oser and the faster, bridge-playing crowd, and she was an exemplary member of the Mothers' Club, too. She had a foot in both camps . . ."

Anne:

I was giving a party and somebody said something to me about that girl. Jim was so good and kind, I couldn't imagine him having an affair. I knew he was drinking heavily. I tried to turn a blind eye to it, but there was no hiding it now. He knew his own capacity and seemed only to drink as much as he needed to cope. He never lost his self-control. He carried on his practice. I knew something was going wrong. I liked to fool myself that Jim and I were an old married couple, united in the kind of middle-aged under-standing and tenderness that comes when much has been forgiven and for-gotten. But I knew, too, that time and chance play cat and mouse with human happiness. I'd seen what unpredictable attractions to some women could do to men, even the best of men. But Norma was too young. She was just the office girl. Only two years older than Betty. She came and went, singing, playing the piano, like one of the family. It was too incredible.

I didn't believe it. Even so, I caught myself no longer looking Jim straight in the face, no longer smiling when he came in the door. It was as if I were the one with the guilty conscience. Worse, I'd find myself trying not to be alone with him, as if to avoid conversation so he wouldn't have to lie, so I wouldn't have to feel disgust. To make me feel more lost and miserable, I was pregnant again. I had turned forty-three in December, the baby was due in March, and my gynecologist in Minneapolis had warned me not to risk having it. I'd almost died with Peggy, now a year and a half old. I didn't know what to do. I tried to talk it over seriously with Jim. But lately, it seemed to me, he answered every question with a joke. That fall, we'd moved at last, after six years, from our old apartment on Main Street. Our new home, what everybody called the "little house on Quality Hill," was small but on the best residential street in town, just across from the Hopes. Jim kept his old offices. When she wasn't away at school, Norma still worked for him sometimes, and if I went down when she was there, it now began to seem as if she ignored me. It also seemed to me she spoke to Jim impudently. And worse, he seemed to answer her in the same angry, confidential tone.

I pulled myself together. I had nothing but gossip and suspicion to go on. Jim had always looked on life with the charitable eye of an experienced doctor who has learned that people can't be other than they are. His very acceptance worried me. He'd never given a hoot about what people thought of him, but I knew how gossip could grow by leaps and bounds if it once got started. Whatever the truth, I knew that for the sake of the children and his medical practice, appearances were going to have to be preserved. In 1930 I'd been president of the Mothers' Club and was scheduled to give the lesson at the January 1931 meeting. I asked Genevieve Thornton to switch with me so I could be hostess that day too. I asked Jim if he'd give a short medical talk to the ladies of the club. Then, though I wasn't thrilled to pieces to do it, I phoned the Thorsons and asked Norma if she would come and sing for us. That, I hoped, would put an end to it.

The Mothers' Club was made up of the most conservative women in town. They were pillars of the Lutheran and Congregational churches. They influenced the *Free Press* through their husbands' advertising. Newcomers seeking to join were carefully vetted. Of course, one had to be a mother. The club was Fessenden's leading defender of the sanctity of marriage, family and the home. Indeed, Mrs. Thornton's talk at just the last meeting had been "The American Home." ("You cannot measure a home by inches or weigh it by ounces. Home is a matter of love . . . .") Her husband, the high school principal, was famous for once, after his boys went drinking with Bud St. Jacque and his gang, refusing to believe they'd touched alcohol. He said, "Look how much water they drank in the morning."

At the meeting before that, Alma Quarve had discussed the six bestsellers of the 1920s, *Main Street, If Winter Comes, The Rosary, The Sheik, The Inside of the Cup* and *Mr. Britling Sees It Through.* Everyone was uncomfortably aware that *Main Street*'s Thanatopsis study club was much like our own club. Sinclair Lewis described it as "such a cozy group, and yet it puts you in touch with all the intellectual thoughts that are going on everywhere." We all knew Gopher Prairie was Sauk Centre, Minnesota, a day's drive away. At our December meeting, Mrs. Taylor, the dentist's wife, had talked about "Foreigners of Prominence," such as Albert Einstein ("Frau Elsa is honest enough to admit she doesn't understand relativity") and Joseph Stalin ("Stalin's mother says, 'I didn't raise my son to be a dictator' "). At the same meeting, someone had played Chopin waltzes, and one of the ladies had read a poem about George Washington by Edgar A. Guest.

When my afternoon as hostess came, I wore a new black chiffon maternity dress I'd whipped up on the sewing machine. I was already seven months pregnant. At the last minute, I straightened my best linen tablecloth on the dining table, and made sure that the candles and glass goblets, and the place cards and favors—little paper cups full of nuts—and the fruit centerpiece looked all right. Our meetings ended with refreshments, which usually meant hot buttered rolls, a Waldorf or potato salad, celery and carrot sticks, stuffed olives, and a pineapple upside-down cake or angel food cake. The club met from three to five so everybody could get home in time to fix supper and their husbands wouldn't be kept waiting. When the first members arrived, there was a burst of cries and confusion, of women saying hello and taking off their overshoes. I took their scarves and coats into the bedroom. I'd arranged chairs facing the piano in the living room. Once they were all there and had settled down, we opened the meeting by singing "America, the Beautiful," as we regularly did.

We'll skip my talk, which didn't amount to much. The program committee had given me the topic "Living Religion," I suppose because I was a minister's daughter. It was hard to know what to say. I knew both Dad and Jim, in their different ways, were the kind of men who tortured themselves trying to find the meaning of existence. Men took themselves, and how they could or should help others, so seriously. I considered myself religious, but I just accepted life as it came, trusting in providence. My own faith was simply to love God and one's fellow man, something, I suppose, to be judged by what you did. Poor Papa. By the time he died, the tide was running against the fundamentalists. But he spoiled me for a lot of ministers. He gave you something that was worthwhile. Something you could use to live by through the week. He preached about the Bible, not about IQ's and improving one's personality. Some of the modern ministers seemed to have a very ambiguous notion of God. I never thought I'd live to see the day when a minister would preach about how to make money. Some blamed the religious decline on the war, automobiles or the popularity of Sunday golf, but it really all boiled down to the growth of science. Even Jim said that . . .

Anne did not preserve her own talk that day in the 1930–31 Mothers' Club Scrapbook, which she put together and which today is to be found in the Wells County Museum at the Fessenden Fairgrounds. Instead she pasted in several articles clipped from the Literary Digest *about foreign missionary work. There is also a clipping quoting Albert Einstein ("A contemporary has rightly said that the only deeply religious people of our largely materialistic age are the earnest men of science . . .").*

Jimmy, fifty-two years later:

". . . Whatever Mother believed, we all went to church. There was no question about it. It wasn't something she said we had to do. We just went. Well, Father didn't . . . No, I don't remember his ever being in church with us . . ."

Peggy:

". . . I'm surprised the rest of us weren't more religious, because Mother was. She definitely believed in heaven and read the Bible every night until she got so old her eyesight failed. She never questioned God's existence. She carried a little New Testament everywhere, a King James Version; she didn't like the Revised Standard one. Mother prayed, too. She was very confident in her religion. Oddly enough, when she got really old, she lost that quality. Toward the end it was more, it seemed to me, as if she were saying things out of habit, almost by rote . . ."

Anne:

Jim came right from a call, his face flushed, a tube of his stethoscope dangling from a bulging pocket in his white coat, the very picture of a country doctor. Norma, who arrived with him, was wearing no makeup, and in her blue georgette with a lacy white collar and cuffs, she looked pale and demure. Jim tried out the piano stool, got up and screwed it up to the right height for himself, then sat down and played an introduction. Norma's pure, clear voice filled the small living room.

> "Out of my lodge at eventide 'mong the sobbing pine,
> Footsteps echo by my side a spirit face, a sign . . ."

The club members, judging by their applause, seemed appreciative—and chastened. It was Betty who surprised me. That evening, when I happened to say Norma looked nice, she turned on me. "Oh, Mother," she said, "how can you be so blind? Can't you see that little floozy puts peroxide in her hair to take away her mousy look? She even had mascara on . . ."

Extract from Jim's talk to the Mothers' Club on "The Prevention of Diphtheria":

". . . The child is listless, down in the dumps and feverish. He may or may not complain of a sore throat. The pulse rate will get steadily more rapid. Toxemia—poisoning caused by bacteria—has led to the death of about one fourth of diphtheria patients on the sixth day. Sometimes a child may seem to be better on the fourth or fifth day, but if he has trouble breathing through his nose, hope is unfounded. It's always a dilemma for the doctor. Once he sees a child is going to die, does he tell the parents right away or let them hope as long as they can?

"There's so much to learn. You heard my wife quote Einstein to show science is making its peace with religion. Maybe so. But preachers don't come up with cures for diphtheria. Missionaries go out and live in grass huts and die young. But what do those natives need? Religion or cures for disease? My father used to tell me a common prayer in the 1880s was 'Save us, O Lord, from diphtheria!' Father said it could get so bad you'd see long lines of teams on the road carrying coffins for burial. He said there was a real reign of terror during a diphtheria epidemic. And so people turned to religion. It's only natural. When people get scared stiff by something they don't understand, they're going to be running to the preacher. Father said, during a bad epidemic everybody was praying to be spared. Nobody prayed that the doctor would come up with a scientific cure. Nobody even thought of it. They didn't know there was such a thing.

"Now, my father-in-law down in Iowa was a doctor in the 1880s. And he became a preacher. A real old-fashioned Bible-thumping Methodist— Hadwen Williams. Now, maybe he didn't know much about psychology and Freud, like we've got today. But he was honest and unpretentious, and I know from Anne he was a powerful persuader. Without a doubt, if those old-timers had the sympathy and human warmth to go with their evangelistic fervor, they changed the course of a good many lives. The old reprobates stopped their drinking—at least for a week or two. Oh, you ladies may chuckle at that—I see smiles out there—and maybe you'll say they only changed on the surface. That was probably true. But, you know, it helps when people hide their bad side. Especially in a little town like this. We've all got to live together and get along, so maybe what happens on the surface matters more than we think it does. Of course, you can get a lot of hypocrisy, too. That old-time religion had its share.

"Reverend Williams died five years ago, and that old-fashioned kind of preacher like him is pretty much fading out. And so have the worst ravages of infectious diseases. Curious, isn't it? My wife talked about religion today and I'm talking about diphtheria. Two subjects that don't seem to have much in common. Or do they? I've often wondered why Reverend Williams would give up being a doctor to become a preacher. And you know what I think? My guess is that he somehow sensed that we needed tent meetings because we didn't have diphtheria antitoxin. In the 1880s there was so much fear. Every diphtheria epidemic kicked off a religious revival. I think Reverand Williams saw no better way to put to use the store of human affection that made him want to deal with people and help them. He saw where he was needed most. Oddly enough, nobody has yet accused us doctors of making the world irreligious, yet if you think about it, maybe we ought to plead guilty. So I guess you can say, ladies, that you do give us a break now and then . . ."

The Mothers' Club closed the meeting, as it always did, by singing several verses of "Blest Be the Tie That Binds":

> "We share our mutual woes; our mutual burdens bear;
> And often for each other flows the sympathizing
> tear . . ."

Country road, 1920s. (Archives, North Dakota State University)

After a blizzard. (Fred Hultstrand Collection)

A duck-hunting party in Fessenden. Of this group, Steve Litke faces the camera left, Jim is almost hidden behind him, Jess Oser sits across table with her hand to her mouth and Anne is on far right (wearing hat).

Fessenden's first Alfalfa Day, 1928. Mac Solberg, the master of ceremonies, is in top hat. (Wells County Historical Society)

County Fair in Fessenden. (Wells County Historical Society)

Chariot Race at County Fair. (Wells County Historical Society)

Fessenden Golf Club.

Anne driving to Iowa with Jimmy and Billy.

"I like your size, I like your eyes, that's no surprise, who wouldn't?"

Critchfield family in Fessenden, 1930. Back: Jim and his mother; front: Jimmy, Auntie Kay holding Peggy, Anne with Billy, and Betty.

Peggy, Pat and Betty outside the house on Twelfth Street in Fargo in 1938, at the time of Jim's death.

Hadwen.

Jessie.

Jim.

Anne.

Anne's last picture, 1982, with Peggy.

Jim

"Let the drums roll out *(Boom boom boom!)*
Let the trumpet call *(Ta-ta-ra-ta-ta-ta-ta!)*
Let the people shout *(Hoo-ray!)*
Strike up the band! . . ."

From the Wells County Free Press, *March 5, 1931, article written by Jim himself:*

"MIGHTY MAMMOTH MINSTREL SHOW WILL OPEN NEXT MONDAY

"Tuneful melodies, rapid-fire fun and clever specialties will mark the American Legion's Minstrel Show which will hold the boards at the Auditorium on Monday and Tuesday of next week, and you'd better be there. A mammoth chorus of forty-five voices under the baton of Dr. R. J. Critchfield has developed into a fine group rendering snappy tunes and popular ballads with feeling and expression as well as majestic power . . . If you miss this show you might just as well go out in the alley and die, for everybody else is going, and you just simply won't be counted among the living if you don't come.

"Fun? You said it, sister, and when the show is over the Legion boys are going to furnish hacks to take care of the customers who are overcome with laughter. Two doctors and a nurse will be in attendance to take care of the crowd that will storm the theater in the last-minute rush for tickets.

"Tingling tunes and dreamy melodies are going to be featured by these happy harmonizers. The 'dark yaller' boys who pull the jokes and sing the solos are past masters of the art and can make a wooden Indian laugh. And that chorus, handsome, beautiful males, forty-five of them, and sweet vocal singers they are, every one. The pick of the high school Carusos will lend their talents to the affair. Those vaudeville specialties which will follow the big opening are worthy of the honor place on a big-time circuit, and Al Jolson himself would turn green if he could hear these blackface babies warble and see them strut their stuff.

"The third part is entitled, 'Rastus Goes to His Own Funeral,' and the scene is set in No-Man's-Land Somewhere in France. The Darktown Jubilee that winds up the show is a tuneful and absolutely authentic sketch of life on the old plantation 'befo' de war,' introducing Uncle Rastus, Tambo, Bones, Mellonrine, Snowball, Rev. Giblets, Slofoot, Kroflite, and the Interlocutor, with all their friends at the Jubilee. A musical melange of Old Time Favorites and the Flaming Jazz of today. It's going to be hot and full of pep and ginger. Better be there. Our happy 'culled' boys will impart a true Dixie flavor to the show. We warn you to watch out for their jokes. The Darktown Jazzbo Band has been engaged at tremendous expense . . ."

Letter from Anne, dated four days later and mailed from Minneapolis to her sisters, Mary and Helen, in Iowa; unabridged:

"128 East 18th St.
Minneapolis, Minn.

"Dear Girls:—

"I'm wondering every day how Helen is, with the baby coming? Hope she's feeling O.K. I'm now here in Minneapolis myself—Now prepare for a shock for I'm expecting the stork myself. Haven't told you before because I was afraid you'd worry. You had troubles enough of your own.

"I'm feeling just fine, though. So now Helen will be wondering every day which baby will arrive first. I've been downtown today trying to get a few things I needed. Am staying with Kay and am going to Eitel Hospital, as Dr. Litz does most of his work there and it's within walking distance of Kay's. Won't write much today as I'm a bit tired. Did you get the pillow, Helen? I also sent a bunny wrap, as I had another one given me. Must run and mail this—Heaps of Love—Louie."

Betty:

". . . The affair became flagrant about the time Pat was born. Dad never wrote Mom all the time she was in Minneapolis in the hospital . . . I think he was trying to pull Mother down in some way. I became very protective of her. Much later, he wanted Mother to always sit close, where he could touch her. By then, it had all been sort of a bad dream. Many men in Fessenden had affairs.

"Daddy used to criticize Jimmy a lot. He felt guilty. He'd say, 'Oh, you think you're so pure.' I think, in Fessenden, once he'd turned forty, he began to feel that life was slipping by. Everybody was always complimenting Mother. They told him, 'You have a perfect wife,' 'Anne is the perfect woman,' 'If I had your wife, I wouldn't tear around.' Then he got mixed up with this babe. I felt it was a reaction. I felt then that any young girl can make a fool of an older man . . ."

Jim:

We had to be careful. Just about every time we were out joyriding or dancing in a roadhouse out by Harvey or Carrington, some patient of mine was bound to turn up. You'd think the whole countryside was deserted, with nothing moving but my Buick chugging along, and there they'd be. As part of her Flaming Youth pose, to show how daring she was, Norma was smoking too much. She also drank, though not openly, from a hip flask I carried in the car. Instinct told me it would end badly, but we were having some high old times. I wasn't kidding myself, I knew what I was doing.

I sometimes wondered if Norma did. People who know nothing about life tend to picture life and what it takes to make it work from what they read or see. In spite of going to college, Norma was as stuck as she ever was on confession magazines, the ones with articles like "What I Told My Daughter the Night Before Her Marriage" or "Seven Movie Kisses." She seemed to get most of her ideas about love and sex from them, and from movies and the romantic songs she sang. "Don't you ever listen to the words?" she asked me one time. "Sure, but I don't always believe them." "I do," she said. "Silly me." I think she really did.

She never missed a movie if she could help it. In Fessenden, this meant the Auditorium, where, until we got talkies in 1928, a formidable old maid named Caro Prescott played the piano at every showing, her hands pounding the keys, her eyes fixed on the screen. Caro was good and somehow that metallic piano-key sound—*jingle ping tink tink*—mixed with the flickering images on the screen in the dark theater with its old, stale smells of varnish, tobacco, sweat, mildew and perfume, cast a kind of spell over you. Even after talkies came in, when the lights went down and the picture came on you got a sense of space and life opening up for you. Movies seemed like life, but they seemed bigger than real life too. Norma got totally swept up in them. She'd be right up there, poo-poop-a-dooping to "I Wanna Be Loved By You," doing the tango with Valentino, slithering around the Golden Calf like Theda Bara, or, the best fantasy of all, the Star at last, in glittery silver and white, hailed by a chorus line of men with top hats and canes who danced just for her. "I like your size, I like your eyes, that's no surprise, who wouldn't?" they sang, like something out of a dream.

From movie handbills, Fessenden's Auditorium, winter and spring 1930–31:
    ". . . LADIES MUST PLAY and their favorite game is man-hunting . . ." "NEW ORLEANS . . . a night of revelry, of music, laughter and love, when two hearts strike fire and burst into flames!" "SCARLET PAGES presents the soul secrets of two women bared to a gossip-mad world. Blood red with scandal! Ruin to the girl who puts love before honor!" "FLAMING YOUTH . . . neckers, petters, white kisses, red kisses, pleasure-mad daughters, sensation-seeking mothers . . ." "MARRIED FLIRTS—Husbands! Do you flirt? Does your wife always know where you are? Are you faithful to your vows? Wives! What's your hubby doing? Do you know? Do you worry?" "TWO MEN AND A MAID on the fringe of civilization . . . Where men want to forget and women don't remember! Where love is wanton and hate is deadly!"

Jim:
    . . . And Norma, so slight and blond, almost pathetic in some cheap, thin dress, with her bright red lipstick and hair curled in waves, half Poor Little Match Girl and half Betty Boop—Norma believed this was the way to think and act and feel. Hardly a conversation with her took place without an element of make-believe. And a man had only to come into the room— whoever it might be, somebody important or the delivery boy—for her eyes, her face, her voice to change, even the way she held her body. I think she had this fantasy that somewhere, somehow, if the great producer could only hear how she could sing just like they did in his movie musicals and see how well she was made and the pale blondness of her skin and hair, he'd recognize her star quality and all her dreams would come true. And she'd be in heavenly Hollywood, all glitter and gold and music, Hollywood with its big green swimming pools and champagne baths in the purple dawn.
    I knew many girls must have such dreams, but I hoped when she was let down, it would happen gently. Even so, sometimes all the talk of her voice, of her hair, of her figure, got my goat, and seeing this she would, if she got mad, say any bad or four-letter word like some tramp. She could also be wildly superstitious—she was afraid to walk under a ladder, of Friday the thirteenth, of a black cat crossing her path. She never missed reading her horoscope. If she sometimes lived in a shallow fantasy world and seemed so vulnerable and innocent I'd feel sorry for her, I'd found she could have a hot temper. If she lost it, she could always insult a waitress or squash an insect without a pang. In politics, she talked like the most bigoted illiterate out in

the sticks. She liked to hear about murders, and got indignant if some accused rapist or killer got off with a light sentence. When I complained about money, she'd say it wasn't her headache, and when flinging away some hard-earned medical fee in a clip joint, she'd be humming "My Blue Heaven" with a light heart. Little by little, if I went on the wagon and we stayed away from each other long enough, I'd feel guilty about the whole thing and grow cold to her and want to break it off.

For some days I'd work furiously, and enjoy it, answering calls way out on the prairie, going anywhere in the worst weather, atoning for my sins. Then, going in and out of the cafe at the Conner Hotel, I'd see all the same old bankrupt farmers hanging around the dingy lobby, defeated faces among the grimy leather chairs, stale air and spittoons. They'd talk in querulous voices about crops and the weather and who had lost his farm this time. Stock still brought fair money, but machinery was going for a fraction of its value. Lousy yields and the lowest prices in forty years meant much of the last harvest was a dead loss. Many crops were plowed under. There were always new foreclosure and farm sale notices posted and always somebody to say, "Hard times, ain't it, Doc? I suppose you're not doing very well either." Sometimes all the hoping against hope got to be too much. What wasted days, what dull nights of no interest the six years in Fessenden seemed at such times! Empty golf games, pointless talk, vapid boosterism that never led to anything. Futile pursuits and dismal conversation about the same old boring topics taking up the better part of the day. Sometimes I'd feel I was suffocating in this town. I was forty-two and felt condemned to live out a shrunken life. Impossible to escape. I might as well be in a madhouse or a prison.

Some nights, I didn't sleep well and ended up taking a slug of whiskey, something I was also starting to rely on to get me through the day. I'd pay for it and suffer a hangover the whole next morning. Maybe the following nights, too, I'd sleep badly, tossing and turning, anxious, worrying, trying not to disturb Anne when she was still there. I was fed up with the town, fed up with my life, fed up with being so scared. A drink softened up the sharp edges. After a really stiff drink, the panic went away and I'd feel my inside sort of smiling at me. I was starting to notice I didn't look too good. Sometimes if I caught my reflection unawares in some mirror, I'd be struck by the dark shadows under the eyes, the faint tremor at the corner of the mouth, the tic that appeared in a facial muscle when I got too tired.

All attraction to the girl seemed to be over, and then . . . I'd slip into the Auditorium some evening for a little escape, maybe a drink or two under my belt, and I'd sit there in the dark, watching the screen, its emotion heightened by the music of the soundtrack—and maybe Norma would slip into the seat next to mine and she'd look at me without any affectation, a softer expression on her face, saying what she felt, glad to see me. And I'd feel my pulse start beating faster and a lively, youthful feeling surge through me and the warmth and comfort of her presence beside me . . . Oh, let the saxophones wail and the bottle make its rounds and the dancers turn and sway . . . She had her faults but she was a sweet girl and she was there, someone to quell the panic and push the awful sense of futility a little bit further away . . .

Jimmy:

". . . As you came down the front stairs from Father's office, to the left was the shop of an old harness maker. He was like Doolittle in *Pygmalion*—Eliza Doolittle's father. Now, this man, he was a very good harness maker and he had a big shop with all kinds of leather and he sat there and worked and sang parodies. I used to just love to go in and listen. Remember 'Every Day Is Ladies Day with Me'? He had a parody of that:

"If you know a lady and she wants a baby,
    Just send her round to me . . .'"

"I'd hear Father and Norma, or Betty, singing the straight version of all these songs. Then I'd go down and offer to help work on the leather and he'd sing all those dirty parodies. It added a little spice to the life of us boys . . ."

Betty:

". . . About this time, we got hold of one of Daddy's books. He'd inherited it from his office's previous tenant. It was *Disorders of the Sexual Function.* It was not very medical. A bit gamy. One day it was gone. Somebody had stolen it. It had been published in 1908 and I'll never forget a sentence about contraceptives: 'Tablets aren't very good but very convenient because they can be carried in a vanity case.'

"One day, Jimmy and a friend of his got their hands on the book and learned the terminology for a very frigid woman and a very hot woman. They memorized the medical terms for this. When I came home with Helen Hope or somebody, they called me one and her the other. The book was supposed to be hidden. But then we knew they'd read it. Father was very angry with the boys.

"That February, he was gone almost every night, holding rehearsals over at the Auditorium for the minstrel show. Daddy was good at things like that. He put on three while we lived in Fessenden. This time, rehearsals were going on for six weeks, because it was going to be the biggest production he'd ever directed, with a lot of painted backdrops and fancy costumes. If you counted the big male chorus, the band, all the specialty musical acts and the 'minstrels' who blackened their faces with burnt cork and sang and cracked jokes in Negro dialect, why, close to a hundred people were going to perform. Poor Mom was having to miss all the fun, because she was down in Minneapolis having Pat . . ."

Jim:

While I was still in my undershirt, I lathered my face with soap and shaved real close. Then I wrapped a towel around my shoulders and started to put on the blackface greasepaint, sort of singing to myself, ". . . Make my bed and light the light, I'll arrive late tonight . . ." When I got done, I hollered to Betty to come in and help me with the white shirt, detachable collar and big floppy bow tie so I wouldn't get makeup all over them. When she finished and I said, "Well, how do I look?" she stepped back a ways and said in a deep bass voice, "GENTLEMEN, BE SEATED . . . Ladies and gentlemen, it is with great pleasure that I introduce you tonight to that incomparable comedian, Mr. Kroflite—raring to go! . . . Why, Kroflite, why are you still standing? I said, 'Gentlemen, be seated.' "

"Dat's de trouble, Mr. Interlocutor," I said in my minstrel-show voice, getting into the act. "You said 'gentlemen' and ah don't know what to do . . . Anyhow, ah'se standin' because ah got a pain in the seatus."

"A what?" Betty started to giggle.

"A pain in the seatus."

"Oh, you mean appendicitis?"

"No, sah, ah got kicked by a mule this moahnin' and ah know whereof ah speaks . . . Say dere, Uncle Rastus, who was dat lady ah saw you walkin' down the road wid last night?" I answered myself in a scratchy falsetto. "Why, Kroflite, you'se all wrong. Dat was no lady, dat was mah wife. Hee haw." I was already lit.

Betty, forty-eight years later:

". . . Gosh, we were racist in those days, when you look back on it. I was going through a trunk down in the basement the other day and I came across one of Daddy's old minstrel-show scripts. It'd been published in 1928. In the Introduction, it said that Al Jolson and Eddie Cantor were the two top 'blackface comedians.' It told about how they'd 'studied the peculiarities of speech and the mental processes of the darky and find in him a mine of humorous ore.' And I'd always thought Stephen Foster's songs were folk music, you know, 'Old Black Joe.' The old script says they were mostly originally written for minstrel shows too. I suppose in a little town like Fessenden, where hardly anybody had ever seen an actual black, there was a kind of innocence, at least ignorance, about it. 'Amos 'n' Andy' was the most popular radio show then. Everybody listened to see if Andy was going to marry Madame Queen, and we all knew 'Brother Crawford,' 'Lightin'' and 'The Kingfish.' And who can forget 'Buzz me, Miss Blue,' 'Check and double-check,' 'I'se regusted!' and 'Ow wah! Ow wah!' No wonder the civil-rights groups raised Cain. And the minstrel shows were a lot worse . . .''

Jim:

By the time we got there, the Auditorium was filling up fast. A struggle was already going on out front between people trying to get inside to claim seats and those whose seats were already staked out with coats and companions, and who wanted to get out to smoke or just mill around. Some were going in, some were coming out, everybody was pushing and wrangling; it was a real uproar. Inside, the theater's slanted floor had rows of wooden seats nailed to scantlings, and though there were a few side boxes, it was first come, first served. In all the noise and confusion, the crowd was well dressed. Just about every man wore a suit and tie and many of the women had hats; that night, it was easy to imagine that we'd turned back the clock and there had been no Crash.

There was a canvas drop curtain, the kind with a chain-weighted bottom so it could go up and down real fast, and it offered a painted view of Swiss scenery surrounded by advertisements. We were all there: G. L. Hope's Ford Garage ("Bargains in Used Cars"), Swan's Dry Goods, Quarves' Viking Store, Minnekota Elevator Company, Otto Neuenschwander—Funeral Director and Embalmer, R. J. Critchfield—Physician & Surgeon, Anthonson Blacksmithing and Horseshoeing, L. V. Kunkel for Draying and Hauling, the Ben F. Oser Model Clothing Store, and the Conner Hotel—European Plan, Rates $1.25 to $1.75.

Backstage, men in blackface crowded into the tiny dressing rooms, where their wives were helping them put on their makeup and costumes. Mirrors blindingly reflected naked light bulbs and faces glistening with heavy black greasepaint, all the bright red lips, woolly wigs, stovepipe hats, big bow ties, black coats, flowered or checkered pants. There was a pungent smell from the greasepaint and that electrically charged excitement of a working theater. Some of the men who were already made up and dressed stood around drinking moonshine whiskey from paper cups. I joined them for a shot, butterflies were churning in my stomach and my mouth was as dry as sandpaper. "Five minutes, everybody!" somebody called.

The end men and minstrels were soon taking their seats in a big semicircle of chairs facing the curtain. All were in blackface and gaudy costumes except the Interlocutor, who wore no makeup and was in a tuxedo. Behind them, the fifty men in the chorus—the biggest we'd ever had—were taking their places in the bleachers. They wore black suits, and about half of them were high school boys. Back in Hunter, we'd had more traditional shows. Then, after the curtain rose, the company paraded to their chairs. The Interlocutor cracked jokes with the end men the same as we were doing, but for the finale everybody passed in review in a "walk-around." We'd always had vaudeville and musical acts in between the minstrel skits; both Norma and Betty were coming on in different numbers tonight. The old-time show ended with a burlesque on a play or an opera. Ours was going to be a little more like a Broadway revue, mixing plenty of hit songs and jazz with the traditional minstrel-show tunes.

"Everybody in their places onstage!"

There was a lot of frantic movement. I waited until they were all set, then ducked under the small entry into the orchestra pit. After nodding hello to the band members, sensing the atmosphere of excitement, I stepped up on the podium. A hush fell over the theater as I raised my baton and led into the first brassy notes of the overture, "Strike Up the Band!" This was followed by an old-fashioned medley—"Swanee River," "Dixie," "My Old Kentucky Home." After "Mammy," the curtain rose and the chorus went into its jazz numbers: "Sweet Georgia Brown," "Avalon," "Somebody Loves Me," "Crazy Rhythm," "Who's Wonderful—Who's Marvelous—Miss Anabelle Lee," "Singin' in the Rain" and "Did You Ever See a Dream Walking?" In the burst of applause which followed, I bowed into the blinding spotlights to the audience—just a blur of faces—and back to the chorus. There was an exchange of jokes for some minutes now, so I stepped to one side of the pit to get a good look at the stage. In the bright red and white spotlights, the sweating, shiny black faces with their flashing white eyes and teeth looked fantastic. The shifting lights, as the spots played first on one speaker, then another, made the whole lineup of minstrels look as if it were bursting with hilarity. They shouted their lines so loudly and in such an exaggerated fashion, the audience responded with waves of excited laughter, even when the words weren't intelligible or made good sense if they were. Everybody seemed to have a glow on.

"Well, Mr. Bones, how are you feeling this evening?"

"Ah'm feelin' kinda spiritualistic, Mr. Interlocutor."

"How is that, Mr. Bones?"

"Oh, sorta *medium*. Yassuh, Mr. Interlocutor, ah wants a divorce. Dat woman of mine she jest talk, talk, talk, night and day. Ah can't get no rest and all de talk is driving me crazy."

"What does she talk about?"

"She don't say."

"Mr. Bones, where's your chivalry?"

"I done traded it in for a Buick."

The Interlocutor went down the line.

"Mr. Rastus, do you know what is a dry dock?"

"Yassuh, that am a physician who don't give out prescriptions for alcohol." That got a big laugh.

"Tambo, if you get a letter from the Ku Klux Klan, what are you going to do with it?"

"Read it on de train, man, read it on de train." The faces in the audience all seemed to have a lively expression, even when they were not listening to the jokes or taking them in. Everybody seemed to be caught up in the same restlessness and excitement. It was going well. At rehearsals, I'd kept drumming in how speed and volume mattered; the jokes were so corny and bad, speed and style were everything. The louder and snappier, the better.

"That's crazy, Mr. Bones! How did Noah manage to have beer aboard the Ark?"

"He had to bring two of every kind of animal aboard dat old Ark, Mr. Interlocutor. Even two blind pigs!" It was going all right. The boys were throwing themselves into it and the audience was warming up. There were the usual wife jokes; the Interlocutor asked Tambo if his wife picked out his clothes.

"No, suh! She jes picks my pockets!"

And the mother-in-law jokes: "She don't eat much. She's too busy talkin'." I went back to the podium to introduce Tambo singing "Mississippi Mud" as he played a banjo, then Bones with "Can You Imagine That?" Then it was time for Mellonrine, "that black baby with the itching feet," who did a clog dance to "Are You from Dixie?" My own number was right after that. I went backstage and had a quick one. I was feeling no pain. Onstage, the Interlocutor was making the introduction. Betty, who was going to play the piano accompaniment for me, struck the first few bars. I went out into the spotlight, moistened my lips and with cardboard hat in hand, began to sing, starting out real slow in a hoarse, mock-whisper:

"Pack up all my care and woe
Here I go, singing low
Bye bye blackbird
Where somebody waits for me
Sugar's sweet, so is she
Bye bye blackbird . . ."

I couldn't see out into the audience. In the blinding lights, all the faces were lost in a blur. But I could sense a kind of continuous, childishly irresponsible gaity about the crowd. It had really warmed up. I wasn't surprised to hear some people clapping to the beat.

"Who dat?" I called out with mock indignation. More people joined in clapping. A few started to sing along. I rolled my eyes like Al Jolson and scratched my woolly wig. More laughter. I gave them a great big watermelon-sized grin and sang with all the animation I could swing.

"No one here can love and understand me
Oh, what hard luck stories they all hand me . . ."

That set off a hoot of raucous laughter from the boys on the stage behind me. They were getting tight too.

"Make my bed and light the light
I'll arrive late tonight
Blackbird bye bye . . ."

By the last line, everybody in the theater was singing along at the top of their voices. I signaled to Betty to play it through again, this time really picking up the tempo. The audience kept singing, uproariously now, belting out the words for all it was worth. We were having fun.

"Sho' nuf! Yas suh, boss!" I shouted above the uproar. More laughs and applause and whistles. I caught the infection of their excitement. It was glorious. It rocked the theater.

"Make my bed and light the light
I'll arrive late tonight
Blackbird bye bye . . ."

Further comment from the late Fred Mietz, fifty-one years later:
". . . The minstrel show! Oh, gosh! You know, that's where Jim got so popular. He was musical. He always directed the show. His name was Kroflite, his minstrel name, you know. I was Mellonrine. I would say there were twenty of us in blackface. And an Interlocutor. There was a script. He'd ask

questions. They were all jokes, you know. Jim was good with music. He could sing. The numbers were hit tunes, catchy tunes. At the last one he sang 'Bye Bye Blackbird.' Something with some snap in it, you know, jazz, and how the audience loved it. We also did some old southern songs."

Singing, in a quavering voice; he is eighty-seven:

> "Are you from Dixie?
> Are you from Dixie?

"I sang that and did a clog dance. The shoes had a wooden heel and a wooden sole. I still have those shoes upstairs in a trunk in the attic. With a black coat and top hat and some fancy striped pants . . . *Billboard!* Did you ever hear of that magazine? *Billboard?* That's where Jim ordered some of the stuff, the script and the makeup and the wigs. They were very poor wigs. We ordered cheap stuff. And greasepaint and cream to put on first. It didn't cost much.

"You had to put the makeup on yourself, though some people showed us how to do it. First of all, you just took some cold cream in your hand and rubbed that on and you took tissue paper or toilet paper and wiped most of it off. Then you'd take a real red-orange and just smear it all around your mouth like that, you know. Then you'd take the black and draw an outline around it carefully and then you'd think you had great big lips. And around the eyes, you had to get real close. That blackface was a little bit on the dry order, too.

"Then you put on your wig, a black woolly wig. The shirts were mostly white. White shirts. We put all that on before we put on those collars. They stuck out, you know. That's the last thing you'd put on. They had big neckties or bows that stuck way out. With those stiff collars. We always had help. The women, a lot of them, helped us because if you did it alone it'd be easier to mess it up . . ."

Singing:

> "Meet me tonight in dreamland,
> Under the silvery moon.
> Meet me tonight in sweet . . .

"I forget. I can't remember all the words. It was over fifty years ago. There were so many songs. Jim had us memorize them, you know. I can still sing 'Dixie,' I think, though I may get it all mixed up. The way the Auditorium was situated at that time, we had a big stage, facing east, they even had some box seats, and the floor was slanted so that even in the back you could see. And they had nice dressing rooms and everything. I don't know how many people it held, but it was crowded.

"Lape Brandt—his name was Leo but we called him Lape—he was Slofoot. He came in with great big shoes and he came walking and he had a fishpole. His mouth was all full and his cheeks were bulging out. And the Interlocutor asked him where he was going. 'Goin' fishin',' he says, but his mouth is all full of something and he can hardly talk. He says he's going ice fishing. It's supposed to be winter, see. And the Interlocutor asked him what he's got in his mouth and Lape says, 'Uh, wuh-h-hms. WUH-H-HMS!' And he opens his mouth wide and out comes some noodles or something. So crazy, you know. To make people believe his mouth was full of worms to keep them warm because he was going ice fishing. Oh, God, he was a scream. I don't know if Lape is alive any more or not.

"Jim was humorous, too, and he made a lot of jokes. But it wasn't anything vulgar. And there'd be an umbrella chorus and a pickaninny chorus. Once, somebody was singing and his dog came running up on the stage and sat beside him and howled. I guess he'd been trained to do it. John Thornton and my nephew, Walter Burgstahler, brought the house down dressing like a man and woman and singing 'You'll Come Back.' . . ."

Singing:

> "You'll come back
> I hear you say, Alexandra . . .

"Oh, I can't remember. It was about Alexandra, his wife, running away and coming back. I can't remember the words . . . That clog dance I did was like a tap dance. I got a big hand, but I don't think I deserved it . . . Then Oscar Wesley played a solo on bottles. He had about thirty or forty bottles. All different sizes. And he played them just like a marimba. And when Jim got to the piano! He'd hammer those notes right out and that piano would rock, you know . . ."

Singing:

> "You gotta be a football hero
> To get along with the beautiful girls
> You've got to be a touchdown getter, you bet
> If you wanna get—a girlie to pet. . . .

"No, it was *'a baby to pet'* . . . It's so long ago, you know. I don't know if I have the words just right, but that was the melody . . . Yeah, that was one of the catchy tunes we sang at the minstrel show. Or it could have been a few years later. There was one song we did last, one or two verses. As we got done with that, the curtain dropped. It went something like how there was an end to everything . . ."

Singing:

> "And now it's time to say good-bye . . ."

Betty:

". . . In the intermission, the Girl Scouts did a Great War number. 'In Flanders Fields the Poppies Blow.' All the girls had uniforms. I was the biggest girl but I had the smallest uniform, the only one that fit. We did 'Hello, Central, Give Me No-Man's Land' and a real brassy rendition of: 'How'ya gonna keep 'em away from Broadway, Jazzin' aroun' and paintin' the town? . . .' We practically yelled it at the top of our voices. You could tell Daddy was loaded. He had pants with roses on the seat. A big rose on each side. I darn near died watching him stand up there and direct. Peggy, who was two at the time, was in the front row sitting on Lavonne McKay's lap. Lavonne had a pink dress on and Peggy wet on her. A dark pink spot down the front of Lavonne's dress. A lot of the men were drunk . . ."

Jim:

"Say, Tambo, ah hear they done discovered a machine now that can tell when a man is lying."

"Ah know. Ah married one."

"Rastus, I want you men to do guard duty."

"Gahd duty, gahd duty, what am gahd duty, boss? We ain't been doin' nothin' but K. P. . . ."

After the No-Man's-Land skit, a little boy danced the Charleston and two brunettes from Sykeston sang "Doo Wacka Doo" and "Hallelujah!"

> ". . . Satan lies awaitin' and creatin' skies of gray,
>   But 'Hallelujah! Hallelujah!'
>   Helps to shoo the clouds away . . ."

Then it was time for Norma to do her solo number. I went out front to watch from one side, shouldering my way up so I had a good view. It was worth it. The piano struck up "I'll See You in My Dreams" and out Norma came from the wings, dressed up fit to kill in a very tight white glittery dress. A big boa of white ostrich feathers, which she'd draped negligently over her shoulders, showed off her bare and slender arms. The dress was so tight it forced her to take many small steps to get to the center of the stage, wriggling her shoulders and bottom seductively. She had carefully pow-

dered her arms, neck, face and shoulders, rouged her cheeks and worn blue
eye shading and mascara. Her lips were painted with bright red lipstick into
a Cupid's bow. She was wearing a rhinestone headband, and that glittered
too, over her soft blond curls. Her eyes, under the beaded black lashes,
flashed blue in the spotlight. I gasped with pride at the sight of her. She
looked like a million dollars. All Norma needed was a chorus line of men in
top hats and tails behind her, tap dancing and holding canes. She'd filled her
whole life with fantasy and for once, by God, she was really living one.
There was a piano introduction and then, chin up and blue eyes blazing, she
started to sing:

> "You . . . are . . . my . . . lucky . . . star . . .
> I . . . saw . . . you . . . from . . . afar . . ."

It brought down the house. I never heard such frenzied applause. From
then on, she held that crowd right in the palm of her hand. They kept it up,
encore after encore. "The very thought of you . . . We're happy in my blue
heaven . . . Wake with the singing birds, shout out the lucky words, here
comes the sun!" It was a glorious climax to the show. So it wasn't real life.
So dreamers got punished for wanting too much. They sure had some beautiful dreams . . .

> "I'll be down to get you in a Taxi honey
>   You better be ready about half past eight,
>   Now dearie, don't be late,
>   I want to be there when the band starts playing . . ."

We were singing and laughing and having a grand time as I drove along
the country road. Some of the radiance of her performance, chilled and
sparkling in the March night air, hung about Norma. After the Darktown
Jubilee, our big closing act, with the entire company crowded against the
painted backdrop of an old plantation with magnolia trees, we felt too keyed
up just to go home and go to bed. So we were going for a ride, singing all the
songs of the Darktown Jazzbo Band's final medley all over again, just the
two of us—"I Got Rhythm," "Love for Sale," "Ten Cents a Dance," "I
Found a Million Dollar Baby in a Five and Ten Cent Store" and "Darktown
Strutters' Ball." We were having fun . . .

> "She was selling china and when she made those eyes,
>   I kept buying china until the crowd got wise . . ."

When we passed Steve Litke's place and I saw a light on in the barn, I told Norma he'd probably offer us a nightcap. I swung over and pulled in. I parked and asked her to wait in the car for a minute. When I got to the barn door, Steve was just coming out carrying a lighted lantern. When he spoke his voice was trembling.

"I won't have that woman in my house. She can't come in. You son of a bitch. You've got a family. Anne's about to have a baby."

Jim

Testimony at inquest in Harvey in connection with the death of Gertrude Engelhart Krause, before R. J. Critchfield, County Coroner, October 5, 1931: Under cross-examination by Dr. Critchfield, Heinrich Krause, being first duly sworn, testified as follows:

Q. "Your age, Mr. Krause?"

A. "Forty-nine."

Q. "Now will you, in your own words, Mr. Krause, give us an account of what happened on the morning of October 2?"

A. "Well, about one o'clock my wife waked up and said, 'We're going to Fessenden in the morning.' And I said, 'Oh, Mama, let it go today . . .' Before five o'clock, she waked up again and said, 'We're going to Fessenden. I got to go down before I start my housework.' . . . I took a shave and she got dressed, then we started to make the bed. She said, 'Throw this old blanket in the furnace and bring me a new one.' . . . As we drove into town, I said, 'Mama, it is early yet . . .'"

Q. "What time was that?"

A. "Before six o'clock . . . She went pretty fast. I said, 'Mama, you are going fifty. You always tell me when I go forty to forty-five it is too fast for you.' And she said, 'I've got to hurry today.' Then we came to the hill and she slowed down."

Q. "How fast was she going when she hit that hill?"

A. "About thirty-five or forty. Then she must have struck the gas and brake pedals at the same time. I looked over and said, 'Mama, you got the gas!' And she slipped her foot over to the brake and she must have hit the brake hard. She was kinda rattled already. The car started to wobble, you know, when a car brakes too fast. Then she hit that rock . . . As soon as we hit the first bump, she dropped over the steering wheel. She hollered, *'Ach, Gott!'* and the car tipped over . . . When I came to, I saw flames coming up . . . I worked myself through the window . . . I reached inside and took her and lifted her up and tried to pull her through the window, but I couldn't . . ."

John Toussaint, a neighbor and farmer:
Q. "About what time on Friday morning did Mr. Krause first come to the barn?"
A. "Around six-thirty . . . He said they'd had an accident and Mrs. Krause was in the car and the car was burning . . . We got into our car . . . and we went down there right away . . . The car was ablaze . . ."
Q. "Could you see Mrs. Krause in the car?"
A. "Well, you could see a body that was black all over . . . It was pretty smoky, but you could see her head laying against the window on the cushion of the back seat. She was completely burnt and unrecognizable . . ."

Josephine Toussaint:
Q. ". . . Did you help hold Mr. Krause also, when he tried to get into the car?"
A. "Yes. He cried, 'Let's try to get her out!' "

Dr. J. J. Seibel:
Q. "What was his physical condition?"
A. ". . . burned eyelashes, scratches over the cheekbones on both sides, very deep cuts . . . He showed signs of fainting and vomiting . . ."

Asked why his wife had asked him to throw a blanket, two pillow cases and a sheet into the furnace and make up the bed with clean ones at four or five in the morning, Heinrich Krause retestified:
A. ". . . The lower sheet, it was kinda torn and dirty. She had her monthly and she told me it was no use to wash them any more, to throw them in the furnace . . ."

Krause then admitted he had telephoned an insurance agent in Fessenden, despite the early hour, and asked for a new five-thousand-dollar policy for himself and his wife. Jim took an overnight adjournment.
From the Free Press, *October 8:*
"HEINRICH KRAUSE CONFESSES WIFE'S MURDER MONDAY
"A coroner's inquest at Harvey last Monday into the death of Mrs. Gertrude Engelhart Krause has revealed a hammer-murder that has astounded local residents. Heinrich Krause, husband of the slain woman, confessed at

the inquest that he struck his wife in an argument early Friday morning, loaded her into a car and drove eight miles southwest of Harvey toward Fessenden, ran the car into a ditch and after freeing himself from the wreckage, set fire to it . . . Notified of the mother's death, her two daughters, Caroline Engelhart, 22, and Agnes Engelhart, 18, both university students, came at once . . . Discovery of bloodstains in the bedroom aroused their suspicions . . ."

From Heinrich Krause's confession:

". . . I hit my wife, Gertrude, on the head with the hammer more than once, I think it was two times; then I got up and carried the dead body to the garage and put it in the car . . ."

Jim:

He'd spent most of the night trying to remove the bloodstains from the bedroom walls and floor. At about five-thirty, he called and asked for the insurance policy. Then he put his wife's body in the car. He stopped once at the Ed French farm to burn the bloodstained pillows, sheet and blanket on a straw pile. At about six, he drove the car into a ditch, set it on fire and ran to the Toussaint farm. Popular feeling was so aroused, we had to get Krause out of the county fast. He waived a preliminary hearing at the county court in Fessenden and we rushed him that same day right to Bismarck, where he was later tried and sentenced to life. He told the judge, "It all happened through an argument. I love her yet. I lost my head when we had a fight about money. I intended to kill myself, too. It wouldn't have happened if we hadn't quarreled." This was probably true. Gertrude Engelhart had been a rich widow when Krause, a plumber by trade and still a swarthily handsome man, had married her. It was a second marriage for both of them, and her first husband had left her seventy-five thousand dollars, a lot of money in 1931. Krause knew from a prenuptial agreement that he couldn't get his hands on this money; it went to the daughters. He was deeply in debt. Still, for a crime of passion, he'd gone about it savagely. A basin that we found in the house had traces of blood and hair in it. Gertrude Krause had been a big woman. When I did the autopsy, I found all that was left of her—the charred remains—weighed just thirty pounds.

The Krause murder was just one of the grisly symptoms of breakdown as what was now becoming known as the Great Depression grew worse. The strains from bank failures, low prices, foreclosures, drought, joblessness, anxiety and despair were starting to tell. To make ends meet, I'd run for

County Coroner in 1928 and since been reelected. My very first case had been an old German-born farmer out in Heimdal who'd been about to lose the land he'd cleared and settled fifty years before; he'd strangled himself by twisting a sheet and tying it to a bedpost.

It hadn't happened overnight. Seven thousand American banks, most of them rural, had failed between 1920 and 1930; seven thousand more were going to fail before it was over. The Dust Bowl was also slow in coming. Much of the Great Plains got less than twenty inches of rain in a year. Once settlers broke the sod with their plows and successive generations overgrazed and overplowed, the dust started to blow. In Fessenden, the dry years began in 1924. In 1931, the great storms, blowing away whole farms, like the Armistice Day black blizzard in Kansas, when men would vomit dirt, were still two years ahead of us. Already it was getting bad. We'd go for months without a drop of rain. When I made calls out in the country, I'd notice how some fields were slowly getting drifted over by sand. Roads, trees, sheds, fences and abandoned tools and machinery all showed signs of the steady movement of the soil. You'd see crops that had just shriveled up, cattle that were just skin and bones, abandoned farms with dried-up wells and broken windmills, and even when the sky was clear and as blue as could be, there was always a thick haze of brown dust along the horizon.

When it got real dusty in town, so that Main Street looked like a cavern in a cloud of smoke, they'd string light bulbs across and keep them going night and day so you could see where you were going. Up at our "little house on Quality Hill"—a humorous nickname just like "Poverty Flats" across the tracks, which actually wasn't much different—the dust would seep in everywhere. Anne stuffed rugs under the doors and put wet rags around the windows to catch the dust and keep it from coming in. Even so, a film of dust soon settled on all wooden surfaces. Even food tasted gritty. If a wind came up, several inches of dust might drift across our open front porch.

When it got too bad, and I had to go outdoors, I'd tie a mask over my nose and throat. Then you couldn't drive your car. When I had to make a call way out in the country, I left the Buick in our back shed and hired a team and buggy from a farmer on the edge of town, trying to get horses I could trust to keep their bearings. They'd also need dust masks of gunny sacking to tie over their noses. Sometimes out on those dirt roads, you might get swallowed up for a spell by an impenetrable black cloud. It could get dark right at noon. "That's our good topsoil blowing," everybody would say. At the height of a real dust storm, it was like a blizzard. You couldn't see a house from a barn at ten-thirty in the morning. With that hot wind howling and everything all black, it could be terrifying.

On days when the dust didn't blow and there was a bright blue sky again, Anne would put our baby out on the front porch to sleep. Even when it got real cold. She'd done it with all the kids. When it started to snow and she still put his buggy out, little Billy, now seven, protested, "Mom, the baby will freeze!" "Don't worry," she told him. "I bundled him all up." When she first brought the baby home from Minneapolis, I called him Oscar, saying that he looked like a little Norwegian to me. Then I kidded Anne that he had a closer resemblance to an Irish bootlegger in town and I started calling him Pat. I was just teasing her, but though we baptized him Richard, within the family the nickname stuck. He was a skinny little rascal with big ears.

Once Anne was back home, I told myself I'd break off with Norma for everybody's sake. There were tears and recriminations, also threats. She said she couldn't live without me. She said she'd turn on the gas. And maybe five minutes later she'd be asking if the seams on her stockings were straight. I thought she could very easily do without me if she put her mind to it, and go off and make a life for herself. So I was relieved when she went back to college in Mayville. Some weekends she came back to town but I didn't see her as much as before. I told myself it was over, but when she asked, her voice breaking, "Oh, Jim, what about me? If you run out on me, what will I do?" and when I saw the lost look in her eyes, I could never bring myself to take that final step . . .

Nobody could remember such hard times. Almost every day, you'd hear about somebody's farm falling into the hands of a bank or being seized by the government for nonpayment of taxes, just as they'd done to our farm in Hunter in 1925. Farmers were getting less than twenty-five cents for a bushel of wheat, seven cents for a bushel of corn, a dime for a bushel of oats, two-and-a-half cents a pound for hogs and beef. Who could pay creditors at those prices?

The migrant army we'd first seen in Maddock had swollen to a flood of homeless, jobless men. Fessenden's hobo jungle had spread along the railroad tracks like fungus. There were packing crates, burlap-and-tarpaper shacks, lean-tos, wrecked cars, cardboard shelters; and those without even these slept on the hay at the stockyards. The clothing grew familiar: the filthy old sheepskin jacket, the buttonless suit coat, the pair of cast-off trousers out at the knee or in the seat, the patched tennis shoes, the mismatched canvas work gloves. Too familiar to a county coroner.

Abner Fryer, unemployed, no fixed address, being first duly sworn in at the coroner's inquest, testified as follows:

Q. "You were with Willie Carlson at the switchyard. Will you kindly state in your own words just what happened to Willie?"

A. "We'd been sleeping down in the stockyards and we went up to town and when I got to the depot, Willie left me. I stood there for a little while . . . After a while Hadley came and told me that Willie was hit and I went back and found him under the freight cars and pulled him out. Another fellow came by and asked me if Willie was dead and I said, 'I don't know.' This other fellow was a yard bull, you know, a railroad policeman, so I walked away . . ."

Q. "Did he appear to be dead then?"

A. "Yes. I called him by name and he didn't answer. . . . He was all bloody . . . I mean you could see Willie'd got crushed between two freight cars. Maybe he was trying to get across the tracks . . . I didn't see any bottles or sign of drinking . . ."

Jim:

Willie Carlson's parents, farming people from Wisconsin, came to claim his body. They'd needed money to pay the mortgage and sent Willie off to ride the rails and look for work. As farm prices caved in, there were more and more Willies . . . The automobile, too, played its role in keeping doctors busy. It had promised to be such a wonderful tool of freedom, whirling people where they wanted to go at exciting speeds. Now we were seeing more of its destructive side. As coroner, I discovered how many drivers and passengers were getting killed and maimed in county accidents. Somebody would tip over in his Ford ("fracture of skull and four left ribs, crushing internal injuries") or his car be struck by the Great Northern's Passenger Flyer ("must have been blinded by the sun's glare at crossing"). Or some young couple, just starting out in life, would park on a cold night to smooch ("it is thought fumes escaped from the heater of the car, filling the interior with deadly carbon monoxide gas"). There were the old, familiar causes of sudden death too, the farm accidents, strokes, heart attacks.

If the deaths of Gertrude Krause and Willie Carlson were tragic, what happened to Sven Gustafson was worse. It scared me so bad I began to despair of being able to hang on in Fessenden and thought of taking Anne and the five kids into Fargo, now a city of thirty thousand. Dr. Baillie of Hunter had gone there and I knew he'd help me to start a new practice. I was going to have to do something, and soon.

I'd known Sven—a tall, gray, upright Norwegian farmer of sixty-nine— for a good many years. He'd married a Maddock girl and we knew her family too. For years they'd been childless and then late in life they'd been blessed with a son—young Nels had just turned seventeen. Sven was hard-working, respected. People were to ask and ask, "What made him do it?" We'd never know, but suddenly losing one's farm no longer seemed the worst that could happen.

As I pieced it together, Sven had been brooding over the possible loss of his heavily mortgaged farm. He'd spent his whole life building it up. The day before, he paid off a neighbor for some help and told him, "That's the last three dollars I have in this world." At nine-thirty the next morning, an oil dealer from Hamberg named Liudahl knocked on the back door of the Gustafson house. He wanted to see if Sven wanted any tractor fuel. His creditors later claimed that Sven's farm was not in danger of foreclosure. Maybe this was true. But a man like Sven might think otherwise. He was terribly conscientious. Several witnesses said he himself feared he'd lose it. What we did know was that up until six o'clock that morning, life on the Gustafson farm seemed normal. All three of them—Sven, the wife and Nels —were seen by neighbors going about their chores just as on any other day. Even several hours later, I found everything at the barn and chicken house in perfect order.

So did Liudahl. He kept knocking. Nobody came. He tried the screen door. To his surprise, there was Gustafson seated in a chair across the kitchen table. Liudahl greeted him, then saw the gun in Sven's hand and the dried blood running down the side of his neck and heard the buzzing of the bluebottle flies. He realized he was staring into the eyes of a dead man. Liudahl ran for help, returning some minutes later with George Wynne and his wife from the next farm. They found Sven's brother, Peter, looking around the barn and wondering where everybody was. He had come to help Sven shock some wheat and was just about to go into the house.

All four went inside together. They confirmed Sven was dead. They found the boy in his bedroom. Evidently, after chores he'd gone back to bed. He'd been shot in the back of the head while he slept. His eyes were closed. He must have died instantly. There was no sign of Mrs. Gustafson. They found her in the doorway of a small storage room off the kitchen. I surmised she had been separating the cream when she heard one or more shots. She lay face down in the doorway. From her wounds, Sven appeared to have first shot her in the hand, which perhaps she raised to ward off the blow or to try and stop him. This bullet pierced her shoulder, too. She must have fallen then. Sven fired the fatal bullet into her heart after she'd already hit the floor.

For days after that, my hands would start shaking for no reason. I'd find myself emptying whiskey glasses at a single gulp, absently wiping my chin with my hand. I suppose, like so many were doing now, I despaired and drank, and drank and despaired. I'd think: if patients would come . . . pay their bills. Where were they? Sometimes it seemed as if all I was getting were the child cut up in the mower, the body left hanging until the birds got it, the brutally beaten drunkard's wife, the face kicked in by a horse, the scalded child, the injured thresher, the legless corpse on the railroad tracks, the family whose auto was struck by the train engine, the half-starved old settler dying alone on his farm. I knew some of the patients who had stuck with me were saying, "Even if you can smell whiskey on his breath, he never makes a wrong diagnosis." I clung to the hope there was some truth in it, that my understanding of the human body and its ills had not totally failed me.

Mornings, I'd have a hangover, mumbling at breakfast, "I guess I had a drop too much last night." No word of reproach from Anne; she'd just look sad and resigned. When I'd see patients in my office, sometimes there was an aftertaste of whiskey in my mouth, I'd have a dull headache and hope nobody would notice the bleary eyes and shaking hands. It all came so automatically. "Breathe in . . . Hold it . . . Does this hurt? And this? Do you feel it more on this side than the other?" Writing out the prescriptions, giving the reassurances. "Well, you certainly don't have appendicitis. Just a slight inflammation of the intestine, that's all. Here, just take this down to Fisher's Drugstore . . ."

Always the anxious mothers. "It's Bud here, doctor. For two days now, he's had these spots on his back and chest . . . I figured it might be measles." "No, it's nothing so serious. Just a little hives. All you need to do is apply talcum powder. Keep it dry." Or the elevator operator who'd gotten a hernia heaving sacks of grain, the old man with rheumatism, the girl with anemia, the little boy with mumps. Sometimes I'd find myself feeling cold by the end of the morning, yet perspiring. And always that faint, lingering, bilious aftertaste from too much alcohol. I'd puff on a cigar to get rid of it.

Afternoons, if it wasn't so dusty I had to take horses, I'd head out in my Buick, making calls to the farmhouses. I was familiar, after seven years in Fessenden, with the furnishings of many of the bedrooms and even the individual smell of the kitchens, where I usually went to wash my hands in a basin. A boy of four or five, flushed and bright-eyed, lying in bed under a feather tick. An anxious mother. "I've been wondering, Doctor, if it would be all right to give him something to eat? He keeps saying he's hungry." "He does, does he? Well, a little milk toast isn't going to hurt him, but not too hot." The farmer who drank too much, destroying his liver, protesting,

"I've been taking that Rocky Mountain Tea, Doc." "Lay off those patent medicines, Lars. They won't do you any good. You'll just have to cut out the booze."

From four to six I'd do another round of house calls, but these were usually right in town, so I carried my black bag and went by foot. Sooner or later somebody would offer me a glass of beer. One drink might lead to another. After that first glass, I always got carried away and soon I'd feel irresistibly compelled to stop by one of the bootleg joints, just for a quick one. Once there, I'd get to talking and it would be, "Set 'em up," and a little later, "Set 'em up again, Jake." Often in the illegal places, you'd get some cheap, unlabeled rotgut, the kind that burned your throat and made you want to vomit. Still you drank it down . . .

So, maybe at ten or eleven, having missed supper with Anne and the kids, I'd head for home, just swaying a little on my feet, not so you'd notice. I'd want to talk to somebody but I knew that if I'd had too much to drink, the words got disassociated from their meaning and bore no relation to those strange glimpses of truth that drunkenness induces . . . My God, I'd think, swaying on my feet all the while, I'm wasting my life in this lousy little town, which stinks, and where you can't even breathe for the dust. And the inhabitants . . . They even stole the Christmas tree. What happened was we'd just put it up on Main Street and the next morning it was gone. We found it out in a drainage ditch by the sewer outlet, filthy, the lights and tinsel balls and everything all smashed and broken. It turned out to be some farm boys. They'd gotten drunk and thought they'd have some fun . . . I was forty-two and had spent my whole life in such places . . .

To look back was to see so many missed opportunities it made my blood run cold. Why did I all my life listen with sympathy, telling myself that every man must be satisfied with what he is? Why did I not rage, roar, clench my fists and shout in their faces? Why, why did people persist in doing exactly what they ought not to do? All the waste! The futility, the frustration, the goddam waste! "Set 'em up, Jack. Set 'em up again. Bottoms up. . . ." If I drank enough, it was all so clear in my mind. But when I tried to put my thoughts into words, they no longer made sense. So I would stagger home, stewed to the gills, my speech slurred, my throat raw, afraid I was going to be sick. I'd get to our front porch but the steps seemed to be heaving, the ceiling rose and fell, there were confused noises, I'd make it to the bedroom, the mattress sagged, the darkness spun around, I was dead to the world . . .

I was frightened. Everything was breaking down. And so was I. One night when I reached home, just a little unsteady and ready just to say nighty night and go to bed, I found Anne sound asleep on the couch, an open Agatha Christie in her hand. She liked thrilling stories with happy endings. A clock ticked from the mantel, the only light flowed from a lampshade by her head. She must have been waiting up for me. The heavy flannel bathrobe she wore, an old one of mine, emphasized how plump she had become. Anne was still a fine-looking woman though she'd grown heavier and stouter with the last two children. Her movements were already getting quite matronly. Where the lamplight fell directly on her, I could see how gray her hair was starting to get and the crow's-feet that were appearing in the corners of her eyes.

She looked all worn out. For so many years we had lived together and shared the same bed. Together we had brought into the world five children. And yet I found myself looking at her as if she were someone I hardly knew. Gone was the slim, pale, pretty girl from Iowa I'd married so many years ago. My wife was a mature, middle-aged, careworn mother of five with a husband who had been unfaithful and drank. She'd worked her fingers to the bone and she'd never felt at home on the prairie as I did. She hated those long terrible winter nights when nothing was to be seen but darkness and the wind howled for weeks on end. Was it too late for us to go somewhere else and start again? We'd have to go soon, all of a sudden it seemed terribly urgent to get away, to try something else, something new. In my drunkenness I couldn't think straight, but I felt if I didn't understand what was happening to me now, I never would know. I could feel something cold, cold as death, waiting in ambush, closing in. I was a doctor, I told myself, and medicine knows grief and despair, but I'd felt nothing like this before. Was it too late? Life had dealt me aces over eights, a dead man's hand. At least from death there was one benefit: you no longer went on hurting the people you cared most about. The thought scared me. Was this how Gustafson had felt?

Just then Anne opened her eyes. For a moment she stared at me with confused sleepiness and a fleeting anxiety. Was something wrong? At once her face relaxed into its most kindly and loving expression, as if nothing else mattered but that I was there. She looked at me with the wonderful warm eyes that had never changed. "Oh, Jim," she said with relief, "I'm so glad you've come home." Oh, God, oh, Christ, I thought, don't let me lose her. It came out sounding like a prayer. But I wasn't asking for God's mercy, or any other kind of mercy, and no prayer, in all this life where things are as they are, was ever going to help me now.

Further comment from Jim's sister, Kathryn, fifty-three years later:

". . . I don't think he drank because his life had gone wrong. No, I don't think that. I think he was real happy. I think *they* were happy together. He may have inherited a weakness for alcohol. I don't know how much Father drank, but Mother said he'd go out in the cold winter in his sleigh and give whiskey to the horses and take some himself . . . Jim had lots of patience. Like he'd be sitting on the end of the davenport and trying to get a few winks of sleep. Maybe he'd been out on a call all night way out in the country the night before. And one of the kids would come and crawl up on him and jabber, you know. And he'd close his eyes and not let it bother him. And let them talk. And he'd listen. He was awful good to me . . . I liked . . . I just loved him . . ."

Jimmy:

". . . I remember the Krause and Gustafson murders vividly. Betty and I could hardly wait for Dad and Mother to go away so we could go in and get the coroner's reports out. We read every one of them. And he had boxes. The evidential boxes with the gun and the mat of bloody hair and the diary and the blunt instrument. You might say we tampered with the evidence, because as coroner, Dad had to present them in court . . ."

Further comment from Elsie Engbrecht Kieper, fifty-one years later:

". . . I had confidence in Dr. Critchfield. There was no gossip about him drinking that I ever heard. Why he delivered my daughter in February 1932. If he'd had a reputation for drinking, I never would have had him. My daughter has been a Baptist missionary in Cameroons and Nigeria for over twenty years now. She's a nurse and midwife. But when I had her, I got Dr. Critchfield to come out to the farm and deliver her. Mrs. Critchfield came with him. He was all ready to go to Fargo to take up a new practice, he was all packed up and everything, and he had to go back into town that night— it was just five miles—because the Lions Club was giving him a farewell party.

"One thing I've often wondered about. That night, the night my daughter was born, Mrs. Critchfield stayed all night out at my place. She didn't need to. She could have gone back to town with him and joined the party. I was still in labor. I didn't even have the baby yet. I was a trained nurse. Why did she stay? He came back and delivered my daughter the next morning. I never did ask Mrs. Critchfield why she had to miss out on their farewell party . . . Oh, yes, when my husband paid him, Dr. Critchfield joked, 'Boy, maybe I should stay in Fessenden. I actually got some money.' "

Further comment from Jess Oser:

". . . After the Lions Club party that night, a gang of us went up to that little house on Quality Hill. Anne was out at a delivery and Jim's bags were all packed and sitting around. We all went over and tried to talk him into staying. He had a good practice and all his friends in Fessenden. Why go to Fargo? I think we almost talked him into it, but he said, 'I've gone this far, I'll go ahead with it.' I think he must have felt so guilty . . ."

Betty:

". . . You know, Daddy was a perfectly charming man. There was a big send-off the day he left Fessenden. He went to Fargo alone in February, and Mom and us kids were to stay on until I graduated from high school in the spring. That afternoon, the platform outside Fessenden's yellow depot was cold and windy. There were snow flurries and everybody stood around holding up their collars with mittened hands, blowing out clouds of steam, and stamping to keep their feet warm. Daddy went around, his face rosy with frost, kissing all the women good-bye. Some man said to Mother, 'Isn't it nice to be the doctor?' And she said, 'Yes, but isn't it hell to be the doctor's wife?' And he said, 'Yes, I was thinking of that.'

"The Eastbound was on time, a little after four, whistling as it came in, bells clanging at the crossings, the train's yellow headlight beaming through the whirling snow. It screeched to a stop and Jim Parsons was there with his wheelbarrow to trundle the mailbags they threw off the red baggage car back to his dad at the post office. I was the last to kiss Daddy good-bye. Once he'd climbed up on the train and found his seat, he reappeared in one of the dusty, double-pane windows, grinning and waving. 'All aboard!' the conductor shouted. Almost at once, the train lurched, bumped, and the locomotive hissed, and it slowly gathered speed. The crowd dispersed, some into the depot, where there was a glowing stove. I stayed, watching the train vanish into the snow. The snow muffled sound, and soon there was nothing but that hush common to little railroad stations that stand solitary way out on the open prairie.

"All of a sudden I felt that, with Daddy gone, all that phase of my life which I'd known up to now was gone too, just like the train had been lost to the prairie and the snow. I turned to go and look for Mom, but I was blinded by tears, for I was crying, suddenly sure that a new, unknown life was this moment beginning for Daddy, and for all of us. What would this life be? . . . It also snowed the day before my graduation in May, a freak late-spring snow. It was deep, heavy and wet, and we had huge lilac bushes, all in blossom. We had to shake off the snow to cut the lilacs before the ceremony . . ."

III

AN OPEN PLACE

Jimmy

When I think of North Dakota now, I think of a hot, dry morning in July. Shortly before noon. Hazy with heat, a perfectly blue sky. The thermometer that day hit a hundred and twelve in the shade. We were shocking wheat on a forty-acre piece of land between the railroad embankment and the road that ran in front of the Nielsen farm. Jens and Chris had done the cutting with binders and left, and the girls, after shocking all morning, had gone back to the house too. I was right at the end of a row of shocks and was set on staying to finish it before lunch.

I was hurrying and I got dizzy. All of a sudden I fell backwards to the earth. The sky seemed to jump on top of me. It went round and round. I passed out. When I came to, I opened my eyes but I didn't move. I'd collapsed sort of half in the wheat stubble and half in the prairie grass by the railroad ties. It was that bluish-green buffalo grass that grows in little tufts. Not high grass. Crickets were chirping, a shrill, loud ringing in my ears. There were a lot of grasshoppers jumping about and one or two were sitting on my face. And I was lying there and I thought: how perfectly comfortable this is, nice and clean with the smell of the earth and the grass and, I guess, a little creosote from the railroad ties for the Great Northern train that went by there every day. After a while I recovered enough from the heatstroke or whatever it was to go find the water jug. I sipped that cold water until I was all right. But my whole feeling lying there in the stubble and the buffalo grass with grasshoppers crawling all over was, you know, this is my ambience—I was really at home there. I felt a kind of childish euphoria, everything was good, I felt so peaceful and at one with the earth.

These further conversations with Jimmy, oldest son of Anne and Jim, took place from twenty-eight to fifty-five years later and were recorded stenographically or on tape.

We all followed Dad to Fargo the summer of 1932. It was different from anywhere we'd ever lived—a city—and from the beginning it seemed all challenge and uphill. I didn't like it; my own mood was one of rebellion mixed with hundreds of wonderful memories of Maddock and Fessenden. My first recollection was entering the city's big high school. The natural thing was to go out for football. I was like anybody fighting a system, terribly shy, embarrassed, determined. I was always playing football or basketball. I played every night. The spring of that first year I got yellow jaundice. I stayed home with a terrible fever, coughing yellow bile. What a wonderful nurse Mother was! Always bringing me grapefruit, oatmeal muffins, fresh honey. No one came to see me. No one called. April to mid-May. The day I went back to school, nobody noticed I'd been away. I got mad. That summer I wanted to get out of Fargo. I'd pined all year for Maddock and the farming days with Jens Nielsen. As soon as school was out, I went back.

I was fifteen that summer and Jens paid me a full man's wage—five dollars a day—for the first time. During threshing he gave me my own bundle rack and horses and harness. This old Dane, how shall I describe him? Black hair, mustache, red cheeks, chewed Copenhagen snoose. I could swear like a trooper in Danish at the age of ten. But Jens was never in such a hurry that he would not stop, pause to show me and explain to me why things were done the way they were. The easy way and the hard way. I went there every summer from the age of ten all through our seven years in Fessenden. At first I was essentially an auxiliary force for the Nielsen girls, getting the cows in, digging for potatoes, chasing chickens, filling up water jugs, hauling lunch out with a gray mare named Nell and a buggy. Those girls were really good to me. Rose was indestructible, Aggie quiet and strong like her mother, Edith beautiful and with a good deal of humor. And Chris could do everything. He had a mechanical aptitude his father lacked, whereas I don't think he inherited Jens's love of horses. But everything Chris did, he did at a trot; he was always in a hurry. My folks got rid of me for practically the whole summer. I went over there and became the Nielsens' kid.

By then, Jens was running one of those great big North Dakota farms, though he always stayed with horses. There were three large horse barns, a lot of buildings and, as was common in those days, a well with a windmill, and watering troughs scattered around. The houses—all the houses on farms around Fessenden and Maddock—were very simple, frame, many just one-story. Very few trees. The planting of windbreaks as part of the soil conservation program came after FDR. All the barns were red and all the roads were dirt. Nobody used fertilizer; they just kept using up the soil by planting wheat year after year.

At his peak, Jens had ninety-two horses at one time. Maybe a third were not purebred Clydesdales, but they had a lot of Clydesdale in them. He also bought range horses at auctions that were at least three-quarters just old mustang, probably bred on big ranches out West. When you harnessed a horse in the morning, you'd curry him first, clean the harness and then put this soft pad on his neck. Jens went to great effort to show me just how to drape a harness over my shoulder, how to approach the horse, and how to use my weight to get it up on him. I also helped Jens break in horses, usually in the fall plowing. We used different hitches, but most often we plowed with five horses, two in the lead and three so-called wheelhorses behind. And what we'd do is take one of these young mustangs and put them between two horses. They learned quickly. They had no choice. There's nothing that settles a horse down like pulling a plow.

Before harvesting, in the spring and early summer, we'd go over all the wagons, pulling the wheels and greasing them, tightening up the iron rims, wheelwright work, repairing all the harness, putting new handles on the broken pitchforks. Jens had a blacksmith shop with forges, a harness shop with leather and a general tool shop; it was exciting.

On rainy days the bunkhouse was a marvelous place, because the thresh- ing crews would play cards all day long, and sing and play harmonicas and guitars and tell stories about St. Louie, Minneapolis, Winnipeg, Tulsa. They drank hot water, a little butter, cinnamon, sugar and raw alcohol. No mat- ter what the ingredients, they always called it schnapps. There were two brothers, Shorty and Slim. Everybody knew Shorty because he was a big runner of alky down from Canada. He'd be missing for a day or two now and then. He brought his hootch back in silver gallon cans and he'd take them out and bury them in the tree claims. Every so often Shorty would get arrested and serve a little time for bootlegging. But he was a real hard worker for Jens. One carload, all from Oklahoma and Texas, always came in an Essex, and Tex, who drove it, and the other guys, always had musical instruments. I'd say most of the crew were second- or third-generation immigrants. An awful lot of them were Scandinavian or German farm boys who still spoke with an accent.

Once threshing started, we got up at four o'clock. The bunkhouse was simple. Straw ticks and a sheltered place out back with buckets and barrels of cold water and tin basins on a long table to wash your face in. I don't remember anybody having a toothbrush, but I suppose they must have. Saturday night, anybody going into town would be out there stripped down and scrubbing away, taking a bath in a bucket of water. Some were cleaner and some weren't. Mr. Thomas, the head of the threshing crew and a great big snoose-chewing man from Minneapolis, was famous for never having been known to take a bath. A lot of the threshers shaved every night, I suppose because dust and chaff could catch in a beard.

We'd get called and all stumble out of the bunkhouse and splash cold water on our faces. All farm people bought their clothes at the same place, so everybody looked alike: bib overalls, a long-sleeved Sears, Roebuck work shirt and a bandanna around your neck to keep the straw out. And an old battered hat of some kind. Why we didn't all die of lung disease I'll never know, as we worked in great clouds of dust. After washing, we'd all go down to the barn, take our horses out and water them, then bring them back and feed them hay and oats and put the harness on them. The harness had to be kept clean and properly adjusted. Jens fed his horses just twice a day, as we did later when I joined the U.S. Cavalry.

Breakfast was around five, five-thirty. Oh, gosh, it was huge. Great piles of eggs, bacon, sausage, thick slices of buttered home-made bread, oatmeal, potatoes, great mugs of coffee. There were two cook cars, one to cook in and one to eat in, great big things that got pulled around by horses in those days. They were usually in a farmyard, never at the threshing machine.

When threshing began each morning, the first thing you heard was the "Tooo-o-o-t!" of the steam engine. There was also a special toot for the Tankee, kind of a signal that told him, "Hey, our water's getting low! Get a move on!" There was a certain toot for lunch, and so on. A lot of tooting went on. In the evening, all of a sudden you'd hear this long whistle and then you'd hear the separator clank to a halt. Quitting time was determined by the straw's moisture content, the dew. During harvest, you often saw the sun setting late, maybe nine o'clock at night, and a threshing machine just shutting down. A good crew kept going as long as it could. The work ethic was unbelievable. There was a real tempo about a threshing machine.

The man who ran it all was the separator man, Mr. Thomas. He stood up on top, a great, towering man. He was the one who felt the grain, looked at the sun, smelled the wind, and said, "All right, boys, start." He made the decisions. He was always going around with a long-snouted oilcan, oiling, listening, adjusting, tuning. He had little walkways that ran all over the machine, and all day long he was watching every little piece of it. He was the boss.

Another man ran the steam engine. There was Tankee. And you had a Straw Monkey. Here you'd have this threshing machine spouting out straw and building up a huge pile. It was a real art. They'd consider the wind. They'd take a break and reposition the machine. Or Mr. Thomas would turn it up higher. Or he'd move it here and there. Pretty soon you had these great big straw stacks. The Straw Monkey would bring his rack with two horses and he'd back it in and Mr. Thomas would direct the blower so it would blow straw onto his rack. Then he'd take it and come back to the other end and shovel it into the steam engine.

It took a big crew. Besides them, you had twelve bundle haulers, two spike pitchers in the field and two at the machine and the grain haulers. Maybe thirty or forty men. Jens was always a grain hauler; they took the wheat into town to the elevator. Jens was the owner, the real boss. He took great pride in his horses, and during threshing he had four chestnut horses hitched to his wagon. Two were huge big mares—Bess and Jewel. He also drove them on his bobsled in winter. Anytime Jens drove anyplace, he drove Bess and Jewel.

What you did, you drove your team out to fields where a binder had cut and bound the harvested wheat into bundles for threshing. The bundles were piled to dry in neat shocks which were all lined up in rows, sometimes reaching miles and miles, all the way to the horizon. You'd go to one end of a field and hop off and tie the reins up and get your horses pointed down a line of shocks. You always got on the upwind side. You had a three-tine pitchfork and at first you threw the bundles into the rack helter-skelter. When you had four or five feet of them, you'd start building a load by sticking the pitchfork in the bottom of a bundle so the heads of grain pointed away from you. You'd then reach up and start building a very straight wall with these bundles. The pride of every good bundle pitcher was the ability to build his load up to incredible heights. Once you got a load on, you'd climb up, stepping on the rump of one of your horses. You left a kind of ladder. You'd climb up to where you'd tied your reins on the front pole. And you'd sit way up there and drive back to the machine and take your place in line.

Threshing rigs differed, but the principle stayed the same. After you'd cut the standing crop and gathered it up, you needed to thresh the seed from the stem, separate out the chaff, return the straw to the ground and collect the

grain in a wagon to haul it to the elevator in town to sell. As you drove up to
the rig, you pulled in beside the separator, lining up your rack exactly
parallel with an exposed moving platform—it was on link chains and had
forty-inch hardwood boards which connected these chains. When the front
end of your bundle rack was far enough, you started dropping bundles on
this moving platform. At once, the bundles were carried toward a revolving
cylinder armed with beaters; in the front were about five or six axles with
little sharp knives. Going like crazy. If anybody fell into it, they'd quickly be
chewed up by those knives. It happened occasionally. After it was chopped
up, the wheat passed over a series of shaking screens, sieves and rollers that
further separated the chaff, straw and grain as blowers carried off loose
strands. At last the straw and chaff were blown into the air in clouds of dust,
settling into a big stack. About halfway down the rig, there was a chute
where the stream of grain came out. Here Jens and the other grain haulers
backed their wagons in. You always had one filling up and another ready to
back in.

Mr. Thomas had to decide whether to put his spike pitchers in the field to
make loading go faster, or keep them at the machine. It was a forty-four-
inch Case separator, one of the bigger rigs of the time. It took twelve bundle
racks to keep it supplied with grain; six kept going in a circle on each side.
You'd usually arrive with a full load just as the wagon ahead of you was
moving in to start unloading, so there was time to talk and relax and joke,
and there would be a flash of white teeth in the dust-blackened faces. Sometimes Mr. Thomas shut down the rig to adjust something. Workhorses on a
farm, you didn't have to stay with them, you know. They were so tired most
of the time. Oh, they were well fed—big, fat, glossy animals. You could
jump down from the rack onto their big broad hindquarters and from there
to the ground. They were strong.

I loved it. Every minute of it. I loved every minute of the farm work. I
suppose I regarded it as high adventure. Absolutely.

We all expected to stay in farming all our lives. None of us knew there
was any other world. How would you know? I can remember as a kid of
thirteen or fourteen, working in a wheat field, and seeing a Model T go by.
They'd graded the road by Jens's farm and put gravel on it; that made it
kind of a highway then. At that time it was well known that there were just
thirteen miles of pavement in the whole state of North Dakota, and they ran
from Fargo to West Fargo. After that, you hit dirt. Right beyond that road
was the railroad track. And it was all open. Not a tree. I stopped and
watched that car go by and I can remember thinking, "I wonder who those

people are? Where are they from? Where are they going?" But I never thought of going off myself. It just never came to mind.

You expected it all to go on forever. Just picture those sunbaked plains, dirt roads with clouds of dust as the occasional horse-drawn cart or Model T passed by. You'd find a small family farm every half or quarter section, with cows, pigs and chickens. It was a rural way of life still mostly set by the three-mile-per-hour gait of the horse. At the Nielsens in 1932 we still used kerosene lamps. It was already going, though. By 1937, the last summer I threshed, joining a crew out at Steve Litke's farm in Fessenden, they were already using tractors and everybody was getting mechanized. It wasn't the same any more.

Jens kept his horses to the last. But the day of the steam engine was just about over. Keeping those great monster threshing machines going was getting too difficult. Tractors were appearing, and everybody was talking about the new combines that could cut the wheat, gather it up and thresh it, separate out the chaff and straw and collect the grain in a hopper for delivery to a truck. With night lights, working round the clock, one of the combines could thresh up to a hundred and twenty acres a day. I suspect Mr. Thomas died. The next farm to the south bought a twenty-eight-inch separator in Minneapolis, which was powered by a tractor. It was a lot more efficient and needed fewer men.

That summer of 1932, things began to hit bottom for Jens. Spring wheat, which had been two dollars and seventy-six cents a bushel in 1920, that fall dropped to twenty-six cents a bushel, the lowest wheat price ever. When I went back the summer of 1933, it was down to twenty-five. Mama Nielsen was trying to sell as many eggs as she could, but they had dropped from thirty cents to thirteen cents a dozen. Neighbors were losing their farms. North Dakota was drying up.

Back in Fargo, a big change came in my junior year. I got invited to a party and met Connie Taylor, who became my girl, and Ross Porter, soon to be my best friend. They were in a group of the most wholesome kids you can imagine. Having cracked the ice, I entered a real social whirl. There were a lot of dancing parties and you got printed programs with twelve dances. For days it was a big game for the girls. Connie would meet Lavonne and Joyce and plan who would get what dance, the waltz, the foxtrot, the Charleston, the Big Apple. The boys only found out that night. I earned a letter on a state-championship football team, got elected president of the Sportsmanship Club, played intramural basketball and trumpet in the band. Yet somehow it was an agonizing year, maybe because I was at the height of adolescence.

Many times, I caddied for Father out at the Country Club. He golfed with a group of friends and of course he was very good at it. He'd ask me in a kind of pleasant way. We had kind of a pleasant relationship. The question of saying no to him never entered my mind. If Father said he wanted you to go caddying, I just assumed that was what you did. But you know, I can't remember any football game, any event, any time, in my life, that I participated in that he came to. I don't think the thought ever occurred to him. He saw hunting essentially as a social event with his friends. I think he and Mother had a lot of fun. I can remember them going off golfing and duck hunting and partying and camping. And Mother was always interested and concerned, but there were limits to what she could do.

So it was Jens Nielsen who played the major role in my growing up, along with maybe Mother's brothers-in-law in Iowa, Fay and Victor Collins. We'd usually drive down to Iowa just after school was out, and Victor and Helen, or Fay and Mary, would drive me back to North Dakota by the middle of July. I'd be in Iowa for haying and then get up to Maddock in plenty of time for the harvest. All three of these men gave you the feeling that if they were going to explain something to you, or do something with you, or show you something, you really had their undivided and very genuine attention.

I can't remember Father once showing me anything, telling me anything, explaining anything to me. I had the feeling he used me, that was all. That second year in high school, his health was beginning to deteriorate. This was starting to cast its shadow. Mother was essentially sad and troubled. I sensed sadness and trouble in my own life too, but I probably couldn't have identified the cause.

The summer of 1934, Jens lost the whole wheat crop. There was nothing to thresh. What happened was a great cloud of grasshoppers dropped out of the sky one day, millions of them, flying low, some almost touching the ground, others flying so high they blotted out the sun. They were great big insects, three or more inches long, with black, leathery wings and a smaller set of bright-red or purple wings behind. Wide greenish-yellow backs, but like no grasshoppers anybody'd ever seen before. More like locusts. We'd been hearing about grasshopper attacks since 1931, when the first gigantic swarms appeared. They'd descend on a farm and not only eat all the leaves and stems they could find, they'd chew the binder twine off a sheaf of grain or gnaw on the wooden handles of farm tools. It was terrible. For three years the Nielsen farm escaped. Then they came.

Millions settled, just everywhere, with a crackling roar like burning fields of stubble. Worst was the high-pitched piercing noise they made, a kind of nightmarish grasshoppers' song the scientists later told us was stridulation, made when millions of hind legs rubbed against the whirring wings. One minute it was quiet and the next you couldn't hear a thing for that damn noise and they lit on the wheat, in the grass, on the roof of the house and the barns, on the walls, the posts, the trees. A few got into the house before Mama Nielsen got all the windows shut. There was no escaping them. All of a sudden, right in the middle of the day, the whole farm was covered with a greenish-yellow, crawling, moving mass, and all the while that terrible shrill, screaming sound. Aggie and Edith were caught outside and came shrieking into the house, brushing grasshoppers out of the hair and off their clothes. We ran to round up the stock, and so many insects kept coming, it was soon like a dark blizzard of grasshoppers. They ate every green, growing thing on the farm right down to the ground in a matter of minutes—all the wheat, the oats, the barley, the pasture, they even stripped the leaves off all the trees. In no time they cleaned out several hundred acres for Jens. We and the neighbors tried to fight them with bonfires but it was no use. We gathered a little grain the grasshoppers spared and tried to thresh it but got practically nothing. It was worthless.

Once the grasshoppers left, the bare, stripped earth started to blow. What the grasshoppers hadn't eaten, the dust blew away. Afterward I walked around the farm with Jens. Every place we looked, there was nothing but Russian thistles blowing across bare dirt. Jens was just about a broken man. "I plowed it all and I seeded it and I waited for it to grow and what did I get?" His voice cracked and his eyes were bright with tears. "Nothing." I walked behind him as the Russian thistles blew across the dry, cracked ground, and Jens went along, pulling them away from his fences; wherever they caught on the barbed wire, they stopped the blowing dust and topsoil and it would drift up and catch more thistles. Just wind and dust and Russian thistles. The Nielsen farm was starting to disintegrate. Oh, there was enough to eat, but the great horse barns stood almost empty. In time, of course, soil conservation, crop rotation, tree belts, rural electrification, all the New Deal programs under FDR would rescue towns like Maddock and Fessenden from the Dust Bowl. By then, farming would be mechanized and the days of horses gone forever.

From Chester Zumpf, interviewed forty-eight years later; a farmer in 1934, now a retired implement dealer in Fessenden:

"Those grasshoppers didn't all hatch here. They hatched in Colorado and South Dakota and all the way down the line. The wind blew 'em here. They came in with, maybe, ten thousand feet of altitude. You'd look up and you could hardly see the sun. It was just gray. Solid with grasshoppers. And then if the wind let up or towards evening, they'd come down to feed. When they came down it was just like a terrible storm of grasshoppers. When they got through eating, there wasn't anything around. You could walk on 'em, three deep. They'd jump at you but didn't bother you any. They were the same as locusts, big fellows, with black in their wings, and they could fly almost like little sparrows. If there was linseed paint, they'd eat it right off a house or a barn. Fields that had a little growth on them, maybe six, eight inches, well, when those grasshoppers finished, in a couple hours' time, it was eaten right down to the ground. Nothing left."

Further comment from Agnetha Nielsen Bergsgaard, interviewed on her farm near Maddock forty-eight years later:

"We found out what the Depression was when we were living in Wisconsin. I hadn't been married so long and my husband was working for the Case company. One day, he came home and said, 'I think we'd better start back home for North Dakota. They're laying off people to beat the band down there.' So we came back and rented this farm. We'd saved two thousand dollars in Wisconsin and we put half of it in the Flora bank and half of it in the Hamberg bank. We lost it all. Both banks failed and we lost all that money. So I had chickens. I got seven cents for a dozen eggs. I sold cream, eleven cents a pound for butterfat. We milked and separated that, you know, and sold it at the creamery. And we raised our own garden. So we could keep on living. That's what my husband said, 'We get back out on the farm we can always get some food anyway.' And that's what we did. We could always eat.

"We bought the farm in 1938. We were sitting at the table, making out the contract and we bought it for thirty-four dollars an acre. Afterwards I made some coffee and we turned on the radio and heard President Roosevelt say we might have to go to war with Germany. 'Don't be surprised if we're in it,' he said. We had grain bins all full of wheat. We hadn't sold it, because it was only about seventy-five cents a bushel. For a couple of weeks, it went up to seven dollars a bushel. Well, we made a payment on the farm for three hundred and forty dollars that fall, and the next year we paid the rest of it and we've owned it ever since. Without a cent of anything against it. This spring, two quarters of land down the road here sold for eight hundred dollars an acre. And it was just hills and sloughs. I don't know why in the world anybody would pay eight hundred dollars for that poor a land . . ."

Jimmy:

In the spring of 1935 I was named "Representative Senior," the biggest honor Fargo High School had to give. It stunned me. I'd been genuinely shy and unassuming and had no feeling of being outstanding. I went to school most days wearing a rather peculiar light tan corduroy jacket Mother had made on her sewing machine. The award was given at a big general assembly in the school auditorium. Claire Putz, the girl chosen, and I were called to the stage. Everybody cheered and applauded. The commander of the local American Legion post gave us each a check for ten dollars. Mother was there; she'd been invited especially and was pleased as punch. I don't remember Father taking any notice of it at all.

Betty

Just after we moved to Fargo, the summer of 1932, Mother took Grandma Critchfield down to Knoxville, Iowa, to visit McLain in the veterans hospital. He'd been there ever since his brain was injured in that plane crash during World War I. Mom took the three boys along with her. We'd moved into a house on the north side of town and the Hopes were visiting from Fessenden. Mr. Hope had fallen asleep at the wheel and woke up when his car hit a passing train at a crossing. He walked for help with a shattered kneecap. Anyway, the whole family of Hopes came to our house in Fargo to recuperate. When Mom got back from Iowa, she hunted all over for the toilet brush and found it in the kitchen. Helen had been using it to scrub vegetables.

In that first house in Fargo, a family named Hilliard lived next door. By Martin Hector's vacant lot. Mr. Hilliard wore shorts and a goatee. The shorts came below his stomach and one day his little girl stuck a nasturtium in his navel and he left it there all day. Mr. Hilliard was very congenial. He'd call over, "Yoo hoo! Let's all come out! I've got a good dirty story!" Daddy was always joking too. One time, a man had been chasing girls in the park and Daddy said, "I just wish he'd jump out of the bushes at Betty. She'd scare 'im." Another time, when Aunt Helen was visiting from Iowa with her two-year-old and a newborn baby, Daddy said, "You people in Iowa breed just like rabbits." That didn't go down so well.

Extract from interview with Harry Critchfield's wife, Kay, fifty-one years after the time in question:

"The first time I saw Jim was in 1932, not long after the family had moved to Fargo. He was a good-looking man, not thin but more husky than stocky, and he was always cracking jokes. Well, Harry and I hadn't been married very long and I had just met Jim and he came and sat down beside me. And he sat on a hot-water bottle. On the davenport. Right next to me. I don't know how come it was there, but he sat on a hot-water bottle. And he was sitting there and pretty soon he started to sweat. And he jumped up and said, 'My God, I thought I was getting all excited about your wife, Harry!' I was really embarrassed. I liked Jim . . ."

From Harry, same interview:

". . . Jim was a better-looking man than I am. Oh, not as handsome as Ray, but Jim was nothing to be sneezed at. We got along fine all those years on the farm. He never got mad nor bossed me around like Burke did. Jim was . . . he was . . . an awful nice fellow."

Betty:

That fall, I entered the Agricultural College in Fargo. To enroll, I had a swagger suit, a blouse that came from Bonnie Miss, another blouse, a matching hat and a blue-and-white-striped dress with a tied collar. I wore it to the Freshman Mixer. Mom made it out of a pair of pajamas. That Christmas, she borrowed fifty dollars from one of Grandma's former maids and bought me a coat and green wool dress. All my boy friends were tall—six foot two, six foot four. Daddy was only five foot seven or eight. I loved the college dances. I played the piano and sang torch songs a lot in those days. "As you desire me, so shall I come to you . . ." "I Surrender Dear . . ." "All of me, why not take all of me . . ."

From Billy:

". . . Every time Betty got interested in a new boy, she'd make hot-pan holders for her hope chest. Then she'd give them to Mother when hope began to fade."

Betty:

After my first two quarters at college, I had to drop out and work for Daddy for two years. Daddy hated being without money. Our second Fourth of July in Fargo, in 1933, poor as we were, he went out and bought fifty dollars' worth of fireworks—Roman candles, sky rockets, pinwheels, gaudy displays, sparklers for the kids. Pat, who was two, was afraid of the noise; he cried so much we had to take him inside. Peggy was a dark, sweet, quiet little girl. She always slept with me. Terribly shy. Daddy used to hold her on his lap at the table and say, "This little girl is my favorite . . ." Billy was more self-reliant. Smart as could be. Even when he was ten years old, he read all the time. If somebody asked, "Where's Athens, Billy?" he'd say,

"You mean in Georgia or Greece?" He'd go out in the wintertime on a pair of old wooden skis and cross-country ski for miles along the Red River.

About the summer of 1934, we began to see headlines in the Fargo *Forum* like "HITLER IN NEW DRIVE AGAINST JEWS." But it wasn't until the Czech crisis, four years later, that the terror, invasions, concentration camps and all started to become real. Until then, the Depression was all people worried about. FDR and his New Deal for the "forgotten man," and how the only thing we had to "fear is fear itself." That and other things at home: the St. Valentine's Day Massacre, the Lindbergh kidnapping, lynchings, the Scottsboro boys, the exploits of Dillinger, "Public Enemy Number One," the Dust Bowl, the shooting of Huey Long, the Joe Louis fights, the crash of the Hindenburg. Or how Virginia Bruce, a Fargo girl, had become a Hollywood star and married John Gilbert, every girl's dream come true.

The second year I was his office girl, Daddy was county doctor. All the free patients came to him, the really down-and-outers. Destitute families on relief rolls, badly nourished children who didn't get enough to eat, uprooted and homeless men who drifted in from hobo jungles. Every Friday evening, all the people who had syphilis would come for their bismuth and Salvarsan shots. I was always afraid I'd prick myself with a needle. One whole family had syphilis, and even after Daddy was no longer county doctor, they still came to him. They didn't have a cent, but the father was a barber. Daddy said he could pay for the shots by giving our family free haircuts. Mother went once and said it was awful; the barber cut too much off. She couldn't go anywhere for weeks and was madder than a wet hen.

Once while he was county doctor, Daddy had to take out ninety pairs of tonsils in just two or three days. He was the only doctor for the county hospital, or what most people in those days called the Poor Farm. And I can remember Daddy and the other doctors in the building sitting around Daddy's downtown office on Broadway and telling about their cases. Vivid stuff and always distasteful. One time, I went with Daddy on a call. It was to visit a little hunchback. It was a dismal, old-fashioned house, dark and gloomy. We entered her bedroom and there she was, sitting up in bed, all made up fit to kill. Daddy pulled her lip down and it was bright blue inside. Terrible heart condition. She died that night. They took her to the funeral home and I went along with Daddy while he did the postmortem. They used suction to bring out the natural fluid. Slit her down the middle, pulled it open with forceps and there was a little shriveled-up lung in one corner and an enormous heart. Suction tubes were attached to a water faucet. They made a slurping sound. Slurp, slurp. I got sick.

Another time, a whole family got the "itch." Daddy put sulfur on. It smelled terrible. He told them, "This will scare it away if nothing else."

In 1935 I went to business college from January through April. Somehow I bought myself a blue velvet dress with brilliants around the neck. The first day, I happened to meet Mother on a bus. "Oh, Mother," I said, "you'll never guess who's in my class at business college. Agnes Engelhart!" Mother looked blank. Then it came to her. "Oh, *she's* the girl whose stepfather murdered her mother and burned up the remains in a car. Only thirty pounds left. Later, poor Agnes accidentally ran into an old lady, who died from her injuries. And *that* old lady's brother had murdered a grocery-store owner over in Heaton. It was in a grain elevator, as I remember." Then Mother noticed all the bus passengers were listening. She was terribly embarrassed.

In May I was asked if I wanted to work for an outfit called the Ideal Finance Company, which had a small, seedy office downtown. It was at the height of the Depression and a depraved job if there ever was one. We'd give little bits of money to poor and desperate people at exorbitant interest rates. We'd lend them a hundred dollars and they'd have to pay back twelve-forty a month. The boss was terrible. He'd come in loaded in the morning, smelling of gin, and go to a cheap hotel two blocks away and shack up all day with some woman. She was apt to come to the office and throw ashtrays at him. Sometimes he'd come in all scratched up. Then she'd call to make up and say she had bean soup ready. It was a kind of signal. Every morning, he drank beer with an egg in it. He was also in the habit of swallowing his phlegm. He was practically illiterate. I got sick and tired of working there. I was only twenty-one and Saturdays I'd be alone with all that money. Sometimes we had as much as fifteen hundred dollars in the safe.

I was getting more and more worried about Daddy. In Fessenden, he'd always worked hard. He'd received patients from breakfast until noon, kept up a maternity practice, performed operations and taken the really complicated cases to hospitals in Harvey and Carrington. And day in, day out, in any wind or weather, he made calls all over the country. Everybody said how skillful and kind he was and what a good diagnostician.

Now it was too much for him. As county doctor he'd receive forty patients one day, and the next it would be forty-five, and the day after that fifty or even sixty. Sick people never stopped coming. Taking care of all who were seriously ill in a good hospital according to modern scientific principles was impossible: Those without money had to go to the county Poor Farm, where he was the only doctor. That was it. I saw what a beating Daddy was taking from it. The patients were too many, the time he could spend with each was too short, every examination had to be kept brief, he could just ask a few questions and hand out some prescription. Even when he stayed on the wagon, it got too much for him to handle. Maybe it was too much for anybody. Certainly for Daddy, with his drinking problem and sensitivity about what happened to his patients.

From a 1983 taped interview with E. Louise Gronlund, retired former director, Community Health Center, Fargo:

". . . In January 1934, I had just joined the city health department as a staff nurse. One time we were assigned to a prenatal clinic for welfare patients. It was run by a county doctor, who was Dr. Critchfield. I have a mental picture of him as not too tall, with a rather stocky build, a mustache and glasses. But that's fifty years ago.

"The county doctor's job was to treat welfare patients and those out at the county farm and hospital, what mostly people just called the 'Poor Farm.' They had a farm and several barracks where about fifty men lived and there was a hospital with seventy-five beds and a cemetery. They still call it 'Potter's Field.' There's always some men who can't support themselves, or don't have enough money in their pocket to go rent a room, or who work on farms in the summer and spend whatever they earn on liquor. Homeless men. We still have some, but then a fourth of the labor force was out of work. You saw defeated men without jobs everywhere. There were breadlines, you know, and soup kitchens, and in 1932 General MacArthur used tanks, bayonets and tear gas to clear the Bonus Army out of Washington.

"The hospital patients out at the Poor Farm came from families on welfare who went there for surgery or a delivery or treatment for chronic illness. For example, every fall, the city health officer examined all the first-, fourth- and seventh-graders in Fargo. Tonsillectomies were routine in those days. A doctor would look and take them out. They all did it. Nowadays, medicine has swung the other way. But if he recommended tonsils be taken out, the parents might tell nurses on follow-up visits, 'This is a total impossibility. We have no money.' Then those children would be put on the county doctor's list. Sometime in June or July, he'd do a whole raft of tonsillectomies, forty or more in a day. There were scads of poor people who couldn't get it done any other way. I'm sure things went pretty fast out there some days. There was a lot of volume.

"Dr. Critchfield was the only doctor for all those people. There were close to seven hundred welfare families, plus all those homeless men. He was under a lot of stress. Nowadays if a welfare patient needs hospitalization, they go to an ordinary hospital while the county pays. And homeless men are taken care of in winter by the Salvation Army or New Life Center. I don't think his job was looked down upon in any way. It always carried a commensurate salary. I think Dr. Baillie was county doctor once too. And he was a fine, wonderful doctor. But they did have trouble sometimes in talking somebody into the job. It was terribly hard.

"Then, Dr. Critchfield just missed the big change in medicine. Sulfa came in about 1938. We started using it then in pneumonia cases or for sick people at home who got secondary infections. It was the first time we really had something that could snatch them away from death's door. But the old-time country doctor supplied something people needed too. He was part of the community, the family. He was who you went to for everything. It's a cold, cold situation for a sick person when they look into the doctor's eyes and only see dollar signs. You talk about the milk of human kindness. Some of those old-time doctors really had it.

"I know he drank. Maybe he found his work too depressing. You just don't know how much anguish he felt. Maybe he hadn't felt able to stay a country doctor and make all those long trips out to farms any more. Maybe there were things he felt physically that he wasn't talking about. In Fargo, he'd have patients gathered at the Poor Farm and those who came downtown to see him at his office. This was at the height of the Depression and city people seemed less self-reliant than they did in the country; they couldn't feed themselves. There were many times I went into homes on a school visit or sick care and the mother of plainly hungry children might say, 'Oh, the doctor was just here and, bless him, he went to the store and got us some bread and milk.' You went into houses where the parents trembled because they'd starved themselves to feed their children. Or the children suffered lethargy and sleepiness from hunger. Or they couldn't go to school because they didn't have shoes or go outside because they didn't have a coat. In the thirties, you saw such things all the time. Out at Potter's Field, if somebody died without relatives, without money or anything, that's where he went. They've got a good many unmarked graves out there, I think. Dr. Critchfield had to examine the bodies and sign the death certificates. It was grim.

"Sure it could get to you . . . I'm not sure, but I think . . . from my experience of doing house calls in the Depression . . . that for years deep inside me I had a holy fear of going hungry. I never *was* hungry. But a nurse saw so much. Nobody had any money. Nobody. Some families didn't have so much as a crust of bread. They got sick. And it got to you. Oh, I loved my work. But all of this used to stick in my mind. Of course, nobody in those days could foresee what would happen or how soon the recovery would come. How did you know what was going to happen or that you were going to come out of it?"

From a taped interview with Ed Brekke, sixty-eight, retired schoolteacher, in Fargo, 1983:

"We only lived in Fessenden a couple of years and moved away in 1929. But I remember Doc very well. I used to caddy for him quite regularly out at the golf course. My folks ran the Fessenden Cafe and he would drop in to talk and have a cup of coffee. We used to have a Victrola there that played "Ramona" and "Girl of My Dreams," all those old songs. Once, Doc Critchfield asked me to go with him to a golf tournament up in Harvey. I was happy to go and he picked me up in his Buick. He had to stop on the way at a farm to see a patient. He drove pretty fast. He had kind of a fragrant aroma like bay rum and smoked cigars. He had a little mustache and of course everybody knew him and they'd call, 'Hey, Doc!' He was a heck of a nice guy. I loved to be with him. He was so kind to me. I was just twelve or so and he treated me like a grown-up.

"So the next time I saw Doc it was kind of a shock. I was seventeen and I was playing the piano at a roadhouse in Minnesota about five miles outside Fargo. Little place called Dilworth. The name of the nightclub was La Florentine. Later they called it Venice Gardens. It was run by an Italian, Carmine. During the Depression, I had to take work where I could get it. These two Italian boys, Joe and Tony, were good musicians. Joe played a beautiful guitar and he knew chords and taught me a lot. Later, when I joined a fraternity at college, they thought I was the finest piano player in the world. Jitterbugging was just starting to come in and they'd swing the old fox-trots. When we got wound up, we'd play, 'Hold That Tiger!' Except we sang a dirty version in Italian. And all those thirties songs: 'Try a Little Tenderness,' 'Shanty in Old Shantytown,' 'I Can't Give You Anything But Love, Baby.' Maybe 'My Wild Irish Rose' for a waltz set. And, of course, 'Brother Can You Spare a Dime?'

> " 'Once I built a railroad, made it run
> Made it race against time.
> Once I built a railroad, now it's done.
> Brother, can you spare a dime?'

"Remember Rudy Vallee singing that? La Florentine made people forget the Depression. It wasn't a dump. It was quite classy in a way. Carmine's wife—Blanche, I think her name was—stood by the door, very well dressed, and she welcomed the guests. I know one thing about her. She went to the hairdresser every day. Quite vain, I thought. But then, I was only getting fifteen dollars a week.

"Yeah . . . La Florentine. It was a wide-open nightclub and they ran it until three o'clock in the morning. People would start drifting in after nine, and by eleven you had maybe a hundred and twenty or so. A good-sized crowd. A dance floor with tables around it. A bandstand. Slot machines. A gorilla who served as a bouncer. A bar where they served setups for bootleg liquor or beer. Beer was back in. It came back in 1933, you know. 'Happy days are here again! The skies above are clear again!' . . . There was a crooked crap player, a guy from Alabama we called 'Alabam.' He could palm loaded dice and used to get guys into crap games and take them to the cleaners. Those guys would do anything for money. Oh, no big rackets like gangsters or anything. More like con men, you know, short-change artists and flimflammers.

"La Florentine had to be way out in Dilworth, because a lot of people in Fargo in those days were morally very strict. Dilworth was a tough little railroad town. A lot of Italian immigrants. One of the Italians opened a dance marathon, where couples would dance for days and days for a crack at the prize money. 'The Walkathon,' that's what he called it. Crowds would come out from Fargo in the middle of the night sometimes to watch. Some of the dancers would maybe be trying to catch a little sleep, sleeping on their partner's shoulder. And then somebody in the audience would throw a dollar bill out to make them dance faster, maybe something like the Charleston or shag or the Black Bottom . . . And they were damn near ready to die, you know. People liked to come out and see them suffer. It made a lot of money for Dilworth, brought people out there.

"La Florentine had no connection with it except that the Walkathon was a big deal and La Florentine was a fun place to go. Anyway, in 1934 it was going strong and I saw Doc Critchfield out there three or four times. Drinking and dancing. He was with this little blonde. Norma Thorson. I heard she'd followed him down from Fessenden. Norma was a sexy, pretty girl. I would say, quite vivacious. Oh, Mrs. Critchfield had it over her a million times, she was a beautiful woman. It was more a case of 'I love my wife, but oh, you kid!' This young lady was pretty and I think she had a fairly keen mind in her way. Maybe her judgment wasn't too good, but I think she was a sharp little dish. She was awful young, but I think he kind of compensated for that by acting young with her. You know, 'You and the night and the music . . .' Doc was a gay, happy sort of guy.

"I didn't want to talk with him. I'd known him when I was a young boy and I kinda had the idea that he didn't want anybody to see him. And I didn't want to go up and talk to him when he was with his girl, you understand. I tried to keep my face turned when he was around, because I thought it might embarrass him, seeing me. So I didn't want him to recognize me. When I looked at him it was out of the corner of my eye. I knew he had a wife and five children at home. And I had a strict mother, who'd taught me this was no way to live.

"Doc looked the same as ever. They were having a jolly time. Having a few drinks. And just dancing. I think they always came alone. I don't think I ever saw them with anyone else. Evidently he thought it was worth the risk. My own name for that is female-itis. And I notice people can lose their heads completely when they get that disease . . .

"I would say people not knowing much about each other is a normal state of affairs. What did our parents know about us? Or what do we know about them? People are what they are because of what happened to them. Life had made Doc what he was . . ."

Further comment from Jim's niece, Barbara Dunn, youngest daughter of Dr. Ray Critchfield.

". . . That family, I'm telling you. So much was going on and they kept everything from us. I keep wondering why the older generation tries to protect the younger generation from what life is really like. We all grow up and then we think, my gosh, look at all my relatives, they're all so neat and sweet and good and everything went so well for them, and here I am, screwing up my life. And, my gosh, it turns out you're really just one of the normal people . . ."

Further comment from Helen Collins:

". . . The only time I really saw the kind side of Jim was when I was up at Fessenden one summer. One night, I just felt terrible and he said, 'I think it's those meatballs, because I do too.' None of the rest of them had ever had food poisoning. Finally I got some relief, but he told me if I hadn't he was going to pump my stomach because he thought it was going to get me. I was terribly ill. And he was much the same way. And that's the only time that I really had much kindness from him . . . Well, he knew I was getting pretty white around the gills . . .

"After they moved to Fargo, we drove up one time, taking Jimmy home, and she had this electric stove they'd bought in Fessenden, but they didn't have the money to have it hooked up. And she was doing all the cooking and everything for the family on a little two-burner gas stove down in the basement, where she laundered her clothes. No way to bake or anything. I felt so sorry for her . . . Things weren't right then, but I didn't know much about it . . . I don't know, because you can't tell about somebody else's life, but I think she pret' near cared too much for him, did too much. He always knew she'd look after everything . . . She was the commanding presence in any house she was in. But if anybody was to kinda go without, I think she was the one. But she never let on. You just saw what you saw. I felt so sorry for her . . ."

From Billy, twenty-five years later; like many of the interviews, subject to the express qualification: "as far as I can remember":

". . . He smelled kind of alcoholic. I always hated to ride in a car with him, because he smoked cigars. He was always sort of unpredictable. I guess we weren't on the same wavelength. His office downtown in Fargo was depressing. Jars of unidentifiable organs pickled in formaldahyde. A slippery black leather sofa and old wicker furniture. Dirty. I always felt we weren't very closely related. He had a mustache. Later, when he was at the Veterans Hospital, he was wasted and pathetic. He read things like *True Detective*. I was already into hardbacks.

"Every Saturday, I'd go to Dad's office and ask for money. I'd sort of have to haggle. I'd ask, 'Dad, can I go to the movie today?' He'd reply, 'No, I can't afford it.' 'Aw, c'mon, Dad.' 'Well, here's twenty cents.' It was always the same. Ten cents for the movie, five cents for a hamburger with onions and ketchup, and five cents for broken-up milk chocolate. I'd go to the movies by myself, as usual. I was about ten or twelve. The first movie I saw had a song in it: 'Jeannine, I dream of lilac time.' I think it was a World War I movie, *Roses of Picardy*. There was a French chick with a Dutch bob. Then a Lon Chaney picture. A horrible, deformed guy. He couldn't walk and had to crawl up huge steps, Spanish steps. It was very vivid. It was agonizing. It seemed like you had to drag yourself up, you know.

"One time, Betty had an apartment downtown. She had a canary in a birdcage and there was a horrible figurine: a nude lady, stylized and painted silver. I put handkerchiefs around the top and bottom one time. Once, I was visiting Betty's in the summertime and I went to see *Werewolf of London*. I'd only been at Betty's a few days and had to walk back that night through strange streets.

"In Fargo there was a barber or beauty shop downtown on Broadway where I wasn't supposed to go. There was some sort of bad woman there. I have only this vague impression. When I was older and learned who she was, I was disgusted by the whole thing. It was just the conventional reaction, believe me. Strictly conventional . . ."

Anne

A June evening in 1935. I asked the long-distance operator for Ray's number in St. Paul. He was at home. He sounded tired. He said he'd been in surgery all day. When I heard his voice, I was so relieved I lost control for a minute. Then I pulled myself together. I told him it was Jim. He'd been drinking so steadily and so much, his nerves had come all unstrung. For days in a row he hadn't come home, and when he did, he staggered in and passed out, the stench of alcohol on his breath and dried vomit on his clothes. When he woke up, he was deathly pale and his hands shook. Ray said to take my time and tell him everything.

"He can't seem to sleep at all," I told him, "and his appetite is gone. He's been in a kind of stupor for the last three days. I think he's got some whiskey somewhere in the house, but I've looked everywhere and I can't find it. He keeps going on to me about how good I am and how ashamed of himself he is and how he hates the way he's been acting. He says he's so sick and tired of always going on the wagon, and his health is so bad, only to fall back again."

But the binges when he was drunk and delirious for days on end, disgracing himself in the bars downtown and staggering down Broadway were not the worst of it. He'd become seized by the idea that his vitality was gone, that he'd somehow squandered his capacity for living, and was done for. I managed, at last, to blurt it out. "Oh, Ray, he's threatening to take poison and kill himself. Can you come? I don't know what to do."

There had been some terrible scenes.

"He'll sit here and argue with me by the hour. He says he's going to make an end to himself. Oh, God, and then I try to talk to him and persuade him out of it. Jim, I tell him, if anything happens to you, what will become of me and the kids? I tell him I just couldn't face it without him."

I talked and talked. About how Jim would stop drinking and try to keep sober and get back his health. And how somebody would offer him a drink somewhere and another binge would follow, until he'd come home looking so beaten down and desperate my heart ached for him. It was a nightmare, all dammed up inside me. I'd kept it from the children and had no one to turn to or even talk to. Ray said he'd call back right away. The phone didn't ring for almost two hours, and when it did it was Irene. She said Ray had been rushed to the hospital with a heart attack. It looked like a mild one.

Hands trembling, I went out to get supper ready. Creamed wieners on toast, one of the hot dishes I made for the kids now because it cost almost nothing. Jim no longer had the county doctor's post and very little was coming in. We'd spent what little savings we had. I called the kids, who were outside playing. Billy, Peggy and Pat ate hungrily, talking a blue streak as always, but Jim, who came down and joined us, looked very peaked. After being so stocky all these years, he had grown thin. He sipped his coffee and took a bite of bread, which he chewed very slowly, staring vacantly ahead of him.

"Jim," I told him, "you've got to eat something. Don't you have any appetite at all? Here, take some food." But he got up and without a word left the table and went upstairs. I'd told the kids their father was sick; as soon as they started to clear the table and do the dishes and I could hear them all talking, I started up the stairway. Near the landing, I could hear Jim from the bedroom, drawing his breath in long, convulsive gasps. The terrible sound of a grown man sobbing. I ran up. Jim was sitting on the edge of our bed bent over, his face in his hands. I sat down beside him and put my arm around him, trying to comfort him as best I could. We talked and talked in low tones and finally I got him to lie down and try to get some sleep. I could hear Peg and Pat singing over the dishes in their high, childish voices. I sat with my hand on his shoulder until Jim began to breathe regularly, and then I got up from the bed and sank into my old cane-backed rocking chair and rocked back and forth, my face wet with tears, trying to decide what to do. Day after day and especially night after night, it had been going on like this, Jim always seizing upon new reasons for shame and guilt, myself devising new arguments and new excuses for him. I felt I'd gone through the wringer. I had to be careful not to let him be alone for too long, but at the same time I kept everything as best I could from the children, and from all the others, too. I couldn't even bring myself to talk to Betty and Jimmy about their father.

Ray was closer to Jim than anybody in his family; I'd waited as long as I dared to call him, and look what had happened. I'd so desperately hoped that Ray would know how to get his brother the right kind of care so he could get back his physical health and mental well-being. Where could Jim go to recover? Too many people in town still saw alcoholism as a sin, as a disgrace, just as Papa had, and not as the disease I was learning it was. I'd heard terrible stories about the insane asylums where incurable drunkards were sent. If it came to that . . . I'd rather see Jim dead.

The move from Fessenden to Fargo now seemed like a terrible mistake; the work as county doctor had been too much for Jim. But he'd been drinking fairly steadily since 1929, six years now; only recently had he slid toward breakdown. I was aware that Norma, too, was in Fargo. At first, somebody said she'd been a music student and was taking voice lessons. The next thing, I heard she was working as a hairdresser at a beauty shop just a block down Broadway from Jim's office. Betty found out she'd taken an apartment just around the corner on N.P. Avenue; you entered up a wooden stairway out in the back alley. Jim was such a pale ghost of his old self. I wondered how long Norma would stick with him.

Forty-seven years later, in August 1982, the author located Norma Thorson's walk-up apartment at 617½ Northern Pacific Avenue in Fargo. It was on the upper floor of a now nearly derelict two-story building. It was unoccupied except for a tavern, the Silver Spur Saloon, on the ground floor. The upstairs had a haunted air. Torn, shredded voile curtains hung like cobwebs in dirty windows; the interior was dark, unlit, and so coated with dust it must have been undisturbed for years. Two months later, on the night of October 10, when I was out on the West Coast, fire broke out. The tavern was destroyed and the building so badly gutted it was torn down. In another eerie coincidence, the old abandoned building that had once housed the La Florentine also burned down, not so many months later.

Anne:

As always in life, the blow when it falls is less terrible than the fear of it. I never dreamed my marriage could go to pieces. Once I decided to take Billy, Peggy and Pat and go to Iowa for a trial separation, I found I could draw a long breath once more. The children were out of it—at least there were just the ordinary perils like not catching chicken pox or whooping cough and keeping them fed to worry about. Jim, on his really bad binges, frightened me. I was afraid of what he might do to himself.

In Iowa, people were kind. I stayed away from Viola, the little farming community where my two sisters and their families lived. Helen, who had two little boys, had just had her appendix out, and while Mary was as welcoming as always, I was afraid of what their neighbors would say. People talk so much in a small place. So instead I rented a small apartment over a store on the main street in Anamosa. This was a little town on the Wapsipinicon River, five miles from Viola. It was hilly country, with woods and farms nestled into the narrow river valley, and about halfway in between along a winding gravel road was Stone City, which was not a city at all, but a sleepy little village of once-thriving limestone quarries and abandoned stone buildings. Stone City had become famous since it was painted, in 1930, by Grant Wood, who had been born and spent his childhood on a farm near Anamosa.

When word got around how miserably poor we were, people sent clothes to make over for Billy, Peggy and Pat, and they wouldn't take no for an answer. A man who owned a grocery store across the street let me bake bread, rolls, cakes and pies and sell them there. People from all over town sent things they wanted done up on the sewing machine; that paid a little, too. Mary and Fay, who had some land and were running a general store in Viola, helped with a dollar or two now and then. And Jim sent some. I was able to hold my head up. Those were hard times for everybody.

From Billy:
". . . The year Mom left Dad and we went to live in Iowa, I began making paper castles to keep Peg and Pat entertained. Sometimes I also made whole towns of clay, Danish towns with Danish churches, painted pink and white, with gabled, step-like roofs. Once, I made a Lady of Shalott castle and island. The lady looked in her mirror and watched the traffic go by on the road to Camelot. The castles had turrets, walls, vines, towers, stones and bricks, all drawn on construction paper. Cardboard castles. There would be a princess in a vine-covered tower. When they were all done, these castles, I'd strike a match to them. It would be very sad when the fire got up to the princess. Children love that sort of thing. She'd either be a golden-haired princess or else be made of tinfoil with long tinfoil hair. Then she'd either burn or melt."

Jimmy:
"That summer was a time of ambivalence. After Mother left for Iowa in June, taking the kids, I stayed with my friend, Ross Porter. We hung around the tennis courts, helping to roll the courts and string rackets. We played a lot of tennis. Once, the Fargo *Forum* ran a sports story headlined, 'Critchfield Paces Tennis Meet.' Jens wrote that Maddock was having another terrible year, this time from dust storms. I don't know where Father was

staying. Maybe with Betty. The family seemed to be breaking up. Once, I ran into Father downtown and he told me I should go to work, become the family breadwinner, now that his health was failing. He'd lost a lot of weight. I'd never seen him so thin. All my friends were going on to college in the fall.

"At last I went up to the farm at Hunter. Grandma had lost the farm in a sheriff's seizure, but Uncle Burke, now a vice president of the Bank of America in San Francisco, had bought it back again. He wanted to refurbish the old farmhouse, where Betty and I had been born. He left behind a 1933 Ford coupe, an old Model A Father had sold him. I stayed with Grandma in her big house in Hunter and had that car apart and put back together again many times.

"Out at the farm I worked alone. All day, every day. Without talking to anybody. It was nothing like the summers at the Nielsens. Now it was just me and a tractor. I painted all the farm buildings, Venetian red with white trimming, gallons and gallons of paint. I kept thinking: what makes the world tick? Every noon, I'd lie on my back in the grass and look at the clouds in that great, big North Dakota sky. It was like and unlike that time I had heatstroke in Maddock. For some time that summer—though even in my mind I never put it into words at the time—the knowledge came to me that wherever I made my life, it would not be here. It was like the prairie, after holding Father all his life, was now letting me go.

"By God, I was going to college. At last I drove back to Fargo. It was early September. My friends all helped. Fraternity rushing was almost over, but Alpha Tau Omega took me in, no initiation fee and free dues; I had to clean around the house in return. I earned meals by waiting on tables for Dutch Philips, who ran a basement restaurant across from campus. Uncle Burke came from California and said he was impressed with my spirit. I drove his car back to Hunter. Burke had promised to pay a hundred and forty dollars for the summer; he left sixty-five with Grandma and I never saw the rest. I spent seventeen dollars and fifty cents to matriculate. With two other football players, I got the hatcheck concession at the Grand, a movie theater downtown. Ten cents a hat or coat. So I was underway. You had to improvise. So did everybody. It was the peak of the Depression. I was just one of a large minority of penniless students. I never got a dime from anybody. Not Father or Mother or any of the family.

"So I started school at the Agricultural College—the A.C., as everybody called it. I continued playing football, basketball, hockey. Father had an old bearskin coat—it originally had been Grandfather Williams's driving coat, and Mother had brought it up from Iowa with her—and my last year in high school Mother had replaced the buffalo lining with jazzy red and blue plaid and put a raccoon collar on it. I wore it to football games. I still have it. In my sophomore year I sold advertising for the college paper, the *Spectrum,* and had a professor named Leon Hartwell for English who really fired my imagination. I started to think about writing, maybe journalism. With Hartwell's help, I was called in by the faculty and offered the editorship of the campus yearbook, the *Bison,* a job I was to have for two years. The salary it paid—sixty dollars a month—got me all through college. The day I got it, to celebrate, Connie and I went out and bought a record, Glenn Gray's 'Sunrise Serenade.'

"I saw almost nothing of Father. During the Christmas holidays of 1935 I was working at Sears, Roebuck and I ran into him. He said something like, 'Jimmy, if you've got this job at Sears maybe you should quit school and just keep working at it so you can help support the family.' By then I think he knew he was slipping badly.

"That same winter—Mom and the kids were still in Iowa—I was playing hockey down in Island Park and one of the players, Bob Shaw, got hit and thrown up on the boards; he got a bad sliver in his leg. We were playing a night game under lights. The question was, How to find a doctor this late? I obviously didn't have a very clear picture about what was happening to Father, as I phoned and asked if I could bring this injured player to his office, which I did. We hadn't been there long before it became evident from his bleary eyes and trembling hands and the way he tried to master himself and hide his real condition, that he was very drunk, probably too drunk to extract the sliver. It was kind of an embarrassing episode. I think he got it out in the long run, but it was . . . Well, after that I listened to what he had to say, but I no longer considered it was relevant.

"Now, there was one other episode that suggests he did go on practicing as a doctor a bit longer. A year or so later, one of my fraternity brothers, a straight-A student and 'much admired man about campus,' came back late one night full of remorse. He'd been down on Front Street, the tough area of town, and slept with a prostitute. Would I call my father? And I, at seven o'clock in the morning, called Father and Father said, 'Bring him down.' So we went down and this fellow got a shot and went his way. Father was weaker and thinner than I'd ever seen him. And I'm fairly sure he'd stopped drinking by then. This had to be my second year in college, or even the third year, so it could have been as late as early 1937.

"By then of course medicine was starting to change dramatically—into a technology based on genuine science, with sulfa to fight infectious bacteria and all that. The old-fashioned country doctor like Father—making house calls with his black bag—was just about obsolete. And I think he knew it. When he stopped drinking and Mother came back, in 1936, is when we moved into the little brown bungalow near the A.C. that was our real home in Fargo. And he came back and lived there. Not much, but he lived there.

"I saw an awful lot of Father over the years and yet I always felt a great sense of detachment . . . I think he was kind of a theatrical character. I think he enjoyed the role of being a country doctor. He liked showing personal concern and affection for rural people. Look how he liked to put on blackface and come out and sing and perform in the minstrel show. He was the man in the minstrel show.

"He liked being a doctor in the same way. And he played golf with the tradesmen in town and Mother played bridge with their wives. But Father's best friends were farmers. I don't think he ever got farming out of his blood. And by the mid-thirties, the old medical arts of touching and talking were falling by the wayside. I think if you wanted to identify the one thing that probably destroyed him, it was the fact that he was a country practitioner in an area in which the Dust Bowl and Depression were total. There was no way for him to turn. There was no way out . . ."

From Beatrice Carr Sayer, of Hunter, forty-seven years after the event described:

". . . I don't remember seeing Jim drinking when he was a young man in Hunter, because I was never in his crowd. But I do remember seeing him when he was drunk. It was about 1936 in Fargo. Oh, he acted like all drunks, like an idiot, staggering down Broadway in broad daylight. I know my husband used to go to him once in a while in the thirties, and some of the time Jim wasn't in shape to be telling anybody anything. It was when he was in Fargo. I do know he drank an awful lot. And that he liked his liquor. Even as a boy. Yes, I kinda think so . . ."

Betty:

"Jimmy had a terrible experience that year. He was playing hockey downtown, and one of the team got hurt, so Jimmy took him up to Daddy's office. Dad was too drunk to treat him . . . Jimmy always felt bad because Daddy never took him hunting. Daddy was good at all sports—hunting, tennis, runner-up in the state golfing championship. For years we had his silver loving cup around. But he was hard on Jimmy. He worried about his son growing up manly. Mothers are inclined to be more protective . . . Yet Daddy was kind. He had so much warmth. Farm people were his bosom friends . . .

"That year Mom was in Iowa was a terrible year for me. That blonde floozy hung around. I was afraid that if I wasn't nice to her, Daddy wouldn't send money to Mom and the kids in Anamosa. He lived in his office. Mom called going to Iowa a separation. Grandma Critchfield knew about everything. The family's sympathy was with Mother . . ."

Just how and when Jim's affair with Norma ended is not known. It evidently was over by the summer of 1936. The last reference to Norma in any of the interviews was made by Betty in 1959. She was recalling events of 1935–36.

". . . One time that year Norma took morphine in a suicide attempt. Another time she and Daddy rented a hotel room and turned on the gas. He broke the window with his shoe . . ."

At this point, saying, "It's awful sordid, kid, if you're close up to it," Betty couldn't go on and the interview was broken off, as it turned out, forever. She did manage to say, "It's crazy to be crying over something that happened so long ago."

From 1982 interview with Elizabeth Price Pfeiffer, sister of Rees Price and retired schoolteacher in Fessenden:

". . . It was a tragedy for her, too. She should have gone on and studied music. Instead she was a hairdresser. Her favorites were 'My Blue Heaven' and 'The Very Thought of You.' She had a beautiful clear soprano voice."

Mrs. Pfeiffer, a contemporary of the girl called Norma Thorson in this story— as mentioned, not her real name—had kept a copy of her high school annual. Norma had graduated late, having missed a year, and her picture was among those of the senior class. It is a three-quarter portrait, though she has turned her head and is staring right at the camera, her eyes blazing with defiance and looking astonishingly alive. Perhaps it is the dress or the waved blond hair that gives her such a distinctive twenties look—the fun-loving Jazz Baby, the gold digger, the flapper, Flaming Youth personified. There is a small, remote smile as she looks out of the photo so challengingly, and her eyes sparkle, as if she is amused and waiting for something—romance, fun, a high old time— they are a dreamer's eyes. Once she left the family's lives, no further information was sought about her, but in the margin by her picture Mrs. Pfeiffer had noted that she married in Fargo in 1937 and went to live in southern California, where she died of cancer when just forty-eight.

Further comment from Helen Litke Musha:

". . . After Anne came back, they lived in that little house on Twelfth Street. It had a big screened-in front porch. Doc was sick and he was always lying out on that porch whenever I came over for a visit. He wasn't bedridden, but he did a lot of resting. I think he was still practicing as a doctor. I know Mrs. Critchfield told my mother, 'When he got so sick, I had to come back. There's no way I can leave him now . . .' "

Anne:

He must have wanted badly to live. It's hard to break a window with a shoe.

After that, Betty wrote, he and that girl stopped seeing each other. She also wrote how sick he was. And how lonely she was. I said to the kids it was time to pack up and go home.

If I had it all to do over again, I'd be a clinging vine. When I talked to people who knew something about alcoholism, I found they generally felt that a drunkard, if he's going to get well, needs some source of hope or self-esteem outside himself. It was put rather awkwardly, but they seemed to mean some sort of religious inspiration, put plainly, faith in God. Jim, you could say, all these years had put his faith in man. It wasn't enough.

From Peggy:

". . . We'd gone to Iowa and come back and lived on Twelfth Street. I must have been around eight. And I remember going downtown, just walking along Broadway, and there was Daddy. It was so strange, because I hadn't seen him for so long, you know. He kneeled down and hugged me. I can remember him crouching down in the street and hugging me and being demonstrative and affectionate. The memory is so fleeting. Oh, and once on a Sunday afternoon in winter, we went for a walk together. We walked around our block and someone was building a snowhouse. And then we went to the grocery store and I introduced him to Mr. Liederman as my father . . ."

Betty:

"I kept going to an employment agency, trying to find another job so I could leave the finance company. At last I found one at a bakery, which paid twelve dollars a week for doing shorthand, typing and bookkeeping. Mr. T., the owner, was a short, plump man who was always brushing flour from my fanny. Once, they had a strike. Everybody but me and the scrubwoman. Frances, the bookkeeper, got just a hundred and twenty-five dollars a month and she'd worked there for twenty-one years. Finally the union came in and he started giving decent salaries. Every Saturday around two o'clock—quitting time for the weekend—Mr. T. would decide to give dictation. Or he'd say, 'Here's ten letters to type up, Betty.' How I missed college! I would have quit, but Daddy was getting too sick to keep up his practice.

"Once Mom came back from Iowa, we rented a bungalow at 1045 Twelfth Street North, just two blocks from the Agricultural College. The rent was thirty-five dollars a month and Mom paid most of it from Daddy's Eagles insurance; he'd let his other policies lapse. I got eleven dollars and eighty-eight cents a week at the bakery. Seven dollars went for food. I kept the eighty-eight cents for spending money. Every Saturday, Billy would take a white cotton laundry bag over to the bakery and they'd fill it with stale, leftover bread. Sometimes there were stale doughnuts, which Mom would heat up to make edible. There were always six or seven people at home to feed and Billy would carry enough of that old bread home to last us for another week. It kept us going . . ."

Further comment from Rees Price:

". . . It was early 1937 in Fargo. Doc invited us over to have dinner with him, and we went to the Rex in Moorhead. It was supposed to be the best steak club around at that time. Doc liked his steak really aged and in Fessenden he used to have everybody over for steak dinners and he cooked it with mushrooms and tomato sauce. By the time they got one that was aged enough for him that night in Moorhead, it had a lot of mold on it. I never saw a man eat a steak that was that aged before. It just fell apart after it was cooked, you know. But that was the way Doc always liked it.

"I remember we talked about Fessenden. He was interested in how everything was going there, and we had a nice dinner. That was the last time I ever saw Doc. I suppose I hadn't seen him for three or four years before that night. Oh, he was starting to go to pieces a little. He was kinda falling apart or something, just not the same. He just couldn't sit still. And he was thin. He'd been a pretty stocky man when he was up in Fessenden. He was always so healthy-looking, and full of zip. Now he looked so kinda sad and thoughtful, so resigned. His face had that look people get when they've seen too many bad times and are fed up with life and everything. He just wasn't the same old Doc . . ."

Anne:

A year went by. As far as I know, Jim never took a drink. He was sure, at last, that he'd gotten back control of his life. As Betty said, by then it all seemed just like a bad dream. It was springtime, the first of May. Jim had an appointment that day with an oculist downtown. He asked me to go with him.

"I don't know what's wrong, honey," he said. "I'm having trouble focusing my eyes. Maybe my glasses need adjusting." After the examination, the doctor asked to speak to me alone.

"Mrs. Critchfield, your husband is one of two things. He's either taking dope or he's a very sick man."

"I know he isn't taking dope."

When we got home, I saw how scared Jim was. His face was pale and the skin was drawn back over the cheekbones and around the mouth; he looked badly frightened.

"I'm going to St. Paul. Right now. Tonight. I want you to come with me, Anne."

We had to hurry to catch the train, taking almost no luggage. Pat, who was six, had just come home from kindergarten; he was out in front of the house on his tricycle. I took him along and left a note to Billy to watch Peggy when she got back from school until Betty came home from the bakery. I had one extra dress with me, thinking it would only be a night or two. We sat up all night in a coach. By now there was no money for a sleeper.

The next day, Ray put Jim into the hospital, where he was treated with intensive vitamin-B injections. After five days I moved into the hospital with him; they moved a cot right into his room, Jim was so insistent about it.

And so for two months I stayed by his side night and day. They would bring a wet pack. Rubber sheets. They'd roll him up in warm wet rubber sheets. Steaming the alcohol out of him, they said. For an hour at a time. He came out of it very weak. I read to him. Seven, eight hours every day. He wanted Richard Halliburton, but he really just wanted the flow of words. One of the nurses said, "Oh, it's wonderful in this day and age when there's so much divorce to see such a devoted couple."

He would talk. Like a bad little boy, he wanted to confess all his sins. Then I'd read some more. I could hardly stand it. There wasn't anything I could do. Once, they had a band concert and they wheeled him in. They had his hair all plastered down. He would have hated it. One Sunday, I went to have dinner with Ray and Irene, who were looking after Pat. After two hours I went back. The hospital was horrified. Jim had tried to find me, but I wasn't there. He'd fallen out of bed, hurting himself. He was absolutely dependent and devoted. After hell for years.

I asked him one time, "Why didn't you ask me for a divorce?"

"I never wanted to marry her. She was just a girlfriend. You were my wife."

We got twenty-five dollars a month from the Eagles. Disability insurance. That went for rent. Jimmy paid the light bill. Betty fed them. I'd look at Jim's tray. But I thought they might be keeping track, so I didn't eat anything from it. When I'd walk to Union Station to buy a Fargo *Forum* for him, I'd look in the gutter in case anybody had dropped any money. Mother Critch, Ray and Burke paid the hospital bill. The doctors didn't charge anything. Some of them were Jim's old classmates at medical school. Mary would stick a dollar or two into letters. For twenty-five cents I'd buy chow mein, a cup of tea and a biscuit. For six days a week I lived on that, one meal a day. When I was in funds, I'd buy a box of crackers. Nobody realized I had no money. I've always thought that was one of the best things that ever happened to me. After that I could understand people better. Absolutely no money.

Usually when they put Jim into the wet pack, I'd go sit in the hospital library. The nurse would say, "Madam, if you'll please leave the room while I do this." Or an intern would be putting something into Jim's veins. Soon they were calling me back in. "Would you mind coming back and helping us?" the nurse would ask. "He won't hold still at all."

That last year in Fargo, Jim had done no drinking. But it was too late. Once, I asked him, "Jim, don't you crave a drink?"

"I wish I'd never seen the goddam stuff."

Then he began to mentally deteriorate. At a fast rate. They called in the neurologists. One of them told me, "Anything you have to ask your husband, you must ask quickly."

It was absolutely horrifying. Alcoholic degeneration of the brain. In five days I watched Jim go from a brilliant man to a mindless man. A fine mind became a blank. Here and there a word made sense, but not many.

At last they let us take him home. My brother, Hadwen, and Mary drove up from Iowa. Hadwen, after traveling all over the world and being twice widowed, was now spending a lot of time in Florida. He'd built a bed in his car, and we brought Jim home that way. It was a five-hour drive, and when we got to Fargo, we stopped at our house on the way to the veterans hospital, out north of town. Once inside, Jim became frantic.

"I've got to get down to the office," he kept saying. "I've got to get down to my office. I'm a doctor!"

At the veterans hospital he had an older and very sweet doctor, who said to me, "This has been a terrible thing for you. You will be exhausted for weeks to come."

Jim spent that July to the next February—1938—in the Fargo veterans hospital. It was way out in the country along the Red River, several miles from our house. I went every day, walking. I made a friend, Mrs. Browning, whose husband was also a patient, suffering multiple sclerosis. The hospital was a wonderful brick building with great big lawns and lots of flower gardens and trees. I loved to go to the sheds behind and see the guinea pigs and rabbits. So did Peg and Pat.

From Betty:

"It was better with him in Fargo. In St. Paul, Mother was very hungry. Dad got plenty to eat, but she was afraid to touch what he'd left in case they measured what he'd eaten. Uncle Ray paid the hospital bill. Daddy was only in the Army a couple of months before World War I ended, but it was enough to qualify him for the veterans hospital.

"I got up every day at six o'clock. I'd get Peggy ready for school before seven-thirty. Then I'd go to work and come home at eleven, fix lunch and leave. And come home at five o'clock again to fix supper and all. Peg and Pat did the dishes. Every Saturday I'd go downtown to the National Tea Store and buy pork spare ribs and two shopping bags of groceries. Then I'd stop at the public library and fill a third shopping bag with books. Then take the bus. At home I'd wash the sheets and towels in the bathtub with a washboard. I worked at the bakery all through the time of Daddy's illness. Uncle Burke thought Jimmy should go into the CCC, but Mother wouldn't hear of it.

"Peggy was always saying, 'I'm ravished tonight.' She confused ravenous and famished. I used to take her to see Daddy. He was so delighted. Peggy would sit on his bed all day long. She took gum drops and pipe cleaners and made favors and little people. Sitting with her father all day long. And he'd watch her so lovingly. You sensed that when he'd gone, he felt at least something of him would go on living in those little brown eyes and silky brown hair. Peggy would stroke his face and clasp her little hands around his neck and hug him with so much affection."

Peggy, forty-seven years later:

". . . He'd be wearing pajamas and looking very frail and pale. And he always smelled of cigar smoke. To this day I really like the smell of it. Daddy had a mustache and in my memory his hair was brown. I sat in his lap all the time. I don't remember what he said at all. Just that he was looking very pale and I felt very sad and felt he'd been away from home for years . . ."

Betty:

"Mother stayed out at the hospital most of the time. Daddy couldn't bear to have her leave him. He wanted her to be close enough so he could touch her. Mother used to read to him out loud. Everything from *Two-Gun Western* to *Anthony Adverse* to *Little Orphan Annie* ("Leaping lizards, Sandy!").

Daddy had always been an omnivorous reader. He read tons of books. But except for the latest medical reports, he read for escape. That Christmas, I went out to the hospital and played the piano for the patients and sang Daddy's favorite songs. The audience was all old men. Mr. Browning had a cackling laugh. His emotions were reversed from his multiple sclerosis. He wanted to cry, but he'd laugh. Daddy was in a wheelchair. He was smoking a Robert Burns panatela. I sang, 'Ah, Sweet Mystery of Life' and 'Rosary,' songs we'd sung at home. But his favorite was 'Song of Love':

> " 'Once on a time, in a kingdom by the sea,
> Lived a young prince sad and lonely . . .'

"Mother took him lime sherbet almost every day. It was one of the few things he enjoyed eating. She'd ask him how he liked it and he'd say, 'Fine.' She also took panatelas out to him. One day, she was taking him out for a walk and it was too windy to light one. So she stepped into the hospital basement. Just then an elevator came down and a man stepped out. He saw Mom puffing on the cigar and said, 'Well, my Gawd!'

"Every day, Mom walked all the way out to the hospital, three or four miles out in the country. She wore overshoes and used to cross El Zagal Golf Course, which had a grassy bowl in the middle of it. Mother loved to run down it. She'd say, 'I really enjoy running down that slope!' Billy, who was fourteen now, was aghast. He said, 'Well, I hope you don't, and if you do, I hope nobody sees you.' Then Dr. Baillie said she'd better not, with her blood pressure."

From Donald Rock, son-in-law of Dr. Ray Critchfield, in a taped interview in St. Paul forty-five years later:

". . . It was the last week of April in 1938. I drove down with Ray to the veterans hospital in St. Cloud. We were outside on the lawn. It was a nice Sunday afternoon, I remember. Jim had white or grayish-white hair. He shuffled. He wore a bathrobe and pajamas. I'd expected a man in his late forties, and here he was frail and decrepit, like a small, bent old man who shuffled around. I wasn't told why he was ill. Ray, Irene's father, didn't talk about that. I don't remember anything particular about his mind being gone. I think he responded to Ray. We weren't there too long. But what I remember most is that he looked like an old man, like he was seventy . . ."

Anne:

In February 1938, they had moved Jim to another veterans hospital, this time in St. Cloud, Minnesota. It was for mental patients—they didn't say insane asylum any more. Jim had become utterly irrational. Softening of the brain, they said. Alcoholic degeneration. His mind simply faded in that one week in St. Paul. His mind was simply going. There was nothing we could do to stop it. Nothing anybody could do.

One night I was at the Methodist church when I got a message to come to the hospital in St. Cloud at once. I caught the first train. I was met by Ray and Irene. They'd driven down from St. Paul.

"He won't know you," Ray warned. "He doesn't know anybody. He seems to be in a stupor."

We went to the hospital. Inside, a nurse led us through the corridors. A few ambulatory patients, men in dark blue bathrobes and pajamas with blue stripes, sat in chairs along the wall and stared at us as we passed. Orderlies and nurses hurried up and down. Once, we stood aside as a kitchen worker came by pushing a rattling cart loaded with dirty dishes from the evening meal. There was a sharp nasty smell—ammonia, drugs, disinfectant, foul hospital odors. As we followed the nurse, we could hear from the rooms intermittent coughing and moaning. Someone was delivering an unintelligible harangue.

The nurse took us into a room. At first it looked bare, but there was a white hospital screen in one corner. I noticed the windows had iron bars on the inside. A narrow iron bed was hidden beside the screen. Its legs were screwed to the floor. Covered with white bedding to the chin, a body lay on it. One hand, thin and trembling, rested on top of the blanket. The fingers kept drawing in, as if pulling at its folds.

The head lay twisted sideways on the pillow and I could see the matted white hair wet with sweat on the temples, the hollow cheeks and the drawn, clammy forehead. I thought: this can't be Jim. I went closer and looked into the face. I had only to see the blue eyes raised at me, and all the sadness in them, to know the dreadful truth. His hair had gone completely white, he was much more emaciated than I had ever seen him and he had a yellow pallor he'd never had before. In the days since I'd last seen him, he'd become a little old man. He was forty-eight.

His gentle, steady eyes held mine and I bent closer, breathing heavily and blinking back the blinding tears. Ray and Irene stood some distance behind; so did the nurse. Even here the air reeked of disinfectant, and through the walls the muffled sound of moaning could be heard. I felt Jim's chest, his forehead, his hand. His face was burning, the hand cold. I put it back under the bedclothes. His eyes stayed on me and I thought I saw a flicker of consciousness in them. His lips, looking dry and swollen, moved a little. His wasted face looked less lifeless. I bent down and passed my hand over his damp hair, looking intently into those staring eyes.

"Jim, dear, can you hear me?"

Tears were running down my cheeks and I wanted to tell him that we were going to take him home, away from this place, and that somehow we could still make a happy life. I spoke again.

"You know I love you very much."

His lips moved again, there was the faintest suggestion of a sigh. The same flicker of light passed over his deep, sad eyes once more and the intake and release of his hot breath quickened. I leaned forward. His mouth was working. Something stirred within his chest. Then the words came thickly but distinctly.

"How are the kids?"

Ray had to go back to St. Paul. Jim had said nothing more. I was left alone at a hotel. During the night, I was called back to the hospital. Pneumonia had set in. He had on a pneumonia jacket when I got there and was sweating terribly. His eyes were closed now. His forehead was fiery and dripping wet. He had sunk deeper into a heavy lethargy. The only movement was his hot breath in and out. The nurse wanted to change the jacket. She called for an orderly, but she couldn't get one.

"Would you mind helping me?" she asked.

I went over to one side and slipped my arm under his head. He stirred a little and nestled down on my arm.

"Why, he knows you."

"Yes, he does."

I went over to the other side and lifted him and he curled up in my arm the same way and his heart stopped beating.

Anne

Earlier, the doctor had asked me to pick out the casket. "You'll probably go all to pieces," he said.

"No."

"Well, you never know."

He had died in early morning. I waited at dawn at the St. Cloud station. It was deserted. There was a newsstand and I bought a copy of *The Christian Science Monitor*. I looked at the picture page and recognized a familiar painting. It was Grant Wood's *Stone City*.

That afternoon, the phone rang at home and Betty answered. "This is Mr. Moore of Moore's Funeral Home," the caller said. "Which train is your mother coming on with your father's body?" Betty was unable to speak. He said, "Oh, I'm sorry. Hadn't you heard?" She put down the phone and told Billy, "Daddy died this morning."

When I'd left Fargo that night in May 1936, I'd told Jimmy that his father would probably die. He had lived two more years. Mr. Moore later sent a bill for only forty dollars for funeral expenses. I was unable to get the hundred dollars usually given for funerals to widows of Eagles members, because the death certificate mentioned "acute alcoholism." I suppose Jim had done three fourths of his drinking at the Eagles Hall.

He was a wonderful doctor. He was considered the most promising young man in his medical class. He was always on call twenty-four hours a day. He always did everything. He had some terrible cases. Footlings. Malposition of twins. He never lost a mother, never lost a baby . . .

From the Fargo Forum, *May 4, 1938:*

"Dr. R. J. Critchfield, 48, Fargo physician for six years and member of a prominent family of Cass County pioneers, died at 2:30 A.M. Tuesday in the Veterans hospital at St. Cloud, Minn.

"He had been ill for 12 months, suffering from a form of nervous pellagra, but was showing improvement until Sunday night, when he was stricken with pneumonia. Funeral services will be Friday in Hunter . . . Born at Hunter, September 18, 1889, he was the son of a pioneer physician, the late Dr. Henry H. Critchfield, who came to North Dakota in 1886. His mother still lives at Hunter . . .

"Dr. Critchfield was well known in North Dakota golfing circles. In 1925, while living in Fessenden, he was runner-up for the North Dakota state amateur golf title, being beaten in the final by Jim Barrett. Becoming ill a year ago, Dr. Critchfield was in St. Joseph's hospital in St. Paul nine weeks, then entered the Fargo Veterans hospital July 1. He was removed to St. Cloud three months ago.

"Dr. Critchfield married Anne Louise Williams April 19, 1913, in Iowa. Besides Mrs. Critchfield and his mother, he leaves five children: Betty, 23; James, 21, NDAC junior; Billy, 14; Peggy, 8; and Pat, 7, all at home, 1045 Twelfth Street North. Of his four brothers, Dr. L. Ray Critchfield is a pediatrician in St. Paul; Harry, director of Indian agriculture at the Interior Department at Washington; Burke H., vice president of the Bank of America at San Francisco; and McLain, a patient in the Veterans hospital at Knoxville, Iowa. A sister, Mrs. Kathryn Edwards, lives at Mt. Shasta, Wash. . . . Burial will be at Hunter . . ."

Anne:

Jim wanted his funeral like his father's had been. In his mother's house in Hunter and with the same music. The two big parlors were used in the same way. The casket in between. It stood sideways in the door, covered by an enormous American flag. Jim's medical fraternity at Minnesota had sent a big floral wreath. Peggy told me, "This is the saddest day of my life." The old house had fallen into sad disrepair. Jim's mother, who was now seventy-six and lived there alone, had grown much too frail to look after things. The columns along the porch had always been painted white, but much of the color had now peeled away. The house seemed as cold and gray inside as outside. There were conspicuous damp patches on the walls, the curtains looked dusty, the Oriental rugs were badly frayed. It was hard to see anything that was not begrimed and defaced by time. In spite of so many windows, the general effect of color was gray, and the funeral flowers failed to conceal the faint musty smell of decay. A mixed quartet, two men, two women, sang "Beautiful Isle of Somewhere" and "Blest Be the Tie That Binds." The Presbyterian minister spoke briefly about how quietly heroic ordinary lives could be. "How many," he asked, "whom Jim helped through sickness and sorrow will rise up and call him blessed on that last great day of judgment?"

At the cemetery, the pallbearers on both sides raised the covering flag and folded it as the casket was lowered into the grave. The minister threw on the handful of dust. Dust to dust. It was overcast, a gray, blustery day, too cold for early May. The bare, black branches of what few trees there were looked dead. The North Dakota prairie was as desolate as ever. Standing about the grave, besides my five children, were Grandma Critchfield, feeble and tottery and with all the grief of the mother who outlives her child; Auntie Kay, sobbing blindly; Ray and Irene and their four daughters; Harry and his wife, Kay; many Hunter people; college kids from the Methodist church in Fargo, and some of Jimmy's fraternity brothers. About forty students had driven up from Fargo. The minister said, ". . . The Lord gave, and the Lord hath taken away; blessed be the name of the Lord . . . Man that is born of woman hath but a short time to live, and is full of misery . . . Lord, have mercy upon us . . ."

After the funeral, the Aid Society of Hunter served coffee, sandwiches and fruit salad to the mourners at Grandma's house. It was very solemn. Suddenly Peg and Pat came down the stairs. Pat was bare to the waist and wore one of Grandma's best fringed satin tablecloths, which he'd wrapped around him like a sarong. Both were dripping with funeral flowers. They'd made leis out of the funeral wreaths and ribbons. Peggy looked distressed. She held back, a hand over her mouth, and looked ready to burst into tears. Not Pat. He grinned all over his face and showed a large gap of missing teeth. He stopped on the landing near the foot of the stairs in front of a stained-glass window and wriggled his skinny little body. "Hula, hula, hula, hula . . ." he cried. I can see him now.

Peggy, forty-seven years later:

". . . The main thing I remember from the funeral was looking at Daddy himself. I wish I hadn't. He didn't look like himself. Everybody tells me I'm wrong and that he had on a suit, but I have the most vivid memory he was wearing his hospital pajamas. And I don't remember *what* he looked like, just that he didn't look like himself. The coffin was between the living room and parlor in Grandma's house. I can't remember anything else, just looking in the coffin. Oh, and the coffin going down into the grave and some men pulling the flag off. Because that was the American flag we hung up on the outside of the front porch every Fourth of July. We always had the biggest flag in the neighborhood."

Anne

The alarm rings, dreams fade; it's another day. The present is real and concrete—somebody has to get up and let the dog out, wake Betty in time to go to work, feed the kids their breakfast. Even yesterday is not so sharp and clear. With every day, the past loses that quality life has at the moment you're living it. I had to accept that Jim was gone, and that all of our years together were over and there would be nothing more. I was on my own now, a woman past fifty with five children. Somehow I had to find work and make a home for them. I was no longer qualified to teach, and while I could get a little church work and sewing to do at home, they were uncertain and paid little. Yet, somehow I wasn't insecure about the future, worrying about it. I don't know why. How did that old book go?

"The father died . . . Mrs. Pepper had had hard work to scrape together enough money to put bread into her children's mouths and pay the rent on the little brown house . . . 'Poor things!' she would say to herself . . . 'I must get learnin' for 'em someway, but I don't see *how!*' "

Of all the kids, Betty needed help most. She was not in a normal situation, still working at the bakery and almost twenty-four. After the funeral, my brother, Hadwen, wrote, offering me five hundred dollars for ten acres of land in Whittier I'd been left by Mama. On the same land, Papa, as a boy of nine, had held the reins of the oxen while a man went along breaking the virgin sod. There was still time to enroll in the fall 1938 term. I asked her, "Betty, would you like to go back to college?"

"I'd love to. Why?" She said she'd never dreamed of it. Jimmy was a senior that fall. I said, what with the money from the land, we could manage somehow. Betty got a job with NYA, the National Youth Administration, and worked for a professor. She said he mainly kept her busy typing long letters to his family in Woods Hole, Massachusetts. Gamma Phi Beta asked her to pledge. Since we already rented rooms to four college boys, I was counselor to the Oxford Club, the Methodists' college group, and Jimmy was a student there, the Agricultural College was coming to play a big part in our lives. The whole family went to events on campus, and our house was always full of young people.

A little brown house it was, shingled, one-story, five-room, set on a fifty-by-eighty-foot corner lot on the northwestern edge of town just two blocks from the A.C.'s main gate. It was shaded by elms, maples and box elders. We'd lived there two years when Jim died. Though I kept repainting them gray, the front steps were usually scratched up. On the banisters were large pots of geraniums. An old-fashioned wide screen porch ran across the front. Every few years, orange and black box-elder bugs would appear in the trees at the south end. They'd crawl up and down on the outside of the screen, and if you tapped from inside, they fell off.

In summertime the porch was filled with folding steel cots bought second-hand and covered with faded India prints. The bedclothes were wool army and navy surplus blankets and some pink plaid flannel sheets from Mrs. Taylor, Connie's mother. The kids were growing by leaps and bounds, and with them and their friends crawling on and off the beds all day long, the pink flannel usually hung down below the covers like a lady's sagging slip. Peggy and Pat gave puppet shows out on the porch to all the neighborhood children—they had a clown, a wooden soldier, a witch with a red papier-mâché face. Or they'd all go out and play croquet or pom-pom-pullaway or kick-the-can on the boulevard north of the house. It was also the scene of their leaf houses, ghost stories and snowball fights. You could hear their cries the whole day and evening: "It's *my* turn!" "Star light, star bright . . ." ". . . ninety-eight, ninety-nine, one hundred! HERE I COME, READY OR NOT YOU SHALL BE CAUGHT!"

As you crossed the porch and went into the front hall, there was a huge black hall seat, or settee, made of solid oak by my father. He'd copied it from one he'd seen in an illustration of Longfellow's poem "The Hanging of the Crane."

> "The lights are out and gone are all the guests,
>   That thronging came with merriment and jest,
> To celebrate the hanging of the crane . . ."

Once, I broke my toe on it while scrubbing the front porch. It was always piled high with books, musical instruments, the roomers' belongings, sports equipment. It eventually made its way to Idlewild, the Taylors' summer cottage at Detroit Lakes, and left our family for good when the cottage was sold.

Along one wall of the front hall was a coat rack always crammed to capacity with coats—winter and summer coats. People shed their coats there just like snakes. We put ours away out of season. But still there were coats. My goodness, it was terrible. They were always falling down. Overshoes, skates, coats always on the floor, hangers, what a mess! The front door was never locked in all the years we lived there. Over the hall seat was a circular mirror I bought at Woolworth's, there was a scatter rug on the floor and I painted the walls pinkish tan in a stippled effect.

The living room had good oak floors and wainscoting. A sixty-dollar red American Oriental rug got shifted around when it grew too worn and threadbare in places. The davenport was oversized, six inches longer than normal, and it and two overstuffed chairs were covered with blue cretonne slipcovers with floral designs. It was never long before they sagged too. In the afternoons I took a nap on the davenport, detective story in hand. Bill Pepple, a football player from Fessenden who stayed with us all four years he went to college, sometimes crawled between the stool and piano and slept too. I was so tired in those days I could have slept standing up. The piano was an upright one we'd bought secondhand from a storage warehouse. The piano stool came from Mother Critchfield's house in Hunter and it spun like a screw, so the seat would come off. The kids would lie on it and spin, getting dizzy. At Roosevelt Grade School, just two blocks down the street, Peggy had learned how to count time and read music on a cardboard keyboard and sing things like *"Do mi sol mi do . . ."* It was enough to get her started, and soon she was taking lessons. So the piano held her books of Beethoven and Grieg, Betty's torch songs like "Mon Homme" and "It's a Sin to Tell a Lie," Jim's favorites from Sigmund Romberg and Victor Herbert, and all his old 1920s band and minstrel-show music. With so much sheet music it would only take a slight jar to send *"Für Elise"* or "Teaching Little Fingers How to Play" skidding to the floor. On top of the piano were framed photographs of all the kids. Billy said of his, "Who is the man in the picture? Identify him and New York's crime wave is over."

My old pastel to illustrate "The lowing herd wind slowly o'er the lea . . ." was on the wall, as was a pastoral swamp scene Jim had found in the attic of a house where we lived when he was in medical school; it had followed us around ever since. Peg and Pat had a good art teacher at school, Miss Paulsrud, who was teaching them all about "center of interest" and paintings like "Dignity and Impudence," "Feeding Her Birds," "The Blue Boy," "Madame LeBrun and Her Daughter," and "The Horse Fair." In one corner was a small, beveled wooden shelf made by Jimmy, which held one figurine, a tan fawn purchased by Billy at the Treasure Chest, an expensive gift shop downtown. He'd misread the price scribbled on it with a crayon and thought it was twenty-five cents. When the clerk said two dollars fifty, he was too embarrassed not to buy it. That was a lot of money for a high school boy in those days. It took most of his Christmas money that year. The living room also had tan voile curtains which Peg and Pat used to pull back in wintertime so they could scratch their fingernails over the frost on the glass. They'd make the same faces when it tasted like dirt that Betty and Jimmy had made when they were little.

There was an oval-shaped Atwater Kent radio we'd bought in 1931, the year I had Pat. We used to like Chesterfield's "Music That Satisfies," with Ruth Etting, Arthur Tracy and the Boswell Sisters. Now the kids all had their favorite programs ("Jack Armstrong, the Aaaallll American Boy . . ." "A fiery horse with the speed of light . . ." "Who knows what evil lurks in the hearts of men? . . ." Everybody listened to soap operas, too. (". . . the real-life drama of Helen Trent, who . . . fights back bravely, successfully to prove what so many women long to prove in their lives—that because a woman is thirty-five—or more—romance in life need not be over . . .") Peggy even reviewed the soap operas in a handwritten family newspaper she kept up for a couple of years, *The Critchfield News* ("*Against the Storm:* Manwell, Cathy's boyfriend, changed identification papers with Bono, who was going to die . . . *Kitty Keen:* Charles raved on, and he, Bob and Jim talked about going into the trucking business . . .") On Saturday afternoons while I did my housework there was the Metropolitan Opera with Milton Cross. Pat got illustrated children's versions of the librettos at the public library (". . . Isolde gazes at Tristan in terror. 'Must I live?' she gasps, and sinks, half-fainting, on his breast.") For days, Pat would go around the house a hunchbacked Rigoletto, Lohengrin arriving in his swanboat, or what I think was supposed to be a Valkyrie in full cry: *"Yo-ro-to-HO!"*

Then there were the radio commercials. A man kept repeating, "Lucky Strike means fine tobacco." Or there was: "Pepsi-Cola hits the spot; Twelve full ounces, that's a lot; Twice as much for a nickel too; Pepsi-Cola is the drink for you. Nickel, nickel, nickel, nickel, Trickle, trickle, trickle, trickle . . ."

The telephone was on an end table. (Peggy in *The Critchfield News:* "Mother talked on the phone for a century today. I'm not supposed to listen but I have ears. She talked about pensions. And hospital insurance. And getting work. And doctor bills and tonsils and glasses. When she finished talking to Mrs. Browning she made an appointment for Billy and Pat to get their eyes tested . . .")

Behind the phone was a bookcase, which held a dozen novels by Richard Harding Davis, Richard Halliburton's *The Way of a Transgressor,* Tolstoy's *The Kreutzer Sonata,* a German-language mystery titled *Die Verschwindene Miniatur, As the Earth Turns,* by Gladys Hasty Carroll, college yearbooks and high school annuals, a set of Wonder Books, *Heidi, Little Women, Alice in Wonderland,* a collection of Shakespeare's tragedies and comedies, some of Jim's old medical books, the Bobbsey Twins series, Webster's dictionary, a King James Bible, several dozen paperback murder mysteries and a stack of library books. Books went in and out of the house in shopping bags. It got so bad I had to impose a "books and papers" ban at the supper table. You could only bring them on Friday nights. One of Jim's old anatomy books had a large colored illustration of the human body in which all the parts were numbered and detachable. Parts were always falling out. You'd find a liver or a large intestine lying around the living room floor. The kids would joke, "How's your thirty-seven tonight?" "Is your eighty-four working?"

The dining room's most distinguishing feature was a plate rail which went around the entire room about three feet from the ceiling. Peggy once absent-mindedly put a pound of butter on it while leaving the ration book in the icebox. The plate rail held everything but plates: keys, letters, money for the paper boy, beer steins from my father's collection, tickets for sports events or college plays. The south side of the dining room had a built-in window seat which ran under four bay windows, also hung with voile curtains. They looked out on our next-door neighbors, the Newtons, who once had a Peeping Tom. One of the Newton girls, Bunny, a pretty blond, was taking a shower when a man's face appeared in the window. He'd used a piece of our lawn furniture to stand on. Bunny screamed and screamed. Violet, her fat sister, was mad at Bunny for just standing there. She said, "If it had been me, I'd have just reached over and turned off the light." When he heard this, Billy said, "Who'd want to see Violet without clothes?"

The dining table was round and solid oak, an extension table Jim bought when he was in medical school. The extra leaves hadn't come with it, so Jim sawed boards to fit, which we used when we needed to expand it for company. This gave the table considerable personality—you couldn't lean on the middle leaves with your elbows, or the other end came up like a teeter-totter and you got your dinner in your lap. The table was always in use. Here we ate on Sundays and holidays, brooded over jigsaw puzzles and chess sets, Monopoly games, Old Maid and ouija boards, built model airplanes, spread out magazines and newspapers, colored pictures with crayons, modeled with clay, wrote to Aunt Mary and Uncle Burke, puzzled over algebra problems, set sacks of groceries, piled up books or just sat and drank coffee and talked. At the height of the Depression there was a spell when everybody who was without work used to come over and spend hours sitting around our dining-room table, decorating paper plates. Billy fringed a plate with tiny red diamonds he painstakingly cut from an old pack of cards; he put the Queen of Diamonds in the center. Jimmy cut out characters from "Boots and Her Buddies" and "Thimble Theater" in the funny papers and painted on "Pappy," his nickname for Pat, in gold letters. A friend of Betty's named Elaine dropped in out of the blue and did an exotic ram's-head design. After she'd gone, Billy said, "Elaine always looks like she's been up all night." Betty's comeback: "Probably has."

In one corner of the dining room, by the hot-air register, was a big old morris chair, where Betty, when she still worked at the bakery, would sit and fall asleep, she was so tired. Billy used to say, "Betty's spent half her waking life in a pink chenille robe." The stairwell to the attic was always loaded with things left there by somebody intending to take them up later: books, clothes, tennis rackets, skates, Tinker Toys, little trucks that always seemed to have a wheel missing. Like the road to hell, the stairs were paved with good intentions.

Except when we moved out to the front porch in summer, the family slept up in the attic so we could rent both downstairs bedrooms to students. Jimmy put Masonite walls in, dividing it into two rooms. It was dark brown Masonite he got from Mr. Taylor and had been used to line freight cars. It wasn't very strong. You could put your hand through it and people rough-housing sometimes did. One Christmas, Betty and Jimmy used some left-over Masonite to build a big dollhouse for Peggy. In the front room, where Jimmy, Billy and Bill Pepple slept, there was a window seat with two wolf hides and a lot of books in it. Billy used to lie there and read. My dad's old buffalo coat was always lying around. There was an old pre-World War I globe somebody had bought for twenty-five cents at a rummage sale. Billy liked geography, and my brother, Hadwen, who had now been all over the world and was a member of the Royal Geographic Society in London for his work in exploring volcanoes, used to quiz Billy when he came to visit. "What's the highest mountain in Iceland, Billy?" Hadwen also gave Billy a box of steamer-trunk labels from all the famous hotels where he'd stayed, like the Continental in Paris and Shepheard's in Cairo. The boys kept their clothes in a valuable eighteenth-century cherrywood bureau, handed down in my family from the Hadwens in Rhode Island.

In the other room, Betty and Peggy slept in one bed and, when he was little, Pat and I in the other. Billy used to say we "lived in squalor." It didn't seem so bad at the time. It could get terribly cold in the attic in winter. If somebody left a window open, snow might sift in and you'd wake up in the morning to find a little drift at the foot of the bed. We slept under great warm feather ticks, and if the temperature dropped way down I fixed hot-water bottles. When I put Peg and Pat to bed, they always said their prayers: "Now I lay me down to sleep, I pray the Lord my soul to keep . . ." When it came to the "God bless" part, they'd name not only Jim and all the family members, but also Peggy's dolls, including Nellie, who had only one eye left, Rags, our dog, Fluffy and Tiger, the cats, and Mrs. Newton and Mrs. Harmon and all the neighbors. Nobody got left out. In the morning, the kids would leap out from under the covers, make a mad dash downstairs and stand in front of the hot-air register, shivering in their flannel night suits until they got warm.

From Billy:

". . . We always had roomers. Grant and Della were the first. Street? No, that's Perry Mason's secretary. They had both bedrooms downstairs. Mother fixed a kitchen for them in the hallway, right outside the bathroom. It was very inconvenient. There was just the one bathroom for a dozen people, besides a shower Mom had rigged up in the basement (which was too cold and public to use most of the time). Somebody was always standing outside the locked door, calling, 'I've got a hurry call!' I don't know how we managed.

"Two of the roomers were Walter and Julius, North Dakota boys right off the farm. Walter was obnoxious. He was six foot two and frequently phoned his girlfriend, saying, 'Hello, Bunny, this is Wa Wa.' Walter had a habit of waiting for the evening paper and sneaking it off to his room before anybody had a chance to read it. Julius was also uncouth, but he later shaped up and became a smooth fraternity man. One time at Christmas, Betty caught Julius under the mistletoe and kissed him. 'What did you do that for?' he asked. He'd never heard of mistletoe before. Later, Walter's younger brother, Dopey, came to live with us. Everybody called him that because he looked like Walt Disney's dwarf. Then there was Don Bannister, who, after he moved out, came back to our house like a homing pigeon every time he got drunk. And Harold Zumpf, or Zumpfy as we all called him, a big, raw, good-hearted farm boy from Hamberg, near Fessenden . . ."

From Harold Zumpf, a successful Florida construction engineer and real estate developer, fifty years later:

". . . Our dad was born in Germany and believed in work—it came first, second and third. School was considered a sort of reward. It sure was easier than staying home on the farm . . . During my teens we went through the Great Depression and the dust storms. One year, we didn't harvest a single kernel of grain. We had to kill our cattle to keep them from starving to death. The government paid us ten dollars a head. That was what made me tell Dad I wanted to go to college. 'I know we don't have the money,' I said, 'but with your blessing and fifty dollars of the wages I earned on Kittleson's threshing rig, I'd like to see how far I could go.'

"I caught the Great Northern local—we called it the 'Dinkey'—to Fargo with a paper suitcase holding everything I owned. The dean of men signed me up for the NYA and said, 'Here's the address of a lady that takes in roomers. It'll be cheaper than the dorm and it's close.' When I got to the house, Mrs. Critchfield came to the door, and after I told her my name and that we farmed near Hamberg, she said, 'Why, come in. My husband delivered you and I was his nurse.' Don Bannister and I ended up staying in the back bedroom. I was really a dumb country kid. Mrs. Critch understood. I'd confide in her and she'd explain things—never making me feel foolish. Without her help, I don't know what might have happened to me. Later, I got work at the school cafeteria and unloading box cars of lignite at twenty-five cents a ton. When I went back home in the spring, I had more than fifty dollars in cash in my pocket and I felt that anybody could do anything if they wanted it badly enough . . ."

Betty:

". . . Once, two of the roomers brought home a couple of blondes in jodhpurs. Mom kicked them out. One of the blondes stole some perfume of mine from the bathroom and left a damn gold-sequined butterfly . . . Jimmy's gang from college was always around too. One of them, Sammy Starbuck, passed out twice at our house. The second time, they took him over to the Sigma Chi house and he woke up and thought he was dead. I was scared the neighbors would see him being carried out. In the Sigma Chi living room it was pitch dark and cold and Sammy thought it was Hell.

"Another time, Jimmy and some of his friends took Pat and Peggy out to dinner at Powers' Coffee Shop downtown. They had a singer from Jamestown. Jimmy sent Pat up to ask her to sing 'Sweetheart of A.T.O.' Later she joined Benny Goodman's band and had her first big hit with 'Why Don't You Do Right?' It was Peggy Lee.

"Sometimes, Jimmy's gang went riding. Out at the Wanda Clare Riding Stables, they had miles of trails, but you had to be careful if you galloped, as every time the owner took too much to drink, he'd go around closing the gates. They'd also drive out to Dilworth, a little town over in Minnesota that had Fargo's only nightclub. A dump. The Spanish Castle, El Rancho, Venice Gardens, La Florentine—the name kept changing over the years. One time, Jimmy and Ross Porter went out there. It was the night before Easter and Mom insisted that we all go to the Methodists' annual Sunrise Breakfast. Jimmy and Ross came without going to bed. I told them, 'I'd swear my grapefruit tastes like gin. It's like eating a Tom Collins for breakfast.' They were blowing gin breaths across the table.

"As counselor to the Methodists' Oxford Club, Mom was in a spot, as her own children didn't want to go and take part. The Oxford Clubbers were mostly poor, shy, bashful students from little North Dakota towns who lived in rented rooms and were lonely. There were no fraternity or sorority types. They played games. Supper was ten cents, the women's circles at church took turns putting it on. Afterwards, the whole gang would walk across town to our house. Almost two miles. Mother would make black coffee and her famous hot chocolate cake. Sometimes they'd square dance and I'd play 'Little Brown Jug' over and over with a cigarette dangling from one corner of my mouth. Or they'd all come over and listen to the radio. It was always the same. 'One Man's Family' ('. . . dedicated to the mothers and fathers of the younger generation and to their bewildering offspring'). And after that, 'Lights Out.' It was a real scary program and everybody would lie on the living room floor in the dark. It was always something horrible. An amoeba would keep growing and growing. A shrewish wife would turn into a cat. I'd go into the bathroom and turn the water on in the sink and the bathtub and I'd sit on the toilet seat and read a book. Even so I'd hear a lot of loud gurgling and screaming noises. Sometimes Jimmy and his friends would walk in on this mass of Oxford Clubbers."

Anne:

Everybody liked that devil's food cake. One day a woman at church asked me for the recipe. She said her son had eaten some at our house and raved about it. I was embarrassed to tell her. It was sugar and cocoa, lard, water, flour and one egg. No milk or butter. I frosted it with powdered sugar. The secret was to eat this cake hot. That's why it tasted so good.

When it was just the family, we ate in the kitchen most of the time. Peg or Pat said grace, usually running the words together: "God-is-good-and-God-is-great-we-thank-him-for-our-food-amen-pass-the-mashed-potatoes!" *"Please* pass the potatoes." "PLEEZ pass the potatoes!" Sometimes I'd make a terrible face and tell them about the Goops, "The Goops they licked their fingers, the Goops they licked their knives, the Goops they lived such disgusting lives!" Peggy would look horrified, but I suspect Pat rather relished the notion of being a Goop. She was so good to him; he might poke, pinch or hit her, but she'd never fight back. (Peggy in *The Critchfield News:* ". . . The first fight today was between Pat and I. I sat down to lunch first. Then Pat got a chair and came. He moved his chair real close to mine. Then he complained that I was sitting in his chair. Don't you think I am right?" After this, printed in childish capital letters, was "LIKE MUD, BY PAT."

The kitchen had an old gas stove, a table covered with oilcloth, wooden chairs, a pattern linoleum and a corner sink where Peg and Pat did the dishes at night. The curtains were fiesta-colored: orange, green, blue and yellow in panels separated by white rickrack. I bought the icebox from Mrs. Newton when she got her refrigerator. The iceman came every three days and you had to remember to turn up the card in the window with "100, 75, 50 and 25" on it, so he'd know how many pounds of ice to carry in, using tongs and a black leather shoulder pad. Usually, twenty-five was plenty. We got scraps, ostensibly for Rags and the cats, every other day or so from the Liedermans, who ran the Roosevelt Grocery Store down on the next corner. Old Mr. Liederman had come from Germany as a boy. Sometimes I'd find four or five perfectly good wieners and often the small end of a chunk of dried beef, or a soup bone. When Billy found out I was using these for meals, he protested, "Living on scraps? Is it true, Mom? Good God, eating dog food!" "Oh, I think Mr. Liederman sometimes deliberately puts in good things," I told him. Betty chimed in, "Sometimes the weenies aren't too wrinkled or dried-up-looking." We had certain dishes a lot: creamed wieners on toast, Welsh rarebit, bread pudding, macaroni and cheese, spaghetti, salmon patties—salmon was seventeen cents a can—and our special Sunday dinner of veal, peas and noodles. We were never so poor that we couldn't have company. One time, Ross Porter was at our house on a day we were going to have fried chicken, something we couldn't afford very often. And Betty said, "Go home, Ross. We don't want to share it." But Ross stayed and got fed.

One time, the doorbell rang. Jimmy went to the door and a man gave him an envelope. In it was ten dollars. The man said Jim never sent him a bill and he figured this was what he owed. The same thing happened twice. I canned a lot of fruit and vegetables and that made a big difference. A few blocks north, where the houses thinned out and there were no trees, just vacant lots and open prairie beyond, we had a big vegetable garden. Everybody worked there, and in the fall we'd clear it with the help of all the kids in the neighborhood. Afterward, everybody would stay for a giant bonfire and marshmallow roast. In the backyard we also had plots of zinnias, marigolds and hollyhocks. Outside the kitchen I raised gourds on trellises, built from laths and painted white, and Jimmy built a birdbath out of rocks and cement, with a washbasin imbedded in the top.

The basement had a central furnace, and I usually shoveled in coal and took out the clinkers myself. The coal man backed his truck right up to a basement window and emptied coal down a chute into a bin. Since we had twelve or more people for the one bathroom, I rigged up an extra shower behind the furnace to use in the summertime. There was also a large cement cistern down there; a frog lived inside. One time, a truck carrying wood broke down outside in the street and I offered the man a good price for a whole load of corded hardwood. He dumped it all on the boulevard. The neighborhood kids played in it for days, building forts and having a wonderful time; it was like a giant mountain for them. At last, Peg and Pat and the other kids threw it into the basement through a window, with some help from Billy.

One night, we had no butter. There was no money to buy any. When I told the kids, we just sat there for a moment. Then they roared with laughter. They found the idea of being that poor howlingly funny.

Anne

The Agricultural College had a big cultural influence on our lives. It was so near. The Little Country Theater was under Alfred G. Arvold, a marvelous impresario who'd started out as an advance man for William Jennings Bryan on the chautauqua circuit. He sent plays all over North Dakota, had met George Bernard Shaw and in 1939 put together a touring company of *Peer Gynt* which went about the state giving open-air performances in little Norwegian farming towns. The Little Country Theater itself was on the second floor of the college's brick and turreted Old Main. Its stained-glass windows had scenes from *Peer Gynt* ("Right along the edge we two clove our passage through the air"), *As You Like It* (" 'Who ever loved that loved not at first sight?' ") and *Faust* ("A look from thee, a word more entertains than all the lore of wisest brains"). Narrow, steep steps to the third floor were inscribed with lines from Shakespeare's "All the world's a stage, and all the men and women merely players . . ." And Betty's favorite line: "At first the infant, mewling and puking in the nurse's arms . . ."

Billy:

". . . I can still remember the thrill of the theater, which has never left me. Very exciting. The crowd coming in, everybody converging and finding their seats and getting settled, the houselights dimming. They were all plays by Ibsen and other great dramatists. *Ghosts. A Doll's House. The Cherry Orchard, Wuthering Heights.* Gloom and oppressiveness. They also put on *Our Town* every year. Betty would be Mrs. Webb, pretending to make breakfast and calling upstairs to Emily to hurry up, she didn't want to have to tell her again."

Jimmy, from a letter to Billy:

". . . You and I were raised in rather different ways—living in a city while you were growing up you naturally were exposed to more things and became more of a student. I just lived the normal small-town kid's existence of hanging around farms, playing baseball, swimming in the Jim River . . . To be honest I don't know which is best . . ."

Anne:

Betty majored in speech, and when she started being in plays, the whole family went to see her. She mostly had small roles—Wowkle, the Indian squaw in *Girl of the Golden West;* Rheba, the black maid in *You Can't Take It with You;* the Lady Crook in *Sherlock Holmes.* So she was terribly pleased to be elected president of the Edwin Booth Dramatic Club. She told us that during the initiation ceremonies she had to stand with her hand on a skull, lit from within by a red light, and solemnly intone, "Alas, poor Yorick, as he is now, so will we be . . ." She said her punch line came at the end: "An eye for an eye, a tooth for a tooth! College, college! Edwin Booth!" Her biggest role was "Flora, the housekeeper's daughter," in *Leave It to Jane,* the yearly campus musical show. She dyed her hair bright red for the role and sang her big "Cleopatterer" number in a tight yellow sweater:

> "In days of old beside the Nile
> A famous queen there dwelt;
> Her clothes were few, but full of style;
> Her figure slim and svelt;
> On ev'ry man that wandered by
> She pulled the Theda Bara eye . . ."

Betty sang so awful, deliberately, that a woman sitting next to me said, "My, doesn't that girl have a terrible voice?"

Besides the plays, Mr. Arvold brought many famous artists to the college for his Lyceum series. We all went over to Festival Hall, a white wooden building on campus, for these performances, even Peg and Pat. We had Nelson Eddy, Fritz Kreisler, Marian Anderson, Kirsten Flagstad, Lawrence Tibbett, Yehudi Menuhin, Richard Crooks, Eugene Ormandy, Alfred Lunt and Lynn Fontanne in *There Shall Be No Night* . . .

Betty:

". . . Eva Le Gallienne wore a tight satin dress in *Hedda Gabler* and got whistled at by all the farm boys. Grace Moore was real nasty to a boy from the college paper. Rachmaninoff wouldn't play until they fixed the piano bench but he performed his 'Prelude in C Sharp Minor' for an encore.

Richard Halliburton talked about Africa and said, 'We had this elephant, Elizabeth, who'd been pregnant for two years. I couldn't be held responsible because I was in California at the time.' The audience was shocked.

"Paul Robeson was my favorite. The spring before he came, we received the music for 'Ballad for Americans.' ('In seventy-six the sky was red. Thunder rumbling overhead. Bad King George couldn't sleep in his bed. And on that stormy morn . . . Ol' Uncle Sam was born . . .') Four of Mr. Arvold's speech majors had the speaking parts. Mostly we just shouted out phrases on cue, like 'Coal miner!' 'What *is* an American?' 'What religion?' Robeson sang the rest. ('. . . For nobody who was anybody believed it, everybody who was anybody they doubted it . . .') It was in 1939 and Robeson gave a ten-minute speech about Russia, where he was living. At the Edwin Booth Club luncheon, I sat between Robeson and his accompanist, Lawrence Brown. When the waitresses brought chicken pot pies with orange slices on the side to everybody else and forgot to bring me one, pompous President Eversull, the head of the college, told them to go ahead and eat, saying, 'We have Betty on a diet. All she gets is the orange slices.' Robeson and Brown politely gave me theirs and that's all I got. Later Robeson sent me an autographed picture, saying, 'It was so much fun singing together.'

"Mr. Arvold was very fat. He had a huge stomach, though he always walked home a mile for lunch. He had eyes like gooseberries and did not encourage familiarity, though he had a very nice wife. Old Main had equipment in its bell tower that transformed ordinary records into a bell and chime effect. It played pieces like 'Beautiful Isle of Somewhere' every day at noon. One time, some boys snuck up to the tower and played 'Red Hot Mama.' Mr. Arvold was furious. He got red in the face and nearly had a heart attack. Usually, he completely intimidated his students."

Anne:

He had a great fondness for elaborate public spectacles. In the fall, the students in his Pageants class put one on at El Zagal Golf Course, with covered wagons and Indians. Lilac Day, staged by his Festivals class, came in May. Since Betty was in them—usually riding a horse—we all had to go and see. There was a queen, wearing a lavender dress and a silver crown, and a prince, both of them chosen from the class. The queen was attended by fifty-two maidens . . .

Betty:

". . . Mr. Arvold liked to do everything on a grand scale. He'd go through the enrollment records and pick a girl from every county in North

Dakota. She wore a pastel gown of her own, and Mr. Arvold supplied a lavender sunbonnet. He also hired eight horses from the Wanda Clare Riding Stables. Two or three girls who'd grown up riding would take the fractious horses. I'd end up with some very docile, half-dead old mare. Somebody would always say, 'Gee, Betty, you sure can ride.' The college band would group itself across from the Old Main front steps. A big crowd gathered to watch; Mom and the kids always came. Down the steps came the queen and fifty-two maidens. We eight horse riders had been practicing, and we'd come riding up and perform figure eights and cloverleafs before the steps. Then, from a distance, the prince would come up the winding college road to Old Main. One year, it was Abner Selvig on a white horse, tights and a suit of mail made out of silver bottle caps, scared to death. Abner had never been on a horse before. But he'd enrolled in the class. Everybody was cheering and hollering, 'Heigh-ho, Silver!' Mr. Arvold, up in the tower, would be watching to see if anybody giggled. Abner dismounted from his horse, climbed the steps to the queen and took her hand. Then the band would play and the entire crowd sang 'Lilac Days,' composed by James Golseth, Class of 1935.

" 'Lilac Days, Lilac Days, we welcome you,
Lilac Days, Lilac Days, bring Spring anew . . .'

"The horses, frightened, reared and whinnied. Abner led the queen down the college road, followed by the fifty-two maidens in their sunbonnets, the eight girls on horseback, the band, the crowd and an unobtrusive workman carrying a lilac bush and shovel. At the road, they'd ceremonially plant it. Mr. Arvold's grand scheme was to plant lilac bushes on both sides of the highway the whole ninety miles to the University of North Dakota at Grand Forks. After this ceremony, I'd have to change directly into a pink organdy formal for the Lilac Day Dinner. Boy, did it smell horsey! The food was brought up from Ceres Hall, the college cafeteria, to the Lincoln Log Cabin, another of Mr. Arvold's creations, where we had banquets. Everything was lilac-colored: lavender mashed potatoes, lavender cookies, lavender ice cream, a glass of grape juice, a grapey salad. Mr. Arvold never took much part in these affairs. He only masterminded them behind the scenes . . ."

Billy:

". . . By the time I was twelve, my lifelong habits were already established: going to the theater, drinking tea, reading detective stories and taking long walks. I'd go north of town, out behind the A.C. There was an experimental farm with windbreaks out there and I always used to climb up on one pile of dirt. It must have been about twelve feet high. Sort of a mountain substitute. The North Dakota plains seemed windswept and unfriendly. I instinctively sought out any sign of topography. We went skiing in the wintertime. We'd go over to the Red River and slide down its banks, which were about two ski lengths long . . .

"Books were everything to me. I introduced the kids to Robert Frost and *The New Yorker,* though Pat discovered the opera books by himself. High school was a trauma. I was very hard up. I worked for NYA. It was set up to let students eke out a bare existence. Like being on relief. Only the real crumb bums, the ones that smelled of poverty, were on NYA. I earned six dollars a month, sorting cards in the dean's office. God, that old farmer's jacket I used to wear! Shiny on the outside, with an imitation-leather collar. Grim! Uncle Burke came through with twelve dollars for an overcoat, but the cheapest one was sixteen. It was the only thing he ever gave me, but I came to think of it as a typical Uncle Burke gesture—not that he gave you, but that he never gave you enough.

"Burke would pop in every once in a while and interfere. He was the most gregarious and family-oriented of Father's brothers. Though he married twice, he had no children of his own. Once he became a vice president of the Bank of America in 1934—one of fifty-three—we thought of Burke as our Rich Uncle. After he left the bank, in 1942, he went into wine and then became what he called 'Grain Bin King of America.' He turned out log-cabin-like nail-less wooden bins to store the big wartime wheat crop. When peace came, he converted them into 'Critchfield Cottages' and sold thousands to college campuses as cheap housing for married veterans on the GI Bill. He even tried to sell some to Israel. They were eyesores and terribly cramped. For his retirement, Burke bought a beautiful country place in the Napa Valley, Glass Mountain Ranch—the mountain was obsidian. But he couldn't resist making a fast dollar, and though he was in his eighties he turned it into the Critchfield Tree Farm. People from San Francisco drove up to cut their own Christmas trees. I used to joke I kept running into widows and orphans who'd been bilked by him. Uncle Burke's last grand gesture came in 1970, when he promised to leave the Agricultural College—now North Dakota State University—one hundred thousand dollars in his will. But before he got around to doing anything about it, he had a stroke and died and NDSU never got its money. With all his faults, Uncle Burke was kind of fun to be around. He had life to him.

"In the spring of 1939, when Jimmy was getting out of college and thinking about a job, I carefully researched my atlases and geographies and selected two ideal American towns. One was Eureka, California, and the other

Nevada, Iowa. I was about thirteen at the time. Years later, I passed through Eureka several times. It was a real rough lumber town where the sun shines twice a year.

"Jimmy used to send me on errands to the house of Connie, who if not the girl next door, was the girl who lived five blocks down the street. They'd been going together since high school. It was an apple-green house. One time, I got up early and threw stones at Connie's window. I had a message to convey from Jimmy. I can remember her and Jimmy lying on the sofa together, napping, sort of, right in the bosom of the family. Connie was great-looking, but not pretty. Tremendous homegrown style. She and Ross talked about everything. One time when she came over, she'd been reading *The Good Soldier; A Tale of Passion,* by Ford Madox Ford. Connie had a way of giving you uncalled-for compliments. Like she'd say, 'Bill, it's so wonderful to go places with you because you know so much.' "

From letter by Connie to Billy nine years later when he is a student in California. It is postmarked Vienna but inside she has written, "From Behind the Iron Curtain."

". . . Greetings and Happy New Year, Comrade and Brother Bill (in case the Russians are now censoring the mail & also in case we don't get out so we can be gang bosses in Siberia). One must really do long-range planning here in *'Wien, Wien, nur du allein'*—home of music, wine, women, thieves and intrigue. Billy, I'm hot on a new idea to spend the Critchfield millions—namely, Uncle Burke's—with a few dollars of the rest of ours invested. How about a hunting, fishing and skiing lodge in the West?"

Anne:

One time, Bill and I were walking Connie home. Just as we crossed the railroad tracks, two hoboes came out of the darkness behind some freight cars and approached us. One asked gruffly, "Hey, what town is this?"

"Fargo, North Dakota, the great metropolis of the Northwest," Billy told them.

After we'd walked on, Connie said, "You really boomed that out in a bass voice, Bill."

I told her he'd always had a bass voice, even as a child. He cried in a bass voice.

That last year of college, Jimmy was president of his fraternity and lived at the A.T.O. house, just a block north of us. In the spring, he was offered a regular commission in the Fourth U.S. Cavalry. The Army was rapidly expanding, and West Point couldn't provide all the officers they needed, so they were starting to take a few from R.O.T.C. The major who came to interview candidates was from the cavalry himself, and he and Jimmy got to talking horses. Jimmy was also offered a newspaper job in Iowa, but the Army paid a little more and he and Connie wanted to get married. So he joined America's last horse cavalry, serving first in South Dakota and Kansas and then guarding the Mexican border in southern California. "It's a marvelous life," he wrote home, "riding around on horses and brandishing sabres." Shortly afterward, Poland was invaded.

He didn't get his first leave until Christmas. One Friday night in December, a whole gang of students who'd been downtown drinking decided to come out to our house. There were fifteen or so and it was getting so boisterous, I decided to make Welsh rarebit, hoping they'd quiet down if they ate something. Connie and Betty were helping me in the kitchen. Billy was getting disgusted. All of a sudden, in walked Jimmy in his calvary uniform, boots, breeches and all. He got all the way out to the kitchen before anybody realized he'd come home.

The next summer, he got permission from his commanding officer to marry. He asked Connie if she could be ready in a week. We all tore into it. It was a lovely wedding at the First Methodist Church. All the women there helped. Jimmy spent the whole afternoon gabbing with his friends about whether America should get into the war or stay out. He had to rush and pack his bags and lock them in the trunk of his car at the last minute. He and Connie had been living on snacks, so I made macaroni and cheese with a tossed salad and fresh rolls and coffee and made everybody eat before going to dress for the wedding . . .

In the summertime, the kids loved to go down to Detroit Lakes, where the Taylors had their cottage, or for longer stays in Iowa with Mary and Fay, who hadn't had children and enjoyed them. Viola was just a little farming village in the heart of Iowa's Grant Wood country—all rolling hills, cornfields, woods, limestone bluffs and meandering creeks and rivers. It was another world from North Dakota, and the kids helped mow hay, put up bales in the barn, get the cattle in or, in the evenings, they'd sit and listen to Mary play Chopin or Rachmaninoff.

From a letter by Mary to Billy:

". . . Iowa is lovely now, after freezing here several times much too soon for the good of the crops. The flowers are mostly gone, the leaves are falling, and the grass is very green. I invent all the excuses I can to be outdoors, for these days are rare indeed. About an hour ago, a big flock of geese went directly overhead, about three hundred, I'd judge. They were flying quite low and were straight up from our front yard. The sun shone on them, and they looked golden with black tips on their wings. I don't suppose they were golden at all, but it was a most beautiful sight. One of the compensations for living in a rural locale . . . Your mother picked and hulled a half bushel of walnuts when she was here . . . Remember to drop in whenever you can possibly make it. You are so very welcome. I have got over being surprised at the affection you kids have for Iowa, but we do appreciate it. Come whenever you can . . ."

Billy:

". . . A year after Father died, I spent the whole summer of 1939 in Iowa. Uncle Fay gave me the job of weeding his goldenseal roots. Every afternoon at six o'clock, the train passed through the kiln ground behind Uncle Fay's fields on its way to Stone City and Anamosa on the Wapsipinicon River, and it would blow its whistle. You could hear it coming from down over the hill in the trees. Soon Aunt Mary would come and call us to supper. It seemed like every meal we had leftovers. I don't know what left over from. Mom said it was because Aunt Mary *liked* cold food. I'd go up the road to Aunt Helen's to get filled up on pork chops and mashed potatoes and gravy and chocolate cake.

"I worked all summer and earned twelve dollars. Uncle Fay was to pay by the bed and I guess I was sort of slow. During the summer I read the full-length Nero Wolfe mystery novels in Aunt Mary's huge stacks of *American* magazines. She'd saved them all through the nineteen thirties, and they were all piled up just inside the attic door. It was across from the upstairs guest bedroom where we slept, and we'd sneak one or two magazines out. Eventually, all the family came to spend cozy afternoons becoming acquainted with Wolfe, Mignon G. Eberhart, James Hadley Chase, Fanny Hurst and others. The stories were dramatically illustrated. Aunt Mary believed in naps. She always seemed surprised, though, that we'd go up and appear to nap for such a long time. Actually we were all reading murder mysteries in her *American* magazines.

"Sometimes I'd take a battered copy of *American* and take it out to the meadow of sweet clover by the creek and occasionally slip into the women's stories. You know, the ones that are all alike. I used to like to go down by the orchard, where there was a grove of pine trees. During the Iowa summers, I slept out on the back porch. Aunt Mary and Uncle Fay would tell me about all the different kinds of birds and plants. Everybody kept milk cows then, so the pastures were like parks. You could walk under the big lime bluffs along the creek all the way to the Wapsipinicon River and Stone City. We used to like to climb up the same hill where Grant Wood had stood when he painted *Stone City.* Not much had changed since 1930. We could see the same stone church to the left, the limestone quarry that cut deep into the facing hill, the store, water tower, windmills and farms across the Wapsipinicon, and the road from Viola crossing the bridge and winding like a ribbon over the hills toward Anamosa and out of view. *Stone City* and *American Gothic,* which he did one after the other, were Wood's first two paintings in the humorous midwestern style that made his work such a hit in those days.

"I'll never forget a lovely ramble we took in Iowa through a hill of black-eyed Susans. Through the kiln ground, where they'd once baked bricks, across the tracks and the creek, up a little gully and onto a lovely hill just covered with daisies. It was that same summer, and Jimmy and Connie had driven down on their way to Fort Riley, Kansas. Jimmy took pictures with his Kodak, while Peg and Connie picked black-eyed Susans. Those daisy pictures still have a lyrical quality. Nothing special happened. It was just a perfect morning . . ."

From a letter by Pat in Iowa. It is to Anne and begins: "Saludos amigos! *And how is the gracious lady of Critchfield manor?" He is about ten or twelve.*

". . . This morning from seven o'clock to eleven Viola and its surroundings had the worst and most merciless, terrible, crop-wrecking, garden-demolishing, railroad-destructive rains it has had for thirty-five years . . . I awoke. It was a cold, gray day. Suddenly all the lights went out, plunging the room into ghastly darkness. The sky was black and torrents of rain were pouring down. The telephone rang. It was Aunt Mary, calling that the creek had become a torrent of destruction . . . Adieu . . ."

A postscript adds: "I can whistle now any time you wish. I believe everyone can do things if they try hard enough and long enough, don't you?"

Anne:

Making a home had proved easier than finding work. I took an examination for a postal clerk's job, but while I scored the highest, it was a political appointment and the postmaster wouldn't hire a woman. Then, at last, something turned up. Mrs. Browning phoned one day to say she'd seen an ad in the paper, the city was looking for a policewoman. The starting salary was fourteen hundred dollars. I thought if I got that I'd be rich. I took the test without much hope of getting the job. There were a lot of applicants. Still, all those years of reading murder mysteries gave me some familiarity with terms like alibi, postmortem and habeas corpus.

About two months later, the Police Department phoned one day and asked me to come in. I reported to the station downtown and they gave me some clerical work to do. Soon a tourist-park policeman brought in two boys. One was carrying a brand-new Boy Scout ax. They'd been caught chopping down trees in a park south of town. He left it up to me what to do. That first day and from then on, I was given pretty much of a free hand. I thought: let the punishment fit the crime. I told the boys they must memorize Joyce Kilmer's "Trees." They did. I was to work as a policewoman eight years. Just in my last few months, a big husky policeman came up to me, grinned, and began, "I think that I shall never see . . ."

Also that first day, a middle-aged woman and a girl of about fifteen came in. They were green-looking country women from down in Minnesota, a girl and her aunt. The aunt said, "This girl's father wants her to come home, but she don't wanna go." I checked with the detectives, then told her that since the girl was a minor, her father had a legal right to bring her back. The two of them hemmed and hawed for some time, then the aunt spoke up again.

"Her oldest sister at home, he treats her like a wife. And Emma, this girl, she don't wanna be treated like a wife."

Emma spoke. "I'll wake up in the night and Agnes will be gone from her bed. And I'll hear her in the next room, begging Pa to leave her alone, crying and begging." The sister was twenty, Emma fifteen. The mother was dead. I went over and talked to the chief and the detectives and they asked Emma to come in for questioning. Emma was timid and didn't want to say anything. Life had made her timid. The county attorney swore out a warrant for the arrest of Emma's father on an incest charge, but Emma refused for five hours to say anything more. She'd sit and cry, "Oh, poor Daddy, poor Daddy . . ." Emma's father got fifteen years in the state penitentiary. I brought Emma home and kept her a week with our family. I felt she was more sinned against than sinning. She was very quiet and ate with us. Fargo had no place for juveniles in those days. Mrs. T., the wife of a plumber, agreed to have Emma come in and clean her house once a week. When she heard about the case, she called me up and became hysterical, saying, "That girl's been in my house and contaminated my children." In time, Emma went to live at the Y.W.C.A., got a job as a waitress and later moved to California. I think she always had mixed emotions in regard to me.

I was soon "Critchie" to most of the policemen. The only other policewoman, Lucy Hoffman, was also a doctor's widow. A former Presbyterian, she'd turned Catholic when her daughter decided to become a nun, though she later withdrew before taking her final vows, married and had seven children. I found there were all kinds of policemen. Some had college educations, others hadn't finished fourth grade, many had entered during the Depression, a few had been juvenile delinquents. My favorite was Captain Peterson, a severe-looking but really gentle man who loved to raise flowers and was adored by his children. Jack, one of the younger detectives, who was later killed in a prison break, was one of the kindest men I ever knew.

Fargo in those days had no black families, but it did have four colored prostitutes. When a former navy commander took over as police chief and decided to run them out of town, I was given the unpleasant job of telling them. They were on a much higher intellectual plane than Fargo's white prostitutes; three of them subscribed to the Book of the Month Club. One had graduated from the University of California at Berkeley; she'd had a good job when a new boss, a Southerner, fired her. They were choosier in their clientele, too. The prettiest, Crystal Brown, had been forced into it by her husband, who ran a white-slave ring in St. Paul. When I ran into her at Penney's just before she left town, she asked me to join her for a cup of coffee. She told me how she supported a fourteen-year-old son from a previous marriage at a good boarding school; he didn't know what she did. Some of the prostitutes hated their lives; others were happy. One fell in love with a barber who was almost a foot shorter than she was. A very lovely girl lived in the Gladstone Hotel, and her clientele was made up of Fargo's elite. She was awfully attractive and one of the cops fell in love with her. It was tragic, as he was married to a mousy little thing.

One time, the Greyhound buses abruptly changed schedules, leaving some people stranded overnight. There was a Mrs. John Quincy Adams, who was a courthouse clerk somewhere in California; she hadn't counted on the delay and had run short of money. Three fifteen-year-old girls from Duluth had the same problem. I brought them all home. Mrs. Adams slept out on the front porch with us, and we improvised beds for the girls on the davenport and by pushing the overstuffed chairs together. Billy said, "It's got so at our house you never know whom you'll wake up beside—a prostitute, a stranded bus passenger or a girl being rescued from incest."

As I wrote Mary, it was really very much like housekeeping. You just tried to keep the town all cleaned up. I was given a great deal of freedom whether to arrest culprits or just take them home and try to set them on the right track. Every night, I'd work four o'clock to midnight and I'd make all the liquor stores to see that women weren't drinking at the bar, that there were no minors and that all was being conducted in an orderly way. I'd visit the bus station and the hotels, where I'd go over the registers, and the Crystal Ballroom—Lawrence Welk and his band sometimes played there for dances in those days. I also visited movie theaters to keep an eye out for men molesting young girls. Magazine salesmen seemed to be a generally immoral lot; they frequently got caught "resorting to rooms."

Some people felt sorry for me, but I *liked* being a policewoman. You saw the same people every day. They were pleased to have somebody to listen to their troubles. Sometimes you could help. I enjoyed it. It did seem to bother Peggy, who was innately ladylike, and it may have encouraged Pat to be wilder than he was already, forever getting sent to the principal's office at school. But the three older kids were darn glad I had the job. All in all, it was simply keeping house on a big scale. So life seemed to have settled down for us at last—or does it ever?

Billy:

". . . We were sitting around the dining-room table eating our usual Sunday dinner of veal, peas and noodles with Jell-O for dessert. The living room radio was on low, playing 'Swing and Sway with Sammy Kaye.' Everybody was talking, so we didn't pay much attention when the music stopped and the announcer began to speak. I just heard Mom's sharp intake of breath, saw her face and listened: '. . . in a statement today that the Japanese had attacked Pearl Harbor, Hawaii, from the air . . . A second air attack has been reported on army and navy bases in Manila . . .' Ross had just been saying that he'd go to jail before he'd go to war. His brother died that morning at Pearl Harbor and he enlisted the next day . . ."

Anne:

Grandmother Critchfield was spending more and more time with us. One hot July afternoon, she told me she was ailing. She got severe pains in her stomach, she said. "I'd like something hot, Anne," she told me. "I'd love some chicken soup." After she sipped some and swallowed one of the yellow Nembutal pills her doctor had prescribed, I brushed her hair and rubbed her back. The front bedroom was empty, so I'd put her in there. "Anne, you're so good to me . . . You're so good to me . . . You're so good to me . . ." She must have repeated it about twenty times as she drowsed off to sleep. I went down to the police station to ask the chief for the evening off. I wanted to stay home with her. While I was gone, Betty phoned.

"Mom!" she exclaimed. "You'll never guess who's here. Your little boy's come home!" Billy had come all the way from Seattle for sixty hours' leave before going back to join Navy boot camp. I rushed home. Sometime later, I was ironing and went in to take a look at Grandma. She was a pale, yellowish, unnatural color I hadn't seen before. I called to Betty. "I can't hear Mother breathe." She was eighty-two. Burke and Ray came as soon as they could. They were terribly shocked. I told Billy I'd have to go up to Hunter with Burke to help make the funeral arrangements. He fussed. "Oh, Mom, you can't go! Grandma would pick now of all times!" Of course I did. It was the last of the funerals in that house . . .

Further comment from Merland Carr, of Hunter:

". . . His wife lived on almost forty years after Dr. Henry Critchfield died. She was a very independent old lady. Used to live in that great big old house all alone. She'd come down and collect her own mail at the post office every day. Never sent anybody else. She walked down herself. A year before she died, she couldn't pay six hundred dollars in back taxes she owed on the house. I expect she never told anybody . . ."

From Jim's sister, Kathryn:

". . . She used to say Father had performed the first appendectomy in North Dakota. I don't know if it was true or not, but they'd come out in the eighteen-eighties, when it was just being settled, and he'd brought all those fast horses with him, race horses from Ohio. Mother was overcome when he died. I don't think she ever got over it. Her hair turned white right away, and she'd been so pretty. There was never any money. Uncle Lyman came up from Ohio for Father's funeral and he was going to collect, but he antagonized people. They said we'd have got a lot more if just one of us had asked for it. I think it was too hard trying to raise six children. One time, we went to stay with Aunt Matilda in Minneapolis, and when we went to go home, she told Mother, 'Don't bring those boys back until they're all over twenty-one.' "

From Jimmy:

". . . I remember it was a Saturday at Camp Lockett, California. I was a young squadron commander and I was sitting on my horse at the head of a column of troops that were getting ready to march out on the parade ground. And one of the orderlies from headquarters trotted up on a horse, saluted, and said, 'Colonel, I have a telegram for you. It just came.' It said, 'Grandmother passed away yesterday, Mother.'

"And I folded it up, put it into my pocket and thought, 'She was a great lady.' That was the last parade, I think, I ever went to. Right after that, we left for North Africa . . ."

Extracts from two V-mail letters home, the first from Jimmy in Europe, dated January 1944. A battalion commander, he is a much-decorated combat veteran after fighting in North Africa, Italy, France and Germany:

". . . Christmas found my battalion getting a much needed rest near Strasbourg after one hundred and thirty-two days of continuous combat from the Riviera to the Rhine. I haven't missed five minutes of duty until now and am beginning to feel like a fugitive from the law of averages; however, at present am in a rest camp recovering a little vim and vigor back. Felt quite exhausted, more mentally than physically, when I arrived here. Expect to be back with my unit next week . . ."

The second is from Billy, with the Navy in the Pacific:

". . . I guess we're getting rather stale, being on one island for almost ten months, doing the same kind of work and seeing the same fellows every day. It's hard to understand the monotony of it, before we came over here I never believed I'd get so tired of one spot . . . It's just about sunset now, though there's no spectacular sunset tonight as there often is. The western sky is cloudy, there's a cool breeze blowing, and it'll probably rain during the movie . . ."

Billy, forty years later:

". . . All my youth I had a cigar box, sort of a treasure chest. In it were a dried carnation, a U.S. Navy name stencil saying, "February 17, Ship Island, Miss.," a yellowed ivory geisha girl clasping a rose and being pulled in a rickshaw—the rickshaw had a broken wheel—and a Christmas-tree ornament, a sequined-covered bird with a white brush tail. There was also a photograph of me and two other sailors posing with a little old lady in a black coat and hat. It was taken at the Little Country Church of Hollywood on Mother's Day, 1944. She invited two army and two navy men home to dinner. Our hostess was Mrs. D. E. Sharron of Romaine Street. She was about four feet tall and had a black satin hat that opened on top like a clam . . ."

Epilogue

Somewhere in the back of my mind, buried way down deep like something half forgotten, like a dream, there's a hazy picture of a man in a Model T, wheezing along a country road, the only moving thing in a flat and treeless land. The land is so big and empty, it seems as if he ought to be able to see right up to the North Pole, with nothing but earth and sky in between. You can feel the raw chill, hear the wind shriek, see the lonely homestead, way off on the horizon, where he must be going. The dream picture fades into another and he's lifting you onto a barstool and setting a foaming glass of beer in front of you—thrilling, because you're only five years old. And when you find it tastes bad and wrinkle up your nose, he's amused. This fades into other images, just as shadowy. A silver loving cup. A buffalo coat. Medical books. A cornet. A pair of comic flowered pants. A black bag. Forceps. Funny wooden golf clubs. Dog-eared sheet music from old movie musicals. Relics lying around the house as we were growing up. Artifacts from an archaeological dig. Like potsherds, broken bricks, shards of sickles and spears, bits of human bone. Put it all together and come up with a culture. Figure out what they were like. What *he* was like.

"Kind," Anne said. "His own worst enemy." "An easy man to live with," "a wonderful doctor," who "never lost a mother, never lost a baby," "never refused a call." A man who lost control, broke down, failed to adapt, "made a mess of his life," drank himself into an early grave. And Betty: "Everybody liked Daddy because he was real fun." We come back where we started: How much of what he did was decided by his own nature and how much by his culture and time? And what does this say about us and our freedom to choose?

On a hot afternoon one day after the war, in 1948, near Mechanicsville, Iowa, just a few miles from Martelle, where Anne was born and our story began, a farm tractor with a load of hay happened to pull out on the highway just at the exact moment a car came over the next hill at high speed. In the car were Connie and a young man who had just become engaged to Peggy, David Baldwin, the son of Fargo's mayor. Connie was going to Washington to meet Jimmy, and David planned to go on to New England for a sailing trip. The man on the tractor was unhurt, Connie died instantly and David the next morning.

This ended, almost in a matter of days, the Critchfield family's stay in North Dakota—it had lasted sixty-two years in all, scarcely a single lifetime. Yet it had shaped the lot of us, and made us what we were. Anne went off to Germany to spend two years with Jimmy, who was stationed there, and his two small children, taking Peggy with her. Betty was married, and Bill and I —Pat—left for school on the West Coast. Except for Anne and myself, nobody ever went back, and I didn't go back for thirty-four years.

Extracts of Anne's letters from Europe to her sister Mary in Iowa:
"Aug. 14, 1948 . . . When we went to bed it was darker than a stack of black cats. I woke up in the morning and went out on the balcony. A man was driving an ox-cart by the hotel. Then I knew I was in Germany. Our house is 82 Geiselgasteigstrasse, Harlocking, Munich . . .
"Dec. 20, 1948 . . . You should see the fabulous cookie houses in the bakery windows. Frosted Bavarian roofs. I hope the cuckoo clocks came O.K. . . .
"Jan. 9, 1949 . . . So many beggars at the door. Today I had a man and his wife who were on their way to Hanover, no money, no food, she was obviously pregnant, it was snowing and she had some kind of cloth shoes on. Hardly a day goes by that we do not feed at least one or two poor people. Here in Bavaria more displaced people are coming all the time, trying to get away from the Russians . . .
"Feb. 23, 1949 . . . I went to a big card party at the Munich Women's Club this afternoon and won the prize. My playing has picked up a lot . . .
"Feb. 26, 1949 . . . Peggy and I went on a wonderful trip to Tivoli—about twenty miles from Rome out in the country. We had a guide and driver and visited the Palace of Hadrian, an immense place and very beautiful. A lovely walk between cypress trees, so tall & stately & more than four hundred years old. We lunched out of doors and the sunshine was so warm . . . Our

hotel, the Flora, is right across from the Villa Umberto, a lovely park—ancient statues, palm trees, many sidewalk cafes . . . To the Vatican this morning, the Coliseum tomorrow. We bat around all day and fall in bed at night . . ."

"Mar. 22, 1949 . . . Peggy is practicing so I can hardly hear myself think. Her instructor, Herr Paul Engler, is a Sudetan German who used to conduct the sixty-piece orchestra in Marienbad. He likes her to play loud. She's working on Liszt's *Liebesträume,* Beethoven's *Sonate Pathétique,* a Chopin nocturne, Friedrich Burgmüller's études, several sonatas by Mozart and a whole bunch of Schumann lieder . . . I am going to Dachau tomorrow to a bridge party. One of their worst concentration camps was there. I have never visited their horror places yet . . ." *(Later she did and wrote Mary:* "After seeing those gas chambers & ovens and hearing about the most unimaginable atrocities from some of the old prisoners, I felt sick. One keeps asking oneself, 'Why? Why?' . . .)

"May 30, 1949 . . . Well, another year has rolled around and Memorial Day is here. Last year Connie and I went up to Hunter a few days before and trimmed the grass around Jim's grave. I miss Connie very much. It will be a year since the accident . . .

"June 10, 1949 . . . Our dining room has both my blue rugs in it, the dining table at one end and Jimmy's new grand piano—a Bechstein—at the other . . . Did I tell you about the boy I met at the displaced persons camp where I do volunteer work? His father was sent to Siberia, his mother to work in the mines and the children tried to escape to Germany but the Russians caught them at the border. Just this one boy got out . . .

"Nov. 25, 1949 . . . Thanksgiving we all went to *La Bohème* at the Prinzregenten . . . I was thinking yesterday how shocked you would be at the Bavarians' immodesty. The men go up to a tree along the highway and don't even bother to turn their backs. At home they'd be arrested for indecent exposure . . . It is snowing on the Zugspitze, so Jimmy and Peggy are going skiing Sunday. Last week they skied at Garmisch . . .

"Jan. 2, 1950 . . . I am dead, such a strenuous holiday, parties galore. We were having a dinner on New Year's Eve for forty people. At noon that day, George and Elsa, our servants, quit. George told Jimmy he wouldn't work on New Year's Eve and Jimmy said forty people were coming and they'd have to or quit. Nancy Tanner lent me her maid and fireman and his wife and they simply took over and everything went beautifully. We had platters of sliced beef and pork bought at a German market and much better than our frozen meat at the commissary, cranberry jelly, chicken-and-almond mousse and shrimp in aspic. I put the mousse in a bed of lettuce leaves surrounded by deviled eggs frosted with whipped cream and mayonnaise with a slice of stuffed olive. It was in big round molds with the center filled with carrot curls. The aspic was in three shell-shaped molds in lettuce leaves. And we had hot rolls and coffee and platters of cookies. For *hors d'oeuvres*, I had ground beef in barbecue sauce in pie-crust blankets and rolled-up green pinwheels and tiny cheese sticks. I took the stuff out of the molds just before the guests arrived and dashed upstairs and put on my black evening dress and pearls. It was the prettiest buffet I ever had . . . Peggy and I are going to Vienna next month to see *Lohengrin* and Verdi's *Otello* at the Staatsoper . . .

"Mar. 4, 1950 . . . When Jimmy gets married again and I come home next fall, I doubt if I will build a house. I think about two rooms somewhere would suit me. Just a place to come home to. I expect to be batting around here and there. I've never stayed alone in a house overnight since I was married, except the time Peg and Pat had their tonsils out. Then, too, if I put all my money into a house, I could sit and starve in style. I'll have to help the two younger kids through college, I expect. I've always been hurrying so much, it seems funny to be planning a leisurely existence. However, I do not worry about the future at all."

Two years before she went to Europe, Anne's brother, Hadwen, had died at a trailer camp in Florida. He had never completely recovered from a car crash in 1935 near Muncie, Indiana, in which his wife was killed and he, at forty-nine, suffered a head injury. Three years later, while traveling in Mexico, he collapsed in Monterrey and was brought back to Iowa for brain surgery. He rallied enough during the war to work as a Far Eastern expert in the censor-ship bureau in San Francisco and was planning a return to the Philippines when death came. To everyone's surprise, since he was thought to be poor and improvident, he left each of his three sisters close to ten thousand dollars in investments. These grew, and with Social Security and a little help from her sons, Anne had a modest if ample income. She would never have much money.

"Aug. 8, 1950 . . . Peg and Pat are out mountain climbing. We are in Switzerland and having a marvelous trip. Started at Munich, ate lunch in the mountains overlooking Innsbruck, then over the Brenner Pass, stayed all night near Cortina in the Dolomites. On to Venice (hot & crowded & stayed only two days). We found a lovely peninsula on the southern tip of Lake Garda—swimming, lovely hotel, palm trees, straw market, 13th-century castle complete with moat and drawbridge, millions of pink, white and red oleanders, and grand old Roman ruins. It's the summer home of Catul-lus, which is being excavated. From there we drove along Lake Como, lovely but not as lovely as Lake Garda. Up—up—up with our ears popping, one hairpin turn after another, to St. Moritz. Sunday morning we were staying in the little town of Samaden on the outskirts (St. Moritz was too crowded) and I awakened to the sound of sleigh bells??? It turned out to be a herd of goats being taken up to the mountains. A little while later, a band played church music out in the square . . . After having driven all over Paris (which is a madhouse) & the Alps, I feel able to cope with almost any driving . . ."

Bill had joined the family in Europe the summer of 1949, and in 1950, when I was nineteen, I was sent a boat ticket to come over too. Anne—that is, Mother, as I'll call her, since I'm in the story here—and Peggy met me in Paris, where we had a suite at the Continental (breakfast every morning on our balcony overlooking the Tuileries). We drove to Salzburg and Hallstatt and Wolfgangsee, then after a few days in Munich, to Cortina and Venice as mentioned—climbing in the Alps and swimming on the Lido—and ending the two most idyllic months I've ever spent on Lake Garda's almost-island of Sirmione. As in Mother's letter, Sirmione in those days had a grand hotel, a fishing village, the castle and the ruined villa of Catullus, Julius Caesar's favorite poet, who had lived at the very tip of the peninsula, where cliffs dropped down into the water. ("Dear Sirmio, that art the very eye of islands and peninsulas—Joy of all joys, to gaze on thee once more . . .")

There was a sort of magic about the place. We'd gone there by accident. Peggy had seen a sign, "Sirmione—Straw Hats," and Mother, who was a good sport about doing what her children wanted to do, turned off as I groaned and we found ourselves on a long causeway, or what looked like a causeway but was really a road on a long, extremely narrow strip of land reaching into the lake. The banks fell away sharply to reeds and the water was that wonderful blue-green you sometimes see in Italy. All of a sudden the land broadened out and there was Sirmione.

It was our best discovery all summer. We took rooms at the Grand Hotel Terme, which was empty except for ourselves and a party of singers from La Scala, who sometimes came out on their balconies and burst into exuberantly passionate arias. A garden of oleander trees was in full bloom down by the lake, and some distance out on the water was a diving raft. Next to the hotel, across a small bridge, was the yellow stone castle. It had its keep, drawbridge and battlements, round towers and courtyards, just like the paper castles Billy used to make when we were kids. In the evening, we crossed the moat and Peggy and I climbed up to the highest crenelated parapet, leaning out to wave at Mother, who took pictures of us from below. Afterward we ate at the village inn, out on a terrace by the lake, under a white oleander in a green tub.

Each day was like the next: sun, silence, blue-green water, contentment. The land was terraced for vineyards and olive or fig trees and banked with rosemary. There were elegant avenues of cypress trees and a few sandy beaches where fishermen mended their nets. Women in black, going to and from the village church, would nod and wish us good morning. Mother's 1949 Ford, one of the first postwar American cars many of the Italians had seen, was an object of great interest. We swam out to the diving raft or lay around on enormous white towels under the oleanders. When the shadows started to lengthen and Mother would begin to gather up her things, we'd daily plead with her, "Let's stay just a little while longer."

Our last night in Sirmione, as we strolled through the ruined villa of Catullus, and a flat, late sun sent long slants of light through the olive trees, it came to me all at once that my universe had culturally exploded. I saw that we had left North Dakota forever. Its rules for life and solutions to its problems, handed down father to son, were the rules worked out by a people who happened to inhabit a certain place at a certain time. Now I saw that we had left those ways, just as we had left the people. Our homelessness had set us free. We could be anything we wanted to be. I thought of Mother and how, wanting something more than the familiar but restrictive life of her small-town Iowa Methodist society, she'd set off, as young Anna Louise Williams, looking for a sort of open place. Not in the physical sense, though North Dakota was that, too. But an open place of the spirit. Not cramped and narrow and all bound up in ties to a past culture and time, but wide and boundless and free. Now we, her children, were doing the same thing, though our ties had been broken for us and, coming along forty years later, just as America was entering its postwar imperial age, our open place was going to be the whole world.

So began what became a lifetime journey for me. In it, Mother would be remarkably supportive, though it kept me out of the country years at a time. Once, when I was about thirty, and Jimmy and Billy were pressing me to stay home, get a job and settle down, she quietly slipped me the money to buy a ticket back to Asia. Like the time she sold her Whittier inheritance to get Betty back to college, she had an uncanny instinct for doing the right thing at critical moments in her children's lives. Like all good parents, her love was selfless and unqualified.

She lived just five years short of a century. Like many people up in their nineties, Mother never expected to live so long. Just while she was alive, average life spans had gone up forty years. As time went by and decade succeeded decade, she stayed healthy, despite a little shakiness diagnosed as Parkinson's syndrome. These were pleasant years. She spent her summers in Iowa, where she built, doing the carpentry herself, an outdoor studio with windows on all sides on a grassy slope behind Mary's house out in the country near Viola—she got her "two rooms." She traveled the rest of the year to stay with her children on both coasts or friends, some of them going back seventy or eighty years. Once a year she went to New York to see the Broadway shows. She avoided flying if she could, riding coast to coast in marathon bus journeys, to the dismay of her children (who never went by bus). She said she liked the people she met. At last she entered the jet age, flying to Bangkok to see Betty and her husband, who was managing a Thai factory there, when she was eighty-two, and at ninety-one, she went back across the Pacific to spend six months with Peggy and her family, who were now living in New Zealand. She was just as amazed as everybody else at how small the world had become.

From letters by Anne to Betty, 1965–73:

". . . Billy is back in Berkeley, mapping pines for his atlas on where they grow all over the world. He's going to India and Pakistan soon to visit scientists who work in forestry . . . Jimmy says Pat's new series from Vietnam in the Washington *Star* is the best reporting he's done since Kashmir. It's called *The Lonely War* and deals with the life of Vietnamese villagers and the GIs and young American officers who are out in provinces remote from Saigon . . . Jimmy is working at the White House some days. He'd worked with Scoop Jackson, and Nixon asked Jackson if he knew anyone who knew a lot about energy and the Middle East and Jackson said Jim was his man. So the President asked him to be on some committee . . . It was so much fun to visit you in Bangkok. The only trouble with taking a trip, you get an itching foot and want to go again. Well, as my Quaker ancestors would say, better to wear out than rust out . . . Sometimes I think about the days when I was a girl growing up and how we were entirely satisfied with our own country and lives. I never expected to go abroad at all. If anybody had ever told me my children would someday be scattered all over the world, I would have thought they were absolutely mad. Life was quite placid and pleasant in those days . . .

"I came home from Washington by Fargo and some friends took me out to dinner at West Acres, a wonderful new shopping mall with two theaters, candle shops, eating places—you name it, they have it. The big department stores are gone from downtown. All of Front Street has been torn down. There's a big white Medical Arts Building and a twenty-two-story apartment house for poor elderly people who pay rent according to their ability. Some as low as $25 a month. The city has built past the old County Poor Farm, which has been torn down. I saw only one person I knew at the police station . . ." *She was still cheerfully adapting, even to shopping malls . . .*

Her prayer, the common one, was to live long, but not *too* long. Yet she did. One year, when she was eighty-seven or eighty-eight, people were saying, "Anne's remarkable. She has so much energy and still drives a car and everything." Then came a broken hip and general collapse and it became, "Anne *was* remarkable." A slow, gradual decline set in, at last, and continued seven years, year by year. She had to give up travel and seeing most of her old friends, gardening, cooking, watching television, reading, in time the ability to write her own name, or to see more than a few yards away, eventually the power to walk or stand or feed herself. At last she lay, a tiny white lump of bedding, next to a picture window overlooking a parking lot in a room with a number over the door.

Mercifully, by the time some seizures hospitalized her at ninety-two, compelling us to put her in a nursing home, her mind had faded. If, in a rare moment of comprehension, she would ask, "Where am I?" we'd answer, "In a hospital, getting well" and it seemed to satisfy her. She was spared the shock of those who fully had their wits about them, the shock of having been taken from home to go to a strange place to eventually die.

Since the seizures came during a visit to Bill, the nursing home was in Berkeley, not in Iowa. It was just a half-hour walk across campus from his house. At first it was horrifying to go in and find her sitting there, bent over, head down, in a row of old, old women sitting white-faced and silent in their wheelchairs on both sides of the entrance hall, the very picture of senile old age. It was worse if one might cry in a quavering voice, "Please, nurse, I have to go to the bathroom," and nobody came. Nurses in white did hurry by, preoccupied with their charts and trolleys of medicine, busy like the kitchen help with their trays of food. The nurses did their best, but they had seen too much incontinence, dribbling, blindness. It was routine. Not to the patients. Uppermost in their minds was the thought: my God, this has happened to *me*.

Our nursing home was probably no worse than any other; I suspected, and we tried to persuade ourselves, that it was better. It went in for determined brightness, a kind of desperate gaiety. That it could be sometimes pleasant owed much to the dogged endurance of a number of black practical nurses who had worked there for years and years. Brightly colored curtains on big picture windows framed views of a decaying neighborhood with falling property values. Numbered doors. Numbered trays. Numbered clothing. The "homelike" Green Room, where the big color television seemed to go day and night. The sign by the front door, "WE CARE." The professional cheeriness of the staff with the patients. "Are *we* having *our* lunch?" There was that lack of privacy and increased noise of any public institution. The sharp smell of disinfectant. The incessant banging of plates and trays in the kitchen. Chimes summoning the staff, telephones ringing, voices amplified on the intercom, the hum of electric polishers and vacuum cleaners, the buzz of central heating, the rev of engines in the parking lot, toilets flushing, doors slamming, the confused wails and cries of senescence. There was also a sense of confinement; patients couldn't just up and walk out the front door. Every so often, one did and would be found several streets away and be brought back. One day, one of them, utterly confused, but more spirited than most, screamed, "Help, police! Get me out of here!" Mostly the patients were calm and quiet, patiently waiting, waiting . . .

Visitors came and went. Mother saw at least one of us every day, Bill going at night to feed her, Peggy or I at noon. There were occasional visits from grandchildren, great-grandchildren, cousins, in-laws, old friends. Some acted naturally, some took on patronizing voices, especially loud or hushed. A few, if they were already old themselves, could scarcely hide their horror at what might lie not too far ahead. There were those who didn't come at all and tried to justify themselves. "She wouldn't know us." Or sent huge, expensive bouquets, too big to keep in the room. Mother never complained. Somehow she survived it all for three years.

What saved us was the garden. There you could be alone, escape the noise, the faces of strangers, the claustrophobia. It was like a secret hiding place; nobody else ever went there. You entered through a wooden gate behind a toolshed at the far end of the parking lot. There, behind shrubbery, out of sight, was what had been an old-fashioned backyard. It had once belonged to the house in front of it, an old wooden pile of Victorian Gothic fallen into disrepair. A sign in one of the windows warned, "This Neighborhood Organized Against Crime." Rock drifted faintly down from the open windows of rented student rooms, "Video killed the radio star . . ."

The nursing home had once installed a walkway of wooden planks for wheelchairs, then blessedly lost interest in further improvement. Deep green grass grew rank and weedy; from a hectic green tangle rose the dense foliage of an old apple tree, two dying fig trees, a white-barked birch, a soaring redwood. Two swings hung on rotting ropes from the branch of a live oak. Cataracts had taken away much of Mother's sight, so to her it all looked lushly green and beautiful. She heard the birds, saw the clouds and sky and turned her face up into the sun. She talked less and less, though she was still full of surprises. One day, out of the blue, she declared, "I wish I'd been an architect." Her mind was going. Some days, it seemed quite blank. Like other extremely old ladies, drilled by Edwardian mothers in childhood, she kept her gracious manners to the last. But conversation was something else. In time, I discovered that at sometime in her life, Mother had memorized a good deal of poetry. All I had to do was find a poem she knew, say the first words, and she would quote the rest. It was a way of getting her to speak.

So, in this forgotten place, the last three years of her life, hour after hour she recited the words of Tennyson and Whittier, Shakespeare, Burns, Keats and the Brownings, Gray, Kipling, Riley and Field. "Abou Ben Adhem," "Elegy Written in a Country Churchyard," "Little Boy Blue"—("Now, don't you go till I come," he said, "and don't you make any noise! . . .")— voiced with such expression it came as a shock when a verse ended and she retreated to that far-off place her mind now seemed to inhabit. She knew more fragments than complete poems and it was not until I came across Peaslee's *Graded Selections for Memorizing,* published around the turn of the century, and the *McGuffey Readers,* that I knew their source. She was most fond of the closing, elegiac lines of William Cullen Bryant's *Thanatopsis:*

> "So live, that when thy summons comes to join
>   The innumerable caravan that moves
>   To that mysterious realm, where each shall take
>   His chamber in the silent halls of death,
>   Thou go not, like the quarry-slave at night,
>   Scourged to his dungeon, but, sustained and soothed
>   By an unfaltering trust, approach thy grave
>   Like one who wraps the drapery of his couch
>   About him, and lies down to pleasant dreams."

Almost surely memorized at least three quarters of a century earlier, most probably as a seventeen-year-old teacher in that one-room schoolhouse in Hardin. Her other favorite, the "Twenty-third Psalm," must have gone back to childhood. She said it with great conviction.

". . . Surely goodness and mercy shall follow me
All the days of my life,
And I will dwell in the house of the Lord forever."

She outlived Betty, who died peacefully, aged sixty-six and a grand-mother, sitting at the table in her home in Seattle on December 2, 1980, which happened to be Mother's ninety-third birthday. Betty's husband found her when he came home from work. Spread out on the table in front of her, in envelopes ready to mail, was Betty's annual newsletter about old friends from Fessenden, something she'd started doing in recent years. World War II had scattered Fessenden's young people, like so many Americans of their generation, across the world. Afterward, few went home to farm or stay. Instead they entered all kinds of professions and lived all over the country. As the letter showed, her contemporaries, now in their late sixties, were part of mainstream America: ". . . thinking of retirement . . . went to Europe in May . . . children are grown, married and dispersed . . . traveling in their camper . . . proud grandmother of five . . . in Honolulu over Easter . . . back down in Arizona . . . recovering from heart attack . . . a two-week Caribbean cruise . . ." There was mention that "Bud St. Jacque has retired in Long Beach and enjoys puttering around his roses—don't we all?" Betty was nostalgic about her lost Eden: "The other night I was going through my old sheet music and ran across 'Home'—reminded me of my last Alfalfa Day, when I sang it with the band wearing one of my dad's sports shirts . . . 'When shadows fall, and trees whisper day is ending, my thoughts are ever wending home . . .'" Bill broke the news of Betty's death to Mother. She seemed terribly shocked, but never spoke of it again—perhaps, we speculated, blocking it out.

Toward the end, she began to have what Bill called her "manic" days. After weeks of resting peacefully, she would be seized by a kind of frenzied vitality. She might talk twenty-four hours, hardly stopping, and then collapse into a deep sleep for two or three days. The doctor said it was a not uncommon geriatric phenomenon. I happened to be there during the last of these. When I arrived at lunchtime and entered her room, instead of the usual drowsy figure, I was greeted by a robust, "I'm starving! When do we have lunch?" She rambled on animatedly. "I'm not sick. I don't feel the least bit sick. I'll be up and navigating about in no time." That noon, wrapped in a steamer rug and pale blue shawl, her face framed in a cloud of white hair, wearing glasses, she looked as if she might. Somehow she did not look ninety-four, mortally ill with arteriosclerosis and Parkinson's disease, almost blind, her frail little body shrunk to skin and bones, weighing just seventy-two pounds. If the nurses let her, she tried to curl up in bed in a rigid fetal position; they found it was getting painful to her to be moved at all. Everything was going but the heart and lungs. But as she proved with gusto, the essence was still there.

After a trip to the garden and lunch, which she always took on a tray in her room, the nurses put her to bed. Ordinarily she would have slept, but she showed no sign of calming down. I took out what we called the "family history," notes from interviews with her I'd done twenty-three years earlier. She liked to have them read to her, as it brought back memories. That day, she kept interrupting. I'd read: "The front door of the house on Twelfth Street was never locked all the years we lived there . . ." and she'd break in: "We didn't have the key! The landlord never gave us one." I'd read: "I was never insecure about the future, worrying about it. I don't know why." And she'd interrupt, "Oh, you knew you wouldn't starve, for one thing." She smiled, as if thinking of those days made her happy.

I came to Jessie's final entry on the death of Hadwen in their journal: ". . . from earth into the beauty of Heaven was to him but a step. Now I am alone . . ." "She was a lovely woman," Mother said. Then, after a pause, "But, you know, they bickered a lot." At random I chose a passage about how Betty had once kissed one of the roomers under the mistletoe. She laughed. "That was funny. You know, Julius just looked flabbergasted."

I read about her arrival in North Dakota as a young schoolteacher in 1910. She listened attentively, then grew agitated. "Somebody's got to write to Jim," she said anxiously. What could I say? He'd been dead for forty-four years. She seemed to know it herself, for she asked right away, "Tell me, are all the Hunter boys dead?" Again I didn't know what to say and flipped the pages at random. There was a quote from Jimmy as a little boy in Maddock: "It was the only time in my life that Father ever laid a hand on me."

"One little slap," she said with feeling. "It didn't amount to anything."

Turning back to Iowa, I found her wedding day. I read how Reverend Williams had told her he wished she were marrying Forrest instead.

"It was an awful thing to say to me. He said it to *me.*"

And Father's courtship. I remembered her once saying that even if she'd known how things were going to turn out, she still would have married him. I read: "Jim Critchfield always played the piano . . ." She smiled and said, "Do I remember? It's one of the things I remember the best." Still smiling, she closed her eyes. I thought she was falling asleep, but she opened them at once and went on speaking.

"I've often wondered about that matrimonial fling. Oh, Jim always liked it on the farm. I don't suppose he'd have been happy if he'd had to have stayed there though."

What did she mean? Before I could ask her to explain, I felt her trembling hand on mine. "I wish you'd write this, Pat. You're used to writing now. I wish you'd write about North Dakota. . . ." A pause. ". . . and Iowa." Another pause. "I wonder if the Hunter boys are all alive . . ." What to say? And what if I did as she said? How could I write about Father? I asked her. "How can I write about somebody I can't remember at all? I mean, say of all the people we know, who is like him?"

"You are."

That was the last conversation we had. Whether senile dementia or solemn last wish, I took her words seriously. Now a gray-haired, middle-aged man, I went back to the North Dakota I'd left at seventeen to begin research into what she'd said. It was many months before I returned to the West Coast, flying in on a Sunday night, too late to visit the nursing home. The phone rang Monday morning just before seven. It was Peggy, calling from the apartment over by campus where she'd been living since her divorce. (We still saw her ex-husband, who'd sung in movie musicals as a boy, in the odd film on TV, one of a group around a piano with Bing Crosby in *Going My Way* or a choirboy in *Mrs. Miniver.*)

"A nurse phoned," Peggy said. "She said Mother was unresponsive when they went to wake her this morning." Her doctor had come and diagnosed a cerebral thrombosis. In less than three months she would be ninety-five. Within the hour we were at her bedside. I phoned the office of Bill, a research scientist, and he came at noon. Except for a few years at Harvard, he'd been at Berkeley since his student days. Jimmy, now a business executive, was on a holiday with his wife in the South of France. His secretary was trying to reach him and arrange a flight from Nice.

For the next three days, we stayed at Mother's side, holding her trembling hands, wiping her forehead, wetting her lips with a cotton swab. The first day, she watched us with a fixed, concentrated gaze, unable to speak. Once, she went into Cheyne-Stokes breathing—the long, still pauses between gasping breaths that signaled her own mother's death. The head nurse said she expected death in an hour or two. Even so, Peggy and I felt we should softly sing some of her favorite songs, ones like "Froggie Go A'Courtin' Ride,"

"Skaters Waltz," "Now the Day Is Over," songs we used to sing as children when doing the dishes. I stayed with her that night, and the next day, as she sank into a coma, her eyes closed, we sang her favorite hymns. That evening, while Peggy was alone with her, there was an awful rattle in her throat and the nurses feared she might drown in her own phlegm.

The third night, Wednesday, I sat up with her again. A year before, when I'd told her of Forrest's death in Iowa, at once she'd asked, "Was he alone?" Now she was breathing fiercely, fighting for every gasp of air, making a hiccup sound. "Your mother's got the real pioneer spirit," the head nurse said. "I never thought she'd last this long. She's a real fighter." I thought of Dylan Thomas's "Do not go gentle into that good night . . . Rage, rage against the dying of the light . . ."

Nurses came and went. One said to watch for sweetness of breath, another for cold feet, both sure signs. A male nurse tried to get a few drops of orange juice down with a syringe. She hadn't been able to swallow anything for over thirty-six hours now and there was a danger of dehydration. Everything was aspirated into the lungs. "I'll keep trying," he said. "Pneumonia is better than dying of thirst." I telephoned her doctor. He hadn't come back since he'd diagnosed the stroke. "An I.V. is possible and it is up to the family," he said. "We could rush your mother to the hospital. In view of her age and condition, I personally would not favor any artificial life supports at this point. Just make your presence known to her. She mustn't feel alone."

I knew he was right. There was no position now in which she could lie without pain, there was hardly a spot, or a limb, in her body that did not ache or cause her excruciating pain if she was moved. To live meant prolonged suffering. Yet how hard she was fighting to hold on. I kept wetting her lips and the inside of her mouth with a swab dipped in cold water and wiping her forehead with a wet cloth. Just before midnight and he went off duty, the male nurse came back. He tried and said he thought he'd succeeded in getting a few drops of orange juice down.

"Her hands," I said. "I can't feel the nervous tremors in her hands. She's had them for years."

"It's the central nervous system. It's going."

A new shift of nurses came on, nobody I'd seen before. Hours passed. I kept my hand gently touching Mother's shoulder and sang softly to her, just in case she could feel or hear, "Sweet and low, sweet and low, wind of the western sea . . ." I grew drowsy and lost track of time. Day began to break. Three nurses came into the room to turn her to the other side. I went into the hallway. It was still dark, but the edge of the sky was growing light. Everything was visible, but dimly. The nurses came out. "We're finished," one said. "You can go back in now. She's breathing more easily but still has a temperature."

I went back and sat down. The harsh, raspy breathing sound was gone. I went around to the other side of the bed to listen and could just hear a soft intake of breath. Her mouth was open, as it had been all night as she fought for breath. Her face, framed in her soft white hair, looked peaceful. I sat down, but it seemed too silent and I went back and listened again. This time there was no sound or movement at all. I went to the door. The duty nurse took one look, picked up her stethoscope, ran past me and bent over Mother, listening for a heartbeat.

"She's gone."

Gone? I thought dully, where has she gone? I phoned Peggy and Bill and came back. There was nothing to do, so I gathered up Mother's glasses and dentures from the bedside table. I also picked up a little Raggedy Andy doll she'd liked, a red silk robe I'd brought her from China, a faded little cloth bag from India she used for Kleenex, a book of poems, two books of old songs. A suitcase for the undertaker was already packed. The closet was full of useless clothing. Not much to show for such a long life. Where had she gone?

It was almost nine o'clock before the undertaker came, and by then the room was flooded with light. Bill had sent Peggy and me out for breakfast and tried to close her mouth, but by then rigor mortis had set in. We'd left it open, fearing she might still be trying to breathe. Until the undertaker came, we sat there, still keeping a hand over her hand to let her know that we were there and would not leave her alone.

Years before, she had arranged to be buried, not in Hunter, but in the little Viola cemetery beside her sister Mary. It was just a few miles from where she'd been born, and all her family was buried close by: Hadwen and Jessie and Hadwen, Jr., in Mount Vernon; Eli Johnston and Jessie's mother, Margaret, in Linn Grove; Francis and Mary Williams in Whittier. We took Mother home. It was a long way from that other cemetery, with its grandiose granite monument left half-finished by the sculptor to suggest premature death, up on its windy plain that I knew now was home to me.

And so we gathered at Viola's wooden country church on a fine September day, the white church steeple jutting up into a clear blue sky. Relatives came from Paris, Washington, San Francisco, Seattle, St. Paul, Des Moines, and there were Quakers from Whittier and—just at the last minute—Jess and Ben Oser, he in his nineties and she not much younger, pulled up, having driven eight hundred miles from Fessenden. "We knew if we didn't just get into the car and go, we'd never make it," said Jess. "You know, we thought an awful lot of Anne and Jim." The minister, as we asked, quoted Mother's favorite lines from "Thanatopsis" ("So live, that when thy summons comes . . ."), Tennyson's "Crossing the Bar" ("Sunset and evening star, and one clear call for me . . .") and the Twenty-third Psalm. And goodness and mercy *had* followed her most of the days of her life. We wanted an old-fashioned funeral, so there were lots of flowers and an Iowa niece played "Abide with Me" on the church organ.

From a letter by Helen Collins, Iowa, to Bill in Berkeley, September 26, 1982:
". . . As I think I told you, I could not see the Sister I knew—and finally decided it was her mouth, set so stern and narrow. I *never* saw her mouth like that . . . But what I did notice were her hands . . . And I thought of all they had done—picked potatoes on the farm at Hunter—all the babies she helped bring into the world in Maddock and Fessenden—all the serving and so many things in Fargo. So much *hard work.* But then I remembered how she loved to pick wild raspberries in the orchard at Mary's and get all scratched up. Her hands spoke volumes to me . . ."

It had rained the night before, and when we drove into the cemetery the grass looked trampled and glossy. As the procession of cars followed the shiny black hearse through the gate, the gravel road looked washed, and the white crosses and monuments looked washed too. In the bright sunshine, the long brass handles on either side of the oak coffin glittered with rays of blinding light. Across the road, a clump of young pine trees were a dark green against the bright green of the grass, and behind them, the shivering leaves of tall cottonwoods were a transparent yellow against the light; through the leaves could be seen the bottomless blue sky.

As we left the cars, I noticed the tops of the trees swaying in the wind. It was a glorious fall day. People moved toward the coffin suspended over the freshly dug grave, and a flock of small birds hopping about it tried to make up their minds whether to take flight. Once having decided to do so, they all, one after another, rushed off to the tops of the cottonwoods, frantically scolding and chirruping.

Again the minister prayed. Mother had firmly believed in heaven, at least until she became very old. In times of trouble, she had a way of quoting, "God moves in a mysterious way . . ." I could hear her now, saying once again, "Over the years I've built up a feeling that whatever comes is best.

Sometimes, at the time, life seems pretty hard. But, looking back after a long time, you can see a plan that is better than any we might have conceived." It was, of course, Hadwen Williams's philosophy. Her faith in divine providence was less evident toward the end. Still, it was comforting to think the soul was really immortal. That it could rise again and fly off somewhere near Mars or Saturn, or another solar system, or maybe to some galaxy millions of light-years away. Not Grandfather's white-robed multitudes with golden harps. Just a place to go and always be contented and think and feel in a different and better way. Or was it more honest to face life with Father's absence of faith, seeing death as inevitable annihilation and trying to have one's fun and lull oneself to sleep in any way one can, convinced that this is all and there will be nothing else?

As we drove back to the city where he was going to catch a plane to rejoin his wife in Paris, Jimmy said, "Well, I suppose this is the end of the Five Little Peppers." On impulse we stopped at Whittier and walked around the tiny churchyard looking for the family graves. Afterward, we peered rather awkwardly through the windows into the locked and deserted Meeting House, with its straight-backed, cushionless pews and bare gray walls. Could we, too, I wondered, if we sat there quietly long enough, experience the Inner Light?

We went our way. Jimmy asked me about the book I was going to write. "What's your story going to be?" he asked. "That's what escapes me. What's your story?"

"Their lives." I'd already started to write the opening scene in my mind. It would be their wedding day, in 1913. Mother had told me how she had gone into the parsonage garden a few hours before the ceremony to pick lilacs.

"Well, he was just an absolutely typical small-town doctor who ran into all the stresses. And her role as the doctor's wife and her behavior is pretty much par for the course in these situations. I think a lot of doctors married women from conservative backgrounds." Jimmy—that is, Jim, as we called him now—seemed to feel that their lives were too ordinary to make a book. He went on.

"It is my observation that she gave and gave and gave and gave. I never heard her say, 'I did so much for him' or 'I gave up so much for him.' Never once. Maybe she was *too* saintly. But I don't think their story is unique. It's been repeated many times and particularly by country doctors. If you look at the incidence of alcoholism and early death among them, it's incredible.

A country doctor lived a terribly hard life. And I think his story, complete with Norma, his drinking problem, and the whole thing was the story of a man who went the same way an awful lot of them went."

I listened to his words and watched the scenery rush by. It was their ordinariness that made them matter. Clouds raced across the sky, and moving shafts of sunlight broke through and radiated on all sides—fields, trees, farms, everything glittered with yellow light. I could feel the faint chill of the glass and lowered the window a little. The cold air felt good. The wind was rising, and cascades of yellow leaves whipped over the ground and flew furiously round and round in the air. Days were getting shorter, nights cooler—the familiar summer look was going, and in the fresh, bracing air I could feel that winter was not so far away. And I thought of the scene at the grave once more: the mourners, the birds, the wind, the light, the whirling yellow leaves. Individual life was by its very nature a tragedy; it came to an end; for all of us it was going to be a short way to that grave. But the ordinary life of a society was a comedy that just kept going on. What was at the heart of those days? Things like the taste of bread right out of the oven when you were good and hungry. The smell of newly plowed earth. A horse munching oats and bending its head to be rubbed. The way the late, flat sun sent long slants of light across the prairie grass. To be sure, memory made it too simple. It was easy to forget the aching muscles, all the dirty work and sweat and monotony and curses. Tending stock, filling kerosene lamps. The worries over sickness and weather and money. Those late trips out back on freezing winter nights . . . Those days. They'll never come again. But somewhere there was always going to be a circus coming to town or a workman walking down a morning street. Or wind blowing yellow leaves or black branches dripping rain. Somebody was always going to be swinging a golf club or a baseball bat or playing a piano or cracking a joke. Or taking a deep breath or drowsing off to sleep or dreaming or waking up. Or passing from youth to old age, and hardly knowing where all the years went. Time, in the instant, in the irrecoverable passing moment, time continuous and remembered, going on and on . . . I wish I'd known them better. And they were with me now. What were they like? . . . Oh, I could guess, I suppose, how he would end this . . . With something like a grand windup number from the band, all brass and drums and oompah-pah . . . Or with a funny story . . . *Well, for Ker-risst sake! Look what the cat dragged in! How the hell are you? C'mon in and make yourself at home. Anne, honey, look who's here! Hey, I've got a good one for you . . .*

Afterword

The reader may be interested in how this book was written. It started out with a series of long daily interviews with my mother, Anne (1887–1982), in November and December 1959, when she was seventy-three. I'd just come home from two years of studying in Europe and was going out to India to teach at a university. A long-standing idea to someday write a book about my family's early years, coupled with my mother's age, prompted me to get her story down on paper before I went. As it turned out, there was no hurry, and these interviews with her and other family members, done at a more leisurely pace, were continued on and off over the next twenty-odd years. In 1979, when Anne's memory was fading, I typed up these handwritten notes and put them together to make the informal family history mentioned in the story. She liked to have them read to her. They came to eighty-one single-spaced typed pages and, together with a few other first-person accounts from letters and diaries, form the basis of *Those Days*.

Those from Jessie, Jimmy, Billy and Peggy are mostly quoted word for word from letters or interviews. The accounts from Anne and Betty have been expanded with additional description and information by the author, though I tried to keep to their exact words in the most personal passages. Hadwen Williams (1854–1926) left behind letters, several long speeches on County Life and over a hundred sermon outlines, carefully preserved by his daughter and Anne's sole surviving sister, Helen Collins. While his final characterization is my own, Mrs. Collins was able to provide a great deal of information about her father, my grandfather, including things he'd said. As with the others, nothing was invented. For example, when no detailed account could be found to illustrate Hadwen's care of the sick and dying during the flu epidemic, I drew upon an actual case history, changing only the family's name.

The major reconstruction in this book was of Jim, my father (1889–1938). Only a few examples of his actual words could be found on record, such as the slangy newspaper article he wrote about the 1931 minstrel show or the courtroom Q-and-A of the coroner's inquests of the same year. The best source for the Hunter years was Jim's sole surviving brother, Harry. Invaluable for the three Maddock years was Mabel Swanson, who lived with the family the whole time. In Fessenden, there were many people who knew Anne and Jim, some in their sixties and seventies, but most of them older. Fred Mietz, the best source on golfing and the minstrel shows, died within a few months of our interviews. The deaths of his wife, Elma, Jennie Miller Anderson and Ben Oser in Fessenden, Mrs. Merland Carr in Hunter and Myrtle Legreid Olson and C. P. Olson in Maddock, all of them interviewed, have since followed. Time and again it was brought home to me that this was a work that could not have been postponed for even a few more years.

That I'd waited so long was because I'd spent the previous quarter century reporting Asia, Africa and Latin America, particularly from their villages. I was unable to resume work on the book until April 1982, when I went back to North Dakota for the first time since the family left in 1948. I'd written so much about how Third World villagers handled change. What about us? When Anne in her last days asked me to write about North Dakota and Iowa, it all fit together. The "family history" was a start. Its time span, 1880–1940, coincided with the sixty years between the disappearance of the frontier in the 1880s and World War II, years that saw the shift from country to city, farm to factory, horses to cars and tractors, kitchen surgery to scientific medicine, fundamentalism to Darwinism, tent meetings to Hollywood movies. Next was needed a week-to-week chronology of what the family members did and another, more general, social chronology of the times.

The small-town weekly newspapers were amazingly detailed and informative. A good share of what I learned about Jim's patients and their illnesses and injuries came from newspaper accounts. Most useful were the Port Byron, Illinois, *Globe* for Mississippi River life and goings on in Le Claire for the years 1900–5; and in North Dakota, the Hunter *Herald,* 1910–20, bound copies of which were made available by Clark Potter, editor, the Casselton *Reporter;* the Maddock *Standard,* 1925–28, Institute for Regional Studies, North Dakota State University; the Fargo *Forum,* microfilm, Fargo Public Library; bound *Forum* copies for 1896, 1910 and 1919 loaned by Art and Angela Jore (including one for Anne's first day in North Dakota); the

Wells County Free Press, Fessenden, 1925–32, again with bound copies (so much better than microfilm), made available by its editor, Charles Eldredge. Charlie, one of many people who went way out of their way to help, let my assistant, Tim Holzkamm, and me set up shop at a big table in the back room of his newspaper office. (The funeral parlor across the street loaned us maroon and black folding chairs.)

Aside from the family chronology, I prepared a cultural history of the times. Then we started taping interviews. It was not until Tim and I got quite deeply into this research that we fully learned about "Norma." In the 1959 interviews, both Anne and Betty had revealed to me for the first time that Jim had been involved with another woman. Somehow, though, I got the impression she was his own age and the affair was short-lived. Now we learned about the abortion, her youth, singing, prettiness, the scandal and that the affair lasted a long time, at least six years and maybe more. I'd known none of this.

What to do? For years I'd planned, now with Mother's encouragement, to someday write a story about the family's life in North Dakota and Iowa. Did she understand the implications? The affair was not something on the fringe of these lives. It affected all of them. Without it, their story would not have been the same. "What will people say?" had been uppermost in her mind most of Mother's life. In extreme age, when death did not seem far away, this changed; truth and reality came to matter more. When I learned of the death of the real-life "Norma" in 1960, I decided to go ahead.

Eventually we amassed several thousand pages of typed notes. Boiling it all down was the hardest part. Selecting, cutting, revising, rearranging. Research was fun; this was work. I ran all of the manuscript through the typewriter six times, much of it seven times.

In all this effort I had the benefit of help and advice from a number of professional historians. At the State Historical Society of Wisconsin in Madison, Janice L. O'Connell provided many ideas, Dale E. Treleven, Jerry Pockar and Grace Hayek helped greatly with research, and Jack Holzhueter and Emily Tari gave expert advice. I also wish to thank: At the Iowa State Historical Society, Iowa City: Bradley W. Williams, Loren Horten and David Kinnett; a useful find was a 27,370-page, 103-volume, 1896–1957 diary kept by Joshua Williams, who, while no relation, went to Upper Iowa University at the same time and knew Beecher Beal, Anne and Reverend Williams. At the Library of Congress, Washington: Betty James, a former colleague at the Washington *Star,* and, during the final checking, the marvelously resourceful Adriana Orr, long the researcher at the Library of Congress for The Oxford English Dictionary Supplemental. Also helpful were two members of the library staff, Rosemary Plakas and Virginia Steele Wood; Mrs. Wood was the editor of Private Zebulon Vaughan's war journal, quoted in Part Two. In Fargo: Barbara L'Heureux, North Dakota State University history instructor, who accompanied me on revisits to Hunter and Fessenden in 1984. Thanks also to NDSU's communications director, Jerry Richardson, and Jerry Lamb, Fargo Public Library; my longtime mainstays in Washington, Peggy Ann Trimble and Robert W. Alvord; my agent, Patricia Berens, of the Sterling Lord Agency in New York, and Norman Kurz of her staff; Dean Eng Wong and Professor Whitney Perkins, Brown University; Wayne D. Rasmussen, chief historian for the Department of Agriculture; Theodore M. Schultz, University of Chicago, for his advice on economics and politics; Dr. William G. Donald, Jr., Berkeley, for clearing up some points on medicine; and Norman E. Borlaug, International Maize and Wheat Improvement Center, Mexico, for his help on agriculture and what it was like to grow up in a small Norwegian farming community in northeastern Iowa. The 1884–1927 journal of Hadwen and Jessie Williams, the Eli Johnston journal, early Quaker letters and other family documents were provided by Helen Collins, Viola, Iowa.

For their help in reproducing the old photographs, I wish to thank NDSU's Mark Strand and Eddie and Elfriede Dyba of Professional Photographic Services in San Francisco. The cover photograph is by Bruce Wendt, Judson, North Dakota, and the black-and-whites are courtesy of the late Fred Hultstrand's "History in Pictures" Collection, North Dakota Institute for Regional Studies, North Dakota State University; NDSU Archives; State Historical Society of North Dakota, Bismarck (with special thanks to Todd Strand); Clay County (Minnesota) Historical Society; Wells County Historical Society, Fessenden; Dalene Battagler, Hunter; State Historical Society of Wisconsin; and Buffalo Bill Museum, Le Claire, Iowa.

Old movies proved to be of great help in their evocation of what it was like to live out on the North Dakota prairie in those days. I wish to thank Bonnie Wadnizak, director, North Dakota State Film Library, Fargo, for her several showings (so I could take notes) of the superb 1915–20 films of North Dakota's pioneer movie maker, Frithjof Holmboe, as edited and narrated by Bill Snyder of Fargo; also the recent movie filmed in North Dakota and set in much the same period, *Northern Lights,* and several one-reel silent comedies produced by Angela Gibson in Casselton. For the interiors of the Hunter hotel and the farm and town houses of the Critchfields there, as well as for such things as a horse-drawn black hearse, a hook-and-ladder firemen's cart, and various models of cars mentioned in the story, I drew upon the marvelous exhibits at Fargo's Bonanzaville, while the one-room schoolhouse in Hardin, Iowa, today long vanished, is closely modeled after one on display at Old World Wisconsin near Madison. I missed the stimulation, as in my other books, which are all set in the present, of living experience. Yet, just as readers sometimes are pleased to run into one of my village subjects in real life, perhaps *Those Days* will have a reader who will someday visit the museum out at the Fessenden fairgrounds and discover the picture of Betty and Jimmy playing in the band or come across Anne's old scrapbook for the Mothers' Club in 1931, just as I did.

Most important, of course, were memories. Among those interviewed, either stenographically or on tape, I wish to thank, besides those already mentioned: Kathryn Critchfield Edwards and Tom Edwards, Livermore, California; Walter Kennedy, Greg Pelp, Chester Martin and Clara Clark, Le Claire, Iowa; Lettie Leamer and Elizabeth Wood, rural Princeton, Iowa; Walter Helble, rural McCausland, Iowa; Fay B. Collins and Hadwen Collins, Viola, Iowa; Barbara Critchfield Dunn, Des Moines; Mrs. Robert Critchfield, Wooster, Ohio; Don and Irene Rock, St. Paul. In Fargo: Gordon Pepple, E. Louise Gronlund, Ed Brekke, Marjorie Paulsrud, Beverly Halbeisen Blanish, Vicky Myrold. In Hunter: Beatrice Carr Sayer, Merland Carr, Emil Moen, Bill and Dale Battagler, Rose Winistopher Rasmussen, Harry and Ella Rasmussen, Kathyrn Garrett, Emil Holzkamm. In Maddock: Edwin Anderson, Agnetha Nielsen Bergsgaard, Edith Nielsen Bjelde. In Fessenden: Helen Hope Graves, Chester Zumpf, Harold and Mai Rita Zumpf, Elsie Engbrecht Kieper, Rees and Helen Price, Elizabeth Price Pfeiffer, Lois Pritchard, Inez Taylor, Jess Oser, Sigrid Quarve Wood, Edith Quarve, Alvin Mohr, Irving Clark, Jim Parsons, Helen Litke Musha, Helen Kotchian, Leona and Roy Kuske, Mac Solberg, Mary Carter and Dan J. Ehni.

My utmost thanks was expressed shortly before his death to the late J. Roderick MacArthur, the moving spirit behind the MacArthur Foundation Prize Fellowships, for the gift of time to do this work.

This is my third book to be edited by Luther Nichols, Doubleday's West Coast editor, in Berkeley, and it's a pleasure to thank him by now as an old friend. I'm also grateful to Loretta Barrett of Doubleday, to my able New York editor, Paul Aron, and to Frank Hoffman for his skillful copy editing.

Particular thanks go to John Bye, North Dakota Institute for Regional Studies at North Dakota State University (formerly and in the book, the Agricultural College). And to Tim Holzkamm, an anthropologist and historian associated with NDSU who, with great good luck for me, was a native of Hunter. Tim worked with me in Hunter, Maddock and Fessenden as we laid the research framework in 1982 and 1983. Years ago, Eric Sevareid, another North Dakotan, wrote, ". . . Very early I acquired a sense of having no identity in the world, of inhabiting, by some cruel mistake, an outland, a lost and forgotten place on the far horizon of my country." In my three-year exploration of this outland, home to all of us, John and Tim were admirably steadfast companions. Indeed, this book took the help and hard work, so much of it given freely and unstintingly, of an astonishingly large and varied group of Americans; it is their book too. Lastly, I want to thank my brothers Bill and Jim and, for her moral support and reading through several drafts, making suggestions, my sister Peggy.

R.C.

Fessenden, Fargo, Berkeley
and Washington, D.C.